PENGUIN BOOKS

EMPIRE MADE ME

Robert Bickers is Senior Lecturer in History at Bristol University.
He has published extensively on Chinese history and is the author
of *Britain in China*.

ROBERT BICKERS

Empire Made Me

An Englishman
Adrift in Shanghai

PENGUIN BOOKS

For Kate

PENGUIN BOOKS

Published by the Penguin Group
Penguin Books Ltd, 80 Strand, London WC2R 0RL, England
Penguin Group (USA) Inc., 375 Hudson Street, New York, New York 10014, USA
Penguin Books Australia Ltd, 250 Camberwell Road, Camberwell, Victoria 3124, Australia
Penguin Books Canada Ltd, 10 Alcorn Avenue, Toronto, Ontario, Canada M4V 3B2
Penguin Books India (P) Ltd, 11 Community Centre, Panchsheel Park, New Delhi – 110 017, India
Penguin Group (NZ), Cnr Airborne and Rosedale Roads, Albany, Auckland 1310, New Zealand
Penguin Books (South Africa) (Pty) Ltd, 24 Sturdee Avenue, Rosebank 2196, South Africa

Penguin Books Ltd, Registered Offices: 80 Strand, London WC2R 0RL, England

www.penguin.com

Published by Allen Lane 2003
Published in Penguin Books 2004
1

Typeset by Rowland Phototypesetting Ltd, Bury St Edmunds, Suffolk
Printed in England by Clays Ltd, St Ives plc

Contents

I

The Empire World

Empire is with us, in our waking lives, and in our dreams and night-mares. British society, politics and culture at the beginning of the twenty-first century are profoundly shaped by the imperial experience. The actual empire with all its frilly finery (which masked such violence) is mostly gone, the governors recalled, bases withdrawn, and the flags pulled down as the bugle played the last Last Post at sunset or midnight. Only scattered crumbs remain, a motley collection of islands and peninsulas and 190,000 residents of what were in 1999 renamed 'United Kingdom Overseas Territories'. The once-powerful Colonial Office, which dispatched officials and directives across the globe, intruding into the lives of colonial subjects from the Caribbean to the Pacific, has been reduced to two very minor committees in different departments of state.[1] No European empire long survived the peace of 1945, but the speed of British empire's passing seemed a mystery. It was a good war for the empire in the short term, and it did not long feel too embarrassed by its Asian collapse in 1941–2 in the face of the Japanese army. United Nations mandate responsibilities substantially added to the bag of imperial holdings, and, having subsidized the war, the United States then underwrote the last decade of confident, assertive British imperialism after 1945 as a bulwark against the influence and expansion of the Soviet Union.[2] But still, in the cold war era the essential pragmatic sensitivity of British imperial practice was hamstrung. The fear of communist expansion prompted inflexibility where there might otherwise have been a defter British touch. In Cyprus, Kenya and Malaya the challenge of colonial nationalism was met with arid, violent repression. By the end of the 1950s empire was generating more enemies – or potential enemies – than friends, both inside and outside the colonial world. The best way to protect and prolong British influence was increasingly seen to be the transfer of power, and so the transfer of problems. It was time to go, and by 1964 the British had mostly gone.[3]

But empire hasn't gone. Its detritus litters once-colonized cities and cantonments, its legacies both tangible – statues, monuments, buildings, roads – and intangible – philosophies, policies, memories. The new states sit within borders designated as such for administrative convenience, shaped by international realpolitik in bold, border-making years. Presidents reside in governors' residences. Parliaments (so-named) meet in chambers constructed for legislative councils in undemocratic times. Repressive legislation introduced during late colonial 'emergencies' is revived to preserve the powers of successor elites. This post-imperial world is at once familiar, stocked with plants and game imported from Britain, with English as lingua franca, and rugby, cricket and football as leading sports – but it is also alien, for all these transplants thrive in new ways in new climates. And empire also lurks in the streets, parks and squares of the imperial cities of the United Kingdom, themselves littered with statues and memorials honouring the imperial great, good, and lost. Empire recognized such debts in stone duly unveiled with appropriate ceremonial. Imperialists put their faith in bricks and mortar, building an imperial heart, constructing sober edifices for the departments of state and the dominions' offices, expressing their ideal in stone in the London and provincial streets.[4] Time, the *Luftwaffe* and the city planners eroded these, but if you stand still in the heart of the metropolis and think and look, you find yourself surrounded by the imperial past. In galleries and museums, too, empire provides the setting and the occasions for the conflict chronicled in the history paintings, and imperialism's new world order infused the evolving vision of the European artist.[5] The fruits of empire line the display cabinets, courtesy of professional and amateur connoisseurs, and courtesy of thieves and looters. Colonialism fostered new forms of knowledge in the work of the archaeologists and ethnographers of empire, and the scholars who ordered what they saw as the great chaos of indigenous culture, the better to understand it, and perhaps the better to control it.

There is little that remains unshaped, in Britain or in the once empire, and there were few who were wholly unconnected. This book is about empire, and specifically about the ways in which it shaped and distorted twentieth-century British lives, about the experience of Britons living and working in a world of empire and then living in a post-imperial world. It searches out one man's story and through it tells the empire stories of his one thousand colleagues, their friends, lovers and relations. Empire was the pre-existing fact of their lives, it was salt to the British diet. The classical age of imperial expansion had effectively ended in 1902 with the close of the South African War. While the new age of imperial retraction began with the loss of Ireland, and with the loss to nationalist activism of small but symbolic footholds in China in 1927, it got much more sharply under way with the transfer of power in India in 1947. This book explores the ways in which the world open to Britons at the imperial zenith (and always kept open by treaty and force, for there was little noonday calm) provided a range of opportunities to the inhabitants of the tiniest villages and towns. Most histories of Britain still draw an artificial divide between home and empire, and between the British and Britons over the seas. They are in fact mostly silent on the matter of empire and the roads to it from the British Isles. But for all that empire was a set of different worlds, with different codes and opportunities, any such divide is artificial.[6] Empire extended the geographical reach and location of British society, and hundreds of thousands of Britons moved backwards and forwards across this nominal divide between home and empire, and across colonial borders. Neither domestic nor imperial history can be understood until both are integrated.

My subjects in this book were Britons: labourers, farm workers, railwaymen, warehousemen, quarrymen. They had served in the army and the navy, as professional soldiers or as wartime volunteers and conscripts. They came from all the walks of British life. This book looks at the lives they lived in China, a country beyond the bounds of the 'formal' empire of colonies and protectorates, whose port cities hosted tiny but influential foreign-controlled enclaves, the 'treaty ports'. A body named the Shanghai Municipal Police (the SMP) saw to law and order in the largest of these bridgeheads, the International Settlement in the eastern port city of Shanghai. This Settlement occupied the heart of the city that was at once China's most important political, commercial and cultural centre. Shanghai was a true capital city for the Chinese twentieth century, but it was subject to the rule and vagaries of two foreign-run administrations (the other was French) that vied with each other and with neighbouring Chinese administrations and local and national authority. Some of the most pressing issues in China's foreign relations began, as one historian has put it, 'at home', and Shanghai caused many more of these than any other treaty port.[7] At the point of intersection between the Chinese residents of the International Settlement and the foreign authorities stood the men of the SMP. A thousand Britons joined the force between 1919 and 1941, all but a handful of them as constables, serving as bobbies on a Chinese beat. They policed this enclave and lived through the glory years of a city and culture in ferment.

It is easy enough now to dismiss empire as a distant, discrete other in the ordinary lives of the British twentieth century, the preserve solely of an *ancien régime* and its upper-class 'white mischief'. The lives and snobberies of the memsahibs are well recorded, as are settler shenanigans in wartime Kenya. A thousand Shanghaied British lives might seem an irrelevance in the empire story. But empire was – and is now – a normal part of the physical and mental landscape of all Britons, however abstractly exotic it seems. In the background to family stories skulks empire, and the historians who write its story are, like Jan Morris, no less 'embroiled in the imperial mesh'.[8] In Shanghai, the distorting prism of the pantomime of formal empire does not affect the vision so much, and we can see the lived thing raw. The story of these Shanghai policemen serves a broader purpose, for these men lived in a world whose contours were mapped out – and defended – by British and other imperialisms. Empire offered them choice, offered to take them away from England, Scotland, Wales, Ireland, away from the limited and the familiar, to live and work in North America, Asia, Africa, Australia. Here in Shanghai, at the margins of formal empire, and at the social margins of empire life – because policemen were marginal men – we can understand what this lost world meant to ordinary Britons, and what it means today to their relatives, descendants and neighbours. So this book is about them. It is also – it is mostly – a book about just one of them. It is a biography of a nobody which offers a window into an otherwise closed world. Richard Maurice Tinkler went to work in 1919 for the Shanghai Municipal Police, and he died in that city from injuries received during an encounter with Japanese marines in June 1939. He was by then no longer a policeman, but he was still in effect one of them, still claimed as such (they even updated his personnel file with the news of his death), and he was living a life many of them also lived in and outside the police service. This is his story; but in many ways it might stand as anybody's story, everyman let loose in an empire world. If 'everyman' is too strong, too loaded now, then we might think of it this way: Tinkler's story involves all the actors in the tale of empire, its proponents, opponents, victims and collaborators, those to whom empire was done, and those who did it. It was a life which still manages to touch us all. Of course, it also seems exotic at first glance – China always seems exotic at first glance – but for all the operatic staging, this is a very ordinary tale.

If you keep your eyes open in Britain you can see just how unexotic China really was, how much a part of an ordinary world of empire; you can also sense the violence of this past. On a central London street a long-past act of combat is frozen in its re-enactment for passers-by. On one side of the monument the Royal Marine Light Infantry are fighting in South Africa, and on the other side raising the siege of Tianjin in 1900. In the foreground a British marine bayonets a Chinese soldier. It's there on the Mall. And there is much, much more. The first hero of the Sudan was 'Chinese' Gordon. The China relics fill the museum cases: the 'Admonitions' scroll in the British Museum, a masterpiece of Chinese art, looted in 1900, lodged in the museum by the end of 1903.[9] Items 'from the Summer Palace in Peking', looted in 1860 during the second China war, now stock national and provincial collections in Britain.[10] Elsewhere there are ordinary trinkets made for foreign visitors which have found their way into museums and collections. China was part of the world of British empire, and Shanghai was the British headquarters, far more so than Hong Kong. In the eighteenth century British traders brought back porcelain and tea to a homeland besotted with chinoiserie and hooked on the green leaf (the Treasury was soon hooked on tea duties). The acquisition of bases in India opened the way for further British expansion eastwards, having given them access on the subcontinent to the one commodity which above all others found a welcome if illegal market in China: opium. In 1792 an embassy, led by Lord Macartney, was sent to China to set trading relations on a footing regulated on British and not just on Chinese terms – which had restricted trading to one port, Canton – and protected by formal diplomatic recognition. This and subsequent efforts foundered on the wariness of the Manchu rulers of China regarding British ambitions. In 1839 continuing tensions developed into a sort of war, settled by the Nanjing Treaty of 1842, which gave the British access to five ports including Shanghai, ceded to them the island of Hong Kong and established the principle of extraterritoriality by which British residents were to be subject to English law, administered by British consuls.[11] Subsequent wars and treaties expanded this presence. British residents built their own suburbs, constructing clubs and churches, stores and shipyards, establishing municipal administrations and police forces. By the 1930s there were some 20,000 British subjects residing in China outside Hong Kong, while tens of thousands more visited as merchant and Royal Naval seamen, or on military postings.

As Britain engaged with China, and as Britons developed their presence there, the country was drawn into the mainstream of the British encounter with the non-European world. Museums and libraries stocked up. Plant hunters went scavenging, and so did missionaries. Scholar-officials found retirement billets in the universities at home, compiling dictionaries, working out chronologies, proving the relationship of the Chinese to the lost tribes of Israel, the implacable obstacles the Chinese written script offered to progress, and the general uselessness of Chinese literature. Clergymen broadcast pulpit pleas for funding for the China enterprise; missionary propagandists described the country and the plight of its pagan souls in every possible medium catering for every possible market. China was always on the menu somewhere: it was a fact of British life. So were the Chinese: Chinese seamen served in the British merchant marine, some of them opening lodging houses and cafés for fellow nationals in London's Limehouse, and in Liverpool and Cardiff, creating little Chinese quarters that loomed large in the lurid, narcotic imagination of the journalist and the popular novelist.[12] Up to 50,000 Chinese men were recruited as mine labour on the Rand in the aftermath of the

1899–1902 South African War, the conditions of their service becoming a key political issue – 'the Chinese slavery question' – in the 1906 British general election.[13] A hundred thousand Chinese served as behind-the-lines labour for the British on the Western Front in the First World War.[14] Chinese resided in other British possessions in south-east Asia, too, and throughout the formal empire, most notably in Singapore, while Britons worked in China as missionaries, or businessmen in every possible line, and visited it as soldiers or seamen.

This Chinese connection is on display not only in museums and public squares, but also in homes throughout Britain, and in the overseas homes of the British diaspora and its descendants. They brought it home with them. I know this because I have seen it there: the carpet in the lounge, bought in Tianjin in the 1920s, the railway share certificate framed on the wall, the lacquerware on the sideboard, the old lapel badges denoting membership of the Shanghai Race Club, the snuff bottles, the opium pipe; the well-thumbed volumes penned by the 'old China hands' – the journalist or diplomat China experts – J. O. P. Bland's *Houseboat Days in China*, Daniel Varé's *Gate of Happy Sparrows*, Anne Bridge's *Peking Picnic*; old photo albums, postcards sent home, indifferent paintings and assortments of more and less art or craft. I have seen it all there because I searched it out. The papers of many of those involved in the British China enterprise now sit in various archives in libraries, local record offices, museums and universities, and such survivals always generate more questions than they alone can answer. It was in one such archive, while I was researching another book, that my entanglement with Richard Maurice Tinkler and his world began. This book was never meant.

This is how I remember it. Roderick Suddaby, Keeper of the Department of Documents, was on duty that day, 16 October 1989, in the grand, round reading room of London's Imperial War Museum. I was there to trawl through papers relating to men and women who had spent any part of the inter-war years in China, and which were deposited there either because they had been servicemen, or because they had been interned by the Japanese during the Pacific war. There is enough in that one depository to make you realize how complex British life in China was. Here are records of ordinary China Britons: soldiers, sailors, oil salesmen, nannies, a gas works superintendent, a jailer and hangman. Some had bit parts in large dramas, but most were muddling through life as best they could. They worked in all possible trades. The papers capture a slice of British life lived out or lived partly in China. These people worked in the large cities opened to foreign residence and partly surrendered to foreign control after the mid-nineteenth-century wars: Shanghai, Tianjin, Hankow. They worked for the Chinese government, in the Customs service, or as military or financial advisers. They worked for the bodies which administered the British settlements and concessions: the Tientsin and the Hankow British Municipal Councils, the Shanghai Municipal Council. They worked for multinational firms, flogging cigarettes in the 'interior', supplying oil for the lamps of China, serving out their time in wretchedly dull little ports with no choice of company except the bottle and/or a mistress. They were not lovers of or experts on China – they were not Sinophiles – nor were they Sinologists. They were not led to China through any particular calling. The fact of empire led them there. The violence of empire protected them or avenged their deaths (through the Royal Navy's China Station gun-boats, and naval landing parties). The papers are full of petty incident, weary moan and minor celebration, but even the dullest bring this past to life. Amongst the collections, Suddaby brought to my table two boxes, containing the papers of an R. M. Tinkler. 'I think you'll enjoy these,' I seem to remember him saying, and he dashed off some detail: how this man Tinkler had been a policeman in Shanghai, how the letters touched on the wars and troubles of the city, and were sometimes fairly frank, and how such candour in his account of an affair with a Russian woman had shocked Edith, his sister back home, the recipient and then donor. Suddaby had been to collect the papers back in 1970, remembering the trip and Edith well. This I remember, and my tatty notes show how I then devoured the documents, trans-cribing huge gobbets and pithy comments (no easy task, for the handwriting is confidently rotten). So I did enjoy them; and I also started to learn from them of the ordinariness of the China life, and how embedded it was in the broader British experience.

The man Tinkler got under my skin. There was intelligence and vivacity in the writing, but a foulness in thought and expression, and a violence which puzzled me. The letters were good stuff still, and I cited them liberally in the papers I was writing and publishing, inadequate as it seemed to do so without a proper understanding of their full context and meaning. There was something in the documents which suggested an acute personal disappointment, and a tremendous waste. For Tinkler, something was changed by China, by Shanghai, and something was broken by it. The documents covered the China life only in part: Tinkler stopped writing home in January 1930. A letter from October of that year from the Commissioner of Police which was lodged amongst the papers refers to 'more than one serious breach of discipline' in the previous eighteen months, and also demotion, but there was no detail, and nothing about this in his correspondence.[15] Tinkler is not indexed or discussed in histories of the British China presence or of Anglo-Japanese relations (and there is as yet no history of the SMP).[16] So I searched the paper trails of his life while getting on with other history business, looking him up in directories and indexes, copying what I found, exploring this lead and that. It was a sideline that might or might not come to something, one of many such which any historian works with. There were some obvious sources. The British diplomatic records dealing with his death led to traces of his involvement in another diplomatic incident in 1934. At the United States National Archives I read the SMP Special Branch's file covering the events in which he was killed (located there because these files had been acquired in Shanghai by the forerunner of the CIA in 1949).[17] But I needed more to be able to do anything with this material, and fitfully sought it. Tinkler's own letters mentioned a girlfriend, Lily Wilson, to whom he'd written a great deal from Shanghai before a breakdown in their friendship, and there was his sister Edith. So, assuming both were dead, I snatched the odd hour in the Probate Registry, looking for evidence which might lead me to Edith's relatives. Surnames change – Lily turned out not to be Wilson's proper name – but I finally found what I needed in August 1994. And to my surprise I was led to Edinburgh to Tinkler's half-brother and relatives, to a box containing a China story, a family story, and a man's story, all lodged safely, quietly away.

These were the makings of the life, but not a book, and they remained simply a distraction. I had other tasks in hand when I flew to Shanghai in 1994 for a three-month trawl through the holdings of the Shanghai Municipal Archives. But I took Tinkler with me, as it were (still under the skin), always on the list of possibilities – a topic to browse for when the other work grew dull. This archive was established in 1959, assembling records from administrative, educational and industrial concerns in the city. Many pre-dated the establishment in 1949 of the People's Republic, and they included the papers of the two foreign-run administrations in Shanghai, and many foreign business enterprises.[18] My other tasks foundered at the requisition desk, for in 1994 the archives I wanted to use were all still closed. But scholars had managed to get access in the past if they were looking at narrow, discrete topics. So I asked for personnel files, if they had them still, for example for this man Tinkler and for some of his peers. And out they were brought, to shut me up until my three-month visit was over. It was strange to have such papers in hand at last, the pages opening up the obscured past, offering explanations, prompting even more questions. You really do catch your breath. You can't focus properly but copy it all, and by hand, quickly; you cannot risk returning it in case somebody changes their mind (which they actually do there, snatching back the file mid-sentence from the desk as the mistake is realized). But at least 130 more such files were brought out before the drawbridge was raised. Of these, forty concerned the men who joined with Tinkler in 1919. And stored there, too, were the papers of the company he worked for after leaving the police, containing traces of his work and his death. So now I felt I really had him.

This is the result, a biography of Richard Maurice Tinkler. Even though his death in the early summer of 1939 was a noisy diplomatic incident splashed on the front pages of the British newspapers, it was a minor one in the great sweep to war, and it turned out to be a complicated affair, awkwardly timed and difficult in detail. The real focus of the British China story that season was Tianjin, in the north, where Japan and the British were caught on the thorns of their different imperialisms.[19] Historians dealing with the bigger Chinese picture have had too much else to choose from to shape and fill their narratives. But that is also why Tinkler's biography is needed, for such straight histories routinely lack the lived life of ordinary people and the events and circumstances that envelop them.[20] This is not a China problem.

There is a large literature on the communities established by Britons overseas in their new domains of Australia, South Africa, New Zealand and North America, or in the settler colonies (Kenya, Southern Rhodesia), but there is far less on the more transient world of empire life and work elsewhere. We have no end of biographies of senior or prominent colonial figures, and studies and nostalgic celebrations of colonial lives. Governor-generals get their lives written up (and stash their papers safely to help the process). The social (and sexual) round and the heightened snobberies of empire make for good copy, allowing the ruling caste to reflect anew on its own importance and quirks, and imperial critics to pillory the immoralities and depredations of that same elite.[21] Sometimes – but often really only in passing – these works turn their attention to the 'other ranks' and to 'poor whites'. The historical literature has recently turned to look at non-elite colonialists, more often than not focusing on issues of gender or race.[22] But we still have very few studies of the British or any other nation's 'servants of empire', while even the workaday deskwallahs – the 'thin white line' – were largely ignored until recently.[23] Their work was dismissed in the aftermath of imperial retreat, their achievements put beyond objective assessment by triumphant nationalist and anti-imperialist narratives which shouted down other histories, as they themselves had been shouted down in the empire age. The other ranks of empire work are obscurer still.[24] Even the five volumes of the new *Oxford History of the British Empire* (1999) do not much notice the men and women who did the job. There's little on the men of the armies of empire, on the navy, the merchant navy, railwaymen, labour supervisors. Nothing on the gas engineers of empire, the road builders, all those who weren't quite *pukka*, and precious little anywhere on policemen.[25]

It might be retorted that there is not enough still on those to whom the job of empire was done – that bayoneted Chinese soldier – whose history was often denied, and nearly always rewritten. The colonial subject – the man or woman policed – needs a voice, a name, a life story. The reproach would be right, and the work is beginning. In *The Seed is Mine*, Charles van Onselen used one black family's experiences to examine in microscopic detail South Africa's hard century, interweaving archival evidence into material from interviews with his main protagonist, Kas Maine, and his family, and composing a compelling survey of a hidden life and world. In *A Mouthful of Glass*, Dutch novelist Henk van Woerden traced the weird life of an even more marginal figure, Dimitrios Tsafendas, who was eventually to assassinate the South African Prime Minister, Hendrik Verwoerd in 1966. Born of an African mother and a Greek father, raised in Mozambique, Alexandria and South Africa, Tsafendas was revealed by van Woerden to have been a man without a home, a seaman without a port, constantly, compulsively shuttling along the supply routes of empires, unwanted, unlocated in the terms then available: nationality, race, class.[26] Maurice Tinkler isn't Kas Maine or Dimitrios Tsafendas. The black sharecropper, the mestizo wanderer and the white colonial policeman are certainly worlds apart on one level, but they lived and worked in empire, and only a closer examination of non-elite life – colonialist and colonized – can bring out more fully the complexity of experience of those in all parts of the web of world empire which had caught and joined them all.

And these men are more marginal than we might think. The empire was never a simple question of black and white, of ruled and ruling. The police (a tiny officer corps aside) were allotted a specific slot in an intricate and fluid hierarchy and expected to know their place (and stay in it). They weren't *pukka*. They weren't men of education or culture, and they were subject to military-style discipline. They threatened the niceties (and often the pretensions) of empire by their very presence. They were treated as servants, but at the same time found themselves issued with servants. They were treated as inferior and condescended to, but at the same time found themselves hectored and lectured about their superiority as Britons and as 'white' men to the Asians in the force and city. Their private social and sexual choices might undermine the public mores of empire. As men at the margins of the British community in the city, and at the same time as the front line between the foreign administration and Chinese society, they might and they did blur the boundaries and fictions on which colonialism rested. Shanghai puts the confusions of empire practice sharply into focus.

The men of the Shanghai Municipal Police force, subjects and servants of British empire (as realized locally in Shanghai), were also actors in modern Chinese history, and not simply as the imperialist villains of the piece. They knew the British empire's security agenda, and at times served imperial interests directly. They served a British-dominated administration which stood outside empire, but was intimately entwined with it, drawing from the same personnel and systems pools, and sharing a common ideology. The SMP was suspicious of nationalism, and saw communism as an enemy (which, of course, it was). In the first half of the twentieth century it struggled against and through the turbulent politics of Chinese urban nationalism. It was also part of a broader struggle against Soviet internationalism, other colonial nationalisms, and Japanese militarism. The archive now in the United States offers much meat for exploration of the role of the force in the tortured early history of communism in China.[27] The SMP certainly got their men, and women. But this was not a political police: its Special Branch was but one department of a large force coping with all the chaos that twentieth-century urbanization could throw at it. The SMP administered a Chinese city at the heart of political, social and cultural change in twentieth-century China, and its policies – and at points its mistakes – fuelled that change. So the history of these men is a part of Chinese history. Until recently the foreign presence in China has not been much studied, and it is still little understood.[28] The Western literature on modern Chinese history – which is dominated by American scholarship – is still infused with anti-imperialist sentiment and assumption (and also at times with anti-British sentiment[29]). The rhetoric and analyses of Chinese communism and nationalism themselves cast long shadows, but the cause lay more in attacks on existing assumptions by politically radicalized younger historians starting in the late 1960s. In their view, analysis of Chinese history was too heavily based on questions deriving from the 'Western impact' on China; in the process the ways in which Chinese people made their own history were obscured. There was some truth in this, and much good work emerged from the shift to what was termed a 'China-centred' focus, but the pendulum swung too far.[30] The nuanced understanding of the colonial encounter which is evident in historical writing on South Asia or Africa is mostly missing from writings on China. So men like Maurice Tinkler get short shrift: they're merely 'imperialists', and especially predictable with it because they're policemen.

The policeman is therefore usually a somewhat anonymous figure in published narratives about Shanghai history, and few have left published memoirs which might give them a voice other than that recorded in official documents and reports.[31] Scholars instead resort to guesswork and cliché, claiming for example that the SMP attracted men 'whose familiarity with ammunition and killing might otherwise have led them into lives of crime'.[32] This book aims to put real men back into the uniforms that can be glimpsed in nearly every photograph of an old Shanghai street scene (sometimes literally so: 'That's me,' said Frank Peasgood, pointing to the photograph of an otherwise anonymous bobby in his friend E. W. Peters's volume *Shanghai Policeman*[33]). The odd Shanghai-based novel aside, the two most prominent

AN INTERNATIONAL POLICEMAN ON PATROL IN THE
CHINESE PART OF THE SETTLEMENT

reminders of the Shanghai police story come through the literature on the history of unarmed combat techniques, knife-fighting and small-arms training, especially in connection with covert warfare in the Second World War (in all of these there was an important Shanghai connection), and through Hergé's cartoon stories of the boy detective Tintin.[34] But there is not much else, and in China even less remains.

The contemporary politics of anti-imperialism still make it difficult to find surviving Chinese actors from the Shanghai police story. The attempts I made to do so were all rebuffed. I met one, by chance, who had briefly been a personal assistant to the Deputy Commissioner of Police, but he was shy of the topic. Such men, some 6,500 of whom joined between 1919 and 1941, are all there caught on paper somewhere, as is the evidence of the trouble they could have been in in 1949. In 1969 the archives staff of the Public Security Bureau in Shanghai – the contemporary police force – combed through the same files that I have used in this book (each one of which was stamped 'Enemy Archive'). The archivists appended to the front of each file a list – headed 'Never forget class struggle' – of the names of Chinese mentioned within in whatever capacity – police officer, crime victim, station coolie. Other documents littering the files make it clear that these men and women were then to be further investigated. Pre-printed forms itemized the 'counter-revolutionary' activity discovered, and postcards were readied, to be sent to their places of work, asking for investigations to be carried out, and for reports. This history was a serious business. I have used these files to reconstruct lives; but they have also served to destroy lives in Shanghai.[35]

This book, then, is a history of the other ranks of empire, of the police force in Shanghai, and of the city itself – which cannot but join the cast – and it is the life of a man. But it is also the record of the journey. Tinkler was not Corvo, nor was he Backhouse: there is no 'hidden life' of a public figure to uncover, as A. J. A. Symons uncovered Frederick Rolfe (the writer Baron Corvo), or as Hugh Trevor-Roper uncovered Sir Edmund Trelawny Backhouse, Bt., eminent Sinologist, congenital fraud.[36] This is instead a record of a life recovered, and of the search for an understanding of a man and his place and time. The death made it all happen; Tinkler would otherwise be just another name. Death is useful; historians feed off it, and it generates documentation; unexpected death – early, violent, disappointing death – is even more so. In Tinkler's case it led to diplomatic correspondence, newspaper columns, probate materials, police investigation files and inquest transcripts. Loss also forces the living to take immediate stock, fixing memories and relationships in time. The living protect the memory and the memorials of those lost to them, keep documents and photographs and lobby to keep their dead somehow alive, and to give the death some meaning. Tinkler's sister Edith did just that, as did his first girlfriend, Lily Wilson. As I looked out from this death I found an ordinary man whose life was unusually and accidentally well documented; and whose ordinary life seems to exemplify the opportunities, contradictions and traps of twentieth-century empire. So I found more than a man; I found a world, and a means of describing that world. I was led back to Shanghai as significant sections of the colonial archive were opened. I was led to Manchester, to the uncatalogued records of the company he was working for at the time of his death. I was led back to the Public Record Office, to military and diplomatic files. I was led to bungalows and sheltered housing, to long chats with the wary survivors of the Shanghai policing days. I was led into contact with sons and daughters, nieces and nephews, grandchildren of the Shanghai police, into a world marked out by a few scraps of paper, the inherited albums, the trinkets, and the family stories attached to them, and the family stories unattached to any Chinese reality. I was led into the British hinterland of this Shanghai story, and shown how clearly it lay within a broader history of men and women living in an empire world. In Maurice Tinkler, and in his peers, we can examine the life and workings of the world that was opened up to empire in the first half of the twentieth century.

So you sit there – as I sat there with the box, in Edinburgh, taking the folded documents from the envelopes, and laying them out for inspection. It is sometimes difficult to make sense of the ordering (they weren't stored for such use, they weren't created with such a purpose in mind), but soon, without even thinking, the sorting-out began: the registration certificates (marriages, births, deaths), the references from employers, the discharge certificates, passports, permits (guns, travel, driving), medal citations and so on, all the shards of a documented life. Some things immediately forge connections, supplying the answers to the questions posed by the scraps from Shanghai, Washington DC, London. Others dismiss your working hypotheses, and show that you've been looking in the wrong places, for the wrong things. The photographs go to one side, but sometimes the inscription on the back raises a puzzled frown: when was he there, and who is she? Here is one diary, here another, both tail off but there is substance enough.

You quickly get the rough outlines of a life stored away, and the significant dates which map out the route. So in that sense the story starts to shape itself from the moment you unfold the first sheet. How to start the story is never really an issue, especially as we know that it hinges on the death. Overall it seems best, and clearest, to start here, with the English beginnings of the China journey, and so start with a birth.

2

Before Shanghai

Shanghai was a city of immigrants, of sojourners who stayed a season, a few years, or even a working lifetime. Journeys to Shanghai began in villages and towns in China and India, and in the villages and towns of Britain. Journeys by Britons to Shanghai in 1919, and for some years thereafter, were diverted by the First World War. This is one such voyage. Richard Maurice Tinkler, always known to his family as Maurice, was born on 29 October 1898 in a house in Yewbarrow Terrace, in the small Lancashire town of Grange-over-Sands, where his father Alfred was an ironmonger. A pretty resort town on the edge of the Lake District, Grange is dominated by the heights of Yewbarrow and Hampsfell at the tip of the Cartmel peninsula on the north shore of Morecambe Bay. The town itself is younger even than the Shanghai International Settlement: it was a product of the Furness railway, which opened in 1846, four years after the Nanjing Treaty. Yewbarrow Terrace, a smart row of shops, sits opposite the railway station across an ornamental garden and the war memorial. In a 1900 photograph the terrace looks idyllic, with Yewbarrow rising behind it. The sight was altogether the antithesis of the urban sprawl that greeted new arrivals as they sailed up the Huangpu river to Shanghai.

Alfred Tinkler, son of a blacksmith, was 30, and before his marriage, on 16 December 1897, to Elizabeth Shuttleworth, daughter of a parish clerk, he had visited Chicago and Cape Town; for what purpose and for how long we remain ignorant. He returned and bought from his father what an 1899 photograph shows to be a prosperous-looking shop. But Alfred was never a successful man; by 1901 he was the proprietor of the Red Lion Hotel in Hawkshead, in the Lake District, but was declared bankrupt in April 1904. The family moved to the nearby town of Ulverston. In later years Alfred was reduced from the status of independent small businessman to that of a store clerk at the Vickers shipyard in Barrow-in-Furness. A daughter, Edith, was born on 27 November 1899, and Elizabeth died sometime after spring 1901. On 30 January 1915 Alfred married Rachel Annie Duston, daughter of a joiner and wheelwright, and mother of his third child, John Eric, born ten months later.[1]

Alfred's steady social decline contrasts with the promise later shown by the two children of his first marriage. By the end of the 1930s Edith was running her own millinery business in Penrith. Maurice was recommended by his headmaster in 1919 as an 'unusually industrious and intelligent student . . . popular with his fellows, and gentlemanly in manner', who did well in his examinations at Ulverston's Victoria Grammar School.[2] The co-educational school, a 'handsome pile of buildings' dating from 1900, was modern in its fittings but traditional in its contrived rituals. The pages of the *Victorian*, the school's journal, offer plentiful evidence of university entries and successes.[3] Beyond lists of certificate and examination passes, however, they provide few glimpses of Maurice's progress in his years there from 1911 to 1915. In July 1915 he passed his Senior School Certificate, the matriculation examinations for the Northern Universities, and he also won the school's Senior Prize for Excellence in Art. Maurice seems to have been impatient. He found Ulverston 'dead slow', he later wrote from Shanghai, and he showed little interest in keeping up with his friends there. His school successes, and the opportunities for university entrance they enabled, were also passed up. The reason may have been family finances; but it may also have been his own desire to cut loose.

Maurice's relations with his father had already come unstuck by adolescence, perhaps because of the second marriage. From an early letter to his stepmother, in 1916, awkwardly and formally addressed to 'Mrs Tinkler', it is clear that they had had little previous communication, 'on account of my aloofness' and, as he put it later to Alfred, because he was a 'thick-headed school-kid'.[4] He certainly looks sullen and 'thick headed' in what seems to be the earliest surviving photograph. After Elizabeth's death, the widower had taken little active interest in his children, leaving them to be brought up by his sister Florence (Fanny), in Penrith. On 20 August 1915, the year he remarried, Alfred wrote out a furious but legally invalid will which concluded: 'To my son Richard Maurice I leave *nothing* for his beastly behaviour towards me.'[5] Five days later Maurice began working at his father's place of employment, as a clerk at the Vickers Naval Construction Works – a location that would probably have exempted him from military service when he was old enough – but in November, having lied about his age, he joined the army instead.[6] Whether he did so because of the state of family affairs, or merely out of a desire to take part in the war, is unclear, although he later refused to quit the forces until, as he wrote to his father in December 1916, 'I have had a chance to show you that I am not what you thought me'. There is irony here. In January 1914 Tinkler's school had been given a lecture on 'The Futility of War' by a representative of the Norman Angell League. Angell argued that the costs of warfare between modern industrial nations now far outweighed whatever benefits might accrue from conquest. Maurice was on the magazine committee that oversaw an editorial confidently proclaiming that Angell's call for a realistic view of modern warfare, *The Great Illusion*, 'ought to be read by all the boys'.[7] Maurice instead sought affirmation of manhood and character in Flanders. He thrived there, but it warped him all the same.

Tinkler trained with the 30th Reserve Battalion Royal Fusiliers at Leamington Spa and Oxford. He was then named for a draft to the 24th 'Sportsman's' Battalion, already serving in France, on 31 March 1916. That day he began to keep brief notes, in a pocket diary he had bought from Boots the chemist, which relate the bare facts of his progress towards the front line, starting with an inspection by the Brigadier-General commanding the Brigade. On the following Monday he had his photograph taken in town, probably the one he sent to his old school, which shows him unsmiling, serious, with puppy-fat cheeks. On Tuesday, 4 April he left Oxford for Paddington, crossing the Channel the following day. Two final weeks of training with 'real bombs' and bayonets followed at the Étaples training camp. Life there also included the odd bout of police duty and rest – 'Lovely day enjoyed it as I did scarcely anything' – and introductions to 'hellish mud', and 'an utter swine' of a Sergeant-Major. On Palm Sunday, probably under orders, he attended divine service at the Soldiers' Christian Association Hut in the camp. He found it 'damnable'.

Tinkler was one of a draft of twenty-eight men of 'fair physique' who joined the battalion on 22 April.[8]

Tinkler – now 4372 Private Tinkler of A Company – found himself on his first front-line sentry duty in a bad trench on Maundy Thursday near Hersin. Easter Sunday was spent under a heavy bombardment and 'hot rifle fire' in the night. They were relieved the following day. 'Cocker killed,' he noted, 'Four days seemed very long as I had scarcely any sleep.' John Cocker, a 28-year-old Blackburn native, was presumably one of the draft who had joined with Tinkler. On fatigue duty that night Maurice heard a nightingale singing in the village at midnight. Back in the trenches on a 'bitterly cold' 28 April, he underwent his first gas attack the next day. On 30 April, the entry reads 'straffed by shrap[nel] 1st time . . . Taylor killed'. Taylor was one of three men who died; ten were wounded. Not surprisingly, the diary starts to dry up. A brief note on the species of butterfly he had seen was almost the last trace he left in his diary of life beyond the trenches, and beyond khaki. After a second spell in the front line Maurice spent a week resting and on police duty at Ablain, before returning to the trenches on Vimy Ridge on 3 July, the third day of the Somme battle. After three days he was invalided out of the front line with an unidentified leg problem, and taken by motor ambulance to a casualty clearing station at Lapugnoy. The problem cannot have been serious, but it kept him out of the firing line for at least a month, which he spent at a convalescent camp in Boulogne. Maurice made a point of not mentioning it in a letter he wrote to his father in mid-July, merely noting that he was non-combatant. He spent a week gardening and walking on the beach in sight of the English coast at Wimereux, north of Boulogne. Time 'passed pleasantly', and he caught up with many acquaintances, all of them, presumably, wounded. Three days of tent erecting in August were followed by a return to the convalescent camp after a medical inspection. Then he returned to Étaples on 13 August, and prepared to rejoin the Battalion. Meanwhile, the 24th had suffered heavy casualties at the beginning of that month, including Private C. W. Sutherland, who killed himself on 7 August.

The Battalion was rotated in and out of the front line as part of the 5th Brigade of the Second Division in Flanders, the tedium of front-line duty alternating with the tedium of training, re-equipping and assimilating new drafts of men. Around a thousand men formed the battalion, the basic infantry unit of the war. They were organized in four companies (A, B, C, D), consisting usually of four platoons each, themselves each split into four sections. Large enough to cater efficiently for all their basic needs, the battalion was small enough theoretically for most men to get to know each other, at least by sight. The 24th Battalion Royal Fusiliers was closely involved in some half-dozen major engagements before the end of the conflict, but spent months at a time seeing very little action. The routine attrition of trench fighting – snipers, trench mortars, machine guns, gas and German raids – steadily culled the Battalion of its men, hardly giving them time for manhood: the average age of one draft was 22.

While Tinkler was convalescing with his gammy leg, 33-year-old Captain Cecil Meares led half of C Company in an attack on the German positions near Guillemont on 30 July, as part of the Battle of Delville Wood. Twelve men returned alive, 105 were lost in the dawn mist and on the German wire, where Meares himself lay hanging. After a period in quieter trenches the whole Battalion, including Maurice, was engaged in an attack near Edmund Blunden's 'terrible' Beaumont Hamel from 13 to 15 November. Advancing over broken terrain a mere twenty yards behind the artillery barrage, the two waves of attackers became mixed up, and the men advanced en masse, precision and tactics replaced by a premodern mêlée. The German trenches captured in the assault were held for two days before withdrawal, a period, Maurice declared, when he feared he would never return. For Blunden, the Division's attack was 'a feat of arms vieing with any recounted'.[9] For the 24th there was less joy: 250 men were killed, wounded or missing. A and B companies were once more gutted at the end of April 1917 near Oppy Wood. During 'considerable activity' near Graincourt in the first week of December Maurice acted with 'conspicuous bravery', while thirteen other men received the Military Medal that month.[10] A photograph taken in July 1917 shows Private Tinkler with a lean face, puppy-fat worn away; he looks older, and stares at the camera, hand on hip, a glass of beer on a stand next to him.

In March 1918 Ludendorff's offensive blew open the British front lines. The 24th were subjected to aerial attack, and then a 'nightmare'

withdrawal that degenerated from a march into a rout. 'The whole countryside', wrote a private in the Battalion, 'was alive with our men hurrying westward.' The 24th was steadily driven back from successive positions around Bapaume over a week of bloody, raggedly confused fighting, and the second offensive in April inflicted further casualties. The War Cemetery near Bertincourt village, from which they were driven in the early stage of the battle, contains almost a thousand Britons. The lack of protection offered by the 'old and dilapidated' trenches they had suddenly to occupy as the front neared the village did for many of the victims.[11] The quieter summer in which the Battalion trained furiously for 'rapid open warfare and attack' after the years of trench fighting was the prelude to the British August offensive. Before it began Tinkler, by now a Lance-Corporal, posed with his section for a photograph. He is almost smiling, and there is a cocky confidence in his face. He received the Distinguished Conduct Medal for his actions during the Battalion's seizure of the villages of Behagnies and Sepignies on 23 to 25 August, taking over command of his platoon, largely composed of 'young untried soldiers' when all his superiors had been wounded. Under his command the platoon 'took part in the hottest fighting. Whenever pockets of the enemy were discovered barring the advance he was the first to dash forward and overcome them.' The citation in the *London Gazette* concluded bluntly: 'He killed many of the enemy.' There were 200 casualties in this engagement, the men advancing on 23 August through 'heavy artillery fire', with little counter battery support. Behagnies was seized by the Battalion on the 25th (it 'shall be taken at all costs tonight' read Brigade Orders that day), and held through a day of counter-attack and heavy shelling. The triumphal tone of the Battalion's War Diary in the latter part of 1918 – the men went 'forward in full confidence that they could beat the enemy, and when they had so thoroughly beaten him, [were] proud and elated to have seen him so thoroughly outmanoeuvred and outfought', reported the Lieutenant-Colonel – contrasts sharply with the earlier pages, where the lists of casualties make for profoundly bitter reading.[12]

To his father Maurice wrote optimistically, and in clichés out of the *Boy's Own Paper* or the *Daily Mail*, which supplied perhaps the only vocabulary front-line soldier and home-side civilian could share. 'I think we have really turned the corner now,' he wrote in July 1916, and he described the strange sight of a sea of poppies and the blood-red symbolism they offered, echoing perhaps consciously images from John McCrae's poem 'In Flanders Fields' (first published in December 1915). 'There is not a patch of ground in Europe where more blood has been shed.' Perhaps out of optimism, more likely out of a desire to avoid saying something more brutal, he added in a postscript: 'That's all over now though.' Otherwise it was schoolboy talk which peppered his letters: '"Très bon" as Mr Atkins says out here'; here, where he was 'learning in the finest school on earth'. And he was, after all, little more than a schoolboy. Within a few months he struck a much harder note. Although still capable of being moved by the pathos of the papers and schoolbooks left behind by a French refugee family in his billet, Tinkler was soon involved in pranks with skulls. He credulously repeated stories of German 'corpse-factories' in which glycerine was extracted from dead soldiers, and demanded the literal decimation of striking munitions workers. The macabre self-protection that is typical of war set in. 'A little humour is useful here,' he wrote in January 1917. Coming off from a midnight bombing raid on a German trench ten months later, in which eleven of the twenty-five attackers had been wounded, he wrote to ask his sister for a sketch-book and some pencils: 'I can amuse myself a bit then,' he added. In return, he sent back captured German gas-helmets.[13] Three sketches survive. A competent watercolour of the 'The Control Post', Ablain-Saint-Nazaire, lists on the back the names of three friends, killed at Beaumont Hamel, Delville Wood, and in July 1918. Another drawing sketched directly into Lily Wilson's commonplace book shows silhouetted soldiers lifting the body of a fallen comrade on a stretcher. His florid script decorates the reverse leaf, inscribing a quotation almost vulgarly at odds with the mawkish solemnity of the image: 'Though the Boche has done/your chum in,/And the Serjeants done/your rum in,/And there ain't no/rations comin',/Carry On.' Nowhere else does Tinkler mention the dead outside his first pocket diary.

The few surviving letters to his family are restrained and mostly pointedly optimistic. His father was ill with the cancer that killed him on Christmas Day 1916, and this illness, and the shock of war on a 17-year-old boy, seemed to effect as much reconciliation as was

possible under the circumstances. 'There have been many moments out here when I have thought that these petty quarrels were too small to think about,' he wrote to his stepmother in September 1916. It must have been distressing to be learning, it seems piecemeal, of the seriousness of his father's condition while he himself was in battle. The family were as keen not to upset him with the truth, as he was not to upset them with his own. One letter from his father had reached Maurice when only 'a few hours before I had thought I would never see any more letters at all'. But such candour was unusual. His last surviving letter to Alfred was written on 9 December, and posted five days later. 'We have in our letters, gone back to a better type of friendship,' Maurice wrote, 'like we used to be when we used to go out for briars at Grange, something we had both missed for some time.' He resisted pleas from the rest of the family to leave the army and come home to see his father. Ignorant of the severity of Alfred's illness, he refused to leave the army through the simple expedient of admitting to his superiors that he had lied about his age. 'I don't want to come home on such an errand. Please for my sake, old man, set

your teeth and wait . . . and then we'll be pals really and do something.'
'It's not a man's game,' he noted, 'I'd rather be up to my neck in mud.'
Alfred died two weeks later.

Compassionate leave seems to have been granted to Maurice on
this occasion. He returned to France writing back about his eagerness
for the remaining family to stay together, but bitter about his prospects
in Britain. The only other known break from France occurred in
February 1918. Maurice visited his stepmother – whom he still
addressed in his letters as Mrs Tinkler – and then spent his last day
before returning in Leeds, visiting a former Ulverston class-mate,
Elizabeth Jane 'Lily' Wilson. Leaving Lily was 'rotten', he declared.
The daughter of the chief engineer on a lake steamer, she was studying
for her BA at the university. The diversion on the way back to France
is the earliest surviving indication that they were sweethearts. Lily met
him at the station and they spent ten hours in each other's company
before he travelled on to London and France. Maurice sent her sketches
and watercolours from the front, but no letters survive.

Tinkler served as a runner from at least early 1917 onwards, carrying messages from post to post. A fellow runner, he wrote in a letter
partly reproduced in the *Victorian*, turned out to be an Arnside man.
They had many friends in common back home.[14] The man was killed
in July 1918. This was a dangerous job, but one which at least left
more room for independent initiative than normal duty, and which
would have appealed to his developing individualistic streak. It would
also have meant missing many of the tedious fatigues and duties of
life both in and out of the trench. As he wrote in May 1918, fresh
from a spell at the front, 'the last time up the line had a much better
time than the company, though I had plenty of excitement'. His awards
testify to his bravery and resourcefulness as a soldier. He fought, and
endured bombardment. Friends were killed almost from his first day
in the trenches, and against the odds and despite the Battalion casualty
lists he emerged physically unscathed. He led, and enjoyed leading.
He killed 'many of the enemy'. If he learnt lessons from the war, they
were that opportunity had to be seized, and that violence achieved
results, or at least that action involved violence. It is also clear that
France was his finishing school, where he grew up surrounded by men,
most of them older than himself (at least initially). The schoolboy

soldier became an adult between 1915 and 1919 in this 'finest school on earth'. He set out to prove himself to his father to be 'not what you thought of me', but this was rendered futile by Alfred's death. However, he continued to write self-consciously in his letters to his sister, aunt and stepmother about maturing, and about manliness. In the photographs he chose to keep or send he seems to have been doing the same. Playing a 'man's game' was a theme Tinkler later returned to in his Shanghai letters. His father gone, he measured his growing up in France against the older men he lived and fought with, and he also sought out the approbation of more senior figures (his company commander in France, more senior officers in Shanghai). But his idea of manliness was also something he constructed himself, and the markings by which he measured it were of his own devising: a man courted danger and displayed his strength; a man led other men; a man lived solo and – as we shall see – a man broke hearts. The manliness of the battlefield was not to be distinguished from the manliness of the battlefield of life.

Before the end of the war Tinkler was recommended for a commission and he was transferred to the 23rd Officer Cadet Battalion back in Britain, with the provisional rank of Second Lieutenant. Somebody proudly kept the *Victorian* updated. But the armistice in November 1918 put an end to all that. The 23rd was based at Catterick, and we have two photographs taken at this time. The first is hardly striking, as he poses with his fellow cadets of D Company in front of Hut 52. The men look awkward in each other's company, and pensive at the change which was due to affect them. The second is a swagger portrait. Posing alone against a bland landscape studio backdrop, overcoat buttoned, collar ruffed up, Tinkler clutches a cane. Looking at Tinkler's photographs of his wartime progress, we see him mature and confidently display officer rank. This portrait is a climax, even if its affectation is clear and almost ridiculous. Maurice Tinkler was marking his progress, and had found his level. But for all that he would not be able to keep it in Britain. Earlier in the fighting Tinkler wrote to his sister Edith that although he would be likely to get a commission if he applied, 'it's no use without £'s'd'. He was obviously prepared to try it out anyway in late 1918, but the plight of the 'Temporary Gentlemen', the non-commissioned classes who were

promoted beyond their station, was a recognized social problem after the war. The atrocious casualty rates of the conflict had dictated that many men were commissioned who ordinarily would never have had the chance. In the field, in an emergency, British society was adaptable; back home during the peace it was much less so. Tinkler never really got his chance, however. Not for the last time, he was prevented at the very last minute from taking a significant step up the social ladder. His rank on discharge was Corporal. He was perhaps a little over-keen on arrival in Shanghai to stress that he was in a Cadet Battalion on discharge, and is listed in the Shanghai Municipal Council's list of its employees' war service as a second Lieutenant, but in a 1922 survey he listed himself correctly.[15] His war service was to become a positive asset in the police, and he was to be given special duties as a result. But the army was a school he graduated from with little to show for time served except a sure and surly hatred of his non-commissioned status. In the army he posed in his uniform as he rose through the ranks. No photograph of Tinkler in police uniform survives. The absence speaks volumes about his sense of self.

Tinkler left the army on 19 February 1919, and returned to spend a couple of months of enforced, but enjoyable, idleness at home. He toyed with the idea of enrolling at university in Manchester but chose not to; he was later reported to have felt 'too old, and saddened, and disillusioned by the War'. He subscribed 5s. to the school's war memorial, but did not join the Old Scholars' Union. Work was difficult to get. Family legend has it that Edith, exasperated by his behaviour, flung at him one day a newspaper containing an advertisement for the Shanghai Municipal Police and asked, rhetorically, why he didn't go to China. 'Fancy 4372 as a policeman,' he had once joked to his father, in a letter home after standing military police duties behind the line in July 1916.[16]

Tinkler had written from France about wanting to escape Britain after the war. He wanted to 'get to some country that is not tied up in the knots of cant and hypocrisy'.[17] There seemed to be no anger against the rights or wrongs of the war itself, certainly none was expressed in his letters home (although this was hardly surprising as all mail was censored). Nor did he express any retrospective discontent in his letters from China. In fact, the war is never mentioned. There might be a host of explanations for such a silence: perhaps it was all too difficult to talk about, perhaps Shanghai was just too much fun and too interesting for him to waste time on retrospection ('I like changes myself' he noted in a wartime letter), perhaps, also, as the evidence suggests, he had actually had a good war. It was the civilian strikers and whiners back home who greatly angered him. Tinkler wrote that 10 per cent of all strikers should be shot, to encourage the others. This violence was obviously fuelled by his sure knowledge of what we know statistically to be true: those who stayed out of the trenches were doubly blessed, as they missed the war and their incomes and standard of living increased.[18] Tinkler's anger was not unusual; angry servicemen and ex-servicemen were responsible for a variety of violent protests in Britain in 1919 and after, against immigrant workers, against delays in demobilization, against unemployment. The anger of the Black and Tans in Ireland was the anger of ex-soldiers fighting what they saw as treason. Tinkler's letters from China abound in angry demands for military solutions to problems, for order, discipline and unity: for Tinkler, any weakness or vacillation in dealing with China was betrayal. Never explicit, but always present, was the sense that it betrayed the Flanders dead. The war, and the army, formed Tinkler in other ways that will be explored later. They provided his first tastes of adult life, of autonomy, and they also rubbed his nose in the stultifying, wasting certainties and rituals of British society.

Disgust with Britain apart, Tinkler may have also inherited a part of his father's youthful inclination to wander which, combined with conditions in Britain for returning servicemen, propelled him away from more conventional courses: his unfinished but promising education, his family and, indeed, from Lily Wilson. His former class-mate was finishing her course even as he prepared to sail, and was preparing to become a schoolteacher. There was an understanding between them, an engagement as she later described it, but he sailed nonetheless.[19] Maurice's feelings of dislocation at being released from the army into jobless civilian life were probably compounded by a sense of opportunities squandered, and increasing distance from his old friends and family. The advertisement Edith showed him obviously served both as a challenge, and as a temptation, although its wording is bland:

OFFICIAL SITUATIONS

SHANGHAI MUNICIPAL COUNCIL, POLICE FORCE – POLICE RECRUITS are now required. Applicants must be unmarried, of good physique, with good teeth. About 20 to 25 years of age, not less than 5ft. 10in in height, chest about 38in fully expanded, and able to furnish excellent references as to character. Salary commences at Taels 85 per month (at an average exchange equal to about £13 per month. The rate of exchange is liable to fluctuation). Men in the Army, Navy or Reserve must obtain full discharge before enlistment. AGREEMENT – for 3 years, with free passage to Shanghai; liberal superannuation scheme and bonus of £2 to outfit. Particulars will not be forwarded to applicants unless they clearly state in writing their age, height and chest measurements and that they are able to comply with the above requirements – Apply by letter in envelope marked 'Police' to Messrs JOHN POOK and Co., Agents for the Municipal Council of Shanghai, 58 Fenchurch-Street, London EC3.

This note was printed in the *People* next to those requiring recruits for the police in the Seychelles ('Sergt. Majs. and Staff. Sergts' were ideal), and in East Africa ('prefer ex-police'); Singapore's Harbour Board sought boilermakers and Road Foremen were wanted for Uganda.[20] These were minor facets of the great movement abroad which had long tempted the British localities. A 1904 edition of the local *Barrow News*, for example, which I searched for details of Alfred's bankruptcy, instead threw up an advertisement from the Commissioner of Emigration which noted that 'Prosperity awaits every willing worker in Canada'.[21] Between 1911 and 1914 almost two and a half million migrants left the British Isles for the non-European world. Between 1919 and 1921 another million left. Such advertisements and the pull of family and friends attracted 200,000 emigrants in 1919 alone.[22] Empire beckoned the demobilized working-class male from the newspaper classifieds.

There has been nothing in this story so far that would suggest China as a destination for this Lancashire native. There were no friends in China, or wartime acquaintances who had been there (or at least, any that we know of). Indeed, in later life Edith blamed herself for Maurice's death because his going to China was 'my idea'. In mid-April 1919 Tinkler wrote to John Pook and Co. as instructed for information about joining the SMP, and the recruitment process was speedily completed.[23] He obtained references from a curate ('fine, clean-minded and intelligent'), a Justice of the Peace, and a local foundry manager. The applicants were usually interviewed by a former army colonel and Charles Mayne, a former SMP officer, and often by senior officers at home on furlough. Maurice passed a medical examination in London on 13 May, and signed a preliminary declaration to work for the SMC. In Glasgow, before sailing, he swore on oath: 'that I will well and faithfully serve the Municipality of Shanghai for the term of Three Years; as a Third-Class Constable of the Municipal Police Force of Shanghai, and will observe and obey all orders of the Municipal Council and Officers set over me. So help me God.' In making this declaration Tinkler joined the service officially the same day, 25 June, and sailed on the SS *Devanha*, with the other recruits of his draft, changing at Hong Kong to a China Navigation Company coaster, SS *Tean* (actually Te-an, a Chinese name). They arrived in Shanghai on 15 August 1919, after a bad journey via Port Said and Penang (which he found 'jolly interesting') and Singapore ('ripping but sweltering hot'). The journey took in the cardinal points of the British imperial system, which effectively girdled the globe. The men sailed second class, itself a foretaste of their intended status in Shanghai, equipped with a passage allowance and a joining bonus. They knew that they would have to refund their passage out if they left the service early, that they were going to have to learn Chinese, that the climate was good but 'very hot' for two months of the year. They were told that the recreation facilities available included a library and a billiard table in every station, a cricket club and a shooting club, and that a houseboat was available for shooting expeditions. 'Promotion is certain for steady and efficient men,' noted the terms of service. Competition for the posts had been heavy; even in normal years there were about eight applicants for every post, and the medical examination was rigorous. But the men were on the whole told very little about the city they were moving to, and knew even less about the culture they were going to confront. But what mattered most, as Maurice noted to his aunt Fanny Tinkler on 22 August in his first letter home, was that 'a white man can get a job out here . . . He can't in England.'

This, then, was how Maurice Tinkler, an ironmonger's son from England's Lake District, came to Shanghai. There is not much that is unusual in this story so far, save that it is recorded in better detail than most narratives of the early life and wartime service of the millions of British men who served in the First World War. A boy effectively runs away from home to join the army at the age of 16, and serves for three years and 102 days. He knows little of the world before he goes, and he can hardly know much more of it on his return, but he has grown and he has lived among men, and has survived when one man in ten mobilized in Britain and Ireland was killed (one in eight of the ex-pupils from his school who had joined up), and five out of nine men sent to Flanders and France were killed, wounded, or missing.[24] This man then plucks a career almost at random from a newspaper advertisement, and within four months has arrived in a city on the other side of the world, having committed himself to three years' service. The world of empire allowed such opportunity. Neither Vickers nor the Royal Fusiliers would have prepared him for Shanghai, but there is much in his war service which – as we shall see – had an impact on his life and work in the city. The war casts a long shadow over Maurice Tinkler's life, and also the lives of his sister Edith and of Lily Wilson. After he left home in 1915 he returned only four times before his death, and three of those visits took place before his departure for Shanghai.

Seventy-four men joined the Shanghai Municipal Police in 1919, and so seventy-four such stories might be written about these journeys to China. Thirty-four men shipped out on the SS *Devanha* from Glasgow with Tinkler, and another thirty-nine sailed from Liverpool on the Blue Funnel steamer SS *Laertes* and arrived in Shanghai on 21 November. The *Devanha* contingent had very little in common except that they had all been on active military service during the war, two in the navy, one as a cadet in the Royal Air Force, and the others in the Infantry or Royal Artillery. Their personnel files give us a sense of the bare outlines of their stories.[25] Harry Diprose joined the colours on 8 August 1914 from the farm in Kent on which he was born, and to which he had returned after his demobilization. James Young was mobilized on the same day and left his job as a railway porter to spend five years in the Seaforth Highlanders, first as an infantry private and then as a machine gunner. Builder's assistant Bert Munson fought for three years in the London Scottish. Hugh McGregor and Allan McGillivray had both left the British Aluminium Company in Kinloch-leven, Aberdeenshire, to serve in the 8th Battalion of the Argyll and Southern Highlanders. Brothers Harry and Walter Hotchkiss left their labouring jobs in a Ludlow quarry to fight. Walter finished as a Sergeant in the Shropshire Light Infantry; Harry survived two wounds and left the Royal Fusiliers as a Lance Corporal. Cyril 'Busty' Bishop, briefly a clerk at Harrods, was wounded five times, earned the DCM and, like Maurice, was awaiting a commission when demobbed. Arthur Wadey helped his clergyman father for a year after leaving school in 1916, then worked as an assistant to the Sussex County Civil Surveyor. In May 1918 he joined the Royal Air Force. Glasgow County Police Constable Charles Henry resigned to join up in April 1915. He was twice wounded, and once gassed, and came to Shanghai with an artificial jaw, demobilized as a second Lieutenant-in-waiting. Stoker Jack Allen also survived two wounds and earned a Military Medal in the Middlesex Regiment. Robert Hall left East Ham Technical College for the Port of London Authority as a clerk in November 1915, but was called up two years later. Walter Webb left the GPO where he worked as a sorter in May 1915, when he turned 18; he fought as a gunner in the Royal Marine Artillery. George Matcham left the Dining Car department of the London and North-Western Railway in September 1914 for the Royal Field Artillery. Labourer Alan Craig spent four and a half years as a private in the Rifle and Machine Gun Corps, and wrote to the SMC's agents in March 1919 that 'having no trade am at a loose end'. Reginald Beer, son of a Devon police sergeant, left his baker's job for the Royal Navy in 1916; like Maurice he lied about his age to enlist. Copenhagen-born Robert Norton – engineer, professional footballer and polyglot – spent two years in the Scots Guards before leaving for a post as a censor after demobilization. William Ryle, an apprenticed engineer's fitter, was invalided out of the 1st/5th Manchester Regiment in August 1916 and spent two years as a munitions inspector before the peace terminated his job. David Bannerman Ross, a Scottish warehouseman, joined the army in November 1914, finishing with two years with the Royal Artillery in France as a Bombardier.

Their colleagues who arrived in November were little different. These flat-capped men, posing awkwardly in the sunshine in one surviving shipboard photograph included among their number labourers, farmhands, a miner, a plumber's mate, a bank clerk, a Royal Naval seaman and a professional soldier. The personnel files of the 1919 recruits show that about a quarter came from London, slightly fewer were Scots (from Aberdeen, Argyll and Elgin), and that the rest came mostly from rural England, from Devon, Kent, Buckinghamshire, Shropshire and Gloucestershire. Many were not familiar with city life. Tinkler was one of the youngest of this contingent, many of whom lied about their ages (Maurice now had no need) to ensure that they stood a chance of getting the job. They were tall; they had good teeth. These were on the whole working- and lower-middle-class men. This social profile fits that of Britain's domestic police forces at the time. It gives the lie to the widely published romantic notions held about such men and empire. They were *not* the wayward younger sons of middle-class families enjoying what was once called a 'gigantic system of outdoor relief for the aristocracy'.[26] They were not seeking adventure in the 'freer' colonial world. Scholars of Chinese and colonial history have long assumed that the Shanghai Municipal Police was composed of romantic adventurers, or violent ex-Black and Tans. Ideological hostility to colonialism, or nostalgic sympathy towards it distort an understanding of the ordinariness of colonial realities. Critics look for and find only violent imperialists; the nostalgic see upper-class, public-spirited, public servants. Both images have their place, but both are too narrow. The SMP recruits were ordinary men. Since Christopher Browning's shocking study of Hamburg police reservists who served as Order Police in German-occupied Poland in 1942–3, and who shot dead at least 38,000 Jewish Poles, use of the term 'ordinary men' – which he took for his title – is hardly neutral, nor is it meant to be.[27] Browning's work argues for a rational understanding of the ordinariness of the men who committed vile slaughter in Poland. No direct comparison is intended, but one lesson of Browning's sober reckoning can be applied to other situations, and in this case to colonial policemen in Shanghai: the extraordinary events of our colonial and domestic history drew on ordinary men.

Literature turns out to be more suggestive of the real atmosphere of colonial policing than most of the works of the historians but it is ultimately still limited. Paul Scott's portrayal of Mayapore Police Superintendent Ronald Merrick in *The Raj Quartet* shows a man handicapped by, amongst other things, the knowledge of his lower status in British India. The policeman is just not *pukka*, and he knows it. George Orwell's *Burmese Days*, and his meditations on service in the Burma police, highlight the distance of the policeman both from Burmese society, and from the colonial hierarchy. In his essay 'Shooting an Elephant', Orwell argued for the absolute impotence of colonial officials like the policeman, but his was an intellectual conceit, that the ruler was in fact the puppet of the ruled. In his *Malayan Trilogy*, Anthony Burgess comes much closer to portraying the men of Shanghai, but plays it for laughs in his portrayal of vulgar, belching Nabby Adams, overwhelmed by bills, by a deep, deep thirst, lost to the 'East'. Scobie, caught in the centre of Graham Greene's *The Heart of the Matter*, is another outsider. Such fictions and representations have their limits when it comes to understanding the Shanghai case. Orwell, after all, was the Eton-educated Eric Blair. Police forces in India and Burma were mostly composed of British officers who oversaw native Other Ranks. Maurice Tinkler and his colleagues joined as constables. The bulk of the Britons in the SMP were constables or sergeants. They still oversaw the activities of Sikh and Chinese constables, but they were themselves the British Other Ranks. Tinkler and his colleagues were sailing out to serve as the lowest echelon of the British presence in Shanghai. In fact, as we shall see, in the community's eyes they were its servants.

Most of these men read of the SMP's openings through the advertisements in the *People* or the *Weekly Despatch* in March 1919, while others were encouraged by personal connections. Arthur Wadey was put onto the force by Constable W. J. Elliot, in wartime a Second Lieutenant in the Black Watch. Hugh McGregor and Allan McGillivray were encouraged to join by Sergeant W. D. McGillivray, Allan's cousin, at home in Glasgow in 1919. Some of these men had returned to their pre-war jobs, but some, like former bank-clerk John Crowley, had 'been away from Banking too long to go back'; others were still awaiting demobilization; the rest, like Maurice Tinkler, and like Alan Craig, were 'at a loose end'. They were lucky to get employment so quickly, and it is perhaps a measure of the difficulties they faced after demobilization that they were prepared at such short notice to leave the homes they had only just returned to, for service in East Asia. Still, if Shanghai was a part of the world most people knew nothing of, it was a part of the empire world, like the other destinations proffered through the newspaper columns in 1919, as the private and government agencies of British colonialism attempted to make up for wartime shortfalls in recruitment. Similarly, in a Europe opened up by European union, Britons of the 1980s and 1990s sought work on the

Continent because closer political and economic integration facilitated the freer movement of labour. British men and women heard of opportunities and sought them out, as building workers in Germany, for example. In the same way, the world opened up by British empire literally broadened the employment horizons of British working-class men and women.

These seventy-four men had served, on average, roughly three and a half years on active service during the war. Like Tinkler they had undoubtedly suffered privation and brutalization, and many had been wounded. They were now expected, within barely six months of demobilization, to act as the guardians of law and order in Shanghai. 'As was only to be expected,' noted the SMP's Commissioner of Police in his annual report for the year, 'a few erratically inclined individuals were found amongst the recruits.'[28] Tinkler was ultimately to be one of them.

3

Shanghai 1919

It was love at first sight. The first time Maurice Tinkler saw Shanghai he knew he had made the right decision. He wrote to his aunt, enthusiasm unconstrained, twelve days after arriving.

Shanghai is the best city I have seen and will leave any English town 100 years behind – that's not exaggerated. It is the most cosmopolitan city of the world bar none and the finest city of the Far East. At night it is lit up like a carnival, and an orchestra plays in the Public Gardens along the river front. (Fountains beautiful trees etc.). Of course, it is not a bit like a European city of the same population, as say Manchester. There is a splendid electric car service and everyone seems to own one of the latest type of American cars. We go about in rickshas mostly and thro' out the East they grow to be a habit with everyone.

This was a rhapsody to light, to modernity, style, display and opulence. And what was there not to love in the self-styled 'model settlement', this neon-lit gateway to China? Shanghai was not only a city of wealth, but a city unashamed of displaying wealth. It was a city in China, but with an orchestra playing soft music in an English-style garden on summer evenings it hardly seemed to be a city of China, at least not the willow-pattern China of the British imagination, or the China which had developed before its opening to the West in the nineteenth century. What had grown up outside the old circular Chinese walled city and which greeted Maurice Tinkler with such dazzling energy was a new urban form, a hybrid city of competing foreign and domestic cultures, interests and power, all of them chasing the Shanghai dollar in order to make a living, a livelihood or even a million (*I Never Made a Million* was the title of one Shanghai memoir[1]). East didn't meet

West in Shanghai: Russia met Britain, Japan met Portugal, India met France, and all met China. And China met China there too. New China met 'Old China'; Cantonese cosmopolitans met wide-eyed students from the inland cities; Singaporean entrepreneurs employed rural migrants from the surrounding provinces. In his first sketch of the city, Tinkler touched on themes that became central to his own singular affair with Shanghai, but which were also central to its modern self: cosmopolitanism, swank, the slowly growing influence of the United States. First impressions count, but although he never lost sight of the fact that Shanghai was a city of opportunity, he also remembered that opportunity for a 'white man' like himself relied on the fact and force of empire.

And it was 'not a bit like' Manchester. Shanghai was doubly foreign: it was a city in China, but it was also a city. Tinkler, like most of his new colleagues, was not an urban man. He had never lived or worked in a city before, and a part of the spectacle that enveloped and enthralled him was the rich newness and detail of an urban panorama. The apprentice wheelwrights, farm labourers and quarrymen of the 1919 drafts were men more used to the hard labour and lean pickings of rural work than to such urban plenty. Their ship had sailed up the China coast from colonial Hong Kong, less developed and somehow staid and dull compared to its northern sister (they were often spoken of as sibling progeny of the British enterprise in China). It then entered the Huangpu river near Wusong, close to the mouth of the Yangtsze. From Wusong the countryside was flat farmland intersected by canals and creeks, and the ship sailed past a mixture of Chinese junks and sampans and modern steamers, including the flat-bottomed gunboats of the foreign powers, imperialism's China watch. Industrial Shanghai came into view first, in the shape of the cotton mills which lined the river in the International Settlement's Eastern District, and the massive new municipal power station (1913). The left bank, Pudong, was home to shipping wharves, a paper mill, cigarette factory, engineering works and the installation of the Standard Oil Company. The *Tean* sailed up the dirty Huangpu through the grey industrial fringe of Pudong's agricultural flats, to the kink in the river where it met the Soochow Creek (as foreigners had dubbed the Wusong river). It then passed the Public Gardens and sailed past the Settlement's emblematic frontispiece, the Bund – home to the temples of the Sino-foreign condominium – before docking at a wharf on the French Concession Bund, the tree-lined but bustling and busy Quai de France.

Tinkler would have alighted onto the wharf crowded with goods unloaded by the waiting labour gangs from China Navigation Company vessels. Rickshaws passed at a leisurely trot (unless the passenger was a European: for, as one British guidebook noted, 'we require the coolie to travel faster than the Chinese do'[2]), pedestrians thronged the pavement and road. There was noise, noise, noise: the clatter of the rickshaws, the unoiled squeak of the ubiquitous wheelbarrow, the cries of the street hawkers, car horns honking, ship horns blaring and steam whistles screaming, and the hubbub of the passing crowd. Pollution from the steam launches and from ships' engines sometimes enveloped the Bund in daytime, blowing into nearby offices. Opposite the wharf stood the offices of Butterfield and Swire (which managed China Navigation), second in eminence only to Jardine Matheson amongst British firms in China – and unlike the Scots firm never tarnished by involvement in the opium trade. 'There is no better way to obtain an idea of the business of Shanghai than a walk along this Bund,' noted the standard guide, written by a local British clergyman, C. E. Darwent. 'Butterfield and Swire's steamers line the wharf; merchandise of all kinds is carried on bamboo poles across the road to and from the godowns [warehouses]. The weights carried by these coolies will astonish strangers.' The 'Mersey is dull compared with the Huangpu,' it continued, which presented 'a scene of far greater animation with steamers, cargo boats, sampans, and craft of all kinds'.[3] Tinkler obviously thought so too; he came back often to photograph the scene at the French Bund. New arrivals in Shanghai often found themselves loaded onto the rickshaws which thronged the Bund immediately on arrival, and being carried to their destination. As Tinkler said, they 'grow to be a habit with everyone', but it was a habit which was taught to Shanghai's recruits the moment they alighted, and it was a habit which alerted them immediately to the ideas they were expected to hold about the relative positions of Europeans and Chinese. Shanghai was no colony like Hong Kong, but Chinese were treated as if they were colonial subjects. These working-class Britons, these quarrymen, labourers and servants, who had joined the SMP as constables, found themselves thrust immediately into a new position of superiority. As Darwent noted, Europeans ought 'in a way assume command' of the rickshaw puller – and by extension his peers and fellow Chinese.

The cosmopolitanism Tinkler noted was obvious from his first step ashore. He did not disembark in the International Settlement, where he was to serve, but in the French Concession. This was a full part of the French colonial empire on Chinese soil, the consul answering to the governor of French Indo-China in Hanoi. Indo-Chinese constables working for the Concession authorities policed this bund. Tinkler later took a snapshot of one, posed in putteed trousers with his head shaded from the sun by a conical bamboo hat, standing awkwardly in front of the French municipal buildings. The French consulate, a 'handsome pile' of the 'modern colonial type', lay to his right. Tinkler's destination, the SMP's Gordon Road Training Depot, lay three miles to the north-west in the Western District of the Settlement. The recruits may have been met by a bus, but let us imagine instead that he took a rickshaw (one with licences for both 'Frenchtown' – as it was colloquially known – and the International Settlement). It is a route he would often have taken anyway, and it would have been one best designed to impress upon a new arrival the variety and colour of the city. He would have been pulled up along the Bund into the International Settlement across the recently culverted Avenue Edward VII, previously a creek demarcating the two areas. Then left along the Nanking Road, into Bubbling Well Road (named after a well at its far end) and then right and north up Gordon Road to the Depot. On this maiden journey much of Shanghai's past and present would have revealed itself. The Revd Darwent was revising his guide the month that Tinkler arrived (sometimes cribbing from earlier publications as he did so), so we can travel with *Shanghai: A Handbook for Travellers and Residents* down the streets of this city and time.[4]

North of Avenue Edward VII the Bund changed from a huddle of commercial wharves to a long, wide, pleasant, lawned and tree-lined extension of the Public Gardens at its far end. Or rather, it was pleasant when the breezes blew the harbour pollution in other directions. And when Tinkler arrived the foreshore was being further reclaimed to cope with the increasing traffic. There were benches on the well-kept lawns, on which all except the Chinese could enjoy the cooler breezes blown from the sea; all except Chinese because these lawns, like the Public Gardens, were 'reserved for the foreign community'. 'Cosmopolitanism' had cold, sharp limits. SMP constables enforced the regulation, which was in the process of becoming a notable political controversy and took shape in the charge that the council's notices were insultingly worded 'Chinese and Dogs not admitted'. They were not, but exclusion became a powerful issue regardless.[5] Shanghai was a colonial city in that the usual demarcation of public and private space by class was joined to demarcation based on 'race' – or rather nationality. There was no segregation of residential space (that was left to the market) but Chinese were subject to exclusions, from private clubs, and from public gardens unless they were British or other colonial subjects. Here, on well-tended lawns, foreign Shanghai sat and strolled at leisure, enjoying the evening air, or taking a break from the steamy offices which lined the Bund and the business district which backed on to it. But even so, 'strangers are usually struck', noted Darwent, 'by the fact that they see "so few foreigners" even on this main thoroughfare'.[6] The empty garden spoke for them instead, and so did the buildings, asserting a foreign presence, and foreign right and might over the Chinese streets and Chinese space.

Whilst traversing the Bund, Tinkler would have passed the buildings and monuments which served in foreign eyes to define the city, the International Settlement and British power in China. First, the imposing seven-storey 'renaissance style' McBain building, home to amongst others, Shanghai's stock exchange, then another in the same manner, the Shanghai Club (1910), all plinths and columns and Ningpo marble inside. Its famous long bar and Elizabethan-style billiard-room helped make it, claimed Darwent, the 'renowned centre of so much of the life of the settlement'.[7] But not Chinese life, and not Tinkler's slice of Settlement life, either, for as an ordinary policeman he would never be able to join even if he had wanted to (it was expensive, and exclusive). The club served Shanghai's British elite. Like other institutions in expatriate British communities it reproduced British class divisions and fractures, which acquired heightened importance in the lands of empire where Britons of all classes were forced to rub shoulders as they oiled the machinery of colonial rule. The potential for social promiscuity was curtailed by strict social taboos and the reproduction of domestic hierarchies through clubs, lodges and other institutions. Keep out, said the club, to Tinkler and his like. Next along was the reinforced concrete Union building, then the three-storey China Merchants Steam Navigation company head offices, and the Hongkong and Shanghai Bank. North of the bank was the Tudor-style redbrick Customs House with its 110-foot-high clock tower. Its bells puzzled Shanghai nights and days with Westminster chimes. Opposite stood a bronze statue to the Customs Service's 'onlie begetter', Ulsterman Sir Robert Hart, Inspector-General for forty-four years, a foreign servant of the Chinese state who ran a service that had been effectively half-colonized by the British.

Banks followed – Russo-Chinese (Italian style), Deutsch-Asiatische (closed) – and then the *North China Daily News* building and the Chartered Bank, before the route turned left into Nanking Road after the six-storey Palace Hotel. From its roof garden (reached by elevators that were amongst Shanghai's first), patrons could hear the band playing in the Public Gardens; the restaurant's vegetables were grown in its own kitchen garden, 'under European supervision – a very important consideration in this part of the world'.[8] Opposite this junction stood yet another statue of another imperial hero: Sir Harry Parkes, British Minister to China, 1882–5, and a tiger of the old school. Parkes had done much to force the second Anglo-Chinese or Arrow war (1856–60). 'The finger of One who rules the destinies of races is clearly traceable in the whole affair,' he wrote, 'It is the cause of the West against the East, or Paganism against Christendom.'[9] With such memorials was the British China life surrounded. On 1 December 1918 the Bund's principal German monument, a memorial to the victims of the 1896 wreck of the *Iltis*, which stood opposite the offices of Jardine Matheson, was torn down.[10] The Shanghai Bund was now resolutely British. North from this junction were the German Club Concordia – now confiscated by the Chinese government and the future site of the Bank of China – the Yokohama Specie Bank, the Masonic hall, Public Gardens, and the large, lawned compound of the British consulate, residence in 1919 of Sir Everard Fraser, KCMG, Consul-General. At the end the Garden Bridge carried traffic over into the northern and eastern suburbs of the Settlement. Close by was the Imperial Russian Consulate, where diplomats orphaned by the Revolution at home puzzled over their future, and the Astor House Hotel, one of the smartest in town.

This was the Bund: foreign commerce and financial power made manifest on the western bank of the Huangpu river. Jostling for position were Chinese banks and companies and the Customs House, lone representative of the Chinese state. Here were the pillars of Britain in China: the Consulate, Masonic hall, the newspaper, the bank and the club. The British were still pre-eminent. German competition was momentarily silenced (German residents had been deported to Europe from all over China; by April 1919 some 2,187 had been repatriated[11]). The American presence was still under the British shadow. Russian interests were suffering from the civil war. The Japanese presence was growing – and had for the first time exceeded in number the British population in the 1915 Shanghai Municipal Council census – and in the years of war the roots of a firmer Japanese grasp on China had been laid. But in August 1919 Chinese labourers sweated under the shadows of Sir Robert Hart and Sir Harry Parkes; Sikh constables kept the lawns clear of Chinese, and amahs accompanying European children to the Public Gardens were still forbidden to use the seats around the bandstand during performances. This was Tinkler's Shanghai.

Nanking (Nanjing) Road, the 'Damalu' (literally the 'great horse road') in pre-1949 Chinese parlance, retains its status today as China's premier shopping street. Tinkler arrived at the moment of its modern birth. He would have passed the Western department stores at the top, including Hall and Holtz (which modelled itself on Whiteley's, Britain's first department store); Weeks and Co. (with stock 'varied enough to suit all classes of customer'); and Lane, Crawford – names still serving twenty-first-century Hong Kong; Kuhn and Co. (jewellers, Chinese curio dealers and agents for Mappin and Webb); Kelly and Walsh (books and stationery); and Edwards Evans and Sons ('a magnificent collection of English books'); and then, after Honan Road, Chinese shops ('The visitor will be surprised ... how thoroughly *Chinese* the Road is,' noted Darwent).[12] The street itself was spectacle. At night it was all neon, fashioned into signs 'increasing in brilliance and intricacy of design'.[13] In the daylight there was less design. A

February 1918 census of traffic conducted in the hours of daylight passing the junction of the Nanking and Kiangse roads counted 30,148 pedestrians, 14,663 rickshaws, 942 carriages, 1,863 motor cars, 2,582 wheelbarrows and 772 bicycles.[14] All jostled loudly for space on the crowded thoroughfare with hawkers and pedestrians. Sikh constables kept a kind of order, confiscating licences from rickshawmen for minor offences (a little ready cash might secure speedier return), and experimenting with a new one-way system in adjacent streets. At the junction with Chekiang (Zhejiang) Road were two new Chinese department stores, beaux-arts-styled temples to the city's burgeoning commercial culture. The Sincere department store (1917) was five floors of shopping heaven (300 assistants, 10,000 lines of imported consumer goods) topped with a three-storey clock tower. Across the way was the six-storey Wing On store (1918), 'classically serene in type', complete with Italianate columns. On each roof was a land-scaped pleasure garden. They were cheaper than the existing foreign-owned stores, and they knew their Chinese market better.[15] Further along the Nanking Road was the New World amusement centre (1915–16), a three-storey building which contained 'an amazing agglomeration of halls, theatres, menageries, distorting glasses, refreshment rooms', in the words of the Revd Darwent.[16] Clerical reticence failed to note the prostitution which formed a prominent part of the attractions offered.

After the old Town Hall (1896), still the seat of the SMC but soon to be replaced by the new administration building – 'a parable in stone', noted the *North China Daily News*, 'commemorating the past, and prophesying an even better future'[17] – the route passed the Louza police station, and then took in the racecourse and Public Recreation Ground – home to a swimming pool and the Shanghai Cricket Club. 'Though the play of the strongest local team is only on a par with that of the English public schools,' noted one survey, 'the Settlement holds its own in inter-port matches' with teams from Hong Kong or elsewhere in treaty port China, and from Japan. (Inter-port cricket had added dangers; in 1892 all but two of the Hong Kong team drowned on their way home when their ship foundered.)[18] There was a nine-hole golf course here, and a bowls club. The Revd Darwent describes the next stage of the route:

The spacious premises of the Horse Bazaar and Motor Company are seen on the right. Shops have taken the place of residences during the last ten years. Here is the Union Jack Club provided by the Race Club for HBM Navy. Over the way is the home of the Race Club . . . now about to be rebuilt. Its well swept gravelled spaces, its air of neatness, its broken outlines, present a handsome appearance. The clock tower is one of the few public clocks which Shanghai boasts.[19]

The traveller passed the turning to 'Love Lane', a whimsical reminder after 'Nanking' and 'Bubbling Well' of names that tripped more easily off the English tongue and places that spoke more softly to the English imagination. Two and a half miles from the Bund he turned right and continued north up Gordon Road. This was named of course for the hero of the 'Ever Victorious Army' (a foreign mercenary band which with official British approval aided Chinese government suppression of the Taiping rebellion in the 1860s) and of Khartoum, the gesture insinuating the China enterprise into the empire epic. Here there was far less of note. The destination came into view. Gordon Road Training (or Western) Depot (1907) was a brick-built, three-storey verandahed building set in a large compound on the edge of the northern industrial districts.

The voyage out was now completed. Edith's joke had been seen through to its logical end, and 4372 Private Tinkler was now PC 72, sworn to three years' service. From the Quai de France to Gordon Road the new arrival would have been soaked in the bewildering novelty of sight, sound and smell, made more curious by the apparently familiar background, a *mélange* of Western-style buildings and shops. Tinkler may have encountered Chinese labourers on the Western Front. He would have noticed Chinese in Malaya, Singapore, Hong Kong. But here he had been thrown pell-mell into a confusion of cultures, styles and languages, Chinese and beyond. In all of this confusion, however, he saw order, the order of foreign administration. From all of this diversity he picked out and noted the familiar. Western achievement, not Shanghai diversity, struck him with most force. The buildings spoke to him through their parables of stone. Tinkler was to live in Shanghai, but in the foreign Shanghai superimposed on the Settlement and city. His own ideas about his individual and 'racial' self, and his needs as a foreigner, an Englishman, could be met only by foreign Shanghai. He needed to see a sharply defined polarity, for East to be confronted with West and for that much-hijacked phrase of Kipling ('Oh, East is East, and West is West, and never the twain shall meet') to apply here as well. But for all the exclusion, and talk of mastery, the city was built on Sino-foreign co-operation and accommodation. Without Chinese entrepreneurs, capital, labour and customers there was no model settlement. For the historian, it becomes nearly impossible to distinguish clearly between the Chinese and the foreign in the making of the city, but for Tinkler it was easy, and it was vital to his sense of self. Shanghai life, Tinkler's life, hinged on the fiction of foreign mastery.

We have some hints about what sights initially impressed Tinkler the most because he made up two albums of photographs after he bought a camera in the summer of 1920.[20] One volume, simply dated 'Shanghai 1920', opens with a snapshot of him in solar topee and cream panama suit sitting slightly awkwardly in the sunlight on one of the rustic benches in the new Jessfield Park. It is framed by a shot of a British gunboat, HMS *Scarab*, and the confiscated German Club

Concordia. It was the Bund which mostly caught his eye. Gunboats fairly dominate the book – and two such boats decorate the first page of the other volume – but then they were a prominent sight moored in the Huangpu, and shots of the river and its busy life are numerous in the albums. Tinkler captured the Settlement's memorials on film – the plinth commemorating the dead ('white', he noted) officers of the 'Ever Victorious Army'; and the Margary memorial, dedicated to a British consular officer killed in Yunnan province in 1875. The British minister, Thomas Wade, took advantage of the affair to force China to open more concessions and further extend British privileges. Cheap labour kept the monuments well tended and well polished, and the metal plaques are captured shining brightly in the snapshot. Police constables were directed to prevent people defacing them, or 'beggars, hawkers and undesirables' from congregating around them.[21] These monuments spoke of colonial power and ambitions, and marked the deaths in action of colonial agents. There are snaps of the Palace Hotel, bridges, municipal buildings, the wide tree-lined streets of the residential French concession, and the Bund-side Public Gardens. In some ways Tinkler's choice of subjects tells us little about his own relationship with the city, because his subjects were often the stand-ard sights laid out in Darwent's guidebook. He certainly had an eye for a good photograph, and a proficiency with the camera. But what is certainly Tinkler is the concentration on gunboats and other military vessels. There is something of an air of personal triumph laid out on this page – British might is displayed in China side by side with German humiliation, and in between it all Tinkler sits pretty, and suavely. There was little of note for him, however, in Shanghai's overwhelmingly Chinese face.

To a man fresh from Ulverston, and from wartime France, Shanghai was intoxicating, and it could not but be so. It had had a good war, and the boom was held back only by restricted wartime access to imports of foreign-made machinery to equip its new industries. The conflict had indeed provided 'a unique opportunity' for the city.[22] An increased demand for raw materials, and the sudden removal of strong European competition gave new opportunities to Chinese as well as to Japanese and American companies, and the rise in value of silver, which benefited the Chinese currency, fuelled a Shanghai boom. So while Europe was bloodily distracted, China strode forward. And as Shanghai earned, it spent, and spent. Shanghai's new rich bought themselves cars (registrations had doubled in three years), hired themselves chauffeurs (a positive menace on the roads), and dressed themselves in the latest fashions. They built Western-style mansions on the Bubbling Well Road; paid for new public buildings as conspicuous acts of philanthropy, and gambled heavily, and illegally, at the 'Wheel' on North Honan Road outside the Settlement. At night they drove up and down the Bubbling Well Road taking in the cooler air and flaunting their vehicles. Caldbeck, Macgregor and Co., 'agents for some of the best champagne on the market', supplied the fizz. J. W. Gande had capacity in their store for half a million bottles of wine and spirits, including 'samples of almost every vintage and brand that it would be possible to mention'. Even before the war, H. H. Bodemeyer was selling twelve million cigars a year in Shanghai.[23] Maurice Tinkler arrived at this moment of great change. Still semi-rural in many ways, Shanghai was on the cusp of a commercialized modernity that would transform it into a city in which people lived and worked and played in ways that we would find familiar. It was beginning the thirty-year spree that would last until communist troops arrived in 1949. Shanghai led China, and it looked to Europe and America for its own lead. For foreign memoirists, pre-First World War Shanghai had been comfortable, but still simple and collegial: 'there were no night clubs, dance halls or even night restaurants . . . most people went to bed at ten getting up at four or five to go riding.' But then came the wartime fortune seekers and Americans – idealistic and brash, and ever upsetting the British good life. The new world was 'glittering and ostentatious, but not too healthy' compared with what former SMC secretary J. O. P. Bland idealized as the 'arcadian simplicity of men and manners' in the old Shanghai.[24]

The new Shanghai and its foreign order that so impressed Tinkler was based on the gunboats he photographed, but also on international treaties and local agreements. The International Settlement was one of three administrations that ran the city. The original walled city lay to the south. This was 'Nantao' to foreign residents, or just the 'native city'. In the main, the British resident saw little of the city, although Darwent encouraged his readers to visit it, despite the 'dreadful smells' which put people off.[25] North of that lay the French Concession, reaching westwards from the Quai de France almost four miles. It was mostly residential with little commerce and almost no industry, and it was popular with British residents and with Chinese political refugees. North again lay the International Settlement – similarly reaching west from its strip of the Bund – but also reaching north across the Wusong river and eastwards for four and a half miles along the banks of the Huangpu. Further north again were more Chinese-administered districts, including Chapei (Zhabei), ever a tempting morsel for expansionist-minded foreigners. The Settlement was ruled by the self-styled Shanghai Municipal Council (SMC). Proudly proclaiming itself a cosmopolitan agglomeration of the fourteen nationalities whose flags were incorporated into the design of its official seal, it was run by a Council of nine men. A gentlemen's agreement fixed its national composition in favour of the British: in 1919 it comprised one Japanese (who had replaced a German representative in 1915), two Americans, and six Britons, elected by the votes of a small proportion of the ratepayers. A land-owning and trading elite had the SMC stitched up between them. About 8 per cent of foreigners had a vote; only 3 per cent could stand for office.[26] More than half of those able to vote in 1918 were Britons.[27] Representatives of the big British firms, Butterfield and Swire (Taikoo), Jardine Matheson (Ewo), the Hongkong and Shanghai Bank (Weifoong) and Sassoons were usually guaranteed a position. It was not, in fact, unlike a British urban municipality complete with property-based franchise, but it looked like a rotten borough, and the Chinese had no vote.

The Settlement's publicists and its romancers long sustained the legend that the strip allotted the British in 1842 was a swamp, a 'wilderness of marshes' and mud-flats. In fact, there were many Chinese houses already there and much of the area was farmed. But the new community needed a founding legend, and this one was a useful lie; it came to stand for a vision of the city's growth from mud-flat to the sombre glories of the Bund, one that was wholly derived from foreign enterprise – 'the men from the West', as one historian had it – and from the introduction of 'progress' in the teeth of Chinese conservatism.[28] The instrument of progress in the settlement was the SMC. The boundaries of the Settlement were demarcated in a set of 'Land

Regulations' which came to be seen as a charter for foreign self-government, and which were devised by the Daotai – the local Chinese administrator – and promulgated on 29 November 1845. After the 1842 Nanjing Treaty and the opening of the port in November 1843 the British came: traders who set about opening branches of their previously Canton-based firms; and missionaries who had been 'waiting for China' in secrecy at Canton, or at training bases in the East Indies. The Settlement was formally reserved for foreign residence initially, but Chinese refugees from the Taiping rebellion fled into it after 1855, and large numbers made it their home thereafter, attracted by the opportunities it presented or the refuge it offered. There were Cantonese compradores – middlemen for foreign firms – and entrepreneurs; overseas Chinese from Singapore and Malaya came to invest in the city's modernizing retail centre. Ningbo families ran the Chinese banking sector; Jiangsu peasants came to provide the labour on which the city still relied in 1919, despite its electric light and power. Pidgin English allowed residents and visitors alike to make sense of this babel of Chinese and foreign tongues.

This perilous squat grew into an assertive, confident and expansionist settlement. Shanghai's British residents developed a hearty communal life too, and christened themselves 'Shanghailanders', an identity available to all who subscribed to a parochial political vision. The community grew slowly and steadily in numbers and complexity over the decades, to 4,500 Britons by 1910, by which year Chinese residents in the Settlement had grown to number almost half a million. To the 138 acres administered in 1846 the British Settlement added 470 in 1848, another 1,309 in 1863 and 3,804 in 1899.[29] A 'Committee of Roads and Jetties' formed in 1846 became the SMC in 1854, convened, as it was thereafter put, for the 'better order and good government of the settlement'.[30] In 1863 the British allotment was amalgamated with the small American settlement north of the Soochow Creek to form the 'International Settlement'. The SMC evolved into a municipal administration largely based on British models. It imported practices and structures as they were developed in Britain, and it recruited trained personnel, engineers, accountants, teachers, health workers and policemen. Revised Land Regulations in 1854, 1869 and 1898 extended its authority over more areas of

Chinese and foreign life and work. The SMC was mostly left to its own devices by the British government and its diplomatic and consular representatives. It was an 'anachronism', admitted the British Minister to China in August 1919, but it was 'a most useful one'.[31] When the SMC needed government help it actively sought it out; during the First World War, for example, the SMC was willing to go as far as it considered prudent, but it resented any interference in its affairs, and tended to act on the implicit assumption that it was responsible only to its ratepayers, and that it was, to all intents and purposes, an autonomous body. Its overt attempts to garner independent status – starting in 1862 and continuing even as Tinkler arrived[32] – were rebuffed, and instead the SMC protected and strengthened itself by making quiet but full use of the advantages of its anomalous position. Its independent-mindedness reflected the fluid identity of the Shanghai British, who wore British, imperial or Shanghailander hats, as and when it suited them.

The International Settlement was not a part of the British empire proper. Only Hong Kong (a Crown Colony) and tiny Weihaiwei (a leased territory) were subject to Colonial Office control. The Foreign, not the Colonial, Office supervised the activities of British subjects in China. Under the treaties Britons had extraterritorial status: they were subject to the jurisdiction of their own consuls, and not to Chinese law. British empire did not respect the limits of the concessions, and Britons used their nationality, and the language of shared empire service, to maximize their opportunities in China, badgering diplomats for support here, and evading Chinese restrictions there with consular connivance. The larger and more widespread the British presence, the more diplomats were drawn in to regulate it, and to curb its excesses. But there were many of them who also saw it all as part of the great game of empire, and in their Shanghai work were doing 'our bit for the Raj'.[33] And, if not a formal part of British empire, the International Settlement was the jewel in the crown of Britain's Chinese Raj, headquartering most of the British business and cultural enterprise in the country, serving as the gateway to the opportunities China offered. It was the great hub of the treaty system which had by 1919 opened up dozens of Chinese cities to foreign residence, and which had opened China's great Yangtsze river to foreign ships and gunboats.

The diplomats lobbied and paraded their plumery in the capital, Peking, but everybody else lodged near the Huangpu. Publicists drew Shanghai into the written world of empire: a handsome series on 'Britons Beyond the Seas' covered Hong Kong and Shanghai in equal measure in 1908, serving as a prospectus for investment, and recruitment, and as a statement of eligibility.[34] The extent of the China trade in terms of global British trade should not be exaggerated, but the Settlement was intimately linked to the world and empire economy. Capital raised on the Shanghai stock exchange, for example, funded investment in the early twentieth-century Malayan rubber boom.[35] And the Chinese enterprise still benefited from an unambiguous British imperialism. An expansionist British state had opened up the treaty ports in the first place, and went to war again in China in 1856 and 1900 to reinforce the victory settlement, and push the door open further as a result. In peacetime British gunboats on the Yangtsze, the Royal Navy's China Station, and troops based in Hong Kong, could fly the flag and punish Chinese transgression. The British Consul-General had equal standing, in theory, with his other colleagues in the Shanghai consular body, all of them deferring to the leadership of the Senior Consul (the longest in post). But he expected to lead, nonetheless, and acted with all due cocked-hatted pomp. The Consul hobnobbed with the SMC's British members, his influence depending largely on how well he got on with them, which in turn largely rested on how well he pandered to their more bullish predilections. But he had no jurisdiction over them, and they ran the show themselves.

By 1919 the SMC controlled an area of just under nine square miles, and by 1925 a total of 7,923 acres in the External Roads areas outside the Settlement (roads built by the Council through Chinese territory over which sovereignty was claimed). It had a population of 620,401 Chinese and 18,519 foreigners (1920 census), only 4,822 of whom were Britons.[36] Inside the boundaries were factories, mills, warehouses and China's busiest harbour. Council responsibilities were supervised by its Police, Public Health, Public Works, Education and Finance departments. Sub-committees drawn from the elected councillors and nominated members oversaw the running of the departments, which were co-ordinated by a central secretariat run by a permanent secretary who had effectively run it as a 'one man show' before 1915.[37]

The SMC also ran the orchestra, a fire brigade and through the electricity department the Riverside Power Station. Aside from a land tax, a general municipal rate and wharfage dues, the council generated revenue from licences which allowed it to regulate taverns, liquor sales, bowling saloons, eating houses, Chinese and foreign lodging houses, Chinese wineshops, food hawkers, tea shops, foreign and Chinese theatres, dogs, firearms, rickshaws (private and public), boats and sampans, motor and other vehicles and pawnshops. This left precious little unregulated. Licensing programmes were further used to prohibit opium shops (by 1917) and, after 1920, brothels. The Council ran five hospitals (including a small mental ward), a sanatorium at Mokanshan, south-west of the city, three cemeteries, eleven markets, a slaughter house, seven parks and open spaces, nine schools, a quarry, a gaol, eight police stations and six fire stations. It published a weekly *Municipal Gazette* and a voluminous *Annual Report* overstocked with statistics and details.

Council statistics told of activity, order and control. The electricity department sold 102,338,137 kilowatt hours of electricity in 1919. Four coal checkers would cost the department 9,720 taels in salary. Grants in aid were made to the Door of Hope (which ran prostitute refuges), the Anti-Kidnapping Society's home, the Foreign Women's Home and the Shanghai Horticultural Society. Then there were fingerprint records dealt with in 1919 (8,453); Chinese arrested for 'begging, hawking and ragpicking', but not charged in August (2,069); cart loads of road sweepings collected that month; dead trees removed; bird's-nests eliminated. The SMP held in stock 32 swords, 58,347 rounds of Webley .45 ammunition and 52 Sam Browne belts. August was drier than average.[38] Such constipated attention to detail was typical of colonial institutions. The lists conveyed the sense of control; landscape and society were identified and regulated. The SMC had mastered the Settlement. Immensely self-satisfied, the Council even commissioned a history of itself from the headmaster of the Shanghai Public School for Boys.[39] Shanghai life belied and bestrode the numbers but despite the statistical bluster and despite the creaking administrative structure, and its corruptions and cosiness, the SMC had created an efficient municipal regime on Chinese soil. It laid and straightened city streets, and kept them clean; it built public latrines and saw that they were used. Chinese reformers contrasted its efficiencies with the problems of their own local administrations. Others, Chinese and foreign, attempted to force the SMC into a more inclusive relationship with its Chinese populace. That inclusiveness might well have started with knowing who they were. Rates records were used to compile lists of foreigners entitled to vote in council elections, but a 1923 note pointed out that it would be impossible to compile a register of Chinese because no record of Chinese householders was kept. The rates were levied on the buildings. Such was the blindness of Shanghai colonialism that it did not formally recognize that its Chinese residents had names.[40]

As the administrative machinery of the Settlement evolved over the eighty years of its history, so did its social and cultural life. For early residents, Shanghai was a dreary exile. Threatened by disease and ground down by loneliness, many men went mad, or drank, or both. Staying healthy in spirit required strong religious conviction, a thick skin, and luck. Shanghai coarsened all but the rich, and not a few of them also. The Shanghailander plutocrat lived in sumptuous style and paraded his exquisite taste, but he was pilloried even in the 1930s as a Philistine vulgarian. Remaining healthy in body proved partly a lottery well into the twentieth century. Typhoid, cholera, dysentery, even bubonic plague took a steady toll. Even the healthiest the night before could be dead in the morning: the death rate of 20.6 per thousand in 1919 was significantly greater than that for England and Wales in the same year (14.0).[41] So the Shanghailander played to clear his mind and keep the body fit. Depending on his interests, rank, status, wealth – and credit worthiness – he played at his mess, his club, his lodge, his sports club, the theatre or one of the fifteen foreign brothels (or the Chinese ones in which the 'salt water sisters' catered for low-class foreigners[42]). He visited one of the houses in the 'Line' on Kiangse Road, or the 'Trenches', the bars and cafés outside the Settlement on North Szechwan Road and Jukong Road: the Shanghai Café Grill, the Golden Eagle Bar, the Rialto Bar, Café Venetia, Eldorado, Café de Paris – resorts, complained missionaries, of 'promiscuous dancing, drinking and carousing during all the hours of the day and night'.[43] He attended church or chapel, danced at subscription balls, feasted at public dinners, drilled and camped with the Shanghai

Volunteer Corps, volunteered to fight fires with the Shanghai Fire Service (before it was professionalized in May 1919), or joined in debates at the North China Branch of the Royal Asiatic Society.

Shanghailanders 'hunted' in the paper-chase, riding a Mongolian pony along a paper trail laid across the local countryside. Maurice Springfield, SMP Assistant Commissioner, and later leader of the special opium squad, managed a pack of hounds which hunted regularly at dawn on weekday mornings, following a Siberian bear-scented drag. (The Shanghai zoo provided the scents.) The Shanghailander rowed out into the Huangpu from a Bund-side boat house, or at regattas held at 'Hen-li'. And then there were those ponies, shipped down south to race all over treaty port China. On race days commercial Shanghai closed down. The ink on the treaties had barely dried before new British residents were surveying likely spots for a racecourse. A ticket to a job in the East was assured for a good sportsman who rode a swift mount: Springfield himself claimed to have clinched his position as an SMP officer cadet by virtue of his hunting and the fact that his father was a master of foxhounds.[44] The race track was nudged west as the city developed, but in 1919 it was still centrally located, mirroring in location its hold on communal life and the community's imagination. These were elite activities. Although anyone could enter the sweep – 'even the station coolies form syndicates to buy tickets', Tinkler wrote in 1923 – membership of the Shanghai Race Club itself was restricted and exclusive. And keeping a horse for the paper-chase was far beyond the means of the ordinary Shanghai British, even if it was much cheaper in Shanghai than it was 'homeside'. Shooting was another matter, and any man with a gun could indulge. Game levels were already falling, and the SMC enforced a closed season, which 'sportsmen' were expected to follow. But for sportsman and non-sportsman alike there was pheasant, bamboo partridge, woodcock, quail, snipe and wildfowl. For one writer in 1903, China was a 'veritable paradise' for shooting: 'one can look on the whole empire of China and say, "Here is my ground, here I can take my gun and my dogs and go just wherever, and do whatever, I please, without let or hindrance; shoot what I will, stay as long as I like without asking anyone's leave, and where keepers and game licenses are unknown".'[45] Men of the SMP could hire a houseboat from the council, and spend a vacation out with their gun. So, for good or ill, the expatriate Briton kept himself busy.

Foreign residents of the Settlement were ever sensitive to the city's poor reputation: the bars and brothels which serviced the floating population of visiting merchant and naval seamen seemed to dominate foreign accounts of the city. But Shanghailanders pointed instead with pride to their efficient municipal administration and orderly polity. This was sound politics, for the Settlement needed to fend off criticisms that might lead to its surrender as an embarrassment by diplomats, or demands for its restitution by the Chinese. The Settlement was, they argued, a model of cultural achievement and one of wholesome social activity. There were daily newspapers (notably the *North China Daily News*), weeklies, a learned journal, occasionally a poor cousin of *Punch*, a short-story club, some local expatriate authors, and a local publisher (Kelly and Walsh). To fill one gap, Mina Shorrock's *Social Shanghai* began publication as a monthly for 'ladies' in 1906, expanding in ambition to cover 'all the brighter phases of life in Shanghai and the treaty ports', recording in words and photographs the social life of satisfied settlement.[46] The Royal Asiatic Society (1858) provided lecturers, created a library and also a museum. Books and journals were imported, and so were pianos, other instruments and sheet music. Travelling opera troupes visited the city as early as 1875, backed by local amateurs from the Philharmonic and Choral societies. The city's cultural pretensions were realized in 1881 when twenty Filipinos were recruited from Manila, taught to play brass instruments, and formed into a motley municipal public band, which played in the Public Gardens, and gave weekly tea dance concerts in the Town Hall on winter evenings. Another council recruit in 1919 was Mario Paci, who turned the public band into an orchestra with world-class ambitions.[47] Dramatics remained non-professional, with the Amateur Dramatic Club (1867) formed to encourage 'amateur acting' and to maintain a theatre. The Russian influx in the 1920s greatly augmented the foreign cultural life of the city, but the Shanghai Settlement from very early on sought to demonstrate its completeness and wholesomeness. It was a bona fide community where men and women worked and played, married and died.

Shanghai histories and memoirs usually paint a picture of a wholly upper-class colonial society. But from the earliest days the Settlement was home to a socially mixed foreign community. There was a sizeable missionary community and a recognized mission 'quarter'. The Council, the utility companies, dockyards, steamship lines and the customs service also needed a cadre of lower-class European men and also women – who came as teachers, nurses, stenographers and prostitutes. For a start, colonialism was rooted in distrust. Common ideas about the Chinese character circulated by word of mouth, but were also compiled into textbooks (such as Arthur Smith's *Chinese Characteristics*[48]). Here all Chinese were deemed to be unreliable, corrupt, inefficient, inaccurate and so on. Chinese labour was felt to need foreign supervision; Chinese supervisors were seen as corrupt or corruptible, and so lower-class men were recruited from Britain, or from the visiting vessels of the merchant navy. And Shanghai's foreign elite refused to be served at the department stores by Chinese staff. Weeks and Co. employed twenty-five Europeans, and Lane, Crawford sixteen and both highlighted the fact in their publicity. These men and women played an intermediary role between the customer and Chinese employees. Racism and snobbery made common cause in the demand for European servants. As in the stores, so in the bed. Taboos against sex with Chinese women were more flexible, but elite men preferred the 'American girls' (initially American, latterly more likely to be East Europeans) on Kiangse Road.[49]

Empire was also rooted in collaboration. Even the vilest colonialist police state required indigenous partners. The British empire was minimally staffed, and relied on establishing relationships with local power holders, or on placing its allies in power. The fewer Britons it sent out the better (and the cheaper). The task of empire lay in keeping up to date, in finding new allies as and when necessary, in re-balancing the local compact. But the settler was the 'ideal pre-packaged collaborator', someone who spoke the same language of empire. The Shanghailander elites might carve up the Council between themselves, but they needed such local collaborators too (and they were also – prostitutes or policemen – expensive items of conspicuous consumption). So, wherever there was colonial power, there were men like Maurice Tinkler. The 1920 census listed bartenders, bill collectors, blacksmiths, boarding- and lodging-housekeepers, innkeepers, clerks, drapers, warehouse- and garage-keepers, commercial travellers, harbour pilots, printers and compositors, tax collectors and undertakers.[50] Most of these people would never have been able to afford one of the 'new American cars' or the 'American girls'. But still, the living was cheap. Essentials – food, wine, clothes, laundry – were far cheaper than in Britain, and credit was standard. Shanghai's lower-class foreigners benefited from the fact of empire, were vital to its functioning, and shared its language.

So they came to join this British transplant on the banks of the polluted Huangpu river. As Tinkler and his new colleagues arrived the city was recovering from an epidemic of choleraic diarrhoea. At least 648 Chinese residents had died. An 'abnormally high foreign mortality rate' for the year was blamed on the world-wide influenza pandemic, which struck the city in March, and recurred towards the end of the year.[51] But expatriate life was generally returning to normal after the European conflict. The pages of the *North China Daily News* for August 1919 offer various examples. Five SMP men, including the cousins McGillivray from Argyllshire, returned from active service on the Blue Funnel line's SS *Pyrrus* on 4 August. The Shanghai Race Club held a 'Welcome Home' dinner for such returnees, providing entertainment in the shape of the Carlton Jazz Four and 'amusing turns' by Billy Weston ('the King of Spoons'). Mrs F. H. Wallace, wife of the master of a customs schooner, died of dysentery and a stroke aged 59. Born in Singapore, she had been in Shanghai for forty-two years. Wearing a 'costume of pale grey and cornflower blue, trimmed with Georgette crepe', Miss Millicent M. Leverston married the manager of the Chartered Bank's Canton branch at Holy Trinity Cathedral ('the most magnificent church in the East'[52]); the Dean presided. Mr E. A. Bernard's Chinese cook was charged at the Mixed Court with theft and forgery relating to an unpaid bill (sentence: six weeks' detention and repayment of the sum stolen). Mrs P. Lambe prosecuted her ex-boy (servant) for recommending a holiday substitute who had stolen her watch (case dismissed as the boy had committed no chargeable offence). In the correspondence columns 'An Indignant Ratepayer' complained about a donkey braying near the St George's Hotel on Bubbling Well Road. 'Settlement Dweller' complained about car horns, which were blown unceasingly from 11 p.m. to 3 a.m. by the chauffeurs of joyriding motors. There was fierce debate over the education of foreign boys in China. Unless watched by their parents (the newspaper editorialized), boys grew up 'tyrannical and capricious in the last degree' due to the 'proximity of the Oriental', who set a poor example through servility and low standards. Bostock's Royal Italian Circus 'surpassed even the highest expectations' before bad weather from a typhoon which skirted the region washed it out. A team from the Japanese trading firm Mitsui won the Hong Doubles Tennis Challenge, soundly beating Probst, Hanbury and Co.

To all intents and purposes, then, the Settlement was a busy outpost of (mostly) British empire life, but it lay in China, a sovereign republic, and it was an increasingly important site in the growing Chinese challenge to international imperialism. While post-war foreign Settlement life seemed to be settling down, China's national and Shanghai's local politics were changing. The *North China Daily News* attacked the handling of Chinese issues at the Paris Peace Conference. Outrage at the Conference's decision to hand over former German concessions in China to the Japanese had galvanized Chinese students and others into an unprecedented and important national mass protest, the May Fourth Movement, which was sweeping the country. In Shanghai there had been an anti-Japanese boycott after 7,000 people, many of them students, held a public meeting in Nantao on 7 May. A students' union was formed and political activists secured a strong adherence to the boycott of Japanese goods organized by commercial, student and native place organizations. A week-long general strike after 5 June heightened political tension. The SMC found itself dealing with activities which were increasingly broadly anti-imperialist, and which questioned its own authority. It struck back by banning 'inflammatory' propaganda and activity, and by trying to split the merchant–student coalition. The strike ended after the dismissal of so-called pro-Japanese ministers of the Peking government, but a victory parade which illegally entered the Settlement on 12 June led to a disturbance in which police shot dead one marcher.[53] There were portents here of problems to come, and there were new worries. The SMP, while conceding that there was 'nothing definite' to link Bolshevik propaganda with the movement, nevertheless felt a need to keep an eye on its role in Shanghai's local politics. Student nationalists were seen as 'earnest' and – 'used in the right way' – as a potential force for good.[54] But the movement had also seen a recrudescence of an increasingly bitter communal tension in the city between Chinese and Japanese, which had erupted in July 1918 when Japanese residents attacked and fought Chinese SMP constables in the Hongkou district. The council largely held the Japanese community to blame, and noted, worryingly, that the Japanese consular authorities appeared to have little control over their community.[55] The national political situation had fed local communal ill-feeling, and the violent activism of lower-class Japanese settlers and their rejection of consular authority would return to haunt Sino-Japanese relations in the Settlement of the 1930s.

Into this changing and increasingly politicized city came the 1919 recruits to the SMP. With confidence buoyed by the strike movement in Shanghai, and as the logical outcome of their increasing social and economic power, merchant bodies and other activists were bringing pressure to bear on the SMC for political reform. In July and August the new Federation of Sheet Unions led protests on taxation issues. A rates strike led to the suspension of collection until late August 1919, a token victory for the activists, but the protests were to turn into demands for greater political representation on the SMC. Although an attempt formally to add Chinese representatives to the council was vetoed, a five-strong Chinese Advisory Committee was created to speak for Chinese residents. Formed in 1920, a new Chinese Rate-payers' Association strove to represent Chinese interests.[56] The SMC had over the years faced challenges from Chinese residents over a variety of issues. Police action and accommodation of elite grievances had mostly seen them off. After 1919, however, the new politics of public activism and revolutionary nationalism would change the Shanghai scene utterly. At a Council meeting on 26 November that year the chairman offered a pessimistic prognosis: there was 'every indication that before too long – possibly within the next few months – the Council will have to face a situation of extreme gravity'. Labour unrest, the anti-Japanese boycott, the spread of 'bolshevist views', the potential for an influx of Russian refugees and the general increase in Chinese political activity posed a raft of unpredictable threats. The SMP needed to be ready, he thought, the number of foreigners perhaps needed augmenting by a further hundred. Acting Commissioner Alan

Hilton-Johnson asked for more Sikhs instead (and more bicycles), an armoured car, use of the fire truck to disperse crowds, further development of locally made smoke bombs, and strengthening of the reserve Special Police. He also wanted the drawing-up of emergency measures to safeguard food supplies, more attention to be given to pro-SMC propaganda, and the preparation of measures equal in all but name to the imposition of martial law should a real emergency arise.[57] Colonial defence had a long shopping list. These SMP recruits arrived, then, at a key moment in modern Chinese history and in Shanghai history. They were recruited to police the city, but would find themselves defending a political settlement that was coming under siege, and acted as if it was preparing for one.

But this was far from their minds. Less than a year after he had left the billets and trenches of France, and one day short of a year since the bloody battle for Behagnies during which he had earned his DCM, Tinkler found himself being woken in bed every morning by a Chinese servant. Such luxury: the 'boy' (no name) pulled back the mosquito curtains at 6 a.m. and served him a cup of tea, 'real China not the stuff you have in England,' he added in a letter to his Aunt Florence. Tinkler had arrived; life already promised to be easier. And now he was to become a policeman.

4

The Shanghai Municipal Police

Shanghai was now home. Although half of those who came out on the SS *Devanha* with him would leave Shanghai before the end of 1922, Tinkler would return to England just once, and would only ever leave Asia twice before his death. Police stations, hostels and company flats variously and anonymously provided the accommodation in which he lived; hotels, cabarets and resorts the world in which he played. The first of his perches was the Shanghai Municipal Police Training Depot on Gordon Road. Here Tinkler and his colleagues were introduced to the SMP, to Shanghailander society and to the city itself. Through this depot the force aimed to turn recruits into policemen, and Britons into Shanghailanders. They would learn about the force they had joined, and the city in which it policed. It would teach them the written regulations as well as the unwritten laws and practices which underpinned British colonialism in general, and the Shanghai Settlement, and the British community in particular. It would make empire men of them.

The Shanghai Municipal Police brought order to the bustling hyperactivity of the International Settlement. Dating back to 1854, the SMP had grown from a small complement of Britons recruited from the Hong Kong police into a large and ethnically diverse force. At the start of 1919, Commissioner of Police Kenneth John McEuen led a mixed complement of 146 foreigners (nearly all of them Britons): a recently established Japanese branch of 30 men whose purpose was to cope with the rapid increase in the Japanese population of the Settlement, especially in the Northern District of Hongkew; 370 Sikhs (first recruited in 1884); and 1,400 Chinese constables and sergeants (first recruited in 1864). These men also helped supervise 470 Chinese and 180 Indian watchmen. The Chinese were mostly beat patrolmen, the eyes and ears of the force, and the core of the detective branch. Sikhs performed traffic duties. The Foreign Branch – in Shanghailander parlance 'Foreign' meant non-Chinese, in the SMP it largely meant British – constituted 'the brain and supervising power of a body inclined at times to be inert and lazy', as former Captain Superintendent A. M. Boisragon claimed in 1905,[1] and their use ensured 'complete supervision of Asiatics'.[2] So in one sense there was nothing at all cosmopolitan about the SMP. Its structure and its duties were organized along strict 'racial' lines and ordered through a raced hierarchy that placed Europeans at the summit. Structure and practice were underpinned by the race assumptions of those who ran the force, of the foreign residents of the Settlement, and in some ways of the experience of policing the Settlement. Such assumptions about the aptitude and skills (and their limits) of different groups were common currency in the colonial era. Part of the popular anthropology of the time, they were demonstrated in every colony, and by all colonial regimes.

The SMP looked like a colonial police force, and broadly followed the standard pattern of Asian forces, although the detail of its structure was as idiosyncratic and syncretic as the Settlement itself. There was no single model even for police forces in the formal empire, which were promiscuous in their antecedents and influences.[3] The SMP was founded on the model of the Hong Kong Police Force, itself based on London's Metropolitan Police. Over the years it looked directly to the Met for ideas about structure and practice, but also stiffened itself with a Royal Irish Constabulary backbone, borrowing a senior officer in 1898 for two years to reform the force, sending various cadets to the RIC depot for six months' or a year's training, and recruiting drafts of men direct from the RIC and the Dublin Municipal Police. Its Sikh element meant that it liaised with the British Indian army experts and recruiters, and recruited senior personnel from colonial police and military forces in Malaya, such as the Malay States Guides and the Sungei Ujong (present-day Seremban) police. Like domestic British forces, it also looked to the military for its leading officers. Informal contacts with forces outside China were common. Officers and specialist junior personnel sometimes spent time on leave with

foreign forces. Senior officers, including the then commissioner, E. I. M. Barrett, took courses for colonial and dominions police officials run by the Metropolitan Police in the 1920s. The force did its best to keep up to date with modern policing methods, wherever they might be best seen, in Britain, its colonies or the United States.

Commissioner of Police McEuen had joined the force as Deputy Captain Superintendent in 1900. He was then trained to what was later described – by a critic of the informality and *ad hoc* nature of the process – as 'a passable mediocrity' in all types of work.[4] 'He chatters the dialect and is keen,' claimed the Council Secretary in 1906, and was 'the only chance of policing the Chinese'.[5] In a sense he had been born for the job which he took over in 1913, for his cadetship was most likely secured by the desire of the city oligarchs to find a billet for a favoured son of the Settlement. His widower father had died in late 1896 while on his way to Britain after being invalided from the post of Captain Superintendent which he had held since 1885. A dry, spare figure, McEuen was later pilloried as a 'notoriously incompetent loafer' by a former acting Shanghai Consul-General.[6] He was a man of the treaty port world, with no strong British roots: born in Hong Kong, he would move to Japan after his forced retirement in 1925, where he would die. McEuen had taken over from the disgraced Colonel C. D. Bruce whose 'infinite charm of manner' and 'distinguished looking' features had not helped redeem him in the face of charges of his own incompetence and cowardice (if not corruption) in connection with the SMC's thwarted occupation of Chapei in 1913.[7] Bruce's predecessor, A. M. Boisragon – something of an imperial celebrity as one of only two Britons to survive the 'Benin massacre' in 1897 that served as a pretext for the British conquest of that West African city – beat 264 candidates for the job, and was ditched as unsatisfactory in 1906.[8] This was a singular run of bad luck.

Still, Shanghailanders were pleased with their force. Shanghai was 'admirably policed', claimed Darwent. The raw police returns published monthly in the *Municipal Gazette* might '*look* alarming', but 'they amount to little'. Almost a third of the June 1919 figures, for example, were 'trumpery ricksha cases', another 40 per cent were 'nuisances'. And 'it is to be remembered that the poorest Chinese criminals have not the slightest objection to spending a month in a nice warm foreign gaol with plenty to eat'.[9] Settlement life was safer, concluded Darwent, than in many Western cities. And it was all a good show. There was the annual inspection parade, when the force route-marched to the Public Recreation Ground, where it was inspected by the Council Chairman, and the SMP stood tall at any other of the many parades that Shanghailanders so liked. A good march through the Settlement streets also served to remind Shanghai's residents where power lay. The reality behind this confidence was rather different. Crime rates had risen sharply since 1913, reaching crisis levels in wartime when the force was understaffed. In the aftermath of the failed 'Second Revolution' of 1913, when Guomindang troops rose against the new tyranny of President Yuan Shikai, China, and East China in particular, was awash with demobilized soldiery, and weapons. Revolutionaries had to live, after all. In 1914 gangs of armed men raided 'shops and houses in crowded and busy places in the Settlement'. There were 98 such cases that year, and 196 in 1916. Two measures helped bring rates down. Nightly search parties were instituted in early 1917. SMP personnel cordoned off street entrances and searched passers-by for arms. And after May 1918, 248 volunteer Special police were recruited.[10] But the murder rate doubled, and the success rate for solving reported property crime fell from 52 per cent in 1912 to 31 per cent in 1916.[11] So the published statistics looked alarming indeed.

A small group of senior personnel guided the force through these challenging years. With the appointment of seven cadets between 1900 and 1914, the SMP hoped to create an officer class, and to solve its long-running leadership problems. These select men were expected to integrate themselves smoothly into elite Shanghailander society and some, like McEuen or Kenneth Bourne (son of an assistant judge at the British Supreme Court), were products of that world, while others married into it. 'There is nothing like having the youngsters of the best leading foreigners,' it was argued, who, after a final education and 'finishing touches' at home, 'could be kept on the straight and narrow by their parents'.[12] The SMP's rank and file were not expected either to assume senior positions or to be acceptable recruits to polite society. Down to 1941 the force would be commanded by the cadets or by appointees from India, although the promotion ceiling was cracking when Tinkler joined. 'Superior education coupled with a long record of duties consistently and conscientiously carried out', noted Commissioner Barrett in 1928, could 'be an invaluable link between the senior officers and the lower ranks whose general outlook on life' they could interpret – so long as this did not wholly exclude 'young men of higher education and breeding'.[13]

In 1919 the authorized strength of the force was: 7 Chief Inspectors, 11 Inspectors (and 5 Detective Inspectors), 11 Sub-Inspectors (and 5 Detective Sub-Inspectors), 96 Sergeants (and 19 Detective Sergeants), and 105 Constables (and a further 4 Detective Constables). Above the Chief Inspectors a cadre of Superintendents was developed in the 1920s. Above that were those 'young men of higher education and breeding', a social world that Frank Peasgood remembered as 'foreign territory to me'.[14] As a new constable, Tinkler faced the possibility of promotion to Sergeant after eighteen months, providing that he passed the examination and that his Chinese was progressing. After a further three years he would be able to sit an examination for promotion to Sub-Inspector, but would then have to wait for promotion based on seniority. There were yearly salary increments, and the possibility of transfer to the detective branch.

At the base of this promotion ladder was Gordon Road, its classrooms and the large parade ground, bordered by the Sikh and Chinese dormitories, on which the British recruits would practise drilling squads of Asians. A 1907 report into the state of the SMP had concluded that the Settlement had long outgrown the force. One consequence was the opening of the Depot in 1908, which marked a new stage in the policing of the international settlement.[15] From November 1909 all new drafts of men began to spend the first months of their service at the Depot, which was designed to serve as the force's anchor: all men were to be trained in one place, and through exactly the same regime. The SMP would know what the men were learning, and it could incorporate new practices and regulations swiftly into its curriculum. Training would filter out the unsuitable, introduce the disciplinary regime the men would work within, and assess potential. The SMP modernized itself in good company: the first Metropolitan Police depot had opened in London only a year earlier. And in 1907 the Colonial Office decided that all future colonial police force officers would undergo initial training at the RIC's Dublin depot.[16] Police forces internationally were beginning to introduce systematic training structures in the first decade of the twentieth century.[17] For the demobilized wartime conscripts of 1919, depot life must have had a familiar feel, with the added Shanghai novelty of being served tea in bed. By the age of 21 Tinkler had seen the inside of two training institutions in the army, and when he summed up this life to his Aunt Florence as 'six weeks' hard training' the 'hard' was probably added as a boast rather than a description. But the gentle morning awakening with the China tea was a prelude to a full day. Reveille at 6 a.m. was followed by a cross-country run, breakfast at 8, school from 8.45 to 11, an hour's study of Shanghainese dialect, 'tiffin' ('the name for lunch in the East') at 12.30, more lessons from 2 to 4, tea (which was 'scarcely a meal in the East') at 4.15, an hour's drill or automatic pistol shooting from 4.30, before dinner at 6.30. After dinner the recruits were free until 1 a.m. when they were required to be in the Depot, lights out.

The SMP's history had been dominated by problems stemming from the ingrained parsimony of the foreign ratepayers, and by the problem of recruiting good men, Chinese and foreign, and, having got them, of keeping them good. Finance was also a recurrent problem for domestic forces. But as the Captain Superintendent noted in 1912: 'the temptation to young men fresh from home to go even temporarily wrong in Shanghai is, as is well known, very strong.' There were two problems: 'as elsewhere in the Far East the restraining influences of home life are to a great extent lacking,' while 'more than ordinary self control is required if he is to retain his self-respect and become a reliable member of the Police Force'.[18] The Depot introduced military-style discipline and oversight for men without family, or who might fall for Shanghai's temptations. Tinkler's wide-eyed wonder at the city's opulence and extravagance needed reining in before it undid him. The punitive culture proved too much for some. 'Sir, I, P.C. 76 D. Craig, beg to report that yesterday I lost my mind to think of my being treated as a child in the police force,' protested one Depot recruit in 1932. Craig was dismissed. 'One's own private affairs', remarked a former policeman in a letter to McEuen, 'were too much spied upon to my liking.' Local recruit John Hooper was last seen walking out of the Depot ten days after he arrived, dressed in his naval uniform: 'He said he would not be a success in the Police.'[19] And the 1 a.m. curfew – monitored by senior personnel who actually checked that men were in their beds – was just one of the ways in which they found their private lives intruded on by their new employer.

Gordon Road also taught these men how to live in Shanghai and in a colonial world. 'We thought we were in heaven,' remembered Fred West, of his arrival at the Depot with his fellow recruits in 1921. They reached it in time for tiffin, a feast already laid out on the table, with servants to serve it.[20] Tinkler learnt useful lessons about foreign life in the city, and about the basics of colonial culture. Chinese were servants, or subordinates, and – as the terms of service pointed out – 'the criminal classes were chiefly Chinese'.[21] Servants needed watching ('the cleanliness of their hands and persons, and the thoroughness with which they do their work' depended solely on the foreigner's supervision'[22]); so did the Chinese police and populace generally. And the East was different in other ways. Expatriate life followed largely unfamiliar middle-class patterns and rituals – tea was scarcely the meal that it was in Ulverston – and it also provided middle-class opportunities, such as paid leave. Shanghailanders also marked themselves apart by using an insider lingo – business was 'pidgin', a servant was a 'boy' – and Tinkler learnt this argot as smoothly as he learnt to sit comfortably in a rickshaw and be pulled around the city by another human being. 'We soon got used to it,' said West of having servants. 'We very soon got to know how to ring the bell if we wanted something.'

The Depot was only as good as its staff. But in 1919 these were good men indeed. Gordon Road was run by an enthusiastic freemason, Irish Inspector Stewart Crommie Young (himself a rank-and-file appointee who would retire as Acting Commissioner and a pillar of the Holy Trinity Cathedral), and William Ewart Fairbairn, Sergeant-Major and drill instructor. Fairbairn was to become an almost mythical figure in the world of unarmed combat and small arms training. In six years' service with the Royal Marines after 1901 he was based variously at Chatham and overseas in China and saw out a stint in the small detachment stationed at the British Legation in Seoul. He joined the SMP in 1907, was soon involved in musketry training and was appointed assistant drill instructor in 1912. By Fairbairn's own account, military training had not prepared him for the roughness of life on the Shanghai beat, especially when the navy was in town and merchant seamen were on the prowl. Fairbairn began studying ju-jitsu with a Japanese trainer in 1908, as well as Chinese martial arts. At the Depot he held evening judo classes, and ran the arms training courses and musketry training; he also devised and oversaw arms training for the force more generally. He brought his experience of Asian martial arts together in the devising of a system of physical training and unarmed self-defence for the SMP which he termed 'Defendu', first publishing a handbook for it in 1926. It offered a 'number of admittedly drastic and unpleasant forms of defence but all are justifiable and necessary if one is to protect himself against the foul methods of a certain class'.[23] After retiring from the SMP in 1940 he ran covert warfare training courses in Britain, Canada and the United States, while his post-Second World War career involved riot-squad training in Singapore and in Cyprus.[24] Gordon Road demon-strated not only that the SMP's pace of development kept up with similar forces elsewhere, but also how integrated Shanghai was into the empire world. It was the location of pioneering innovations in public order policing and combat training that were transplanted to Britain's formal empire, and used in wartime.

A man was expected to leave Gordon Road after about six to eight weeks, with a decent knowledge of how he might begin to carry out his job. The range of knowledge needed by the Shanghai bobby was certainly wide. In the classrooms the instructors and visiting senior officers led the men through the varied topics which constituted 'Knowledge of Police Duties': local regulations, procedures and powers, local general knowledge, geography of China, arithmetic and musketry. For the handful of men with previous police training this would have been partially familiar, but even for them the basic fact of the Shanghai constable's life would have been strange. 'The first duty of a police officer is to prevent crime,' noted a test dictation set for new recruits in the 1920s. But the text, taken from the *Police Guide and Regulations* with which all men were issued, began by baldly stating the singular fact of Shanghai policing, that the new constable 'immediately he starts duty on the street ... is immediately placed in charge of Sikh and Chinese constables'.[25] Becoming a Shanghai

DEALING WITH AN ARMED ASSAILANT

No. 3.—Disarming an Assailant Holding You up with a Pistol. From in Front.

Fig. 39

Fig. 40

Fig. 41

policeman meant learning how to handle the Chinese and Sikhs. They were to be drilled on the parade ground, and then commanded on the streets of the city.

The structure of the SMP was simple enough. Responsible to the Commissioner and Deputy Commissioner were the Director of Criminal Investigation, who oversaw the Criminal Investigation Department (CID), Assistant Commissioners for Chinese, Sikhs, the Foreign Branch, the Gaol Branch (which was responsible, in Ward Road Gaol, for what was in the 1930s the world's largest prison) and the Mounted Branch, which patrolled the outskirts of the Settlement, and which decorated weddings, parades and public balls with its Sikh troopers. An Intelligence Office answering to CID chief William Armstrong dealt with political intelligence, reporting on local Chinese activities, arms smuggling, Bolshevism, wartime enemies as well as preparing reports for British and other consulates. In their classes Tinkler and his colleagues were introduced to the facts of their new life and work through the pages of the *Police Guide and Regulations*. Here was another Shanghai, a weird counterpart to Darwent's city. The handbook provided definitions ('Chattel: Any article moveable or immoveable except land and a dog is chattel. Persons may be charged with theft of a dog under Chinese law'); described procedures ('All cases of death or injury to Chinese police officers must be reported in writing or by telephone to the Deputy Commissioner (Chinese)'); itemized equipment ('The use of truncheons on ricshas etc. is strictly forbidden'); described the structure of police administration; listed local benevolent institutions (The Mercy Hospital for the Insane, the Salvation Army Hostel Men's Shelter); vetoed slang terms in reports and letters, and delivered guidance on the duties and demeanour of the Constable, whose manner was to be 'alert', and who 'must avoid lounging and gossiping'. More than his manner was to be watched: 'when on duty a police officer should allow nothing unconnected with his duty to occupy his thoughts.'[26] Conning the *Police Guide* was the key to passing the examinations at the Depot, and later on for promotion to Sergeant. In its various editions the book mapped out, and remapped, the SMP's Shanghai as comprehensively as the Revd Darwent's guide did the residents' and visitors' city. New recruits still needed to learn their way around physically – and were sometimes route-marched about and then tested on the sights they had been shown – but to function as policemen they needed the *Police Guide*.

Shanghai 'police knowledge' was a tricky subject. 'Before what tribunal should foreigners of the following nationality be charged,' asked a 1925 examination paper: 'British? French? German? American? Russian? Japanese? Unregistered?'[27] Such questions lay at the heart of the peculiar environment that the men worked in. The SMP policed the International Settlement, and was responsible to the Municipal Council, but foreign residents of the Settlement lived under the jurisdiction of their consuls, with the exception by 1919 of former enemy subjects (for China had joined the war on the allied side in late 1917), citizens of the new states of the former Ottoman Empire and Central and Eastern Europe, and after September 1920 of the Russians. British subjects were served by a police court, and by a Supreme Court for China and Korea, founded in 1865 and housed in the British consulate compound. The judge in 1919, Sir Havilland De Sausmarez, had served in judicial positions in Lagos, Zanzibar and the Ottoman Empire before his appointment to Shanghai in 1905, representing a formal link with the colonial world.[28] The US Court for China, established in 1906, dealt with cases involving US citizens. Foreigners who were 'unregistered' – that is, unrepresented by a consul, or who were unrecognized by the consul whose nationality they claimed – came under the jurisdiction of the International Mixed Court, a Chinese body sitting in the Settlement since 1864 which also dealt with civil disputes between Chinese residents, and criminal cases against Chinese.[29]

The Mixed Court was a fixture in the SMP's Shanghai, and Tinkler was to serve there for an eight-month stint in 1920. Foreign 'assessors', usually junior consular officials, sat in on all cases affecting foreign interests, but Chinese prisoners were tried by Chinese magistrates. In 1911 the foreign consuls in Shanghai had taken advantage of the revolution to seize control of the Court. It was perceived as corrupt and dilatory, and year after year there were complaints about either the perceived harshness of Chinese law, or the laxity of sentencing. In hostile foreign eyes the Chinese would never get it right. With the seizure of control, the formal link with the Chinese judicial system was broken – although Chinese law still applied to Chinese subjects.

An SMP officer was now the Court's chief administrator (the Registrar), and a cadre of policemen was brought in to displace and supervise lower-level Chinese functionaries, whose corruption had been such a standard complaint. Opportunities for petty corruption remained and were taken advantage of, not least by the foreign sergeants who often served long detachments there. New recruits were taken in to watch important trials. Earlier reform had also seen the passing of the sight of 'prisoners wearing the cangue [a portable set of stocks] and being bambooed' which became a tourist spectacle, although Darwent pointed out that at the Louza police station 'Permission to see the prisoners in their iron exercise cages may usually be obtained'. A handwritten caption to one policeman's photograph of this sight reads '"The bird cage" and some of the birds'.[30] The SMP kept the Mixed Court busy. In 1919 it processed criminal cases against 38,307 men and women, and 34 unrecognized foreigners, and it heard 1,474 Chinese civil cases and 299 foreign civil cases. Jail sentences were given to 2,132 Chinese, while 63 were sentenced to expulsion from the Settlement – a somewhat peculiar sentence as it was almost impossible to prevent people returning – and 50 of those handed over to the Chinese authorities were executed in the presence of SMP representatives.[31] Many photographs of such executions survive amongst the papers of ex-policemen, testament to a widespread fascination with such violent 'Asiatic' horror.[32]

As well as getting their heads around such jurisdictional confusion, the men had to understand the quirky boundaries of the Settlement. In the Depot classes they were taught local and Chinese geography: 'Where is the Huangpu river?', 'Where is Shanghai?', 'What are the boundaries of the International Settlement?'[33] But they were taught also how such geography affected policing. Another examination question asked 'Under what circumstances would you: (a) pursue a person escaping into territory not under municipal control? (b) having arrested him, what action would you take?' Well might it pose such a query. Boundaries were everywhere. It was possible to stroll from the Chinese city along the Quai de France to the Shanghai Club in a few minutes. Armed robbers found it an easy journey, too. In 1918, 50 out of 109 of those arrested for the crime had come from Frenchtown, and the threat from the 'Southern border' was a big worry for the SMP,

Armed-robbers & armed kidnappers. captured
by the S.M.P & handed over to the Chinese
for execution, being paraded around the streets
of Shanghai as deterrent to others not to join in
their procession.

Top: Execution of armed robbers & kidnappers. Lungwha near Shanghai. Soldiers of Fentien Army acted as executioners.
Bottom: After the execution. Lungwha near Shanghai.

which complained of the apparent French tolerance of 'dangerous revolutionary riff-raff'.[34] Suspects could flee into Chapei, Nantao or the concession. They could be arrested by neighbouring forces, and the SMP reciprocated, but the situation produced thickets of paper and procedure in which suspects could hide. Relations with the neighbours were not always good, and the borders were complicated by the 'external roads' built into neighbouring Chinese territory. When a rickshaw passenger was held up and robbed at gunpoint on one such road in 1914, a Chinese policeman stood watching 35 yards away. He had no authority to act on Council territory – and probably more sense than to involve himself needlessly with armed men.[35] Armed robbery was a high-profile crime, but the quirks of geography and sovereignty made fighting any crime a tricky matter. And neighbouring Chinese forces battled to rein in the SMP in return. Armed stand-offs were not unknown, and the perils of hot pursuit across settlement boundaries were brought sharply home in 1926 when PC Marcus Goulding, who had been in the force barely a year, was shot dead by Chinese police who mistook him for a criminal.[36]

So these were difficult and sometimes dangerous issues and the recruits needed to make a start in learning just how complex their working environment would be. But the first job for most of these men was patrolling a beat, meeting up with Chinese constables and sergeants at fixed points on the quarter hours, and signing their conference books as proof that they were on duty (and also as proof that the foreign constables were properly patrolling their sectors). Effective policing of any sort would have been impossible without an effective grasp of Chinese. Educated Chinese Shanghai residents might well speak English, but the bulk of the city folk policed or policing the city would not. Chinese was vital not only because the majority population of the city was Chinese, but because of the role the foreign branch played in supervising the Chinese majority in the force. Chinese language study was compulsory after 1903, and remained so after men were transferred to stations where they were expected to study for an hour a day in their own time, getting an extra day's leave a month as compensation. Study began at the Depot. For Fred West this was the 'worst part' of his training. Apprenticed to a wheelwright at 14, neither that nor wartime service with airships had quite prepared him for learning Shanghainese.[37] The SMC recognized three levels of ability: Temporary – 'ability to communicate with a native upon any subject of the candidate's choice'; Lower – mastery of a set textbook's lessons (Hawks Pott's *Lessons in the Shanghai Dialect*), translation of easy non-technical passages and department-related easy conversation; Higher – fluency. Men could then choose to study Mandarin, the newly official national language of this polyglot country. But the emphasis was obviously firmly on spoken Shanghainese, rather than written Chinese. (The set texts also partly reinforced the colonial culture the men were learning: 'Translate into Chinese: Chinese are called Yellow men, foreigners White men; the beggars in the city are numberless.')[38] For some men this was a hopeless task; and for most men language remained a barrier, and police practice an impediment. It was easy to rely on the station interpreters in the charge-rooms, and on pidgin English in communication with subordinates and the public. A basic vocabulary would get men by; if they could understand the warning cry 'Jandau' (robber) they could act. 'Oh, Mr Cormie, have catchee information, better we go,' Dan Cormie would remember his Chinese detective colleagues saying to him. And off he would blindly, trustingly, almost helplessly go.[39]

Passing language examinations gave men either a useful cash bonus or a monthly addition to their salaries, and it was a requirement for promotion. The men also had to resit the examinations every six months to retain their bonus unless exempted. Dermot O'Neil found himself on the 'Special Warning List' of men deemed not to be making a real effort in 1936; and this could lead to dismissal, or the refusal of the force to renew men's contracts. The advice that Dan Cormie received when he joined in 1926 was that he should find himself a 'sleeping dictionary', a Chinese mistress who could not speak English. Public relationships with Chinese women were still frowned upon in the 1920s, but Cormie reported that 'most of us' took this advice.[40] In the changed climate of the 1930s one officer's annual report still noted that he mixed too freely with Chinese women, and later noted that he was 'possibly too free with subordinates mainly due to attempts to learn Chinese from all and sundry'. His 'excellent Chinese', helped by his marriage in 1936 to Miss Tsang Mei-yuan, was acquired at the cost of some distrust from his superiors who felt that he failed to keep a sufficient distance from Chinese society and company. The point of language acquisition was command, not familiarity. Tinkler's own progress was smooth; he passed the examination for the higher level in July 1922, and was later exempted altogether from further study.

For all the talk of British control, the SMP, like British domestic and colonial police forces, systematically used strangers to police strangers. Every Saturday morning at 10.30 the British trainees could have watched a motley crowd of young Chinese men, sometimes up to a thousand strong, assembling on the Depot parade ground. A senior officer would arrive and, after they had formed an approximation of an orderly line, he would inspect and question them, 'occasionally pulling down an eyelid where an opium habitué is suspected'.[41] Those who were selected during this brief physical inspection, and who could read and write, were put on a waiting list to join the force. In 1919 only 161 of those who paraded were chosen and passed the tests. These were men who fitted the requirements published in the terms of service.[42] They were of 'good physique' (although Chinese were seen, in contemporary thinking on race characteristics, as unmanly), over 5 feet 5 inches, and had 'some knowledge of reading and writing'. They needed to find a guarantor for their future conduct as it was felt to be impossible to find references for their prior conduct: 'one cannot write to the local clergyman and ask him' about personal honesty or family position, 'as there is no such reliable person or, indeed, anyone who approximates thereto' in China.[43] In the Depot physical training and team sports were needed to remedy the alleged innate clumsiness and effeminacy of the Chinese. In their classes, instructors read out the Chinese Branch manual, and every man copied the regulations into his own notebook. They listened to lectures about practical police work, and spent two hours a day on drill, learning to obey English words of command. A taboo about arming Chinese men, which had been seen as almost tantamount to arming and training a potential enemy force, was broken during the wartime crime wave. They received weapons training for the first time in 1915. This was too late for some. Four had been shot the previous year, two fatally.[44]

The Chinese were infinitely cheaper than Europeans, not least because poorly paid, far easier to discipline, and there was a seemingly bottomless pool of potential recruits waiting to replace those who proved corrupt, inefficient or criminal. They were the front line of the SMP on the streets and in the alleyways of Shanghai. By the end of the 1890s, the patterns of empire thought which had created categories of 'martial races' and hierarchies of 'trustworthiness' among ethnic communities in India began to be applied to China. The SMP preferred to recruit men from Shandong, valued for their physique, but also for their imputed 'characteristic' of being 'loyal to their salt once they feel themselves firmly established as a unit in any concern'.[45] Shanghai men were thought to have 'too many interests in the place'. With officers from Peking and many rank and file from Shandong the SMP also fitted well the Shanghai pattern whereby provincial groups in the city ran different sectors. But it sometimes gave rise to intra-police conflict between gangs of Shandong and 'Kompo' men.[46] Shanghai was policed more intensively than European cities of a similar size and this was only possible because it was policed cheaply. 'The Chinese constable', Commissioner Barrett reminded the SMC in 1929, 'can barely exist on his pay, particularly the married man living out of barracks.' Small wonder then that this combined with the allegedly 'usual custom of the country' to make bribes effectively part of the salary, especially when it was 'realised that the Police can obtain money from gambling establishments by simply asking for it'.[47] The suppression of the legal opium trade – 1918 had been the first full year in which no shops were licensed to sell opium in the Settlement – and the phasing out of brothels served up opportunities aplenty for bribery.

These, then, were the 'Huapu' (Chinese constables), the men Maurice Tinkler and his companions were sent out to supervise, and to lead by example. How would Maurice Tinkler get on with men like, for example, Lu Zhaopeng, CPC 3320, whose copy of the Chinese rule book is now deposited in the Shanghai Municipal Library?[48] Neither man would know the other's name. The CPCs were known by their numbers, and they would know and refer to Tinkler amongst themselves by his. The pay differentials were vast, and patterns in off-duty life very different. There was very little scope for men getting to know each other. And we know next to nothing about the Chinese. Until the late 1930s their names are either not noted or only given in transliteration in the annual reports. Their personnel files are closed. We know from the SMP records the names of those killed on duty, or those who were awarded decorations for bravery or long service. Britons serving in the SMP probably knew little more than we can find out. There are some hints of friendliness. Sam Sherlock sent home two photographs of himself posed in uniform in a photographer's studio, one with a Chinese sergeant and another with a constable. But the relaxed poses are out of colonial kilter, and the familiarity transgressive. Chinese constables were 'funny people to understand they have a terrible amount of pluck and are quick on the draw', reported Sherlock.[49] Jack Darby's papers contain snapshots of him posing with his motorbike patrol companion, Dap Su (Big Xu). But all of these were exceptions.

Race perceptions maintained the chasm in relations that was created by the structure of the force and by language. Maurice Tinkler's letters almost never mention his Chinese subordinates or colleagues. They were not part of his world. Other men's files show an ordinary violence in the relationship. Disciplinary charges for striking Chinese constables were not uncommon. 'Drunk and assaulting CPC 763 on Honan Road', 'attempted to strike CPC', 'Assaulting CPC 784': 'He kicked [the CPC] from behind and then slapped his face and shook his shoulder, later warning him, "You must be careful or I will have you dismissed"'.[50] We can only speculate about the numbers of men who heeded such threats. Some men, as well as foreign civilians, seem to have seen young Chinese constables as a pool of potential sexual partners. PC 14 was dismissed in 1926 for 'grossly indecent conduct amounting to attempted sodomy with a Chinese constable' (who was unwilling).[51] Chinese Police Sergeant Wong Tuk Kwei summed up power relations in 1929 in evidence to a disciplinary board about his failure to stop PC Arthur Benstead illegally entering houses and extorting money from opium smokers: 'As I am a Chinese – he is a foreigner, when he wants to go away I cannot prevent him.'[52] He might of course have been disingenuous, and power relations could certainly be reversed. Young rookies would lack the language or experience to know at times what they were a party to when experienced and corrupt Chinese personnel extorted or stole. One Sub-Inspector had no such excuse after ten years in the force. He accused 3rd grade clerk Hwa Tsz Liang of plotting to 'fix' him with a bribery charge, but the evidence showed that both men were in league with the Hongkew

station gatemen to accept a bribe to release a prisoner. So good relations might result from – and in – shared corruption, which was another reason for actively encouraging Britons to keep their distance. The Sub-Inspector was ordered to resign.[53]

Over two hundred Sikh and Muslim police and gaol staff also passed through the Gordon Road Depot in 1919. Like the foreign branch, Sikh recruitment had been curtailed by the war and the force was desperate for new drafts. The Sikh is the figure above all others who today represents the treaty port period in Shanghai's popular memory. The men served a threefold purpose: economy, defence and display. Eight Sikhs cost the council as much as one European and they were felt to be more reliable than Chinese.[54] They formed a surrogate military reserve for the SMC. Tall and imposing, Sikhs added a touch of imperial authenticity to the squatter settlement. Since 1905 the men had all been recruited through the Indian Army's recruiting staff, but this made them no less risky an asset, as Sikh community politics remained a problem for the SMP. As the century developed there were new threats. Sikhs brought with them empire problems in the form of nationalist politics. 'Seditious propaganda' was found in barrack rooms, and Police Orders were issued forbidding active participation in politics or the circulation of literature in stations. In 1927 the SMP Special Branch formed an Indian Section and collaborated with Indian government agents in the supervision and frustration of Indian nationalist activity locally.[55] In Shanghai dialect slang the Sikh was dismissed as '*Hongdo Asei*' – the 'Red-headed monkey'. For British officers the Sikh remained a distant, even comical figure. Race attitudes encouraged disdain, and the prejudices and caricatures common amongst the British in India were imported alongside the men.[56] Memoirs as well as contemporary accounts dwell on allegations of cowardice, childishness and cruelty. Cormie reported a constable colleague assaulting a Sikh sergeant who objected to being ordered about by a junior officer.[57] 'You couldn't trust them,' claimed another man, 'they weren't truthful.'[58] But relations with their British colleagues could get intimate. Indian personnel, and especially watchmen, often ran a sideline in moneylending. A British man living too fast and too freely could be sure of securing a loan from Sikh subordinates, and so would undermine the disciplinary and race hierarchy. This was very risky, as there was a real danger of dismissal if he was found out (which was useful collateral for lenders). In the empire world, relations between individuals were always made fraught by the confusions of race and dignity, by the power of social norms and peer pressure, and by disciplinary codes and their explicit and coded injunctions.

The Depot made Shanghai men of Maurice Tinkler and his colleagues. There was much to learn that was new, but also much that was obliquely familiar. The men were now in a privileged position in a hierarchy based on race in and outside the force, but they were also at the bottom of the colonialist pile. They learnt in six sweaty Shanghai weeks the race notions that underpinned empire's practice. And they learnt that they were marginal men, whose presence for Shanghailanders was a necessary and sometimes amusing evil. The SMC's 1919 *Annual Report* printed the numbers of disciplinary offences under the headings 'Drunkenness', 'Neglect of duty' and 'Minor offences'. The propensity of the Shanghai bobby to drink was a caricatured matter of public concern. It was almost as if it was assumed that they couldn't read, or would not read the council's publications. Of course, they were tolerated if athletic, good at rugger, or a useful batsman, but they were never a true part of social Shanghai, or Mina Shorrock's society journal *Social Shanghai*. Although there were exceptions, the SMP were seen by the majority of the Shanghai British, as their peers were by other colonial elites, as lacking social background, education, and polish.[59] Their alienation from expatriate society in the city began in the Depot and would be reinforced on the beat. So they clubbed together from the start, on the boat out, looking out for each other, and they began even in Gordon Road to 'learn the ropes', to learn and unlearn the *Police Guide and Regulations*, and to take in the Shanghai police 'canteen culture' and Shanghailander street culture. They were taught pretty quickly what to do by those with more experience of handling a cheeky 'Chinaman', a slow rickshaw puller, a pushy student. And even if discipline was strict, there was old corruption in the force. The sergeants who had stayed at their posts in the wartime period were wary of the new battle-hardened recruits, and there were wartime volunteers returning who knew the ropes, and wanted a comfortable, quiet life.

The SMP needed all its new recruits. There had been no recruitment since 1914 and fifty-five men had been given permission to leave and join up, while another thirty-two had resigned and volunteered despite the efforts of the force, and even the British Consul-General, to persuade them to stay.[60] At least eleven had been killed and twenty-three wounded on active service. At the end of 1919 the foreign branch of the police was 146 strong, against an authorized strength of 238. Where there should have been 105 foreign constables there were only 5. Alan Hilton-Johnson, then acting Captain Superintendent, had himself resigned to rejoin the 10th West Yorkshire Regiment, and he led a contingent of over one hundred Shanghai volunteers seen off from the Bund in October 1914 by 7,000 spectators. On 15 December he had marched the men up to the Central Recruiting Office in Whitehall, where many of them, including a number of policemen, volunteered for service in his regiment.[61]

Many of the SMP's personnel in 1914 had had previous military experience. The force had over the years recruited from visiting military and naval units, from domestic police forces and the RIC, from whom 'fine stalwart young Irishmen' were recruited in 1900.[62] After 1902 it used the Council's London purchasing agents, Pooks, to arrange recruitment. Pooks advertised in the police and the popular press, and sometimes contacted domestic forces directly. The SMP competed with other types of foreign and colonial service – public works, for example – for British men actively seeking overseas employment, but also recruited men who had given no previous thought to working abroad. It certainly needed to recruit in Britain. Recruiting in Shanghai was always tricky. Local foreign recruits knew the cabarets too well, and were often violent in their attitudes to the Chinese. But twenty-seven men were recruited from the Royal Navy China Station ships in 1922 ('they haven't enough brains to answer the telephone', complained Tinkler in 1925). More than eighty-six joined from the Shanghai Defence Force between 1928 and April 1929, and more were to sign on. But as might have been expected, by June that year thirteen had already been dismissed. George Gravenell, for example, was deemed 'unlikely to make an efficient police officer', and 'should be made an example of' for alleged ill-discipline.[63] The prior employment of about a third of the men who joined the SMP between 1900 and 1945 is known, and of these 45 per cent had served in the armed forces.[64] Ex-military recruits often needed as much policing as they gave. A typical report from 1935 on E. W. Peters read: 'Not good at Chinese. Inclined to heavy beer drinking. Usual ex-soldier type – not too reliable but not a bad officer under supervision.' Men recruited from domestic police forces could also be a problem. About 13 per cent of those for whom prior employment is known had police experience – 'we never did it that way in the Met', they would chorus – but such men often complained about conditions and facilities, and their griping affected other recruits.[65] Moreover, in a climate of radicalism at home, police strikes in August 1918 and 1919 had led to the dismissal of some 2,400 men. Through the early 1920s until at least 1928 the SMP brought out recruits in small batches to contain any influence that Bolshevik – or just plain bolshie – recruits might have on their companions.[66] The war provided a twofold opportunity: millions of men were being demobilized, and if the Shanghai police could acquire and mould men who already had an experience of discipline as citizen (rather than regular) soldiers, and who were a fairly representative section of British working-class and lower-middle-class life, it possibly stood a chance of creating an efficient cadre of good European policemen almost for the very first time.

Work on the beat would be the test. McEuen needed his men on the streets as soon as possible. As 1919 progressed the SMP was hard-pressed by the demands of the security situation in the Settlement, by the business of organizing German repatriation in March and April, coping with the May Fourth Movement, and with an influx in April of Korean political refugees, closely followed by early Russian arrivals. The reports on the August 1919 recruits from the Training Depot at the end of the six-week course were optimistic. 'Rather unsettled at present', is recorded in several cases, 'should settle down', usually followed. 'Should turn out well', was the report on Allan McGillivray, whose Depot scores were unusually high. 'Unsettled and careless at present', was the judgement on Walter Webb. The force obviously assumed that the years of harsh discipline in the British army that these civilians had endured would enable them to buckle down into the SMP's intrusive and restrictive regime. As others were to find out to their cost, such an assumption was often wrong. When Tinkler left the Depot in October 1919 a short report was entered in his file, and he was given a mark out of ten for 'Behaviour at Depot, Attention to duties, Ability, Knowledge of Police Duties, Reading, Writing, Grammar, Arithmetic, Chinese'. Tinkler graduated with straight tens, bar one nine for writing. Tinkler began the ordinary duties of an SMP Constable on a salary of 105 taels a month. His training report declared him 'An exceedingly good man. Education very good ... Quiet and attentive to his work.' Such qualities were important, given the constables' role in upholding British racial superiority in the force: 'it is therefore a matter of special importance in Shanghai for every foreign officer to set an example of upright conduct, both on and off duty.'[67]

'Upright conduct' was also exacted through the subordination of the men to military regulation. In 1910 the British Minister to China issued a set of King's Regulations that gave the Captain Superintendent of Police legal powers to punish British subjects in the force. He was appointed as a police magistrate, and could convene a court to try and punish the men.[68] He could also use the Shanghai British courts. Edward Cartwright sailed out with Tinkler, and like his companions had little clear understanding of these regulations. A veteran of eighteen months' service each in the army and the Royal Flying Corps, he had 'come out to Shanghai to make a living'. On 17 December 1919 he appeared in the British police court with another recruit, James Cosson, charged with offences under these King's Regulations. The trial caused a sensation, and was the first and last time that the regulations were enforced in a public court. On 11 December Cartwright had failed to appear for duty at 7 p.m., and was discovered after half an hour in the station canteen. At 11.10 that evening he was, allegedly, drunk. 'I am finished', he said, placed his pistol on the sergeant's desk and left. At 1 a.m. he was not in his room, and he failed to appear for duty in the morning. More insubordination over the following days saw him up before the beak with Cosson, who had sailed with the second draft and was now a warder. Cosson faced similar charges of insubordination and disobeying lawful commands, and Hilton-Johnson, acting Commissioner, was determined to punish the men as an example to the others. They admitted the charges, but pleaded ignorance of the regulations – which Hilton-Johnson was forced to agree were not physically given to the men – and were sentenced to a day's imprisonment and dismissed from the force. 'Do you think you were playing the game,' asked the magistrate, 'setting a good example to the Asiatics in the force?' 'No Sir,' replied Cartwright.

They were not 'Bolsheviks', protested their defence lawyer, they had served their country. Both men were shipped home.[69] The trial hardly did the reputation of the SMP much good. Hilton-Johnson disciplined the policemen as he would his soldiers in the 10th Yorkshire.

Meanwhile, Maurice Tinkler, the new PC 72, walked the Shanghai streets. As the novelty faded, and they patrolled regular beats, the men could look more clearly at their new situation. By virtue of their nationality they had leapfrogged into a different social class, those who were servant-supplied. For James Young, once himself a servant, and George Matcham, formerly a railway dining car attendant, the change must have been even more refreshing. For those who had spent years in dugouts and worse in France and Belgium, the good life must have appeared to have begun. But the initial euphoria at the new way of living soon wore off. Living quarters were crowded, and sanitation was bad. Some barracks had no hot water systems, the men making do with water supplied by hot water shops of doubtful hygiene. The 1 a.m. curfew – which applied to all men living in barracks – was a 'very sore point indeed', the majority suffering through 'the delinquencies of others'.[70] Eight of the 1919 recruits were dismissed on 29 June 1921, in Tinkler's words, 'because they were fed up with the rotten pay and refused to work'. All had been disciplined several times early on after leaving the Depot, mostly for breaking curfew. James Young's excuse on one occasion in June 1920, that he went out with 'missionary friends to spend an enjoyable evening', seems unlikely. All eight failed the sergeants' examination. They requested permission to resign, they 'found it difficult to live on the salaries provided'. McEuen rejected this, but then deemed them to have refused duty and dismissed them, leaving them stuck in Shanghai and 'practically destitute'. As an 'act of grace or charity' – and to prevent their becoming an embarrassment to British prestige – the Council eventually provided third-class passages home as long as they left immediately.[71]

Promotion prospects were poor because the lack of a pension scheme had caused many older officers to stay on in their posts. The Superintendent and three of the six Chief Inspectors had been appointed in the 1880s, and a third of the Inspectors in the 1890s. Many of these men were barely competent at their jobs, and certainly incapable of responding to the city's rapid development. The system of appointing cadets (the two most recent having arrived in 1914) had also blocked promotion for men who had come up through the ranks. Even more worrying, for those concerned with the discipline of the force, was that Shanghai was expensive and getting more so, especially for those with high expectations. Tinkler and his peers threw themselves into as hectic a social life as the Police Regulations would let them get away with. As an SMC Salaries Commission pointed out in 1923:

There exists in Shanghai a standard of living which is extravagant beyond all necessity and beyond all reason, and this false standard of extravagance reacts unfavourably on the life of the whole Community but most unfavourably on new arrivals who perhaps less through the fault of themselves than of their surroundings are tempted to maintain a standard beyond both their needs and their means.[72]

Still, it was better than, for example, Liverpool. After the August police strike there, about 1,000 of that force's men were sacked and replaced from the same pool of demobbed servicemen which had supplied the SMP. There were no annual vacations, no five-yearly seven-month furloughs, and no servants in station houses for the Liverpool City Police. Promotion prospects were dim indeed. The disciplinary regime might have been just as tough, but the Shanghai bobby's quality of life even on the job was far better.[73]

The beat was a lonely affair. It is now idealized, in the era of patrol car policing, as a process that kept bobbies on the streets and involved in the life of neighbourhoods whose inhabitants they could come to know and reassure through their presence. But for the men who walked a beat it was a clockwork monster. A constable was assigned a beat, and had to patrol it at such a pace as to reach a pre-arranged point every quarter of an hour. Failure to make the 'point', as it was known, where conference books were signed by the sergeant who oversaw the constables, could be punished sharply. There was no talking (this was gossiping), resting ('lounging') or delay ('idling'). The night beats in particular were long, lonely and silent. Enjoining others to silence – with a 'civil admonition' – was part of the task, shutting up the singing foreigners, rickshaw coolies and news vendors of the

Shanghai night.[74] It was a 'pretty dry job' remarked Jack Darby of his Shanghai beat in a letter home. 'I go from one week to another without meeting a foreigner on patrol.'[75] The night beat for Dan Cormie lasted from 12 midnight until 7 a.m. with a half-hour break at 3.30 for breakfast. He walked a four-mile route from the Yangtszepoo station in the industrial Eastern District. Cormie was not only alone, but alone in the dead of night in a foreign city, a Chinese city. In the Shanghai shadows lurked for the British imagination the Chinese terrors that filled the pages of the shilling novels and the English stage and screen: Fu Manchu, Mr Wu, Chinatown gangs with their knives, poisons and treachery. And there were the real terrors of the armed robbery gangs – 'when we go out on duty we never know [if] we are coming back', wrote Sam Sherlock in 1929 – and the sobering sights of a city of real poverty – bodies left for collection, babies left to die.[76] The *Police Guide*'s injunction that men must cleanse their thoughts of anything but work was of little use. 'It was enough to try anyone's endurance and many a time I felt like quitting,' reported Cormie.[77]

Small wonder then that men skived where they could. The files record only those caught out, or working at stations with inflexible and unsympathetic superiors: Edward Chambers, 'Off beat eating breakfast', 'Off beat in the New World'; D. B. Ross, 'Failing to patrol his station'; William Ryle, 'Improperly walking beat', 'Absent from beat'; D. D. Anderson, 'improperly patrolling the district and found riding in a ricsha whilst on duty'; John Ritchie, 'found lying asleep and under the influence of liquor'. At least it provided some respite from the humiliation of the beat. The Shanghai policeman learnt from day one that he was a white man, but walking the beat put him on a par with the Chinese and Sikhs, and later with the Russian refugees, and it took him to districts inhabited almost solely by Chinese. He was at their beck and call, and subject to the whim of any passing foreigner with a problem or a caustic remark. 'The constable is constantly exposed to insults,' noted the *Police Guide*, 'and is obliged to encounter many provocations.'[78] And on the Shanghai beat any gesture, any interaction between Chinese and foreigner – or between foreigners in front of Chinese, Sikhs or Japanese – was loaded with the potential for 'provocation': the 'coolie' who seemed to laugh, the rickshaw puller who moved too slowly, the tipsy sailor who sneered in passing. It was a lot to bear. Tinkler was lucky. He was stuck on the beat – 'which I didn't like' – for only five months before he was transferred for service at the Mixed Court, and then in November 1920 he passed the examination with four others for transfer to the CID as a plain-clothes detective. Now, this, this was a white man's job.

5

Shanghai Detective

'Richard M. Tinkler' reads the calling card stored amongst his papers, a new name for a new man. Detective Constable Tinkler was in his element strutting across the Shanghai stage on the pages of letters home to Edith, now working in a Barrow-in-Furness dressmakers. He piled it on thick at times. She could see, laid out in his lengthy, opinionated descriptions, a world recognizable from the popular fictions and sensational newspaper accounts which feasted at loving length on post-war society drug scandals, and exposés of Chinatown opium 'dens' in London: Sax Rohmer's *Dope: A Novel of Chinatown and the Drug Trade* (1919), the acres of newsprint devoted to the case of 'Brilliant Chang', jailed for cocaine possession and supply in London in 1924.[1] In his letters through to early 1925 Tinkler wrote of the raids he made, his life in the police (sending back the odd copy of a report to show what he was up to), and his often caustic views about the SMC. These were the good years, really good years, and Tinkler worked with a steady application that consolidated a cracking start at the Depot. He rose swiftly through the ranks, and was one of the obvious stars of his cohort. His education and aptitude promised to take him far in the force. The personnel file for him in the Shanghai Municipal Archives is pretty slim through to 1929 – a good man doesn't generate much paper – but we can use it, his letters and other documents from the force archives, to get a sense of the world he found as a policeman in Shanghai.

Shanghai gets in the way here. Cities live in the imagination in ways that skew our understanding of how they were lived in. Histories, guidebooks and memoirs can hinder rather than help. It was, remembered Maurice Springfield, 'a city of contrasts with extremes of luxury and poverty lurking in the shadows . . . All the grisly secrets of its waterfront will never be unfolded'.[2] Shanghai 'conceived reptilian life,' ventured American journalist Percy Finch, 'that is the symbol of evil, the dancing marshfires of disillusion, and the effluvia that poisons thought and stifles action'.[3] The city demanded the purplest of prose. Even Tinkler sometimes imagined his work in mythic terms. Opium smuggling in the city, he wrote to Edith, was 'like a romance of fiction'. Like his colleagues he sent confiscated opium pipes home as souvenirs. And 'Paris of the East they call it because of the libertine side of the thing'. In romance Shanghai, in mythic Shanghai, the policeman walks the noisome street, opium's scent extruding from shuttered shops and dank, dark alleyways. In the stark daylight shadows lurk the robber and killer. The gunman fires without compunction so the policeman must fire first. Always at night there is the distant clatter of Mahjong tiles, and the roulette wheel spins. Off duty, the good life swings. Women are laid out for the taking: buy your tickets for a taxi-dancer, take your seat for the cabaret floor show, make your way to the massage parlour. There are Russians, Americans, Japanese, Eurasians and Chinese. The cabarets are plenty, and the partying hard. The navy belts the army in 'Blood Alley' (the Frenchtown locale for a set of seedy, popular bars). In mythic Shanghai jazz and high japes fill the long steamy nights. The memory of Shanghai is imprisoned in the 1930s by the books which appeared during that decade mythologizing the city: Henry Champly's *The Road to Shanghai: White Slave Traffic in Asia*, Mario Fresco's *Shanghai: Paradise of Adventurers*, and E. W. Peters's *Shanghai Policeman*. Through Tinkler's policing years we can get a sense of the ordinariness of everyday Shanghai, of everyday colonialism, of how a man lived in the mythic city, and a sense of how the work made the man.

Five months after leaving the Depot Tinkler had been transferred to plain-clothes duty at the Mixed Court. The Court had certainly been an eye-opener. This was by far the easiest billet in the SMP: fairly routine work, with plenty of time off and mostly plain-clothes duty processing the thousands of cases which came into the Court. It was not a fast route to promotion, but it was cushy, and provided opportunities for petty but systematic corruption – here a lost file, there a misplaced piece of evidence, here a lawyer's interpreter or his tout tipping well (but discreetly) for privileged access to unrepresented defendants, or for special attention to their case.[4] Small wonder that it was the fiefdom of a group of older sergeants who resented the intrusion of the younger men who had been moved in to break their grip on the Court. The workload was increasing steadily, but Tinkler could still relax, indulge his new-found passion for photography, and enjoy a life free – for the first time – from the unpredictability of war, the insecurity of unemployment or the drear routine of the beat. But CID was an exciting prospect. In 1920 the Director of Criminal Investigation was Dumfriesshire-born William Armstrong, who had arrived in Shanghai in 1893 after working as a shepherd and then for a year in the Wigan police. Armstrong had already run the Detective Branch for the best part of two decades, and would run it until 1927. A 'history of one is more or less that of the other', noted the *North China Daily News* on his retirement.[5]

Thirty foreign and 104 Chinese policemen worked in CID in 1920. Chinese detectives ran networks of 'seconds' and informers, and in the Intelligence Office, a 'Senior Intelligence Officer' oversaw the work of 'Intelligence Officers, Assistants and Agents'.[6] The more sensational cases were few: there were ten murders that year, most notably of a Chinese prostitute by an American seaman, Jack Welch, in a Fearon Road brothel – 'You'll be all right Kid', he was heard saying to her as the police arrived, and as she bled to death from gunshot wounds. Welch was found guilty of manslaughter and sent to be jailed in the Philippines. The other notable murder was of Lian Ying, a prominent courtesan, chloroformed and then strangled to death in a car for her jewellery. Some of the jewels were traced, and two men were later executed in the presence of SMP representatives, one having been arrested in the Chinese city of Suzhou. Twenty-nine armed robbers were executed by the Chinese authorities after arrest by the SMP and conviction at the Mixed Court. CID dealt with just over 4,000 reports of theft, with about a 37.5 per cent success rate. One nine-strong gang of Cantonese thieves was found guilty of forty-five charges of theft of property from foreign-owned houses over a two-month period. Three Russian shoplifters were found guilty on twelve counts of theft from stores, and members of another gang – two Poles and a Russian – were jailed and then expelled. CID also dealt with a plague

16-10-21
Crampton &
Tin Hum.

Central

Foochow
Honan

of bicycle theft, a minor spate of bombing, and an attempted political assassination.[7]

At the red-brick Central police station on Honan Road Maurice was put to routine CID work, but re-imagined it immediately through the prism of the detective fiction that he read: 'It's damned queer this "Nick Carter" business', he wrote to Edith, bemused at the new expertise he was supposed to have acquired. The examination had been set around a hypothetical murder case, but now he was hauled out at all hours when a real detective was called for, and a detective he had to be: 'I went along wondering how on earth I could possibly "kid" anyone that I looked like one . . . but I determined to "look like a wise guy" and take it all in.' Tinkler read up the SMP *Rules and Regulations* for the CID examination, and joked about the Holmesian nonsense demanded of him by the Shanghailander populace, but it was the dime novel detective Nick Carter who really provided a language – larded with American slang – and perhaps an image to model himself on. Carter first appeared in the *New York Weekly* in 1886, and was kept sleuthing in various formats, available in Britain, by a number of writers. The detective was strong, clean-living and clean-fighting, an expert sleuth, naturally, and he had even grappled with Chinatown secret societies. It would in any case have been difficult to escape from under the shadows of fictional detectives – and even his CID examination might seem to have provided the bare bones of a detective novel. Foreign residents, Tinkler later joshed, 'all expect us to work a miracle on the spot, to pick up a piece of stamp edging beside the busted safe, look at it sideways, and say, "Ah, this is the work of Wong Ah Nyi, the Hongkew Terror, I will track him with tripe hounds and treacle".'

He mostly took it more seriously, but not just because he worked soberly and successfully at learning the ropes. Fear of going back to the beat was one spur, but detective work gave Tinkler status and an entrée into otherwise closed Shanghai worlds, the hotels, clubs and private houses of the settler elite, where he put his 'cheekier' self to use: 'I have to dash about in the Astor House, the Palace and Kalee Hôtels' mose every day over someone, so have to be.' He got additional salary in lieu of uniform, and an allowance which paid most of a month's rickshaw hire. The work suited his temperament as much as did being a runner in the trenches; it allowed him at least the appearance of autonomy, and he was less obviously in the servant classes. A uniform might sometimes get a man more respect, but it also marked out stark limits to opportunity and behaviour. Police uniform spoke for and over him. Plain clothes gave scope for a bit of dash and a touch of style; smart shoes, well-cut cloth and a natty hat confused class and status, confusion which Tinkler relished. He was confident too, which helped him carry it off. People were 'quite astonished when I turn out to be a policeman. I'm awful swagger sometimes, so that must be the reason.' And with the right attitude and spin, the routine work of CID ('you get used to it here and regard it as a matter of course', he wrote of opium raids) could seem exotic and daring: 'Of course when she knew I was a detective she wanted to know all about the "Opium dens" and she wanted a lamp and pipe,' he wrote of an acquaintance.

Tinkler himself later outlined the work of the Central station detectives when he was senior officer there in a 30 January 1929 report.[8] The staff was bigger by then, but the pattern of work basically the same. Central stretched from the French Concession in the south to Soochow creek in the north, and was bounded in the west by Thibet Road and the Bund. At its heart were the headquarters buildings of Shanghai's foreign firms, but it also contained Foochow Road, with its Chinese theatres, brothels and courtesan houses. (The opium shops had only recently gone, 'a tremendous moral achievement', noted Darwent, but it had robbed the street of 'one of its sights, an opium den').[9] Towards the French Concession were blocks of Chinese residences and businesses. Five men were assigned to detective work, together with a Russian sergeant who was mostly sent out looking for pickpockets in foreign banks, theatres or cinemas. ('85 per cent of the foreign criminal element here in Shanghai', claimed a 1929 report, 'consists mostly of Russians.')[10] When they could they visited bars and taverns, and those Shanghai hotels – the Palace and Kalee – or browsed in second-hand stores and pawnshops. Otherwise they worked on existing cases, interviewed suspects or prisoners, attended court, dealt with the paperwork and supervised the work of the fifteen Chinese detective constables. These were each assigned a sub-district to patrol, keeping an eye on shops where stolen goods might surface, such as a diamond-inlaid gold pin stolen from Lian Ying, which was found in a pawnshop. Another squad remained in the station ready to be called out – for example, on opium raids. Fears of Chinese dishonesty meant that such men were forbidden to respond to enquiries or escort prisoners without a European companion. Foreign detectives were also urged to remember that 'it is always necessary to guard oneself from being imposed upon by Chinese detectives, agents or witnesses by taking their statements with a certain amount of reserve'.[11] In a letter written the day after he had submitted his 1929 report, Tinkler described his foreign detectives as 'rotten'. He was 'not very satisfied' with them, but the month had been 'busier than ever', and over fifty armed robbers, kidnappers or killers had been arrested.

Tinkler's name catches the eye sometimes in the published court reports in the Shanghai press. In a December 1922 number of the *Celestial Empire*, weekly edition of the *Shanghai Mercury*, he is found giving evidence against Joseph Grimble, twice previously convicted and now charged with deception, and with obtaining money under false pretences by claiming to be a representative of the National Bible Society of Scotland. A complaint was made, a warrant issued, and it was not much work for Tinkler to find the man and haul him into the British Police Court, where he gave the initial evidence. Grimble blamed the police. Every time he found employment they came and reported his criminal record. The magistrate declared that 'no man need actually starve in Shanghai', and gave him two months.[12] Here was routine work, hardly any of that Nick Carter detecting, just processing complaints, finding a man well-known to the force with few hiding places in a relatively small community, and seeing the case through into court. Wong Ah Nyi the 'Hongkew Terror' it wasn't. More of these routine accounts of routine offenders and offences lie buried in the newspapers and the Court archives; not much to write home about.

But Tinkler played the detective off duty too, and started to spend time with the journalists of the US-owned *China Press* newspaper close by on Canton Road: 'We have great fun along there at night.' It wasn't 'dry', he wrote, and was 'better than most of the cabarets in town'. Journalists and policemen made use of each other. The detectives could tip off the hacks, or slip them copies of official reports, while the press could play up the role of their 'police friends', in the words of Australian journalist John Pal, or just, discreetly, give a thirsty man a cool drink.[13] The local press – particularly the American papers – was also fuelling mythic Shanghai, sensationalizing shooting incidents, and sketching out the shape of the 'paradise of adventurers'. Passing time at the *China Press* would also have aided Tinkler's hard-boiled role-playing, which took in the American slang, and what were to be increasingly common asides about his dislike of the British, and his admiration for all things American. This was provocative, for few British prejudices were stronger than disdain for the United States and Americans. The pointed adoption of American slang took him, as it took many other Britons, out of the social norm, into a seemingly freer world.[14] It was a mark of a man unsettled, and starting to occupy a defiant, outsider's position that was to deepen with every year that he stayed in Shanghai.

The Americans were also fairly new to Shanghai. Although there had been a large US presence from the very start of the Settlement's history, it was only after 1900 that a sizeable community developed.[15] Initially, the incomers were a motley crowd of beach-combing crooks who, after being evicted from the Philippines, made their fortunes in Shanghai. But with the First World War came a new wave. They set up new social institutions (an American Community Church), new publications (J. B. Powell arrived in 1917 to establish what became the *China Weekly Review*) and new businesses. They took one look at the British-dominated Settlement (where even the China-coast Germans spoke with an Anglicized inflection) and its colonial stuffiness, and made their own fun instead. 'Who is the most generous spender in the Shanghai cabarets?' asked leftist journalist Edgar Snow in 1928. 'Who buys the most dance tickets, the most "smallbottlsvine" ... drinks the most, shouts the loudest, dances the best?' The Americans, was the answer. The Americans were outsiders in the treaty port world, in this 'poorly camouflaged British colony', and Tinkler joined them.[16] 'The English idea of America', Ross McKibbin has written, 'often had more to do with England than America.' Tinkler's America was a reaction first and foremost to the mores and postures of the Shanghai British.[17]

But however much Tinkler talked up his work, it began to grate: 'It's just awful here', he wrote in January 1921:

We are called out at all hours of the day or night to go out on [call]. It might be anything.

You have to throw down everything on a $5,000 embezzlement case, and rush off to see some wealthy foreigner, urgently and chop-chop because his Chinese chauffeur pinched the tool bag.

Some of these people telephone for a detective if they lose their shaving soap, or maybe the canary won't sing.

'Nick Carter' might be visited at home by the chief of police, begging him to take on a sensational case which had defeated the force. Maurice Tinkler was called out at all hours – 'I have no time of my own' – at the imperious whim of settler Britons for mundane reasons. Shanghailanders regarded the SMP as little more than servants and tried to use them to chastise their Chinese domestic staff: 'Say, I'd like you to take my house-boy along and "put him through the third degree". He looks like a smart Aleck,' parodied Tinkler. In the colonial world the fact of domination often encouraged a blasé attitude towards personal safety and security amongst colonists, as well as a blindness to the human presence of the dominated (the house servant was always there, but always invisible). This was partly lazy: as George Orwell pointed out, physical intimacy between colonist men and women and their servants, who dressed them and even bathed them, was common even amongst the most racist.[18] But it was also ideological; a colonist should not live in fear, and the dominated were different and so normal standards of behaviour that applied in relations with fellow colonists need not apply. But it was also caused by the expectation that the forces of the colonial state could be called upon for redress in even the tiniest matters, and that the dominated should contain their own behaviour and learn appropriate fear. In practice, colonial police forces, understaffed and lacking in status, worked to their own agendas. As individuals, SMP men might share the colonists' view, but as a force its reports constantly berated foreign householders for neglecting to lock doors or windows. Tinkler found himself pestered by the peeved. 'One day an old cat of a British lady telephoned for a detective about six times in an hour. I was the first in and dashed round in a richsha, expecting a murder at least. "My doormat was stolen last night. There isn't enough police protection along this street."'

His disillusionment was compounded by discontent amongst the 1919 draft at salaries, prospects and conditions. 'Prices here are out-rageous,' Tinkler complained in January 1921. 'I am very much fed up with the Shanghai Police at the moment, and if I don't get more pay soon will be more so.' He wasn't the only one. A Municipal Salaries Commission had been examining the situation in the light of the increasing cost of living, and in May 1920 acting Commissioner Hilton-Johnson forwarded the men's suggestions for improvements in living conditions, terms of service and an increase in pay. From Tinkler's basic initial monthly salary of 105 taels, a June 1920 example of a constable's monthly spending (messing: 28 taels, washing: 2, servant: 7, clothes and boots: 23, canteen: 15, locomotion, amuse-ments and incidental: 25) would have left precisely 5 taels. There wasn't a great deal left for dashing about the Astor House or for saving. The language bonus really was worth working for, and the detective allowance also helped. Some men were 'heavily in debt due to sheer extravagance', claimed Hilton-Johnson, due to that 'false standard of extravagance' which people tried hard to copy.[19] 'Oh this is a great little old town,' Maurice wrote, 'All the ladies dash about all day in big motor-cars, wearing open work socks and $1000.00 fur coats. Their only occupation is buying more furs and more clothes.' They 'buy new cars as often as I buy new suits', he reported. They didn't, of course, but the sight of flaunted wealth hurt. The increase recommended by the Commission wasn't really going to help, but continuing discontent was averted when all the men were entered for the sergeants' examination in April 1921. It might be 'the most ragtime Police Force in the world' – that Yankee slang again – but it was still a job, and he was doing well in it, getting his appointment to Sergeant in July 1921.

Tinkler's view of the foreign community swung between tart envy, and spitting anger. He was a man constrained by lack of wealth and status; a policeman constrained by prissy politics and sensitivities. The 'Police have no real power here,' he declared in 1921; 'half the wealthy residents in town could cause the Commissioner to lose his job if he annoyed them.' Some on the Council felt the police had too much power, and in the late 1920s the American Council chairman, later Secretary General, Sterling Fessenden battled with Ivo Barrett to recover effective control. 'I wish they would have a real good riot, and murder a bunch of the petty, arrogant, local millionaires and profiteers,' spat Tinkler in July 1921, '*then* they might realise that the Police Force is here.' The 'profiteer' was a middle-class hate figure in the aftermath of the war, the object of an anger infused with anti-Semitism.[20] Anger at the conditions of service, protests against which were then leading to the dismissal of eight of his 1919 colleagues, merged with resentment of the war-rich foreign community, and the continuing politicization of Settlement life. In 1920 rice prices in the Settlement had risen by a third, and the SMC in 1921 decided to enforce the licensing of rice shops in a bid to prevent future profiteering, which it was convinced was the sole cause of the socially destabilizing rise. The shopkeepers objected and closed down. 'Fortunately a show of armed force seems to have settled the situation,' claimed Tinkler after a three-day mobilization of police, Special police and volunteers, although in fact it was mediation that settled it.[21] But he saw the fact of foreign power as resting, not on nuanced compromise with Chinese society and politics, or even on collaboration, but on the fact of armed force. And he saw himself as an agent of that armed force, which his superiors were plainly unfit to lead: 'I wish we didn't have so many rotten Britishers here, and on the Council in particular.'

Tinkler rose smoothly and quickly through the ranks. The average length of service of his 1919 peers was eight years. Seven left before the end of 1919 itself, two being dismissed after trial, and five transferring to the gaol service. Sixteen left the force in 1920: another six transferred to the gaol service, five were dismissed and two invalided (one – four years a prisoner of war – was diagnosed as suffering from neurasthenia, and drink didn't help). Ten more left in 1921, eight dismissed, one invalided, another transferred to the gaol service. By the end of the first three-year contract in 1922, another man had been dismissed – after turning up for the midnight shift 'Drunk and unfit for duty' – and three declined to continue, although all three remained in China. Thirty-eight of the 74 men appointed in 1919 did not begin a second contract, although a number remained in the Council's service. The bald figures might seem to offer little solace for the Council's hope that this cohort would help remould the force, but the early winnowing worked: only six more failed to start a third contract after six years' service, and ten men were still serving at the onset of the Pacific war in December 1941. But, at three years, the median length of service of the 1919 recruits was the shortest of any of the inter-war recruits; and this does not even begin to take into account the fact that most careers in the 1930s were truncated by Pearl Harbor. The average length of service was also the lowest of the immediate post-war cohorts.[22] We can imagine good reasons why the record of Tinkler's companions should be so poor, in purely statistical terms: they were men who had sought a trade in the post-war market, when choice was limited. They had probably chosen swiftly, were unlikely to have considered policing otherwise, and were mostly unemployed after demobilization. So if their chances were not already skewed enough, Shanghai undid some of them.

It was not the healthiest place to work, either. Some men were still scarred by the war. A man 'who, without warning, can throw everything off a table and break things without rhyme or reason is not a person who can be trusted with a loaded revolver', noted a doctor, mildly, of one of the recruits in 1920. At least three were invalided directly because of wartime wounds, and another two indirectly. Eight of the 1919 draft died in service, two in accidental shootings (one on duty), another two shot themselves, the others succumbed to disease or natural causes. Incidental infections affected other men. Venereal disease kept at least three of them off duty for long periods of time early in their careers. Tinkler was hospitalized three times that I know of: from December 1922 for a month for an infection picked up on a shooting trip, in December 1925 with a 'poisoned arm', and for a month in 1927 with typhoid. Photographs of him in Japan in 1927 clearly show the impact of even this 'comparatively mild' bout. By one measure the SMP became a healthier organization as the century progressed: the mortality rate amongst foreign staff fell from just under 18 per thousand in 1900–1909, to 6.5 per thousand in 1930–39, although more men were invalided: 4.5 per thousand on average in the former decade, 6.25 in the latter. Shanghai was probably an unhealthier place to work than Britain: there was what has been termed a 'relocation cost' (the difference in death rates between the colonial and the domestic environment).[23] To the ailments and accidents they might have fallen prey to back home were added local dangers of typhoid, heatstroke, malaria, schistosomiasis.[24]

In mythic Shanghai, also, men self-destructed. Suicide was easier for men in an armed force, who could kill themselves with their own weapons. No two suicides are alike, of course. Those serving officers who killed themselves in the 1920s seem to have done so because of debt, despair, love, disease, dishonour. But the unremitting foreignness of Shanghai, the distance from home and the distancing from home, were all contributing factors. For all the cosmopolitan surface of the city, for all the richness of the settler society, the faces and façades of Shanghai were Chinese. Charles Schooler arrived back from long leave in December 1926 to face another five years' service, this time without his wife, who had stayed in Scotland. We can't ever know, but another stint in Shanghai might have looked like a gaol sentence to some, perhaps to him. Schooler took poison, and was eventually fished out of the Huangpu river. Other men drank heavily. Expatriate society encouraged it, but alcoholism had long been a problem for the force, hardly helped by what politically hostile observers described as the existence of 'a semi-public bar or canteen in every police station'.[25] Recent recruits might overindulge themselves on Shanghai's pleasures, and eventually settle down. But colleagues longer in service unravelled: 'an incorrigible drunkard' (dismissed in 1922 after fourteen years, and dispatched to Britain with 'as little delay as possible'); 'Drunk in West Hongkew Charge Room' ('resigned' after sixteen years' service in 1924); five weeks in the General Hospital 'suffering from the effects of alcoholic excess' (resigned after seventeen years' service in 1924); 'continually absent from work' having recently 'turned to drink' (resigned in 1927 after twenty years' service). It was never an easy life.

In January 1926 agitation began again amongst the men over conditions of service. 'We wanted increased pay, abolition of overcrowding, prehistoric bathrooms and sanitation, etc.,' Tinkler wrote home; 'So far, we are still waiting.' But by July Tinkler had his own room, with a bathroom attached, and an ice-chest. The force had introduced a new level of examination for the move from Sergeant to Sub-Inspector. One afternoon in the old Town Hall building Tinkler took a test containing questions on general knowledge, Chinese geography, arithmetic, general police duties and the particularities of

Shanghai criminal law. He was, he boasted, top of the class by a 'big margin', having proved for example that he knew what to do if 'a tin-canister bomb were brought to the Station by a coolie who said he had found it in an alleyway garbage bin'. He was promoted to Sub-Inspector in 1926. He had also caught the eye of at least one of his superiors, Deputy Commissioner Hilton-Johnson, who left the force to take a new post as Commissioner-General of the SMC in February 1925, and a little patronage might prove useful as well. Tinkler felt that CID chief William Armstrong was too partial to fellow Scots. Class tensions might be expected, given Shanghailander views of the status of the police, but tensions between Scots, Irish and Englishmen in the SMP were also present. Tinkler often snarled at his Scottish colleagues in his letters to Edith, while Dan Cormie, a Morayshire native, found things made 'rough' for him at one station by a Scots-hating superior. When Dubliner Barney Wall arrived in 1932 he found half of the stations were being run by Irish officers, which also led to tensions (although he found it quite useful).[26] The exaggerated ritual life of the expatriate community, with its national day balls and celebrations perhaps added to the problem, but it was mostly a question of the sometimes competing networks through which new recruits made their way in their new environment. For his part, Tinkler sought connections through the United Services Association, and the freemasons.

On the whole Tinkler's response to the problem of pay and conditions, like that of the majority of his colleagues, was to work to seize the new opportunities for promotion offered. Rewards – cracking a forgery case in 1924 earned Tinkler \$75[27] – and advances in seniority, which helped accelerate promotion and pay rises, focused most minds on the job. But other men grafted. Cases of corruption and abuse of power leap out from files – in fact, they led to the creation of files in ways that ordinary policing did not. These men are exceptions; but here I found 1919 recruit Arthur Wadey, a parson's son, prowling the streets in the early morning of 2 February 1919, illegally entering Chinese houses where he could hear mah-jong being played and 'confiscating' – at gunpoint – the gambling stakes. In the words of one of those robbed:

The door was closed but not barred. A foreign policeman with a black (automatic) pistol in his hand, pushed open the door and entered. Grasping the pistol he put his hand on the table and a Chinese policeman outside the door told us to put the dominoes away. The foreign policeman struck me on the knuckles with the pistol, then laid it on the table, collected all the money together and separated the silver from the coppers, counted the silver and put it in one pocket and the coppers in another. He took away 160 cents in ten and 20 cent pieces, $1 and 30/40 coppers.

Here is ex-naval man Mark Bell, sacked after five months' service for entering a house in the early hours of 13 March 1923 and 'making improper suggestions' to a young woman. Here is A. M. Cameron, deemed 'highly Neurasthenic' in 1921, who resigned shortly after unproved complaints were made that he had removed opium and the sum of $120 from 59 Chekiang Road in the early evening of 23 March 1923. Here is Probationary Constable Walter Jarman, accused of illegal searches and theft while on duty in September 1923.[28] The agreement with Bert Munson, another 1919 recruit, was not renewed in 1925. There was that suspicious release of a prisoner on 10 October 1924, and then a few weeks later the queer loss of a packet of opium from the Louza police station property cupboard. Here in May 1929 are constables Cope and Benstead, six months out of the army, extorting cash from opium smokers caught in their own homes. These men were unrepresentative; most of their colleagues worked honestly but such cases give us a sour taste of the corrupting potential of the uniform and status of the Briton on the Shanghai beat, out of the reach of his peers or officers.

Petty corruption was risky business, and pretty desperate, given the visibility of a numbered uniform and the lack of jobs at home: all these men were dismissed. CID was different, as Tinkler noted. 'This job . . . is quite a frost unless you graft which I haven't done yet,' he noted in 1921. 'And you don't get much credit for being honest here,' he continued. 'Everyone thinks a detective "grafts" or is mad. A lot of them do I know.' 'You might be paying for drinks with a fellow when he makes some joking remark "You'll be getting rich now" etc. if he only knew maybe it's the last dollar I have. And whatever you say it doesn't convince them.' 'As I think I said before,' he continued, 'there aren't half a dozen white men in this police force.' He would not even 'swear to the integrity of the Commissioner himself'. Dan Cormie was transferred to CID in April 1929, and worked initially at Central, 'where I might say all the honey was'. His then superior, Cormie claimed, 'made no bones about collecting, he went ahead and collected regardless. He was out to make hay while the sun shone and he sure made it.'[29] The man died in 1936 after twenty-four years of service, leaving tidy sums tucked away in a shares portfolio, so perhaps Cormie's claim has some merit.[30] Fred West remembered being berated as an 'absolute bloody mug' by the senior detective at Bubbling Well for not taking his share of the hush money which came in from local gambling joints or brothels.[31] By the time he left the police Tinkler had enemies enough, and any suspicion of dishonesty would probably have come out. West, who remembered encounters with Tinkler, had little good to say but didn't mention corruption. Tinkler received one commendation early in his career in connection with a case of opium selling and attempted bribery. He was cocky enough, still, to claim to Edith in 1921 that he knew once he was being used by Chinese colleagues for the purposes of extortion, and she tore strips off him for it: 'How did you get that way?' she wrote. But smooth and timely promotion in CID suggests that none of his superiors suspected anything untoward. And there is little evidence of ready cash at any point in his Shanghai years. Whatever else we may and will conclude, he was not dishonest.

CID work at different stations varied a little with the geography and character of the area. In August 1921 Tinkler was temporarily in charge of detective work at both the Bubbling Well and Gordon Road stations; not bad for a 23-year-old with less than a year's experience in CID to his name. 'Bubbling Well is in the country', he noted, but Gordon Road was 'filthy city and gloomy as can be'. He had to keep a second 'boy' at Bubbling Well, an area where rich foreigners lived, where he shared the relative luxury of an Inspector's house with one other Sergeant. His establishment at that point consisted of two 'boys', and one rickshaw coolie – and a fastidiousness in dressing was extended to his servants: 'My boy looks quite a "knave" and even my ricksha coolie is wearing respectable clothes.' He had felt trapped at Central, the only one of his draft left there by 1921, sitting in 'this same darned old room' for three years, but now he was out. The empire world was treating him well, and he was determined that Edith should know it. Both Bubbling Well and Gordon Road were preferable to his next temporary posting, Wayside, where the population, he declared, was Chinese 'with numbers of the worst type of foreigners including a lot of Russians'. In October he was at the Louza station, in charge of two other foreign detectives, and thirteen Chinese. He was formally transferred to Louza the following year, and in 1922 was moved to Hongkew station, 'the heart of Eurasiana, Greater Japan or White Russia whichever you please'. In September 1924 he was transferred back to Central.

The situation facing the SMP had already changed greatly since his arrival. Changes in policing practice, and in international or local legislation, provided three stiff challenges to the force, its authority and efficiency, and its men and their personal probity after the war. The suppression of the legal opium trade, a crackdown on gambling – which was increasingly politicized as an issue in the 1920s and 1930s – and the closure of International Settlement brothels by 1924 forced the SMP to confront Chinese society in new ways, creating new problems, and new temptations. Prohibitions salve consciences, but savvy entrepreneurs love them. The bulk of the work, however, always remained fairly routine, and Shanghai policing was largely the dull business of filling in notebooks and occurrence books, sending chits and memos backwards and forwards, writing up reports of lost dogs and shooting strays. Stations in 1926 were equipped with up to sixty-two types of register and notebook (among them, books for bail receipts, recording the transfer of bodies to mortuary, dog receipts). But we can get a sense of the relative importance of the changing situation facing the SMP in a Louza station monthly CID report for September 1922 that Tinkler sent to Edith. Louza's district included the heart of Nanking Road and the new Chinese department stores. There was not a lot to report: an Italian had his bicycle stolen but it was found the next day; a large amount of jewellery was stolen from one Woo Dau Nyi, but a check of the pawnshops quickly found one valuable item; a pawnshop manager had absconded after fiddling the books; nineteen pickpockets were arrested having taken advantage of the autumn sales; assistance was given to the French police on six occasions, and to the Chinese authorities on five; wanted notices were received and withdrawn; the station handcuffs were out of date; all foreign detectives ought to be obliged to learn to drive. Shanghai's residents, Chinese and foreign alike, called in and called on the men at Louza station.

But opium's shrill voice shouts for its central role in mythic old Shanghai even in these conscientious pages ('Housebreaking. Nil. Last month. Nil'). In eleven raids 70 people were arrested in connection with opium charges, while another 5 were charged for possession on the streets. Four were charged with keeping or selling opium, 8 with conducting public opium smoking. Seventeen men were arrested at 84 Fokien Road on 12 September but charges were dismissed with a caution as they were smoking in their own dormitory bedrooms. 'I have most success', Tinkler wrote casually in another letter,

in raiding opium-smoking joints but any fool can do that. I made 8 raids last month.

You go along with some Chinese detectives, get into the place as quickly as possible and close the exits and watch the intelligent blighters inside gaping open mouthed or pushing the opium pipes out of sight.

Then all of them 'sien-sang, sien-sang, ngoo sang bing, ngoo ih-ding can chuck a-phiem.' First born (= Master) I am sick and I must smoke opium. Strange how many sick people you meet in these places.

The biggest of Dan Cormie's honeypots was provided by the opium traffickers who supplied these men and women, and in the early years of Tinkler's service this trade threatened, quite simply, to destroy the SMP.

Shanghai was the centre of national and international opium smuggling networks and the birthplace, as a result, of new forms of Chinese underworld organization. The most important of these, the Shanghai Green Gang (*Qingbang*), grew headily in the political vacuum caused by the collapse of state power after the 1911 revolution.[32] The impact on the SMP of the opium traffic was breathtaking. 'There is good reason to *suspect*', noted Commissioner of Police McEuen in May 1923, 'that fully one-half of the whole strength of the Force is concerned in some way or other in the business of opium smuggling.' In this long report he went on to outline the organization of the smuggling business, and of the systematic institutional corruption it gave rise to.

I am glad to say that save in a few cases no suspicion has arisen and no allegations have been made that members of the Force have any *active* interest in the business. There can be little doubt, however, that a large proportion of the Chinese members of the Force are in receipt of a monthly Opium 'protection fee' – a fee which is widely distributed . . . among persons having almost any kind of connexion with authority.

Not only Chinese personnel either: 'larger sums amounting to $50 or $100 are mentioned anonymously in the case of members of the Foreign Branch.'[33] McEuen argued, as did his successors, for the resumption of licensed trade, but this was politically impossible: there were international agreements to consider, and it would have dented irreparably the public image of the SMC in foreign and Chinese eyes.

Opium remained a fact of police life. Tourists tried it when the liners called in – 'Wantchee chow opium,' murmured the touts in pidgin English. One opium house, just 200 yards north of the Settlement in Chapei, was reported in 1937 to be visited frequently by 'foreign tourists desirous of seeing a typical opium den'.[34] Police examinations dealt with the normality of it all:

Question 11. A confirmed opium smoker is confined in the station cells, and a small packet of opium found on him when arrested is in the property room. In the middle of the night, the prisoner is taken extremely ill and appears to be dying. Your gateman tells you that if he does not get some opium he will die. What would you do?[35]

The foreign press hardly bothered with it unless there was a novel angle or an audacious twist: opium found encased in zinc bars; opium found hidden on the customs' Inspector General's flagship; a foreigner commits suicide with it. Dan Cormie claimed that most of his peers tried it ('we'd try anything to get a kick out of it'), and less controversially he remembered how police station Chinese staff would sidle out on their breaks, quite clearly heading for a smoke.[36] In various reminiscences, Harold Gill remembered the 'whiff of opium' he often caught when patrolling Chinese residential areas.[37] Opium raids took Tinkler into buildings and quarters of which the swanky Astor House Hotel's guests remained oblivious.

Such raids dented the business of small-time opium sellers and interrupted the quiet life of hapless smokers. But the smuggling combines were too big to crack and the net of corruption so wide that it was quite likely the SMP was often being used by opium interests – within or outside the force – to knock out commercial opposition. 'It is only because of the conflicting interests ... that we ever get information – such as it is – at all,' McEuen noted laconically in 1923.[38] Maurice Springfield led a Special Opium Squad to crack down on the trade. Composed only of foreigners of 'known integrity', who undertook raids in their own time, even they were not informed about any objective until the very last minute.[39] Information usually came from a network of informers, paid 10 per cent of the fines that accrued.[40] For Springfield, this was all 'great fun', but the Commissioner questioned why his men should risk their lives while local authorities elsewhere in China, as he saw it, 'openly enrich themselves by opium smuggling'.[41] In 1925 the Special Squad made 131 raids, snatching sizeable caches of the drug, and in 1926 it was confidently being claimed that it had freed the Settlement from 'opium hongs and their attendant evils'.[42] The business of the large wholesalers was certainly harried and harassed until they withdrew from the Settlement, and this was a signal reassertion of colonial power. But of course it only served to move on the problem, and not very far away either: the gangs settled in Frenchtown.

The point of the opium crackdown was not so much to enforce the law, or even to do 'the "right thing" when others all about us have, by our standard, done wrong', but to prevent the collapse into wholesale corruption of the SMP in the face of the 'extraordinary temptations' placed 'in the way of everyone from Constable upwards' by the traffic.[43] No British government would support an administration that fell prey to the corruption which the opium stand-off brought to the French Concession. Here the French authorities sponsored the growth in underworld influence of Huang Jinrong, chief of their Chinese detective squad from 1918 to 1925, and a key Green Gang figure. This was cynically efficient, initially, but they went even further and in May 1925 formally allowed Huang, Du Yuesheng and Zhang Xiaolin to establish a secret opium monopoly with formal French protection.[44] By 1931 the Green Gang leaders were in the ascendant, and in the words of the SMP Commissioner were 'now advisers to the officials of that Concession and carry more authority and power than the officials themselves'.[45] A clean-up in 1932 saw the negotiated exit from the concession of Green Gang opium operations.[46] SMP actions meant that bulk movement of opium into the Settlement was no longer possible, but the opium problem persisted, and 'many thousands of persons' became involved in transporting small quantities of the drug, and were in their turn preyed upon by 'gangs of snatchers and loafers'.[47]

Opium power also enabled the gangs and other combines to buy and run theatres and restaurants, and to move into gambling, which became the second new threat to the SMP. In September 1922 Tinkler and Louza CID made four gambling raids, netting seventy-two people. Most of them were fined or forfeited bail; two were jailed for a month. Gambling infuses the mythic Shanghai. In the more candid memoirs it is portrayed as something like a game, and not taken too seriously as a policing problem. The SMC had long fought illegal gaming houses. The principal difficulty had been the tangled webs woven out of extraterritoriality, and the application in one small zone of the gambling laws of a host of nations. In 1929 'The Wheel', on Bubbling Well Road just outside the Settlement, was 'owned by the Spanish Fathers, leased by Messrs. Lafuente (French) to an American syndicate in the name of a Mexican citizen. Its employees are Mexican, British, Portuguese, Russian, Spanish, American and Chinese, while its legal advisers are Italian'.[48] Two large syndicates were at work by 1929: an American group, operating under the names of Mexican citizens, and a Chinese-financed Portuguese operation. The Honorary Consul for Mexico was hardly helpful: no warrant could be issued unless gambling was actually taking place at that moment, no raid could be conducted between sunset and sunrise, and anyway, as gambling was not illegal under Mexican law, those arrested could be charged only with gambling without a licence. The Consul was in fact an American, Norword Allman, an ex-US consular officer who had set up as a lawyer, and was later a municipal councillor. He played the system for all it was worth.[49] There were pickings here, too, for those raiding. When the Wheel was raided in April 1928 and the premises kept under guard for a few days, some of the men on duty helped themselves to the food and beer and, for good measure, opened up a case of champagne. The CDI assigned to check the premises daily brought along his wife and a variety of friends to have a look and a trawl.[50]

By 1929 the issue had been wholly conflated with opium power, and the gangs, and was also heavily politicized. Gambling was illegal under Chinese law, and:

We must guard against members of the Police Force becoming involved and swelling the ranks of the supporters of criminals who eventually become so powerful that even the police must seek their assistance in the suppression of crime. This danger is the more apparent when it is realised that the Police can obtain money from gambling establishments by simply asking for it.[51]

Indeed, even in 1940 the then Commissioner of Police's chauffeur sought out the chief of the Louza station Chinese detectives and asked him to 'register his chauffeur name . . . at various gambling dens in

Louza district and thereby enable him to collect money from these places'. He was sacked, poor sap, but somebody must have told him, with reason, that it was the thing to do.[52] Between April and August 1929, thirty-seven raids knocked out organized gambling, at least for a while, but they also revealed extensive and systematic corruption and payment of hush-money to the police that left senior officers 'aghast'.[53] But everyone knew. Dan Cormie's cheerful memoir records one *faux pas* when, as a diligent – or disingenuous – beat patrolman in about 1928/29, he spotted and reported a gambling joint. The station chief sent for him:

'Cormie, what's this that you have put in the report book?' I said: 'Just what I saw Sir, I have grave suspicions gambling is being performed on the premises.' So he said: 'Very well, Cormie, are you sure about that?' I said: 'Yes. I entered the building, I saw the tables and I saw the gambling in progress at the time stated and the date which I mentioned in the report.'

Of course the raid – which had to go ahead as gambling was reported despite the senior's heavy hints – was a flop, but the books showed just who at the station was being paid off, notably Cormie's superior: 'the dear boy was certainly reaping the harvest'.[54]

The third new issue facing the SMP was the suppression of legal prostitution in the International Settlement.[55] Prostitution and mythic Shanghai are intertwined. Darwent's prudish guidebook was superseded in 1934 by *All about Shanghai*, which made a tourist's virtue of Shanghai vice: 'Shanghai the bizarre, cinematographic representation of humanity, its vices and virtues; the City of Blazing Night; cabarets; Russian and Chinese and Japanese complaisant "dance hostesses"; city of missions and hospitals and brothels'.[56] Percy Finch devoted a chapter of his memoir to the cosy delights of 52 Kiangse Road, Gracie Gale's house on the Line, 'purveyor of scarlet romance' in more sedentary years.[57] But after a prolonged missionary-led campaign by the Moral Welfare League ('of Anglo-American hypocrites', sneered Tinkler, who identified the rest of Shanghai's foreigners as members of 'thousands of Morals Farewell Societies'), an unwilling SMC was mandated by its ratepayers at an April 1920 meeting to enforce the licensing of all brothels in the International Settlement.

Once done, a series of annual drawings would successively eliminate licences over the next five years, and all brothels were to be closed by the end of 1924. The police played a key role in identifying brothels, compiling the initial register in June 1920 – so that, if the SMC didn't know the names of its Chinese ratepayers, it could at least identify its 972 brothel owners and their residents – routinely checking the houses and their inhabitants, and enforcing closures. Miss Emily Moore (53 Kiangse Road) and Mrs D. Johnstone (15 Soochow Road) closed down their houses.[58] In fact, the brothels moved out of the Settlement, or reopened clandestinely elsewhere within it, or moved into hotels. The business of sex was dispersed throughout the Settlement and Concession, in some places driving up rents and otherwise disturbing neighbourhoods. Prostitution itself, following British practice, but also reflecting the SMC's own realistic analysis of the situation, remained legal. The Council also feared the corruption that abolition could cause.

The Moral Welfare League next turned its fire on taverns and bars, trying to ban the employment of women, or prevent them frequenting 'premises for the purpose of singing or otherwise entertaining customers'. Such bars were 'degrading for the women concerned and highly injurious to the morals of those attending and of the community'. There were no women employed to dance in Settlement taverns, responded the police, wearily, finding in August 1922 only two women employed at all, excluding those owning taverns themselves, 'highly respectable women with grown families who have made tavern keeping a profession'. The League was generalizing from bars outside the Settlement.[59] Tinkler had a story from a night at one of those bars, the Del Monte: two men argued over a White Russian woman, so she stripped herself naked and offered herself to the highest bidder. Small wonder that the League kept up the pressure. It resumed the attack in March 1926, sending an observer for a late evening stroll through Wayside and Yangtszepoo Road restaurants. In the Moonlight Café (Japanese) he found four women and an infant, and 'one foreign man with a girl sitting on his knee and playing with his shirt front'. At the Minerva, with two foreign men and two women at a table, 'two coloured men entered and asked for a beer'. At the International Bar were two women, 'one we know as a prostitute'. At the Shanghai Grill Room, beer was being served, but no food. A piano was being played in a dancing room. A male visitor was chatting to two women, 'one being scantily clad. One . . . a known prostitute'. Babylon it wasn't. If licensing conditions were being abused, noted the police, then prosecutions would follow, but 'the difficulty of proving whether a woman is immoral or virtuous must be patent'.[60]

Two newspaper reports from early 1929 give us glimpses of Tinkler in action against two more threats: armed robbery and organized kidnapping.[61] On 13 April a stolen pass book was presented at a Chinese bank on Ningpo Road. The police were called and arrested a man who promptly shopped his comrades. With French police assistance Tinkler led a party over to Rue Eugene Bart. They wore body armour – steel vests designed in the police armoury workshops – and broke into the house, rushing a second-storey bedroom where six men were found, one with a loaded pistol. The team headed on to Rue de Marche, where another ten men were found. One drew a pistol but was knocked down. This time no shots were fired, but the danger should not be underestimated: 'we have been lucky' he wrote to his stepmother of the January raids. Armed robbery was a capital offence, and men cornered like this had nothing to lose by shooting. The SMP designed its bullet-proof shields and training programmes to deal with the problem. The shields were useful, but they would not stop a Mauser, so the police fired fast, first and more often. 'The more closely our pistols resemble machine guns,' concluded W. E. Fairbairn, 'the better we like it.'[62] City of Glasgow Police veteran Frank Campbell was not so lucky on a similar raid. He shot his man, but had been mortally wounded first. He was one of fourteen policemen killed in 1927 (three Britons, four Sikhs, one Russian, seven Chinese) in 126 encounters in which shots were fired. Twenty-two more were wounded. Thirty-two criminals were killed.[63] In January 1929 Tinkler had led another two such sweeps. One gang included a former SMP constable, whose force-issue truncheon was found in his room. The other gang, arrested on 7 January and responsible for two kidnappings in 1927 and 1928, turned out to be led by a serving CID interpreter. Having got wind of the sweep he decamped in a car into the French Concession. 'Sensation in police circles', heralded the *North China Daily News*.[64]

In 1921 Tinkler had claimed that Chinese detective corruption was common, and SMP files certainly give glimpses of the porous boundary between the underworld and the force. Green Gang leader Gu Zhu-xuan began in Shanghai as a rickshaw puller before joining the SMP. He later ran teashops, a theatre and a rickshaw company before making 'a little fortune' as a detective in a Chinese force and rising to prominence with 'several thousand followers'.[65] A 1932 report by Superintendent Yao Jialing, responding to allegations that Chinese detectives were playing an active role in gangs 'protecting' opium runners, concluded that of the two Chinese detectives involved one was indeed 'well-connected with the opium gangs'. One of them, Chinese Constable Ting Nyoh-kau, allegedly ran an outfit that trans-ported opium from harbour jetties into Frenchtown. Ting was stoutly defended by a senior British officer, who may have had his reasons, as Yao may have had his, but he opted to resign.[66] Other cases from the archives seem to come straight out of the fervid, race-sodden world of Somerset Maugham, where the 'Westernized' Chinese was always the culprit: a foreign DSI locked into debt with a Chinese detective colleague, now under sentence of death for complicity in kidnapping. A blackmailing Russian lover hovers in the background (and somehow buys a boutique). Nothing could be proved. A foreign Sub-Inspector accuses a clerk of fitting him up with a bribery charge over an opium arrest after he had reprimanded the clerk for inefficiency. Perhaps, but all are dismissed. 'It is possible that he was the dupe of Chinese Constable No. 1486,' noted the Commissioner of another married officer in 1929, accused of conspiring to accept a bribe and release prisoners, but both were sacked.[67]

In CID Tinkler worked day in day out with Chinese detectives, relying on them no less than any other man as his ears and eyes in this foreign city. But we learn nothing of them. One snapshot alone, undated, shows such colleagues, in this case 'two of our interpreters' in a station compound. One of these stiffly posing straw-boatered men, 'Shen', is described as 'very clever (St John's University), but smokes opium'. What are we to make of Tinkler's silence about his Chinese colleagues? Language should have been no barrier. Tinkler had pretty smoothly reached the various standards set and maintained the level at successive six-monthly examinations until he was exempted from further study on the basis of an ability 'to interpret and converse readily and fluently on any ordinary subject'.[68] He was also taking French classes in his own time. The racism that starts to envelop his letters – which was not only anti-Chinese: 'foreigners . . . should be treated as the animals they are', 'Jews and Scotchmen are the curse of this town' – might suggest that he had little interest and even less aptitude for any relationship with Chinese colleagues, and they as a result for any relationship with him. But in fact few of his British colleagues get mentioned either. Tinkler's letters were about Tinkler, Shanghai mores and Chinese politics, or, as we shall see, about what his sister should or should not do.

Tinkler's October 1922 crime report names those reporting major incidents, and all incidents involving foreigners. Otherwise, it notes that 'Chinese were the other victims'. The relationship with the majority Chinese population of the Settlement was always tricky, and any problems could quickly become politicized. There were ongoing minor conflicts about what actually could constitute an offence. In one case, for example, a man seized for letting off firecrackers to celebrate Chinese New Year was prised away from the arresting officer by a good-humoured crowd.[69] More seriously, in March 1931 Acting Commissioner Martin wrote of what he recognized was the 'prevailing impression of the attitude of individual members of the Force towards the Public'.[70] Police reports abound with complaints that the (Chinese) public were slow to report even serious crimes, and often unwilling to be involved as witnesses. The Chinese retort was that 'when they do so their treatment is so off-hand and discourteous that many of them would rather make no report than pay another visit to a Police Station'. Martin put most of the blame on 'Asiatics' in the lower grades, who were 'apt to come overbearing and swollen headed as soon as they have a little authority', but did not exclude some of the European sergeants and new recruits. Men were to be reminded of the need for self-restraint and an even temper, especially in a changing political situation where 'the method employed a generation ago in handling rough uneducated countrymen will not answer to-day when dealing with young men who have been educated and live up to a much higher standard than their parents did.' 'I would like to have a go', wrote Tinkler to his aunt in July 1921, 'at these yellow Chinese swine.' But still, Chinese men and women turned to the police over incidents big and small, and turned in the police for robbing them and insulting them.

Some SMP men were accused of being more than a little off-hand with Chinese lives. In 1922 three Chinese bystanders were wounded in a shooting affray with an armed robber. After a shooting incident on Mohawk Road in 1924, it was claimed at the Watch Committee that 'the two European Constables in question appear to regard Chinese lives as of about the same value as an average sportsman would that of a rabbit'.[71] After a shooting incident in the Louza district in March 1929, the men involved were chided for being 'somewhat reckless' in opening fire in a crowded street: three people were wounded. Small sums of compensation were paid. Commissioner Barrett complained about 'crowds of sightseers who immediately congregate when shooting on the streets begins'.[72] The danger of shooting bystanders (although 'likely to impede promotion') sprang from the small-arms training system devised for the police, which had a distinctive and path-breaking focus on extreme speed, instinctive aiming and realistic practice. Speed was of the essence and 'literally a matter of the quick and the dead. Take your pick.'[73] But speed could mean mistakes.

The incidental and accidental Chinese dead could become political problems for the force. Maurice Tinkler was close to two men involved in the most serious of these before 1925. Here the dehumanization of the Chinese that was implicit in Shanghai racism combined with the ugly logic of maintaining the race hierarchy. One of the few men named in Tinkler's photograph albums is J. F. Gabbutt. Another shot shows Tinkler, cigar in mouth, at Central station with Albert Balchin, a fellow 1919 recruit. DSI Gabbutt had joined in 1912, and had served for two years in France before returning to Shanghai in August 1919. These men were tried, amongst other charges, for malicious wounding and grievous bodily harm at the British Supreme Court, where the SMP itself was effectively tried for torture. Such charges, pontificated the North China Herald, 'affected the prestige of all Western peoples, and if they had been upheld, there was no one who would not have felt that the civilisation on which we pride ourselves had been besmirched'.[74] All three were based at Hongkew, where on 2 February 1923 a 43-year-old Ningbo native, Loh Tse Wha, joined the two dozen servants and labourers at the station as Inspector Prosser's 'boy'. On 5 February he apparently tried to resign suspiciously soon after $400 had been stolen from John Gavan, a recent recruit from the navy. 'It is a matter of pride to get stolen property back', noted Gabbutt. But it was also 'A matter of face-pidgin for me; [the] money [was] lost in [the] station. I thought [that] other boys in the station [were] concerned. I had him out and questioned him.'[75] The 'intensive questioning' used was defended by McEuen,[76] but notions of race and the dignity of the colonist conspired to make the theft seem ludicrously more important than it was, and Loh suffered horribly as the 'face pidgin' stakes were raised and mutiny presaged.

Such accusations were routinely made 'say, twice a month', claimed Detective Inspector Percy Reeves for the defence. But after three interrogations – the last at midnight on 5 February – Loh had been taken to hospital where he spent a month recovering from various injuries including dislocated arms. He testified that Balchin had kicked and slapped him, and that Gabbutt beat him with a belt. 'You know I am "old Shanghai" [Shanghai-savvy],' Gabbutt was alleged to have said, 'if you don't bring the money, I will beat you to death. It is easy to kill a Chinese.' 'I only struck a coolie once in my life,' claimed Gabbutt – hardly helping his case – 'and I got a poisoned finger.'[77] 'The complainant's story', noted the Crown Advocate, prosecuting, 'may seem like a bit out of the movies,' but the evidence was compelling. Loh was, variously, hung up by ropes tied to his thumbs, garrotted, hung from a ladder with his hands tied behind his back while lit papers or cigars were stuffed up his nostrils, and he was stripped and beaten on the genitals. Tinkler was one of the Hongkew men produced in court as a witness. He had seen nothing, he said, and had had nothing to do with the case. There is no evidence that either Gabbutt or Balchin had been involved in the harsher actions, but Gabbutt had tipped the wink and withdrawn, allowing Loh to be taken for a third, unsupervised, interrogation by two Chinese and one Japanese detective: 'it was the usual custom if information could not be obtained from prisoners by the foreign staff, as this method produced satisfactory results,' he explained, blandly.[78] All the men were acquitted, although with a rider from the jury that they were convinced that Loh's injuries had been received while he was in police custody. They were then dismissed, 'to mollify the Chinese', noted

Tinkler to Edith, 'a detestable action on the part of a weak-knee'd Council'. The SMC disciplined other officers as it was clear that the case had been prosecuted with no perceptible zeal – 'you had better keep the ladder out of the way,' advised even the Crown Advocate on a visit to Hongkew station, and he kept the issue largely out of the way in court – and that if the full details had been presented the prosecution would have succeeded.[79] A secret report was prepared after a search of all stations found 'certain articles' – instruments of torture to be precise – at several of them. Clearly, councillors felt, the police had 'for years past . . . dealt with criminals in a manner which at any time, might give rise to a scandal'. ('I caught that thief and bound him to the tree' ran another of Hawks Pott's sentences for translation.[80]) For his part, Commissioner McEuen 'considered that some of these implements might have been placed there intentionally by the Chinese with a view to prejudicing the trial'.[81]

Loh himself might have been one of those 'rough uneducated countrymen', but this case was closely watched, and highly politicized. Two to three hundred Chinese waited at the Court for the judgement. The growing importance of such incidents is also shown by a case the following year. Sub-Inspector Tom Dunne, who had joined with the last of the 1908 drafts and had stuck out the war in Shanghai, was stationed at Louza by 1924. In 1920 either he or his brother, P. J. Dunne, had been involved in an 'alleged assault' on a prisoner. But Tom Dunne was tried for manslaughter only in August 1924. Dunne had rebuked Yieh Chieng-tsiang, 'No. 4 Coolie' at the station, for unsatisfactory work; the man had 'appeared to have been impudent' and Dunne belted him twice round the head. Yieh died the following day. The charge was withdrawn when an autopsy report was presented which claimed that Yieh had in fact died of a kidney disease, 'possibly aided by opium poisoning', and that the blows were irrelevant. The Chinese press thought otherwise, but was shut up when six editors were prosecuted for criminal libel, and when Dunne, sensing victory, took out civil suits which were settled privately. The press interest, claimed Commissioner McEuen, was 'engineered by trouble-makers' who took every opportunity to 'promote hostility to the Municipal Council'.[82] The affair blew over, but it was not forgotten. Dunne himself was dismissed twenty months later and bundled out of

Shanghai to avoid a further court case, after he poured kerosene over his dog and set it alight.

Tinkler himself acknowledged that as a result of the torture trial 'the feeling amongst the Chinese was at fever heat. (They hate the foreigners now far worse than they did at the time of the Boxer rising.)' This wasn't about professional agitators, but about real change in the Chinese political situation, and the development of a new nationalism acutely responsive to the actions of the Settlement administrations and their agents. Foreign residents joked and laughed about 'warlord China'. Since the death of president Yuan Shikai in 1916, central government power had withered and a host of regional militarist power holders had emerged. In late 1924 the two powerful coalitions that dominated the scene went to war. Zhili, which controlled the central government, engaged the Fengtian forces of Marshal Zhang Zuolin. The conflict's impact on Chinese society was like no other struggle since the 1911 revolution, and tens of thousands of soldiers were killed or wounded. The war began in Shanghai, and Tinkler had a grandstand view. Shanghai and Zhejiang (Chekiang) province were in the hands of remnants of a now spent force, loosely allied with Zhili, which served the sensitive balancing act which had kept the various factions at peace. In August, seizing upon a thin but valid pretext, the Zhili forces of the Jiangsu commander Qi Xieyuan began mobilizing for war. On 3 September 1924 Zhejiang forces bombarded them at the town of Liuhezhen. The Jiangsu intention of launching a swift strike faltered in the face of entrenched machine guns, but in October the defenders fled leaving a confused situation behind them: defeated troops, a victor who switched allegiance to Fengtian – which benefited from a similar coup in Beijing helping it to defeat Zhili comprehensively – and the threat of disorder and conflict spilling over into the concessions.[83]

None of the Chinese combatants wished to provoke the foreign powers, and the concessions remained untouched though hardly wholly uninterested in the outcome. In September 1924 Tinkler wrote home gleefully that 'we have a war here at last'. From 3 September he was detective in charge at Central, but was also 'on special work in connection with the war (chiefly being the defence of the settlement)'. On 4 September, together with fellow recruit Hugh McGregor and a

Chinese detective, he drove out to a front-line village, penning a report on the day's activities there, and the weaponry available. They were investigating 'rumours of a Chekiang retreat', which would wash up on the Settlement borders, but he saw no sign of it that day. 'We got a few bullets close to our heads', he told Edith, but 'I have quite a few souvenirs'. He still liked his battlefield trifles. Four days later they went out again for another brief visit. He sent the two reports back to Edith (the soldiers really were equipped with umbrellas, he told her, referring to the standard caricature of the unmilitary Chinese soldier, 'but the war is going to be very serious for all that'). Quite what she made of all this we cannot tell. He had written her a closely typed lecture on the politico-military situation. But, he added, 'you need not worry. It's fine to watch other people fighting when you have nothing to do but criticise.' He was there again in October, scouting around as the Zhejiang forces retreated, sallying out to the town of Songjiang by train, and examining the abandoned Jiangnan arsenal on 13 October. Tinkler was plucked out for this task by Acting Police Commissioner Hilton-Johnson, as likely as not because of his wartime record. Here was happiness indeed. War might force the issue of imperialism's position in China generally, and in Shanghai in particular. But war also gave Tinkler an escape from the constraints of normal CID work. It was also rather better than the task of many of his colleagues who for some weeks manned one and a half miles of the Settlement defences, although as he put it seven years later, 'on occasion, I was under rifle, shell and machine gun fire miles from the Settlement'.[84] The SMC declared a state of emergency; swept the city for 'loafers, known bad characters, gaolbirds' interning 500 of them briefly before expelling 170 men into Chapei. Tens of thousands of refuges sought sanctuary in the settlements. The war fed crime. 'Automatic weapons were being sold freely by soldiers on the borders of the settlement.' Other demobilized or deserted troops used their weapons instead. The armed robbery rate doubled.[85] But the war had its uses: the SMC took advantage of the fighting to extend its control in small but useful areas. Judging that with the confusion and uncertainty in the aftermath of the fighting the 'psychological moment to take this action had arrived', it completed the extension of the outside Great Western Road.[86] This was a small gain, however, and the war's greatest impact was the destruction of the existing political and military order from which emerged a new anti-imperialist nationalism which sharply challenged the foreign presence. Renewed fighting in and around Shanghai over the winter was to see the emergence as the dominant power holder in the region of a former subordinate of Qi Xieyuan, Marshal Sun Chuanfang.

In these early years Maurice Tinkler showed great promise, and Shanghai police work delivered responsibility, recognition, patronage, excitement, and – eventually – a reasonable quality of life. He hadn't come unstuck on the beat like Wadey or in CID like some of his colleagues. He hadn't come down too hard with disease, hadn't grown disillusioned and resigned, or erred and been sacked. Professionally, the empire world was treating him well. Certainly there were moments when, after the initial euphoria wore off, he was disillusioned and angry with the SMP, but he settled into it. People in organizations grumble; it lubricates life and work. Dan Cormie's chief gripe was the 'Old School Tie', the persistence of nepotism in appointments and promotions.[87] Tinkler was angry at the Shanghai settlers who reminded him regularly of his lowly status; he was angry at 'profiteers', at that 'weak-knee'd Council'. And Tinkler's work accelerated a growing alienation from his fellow Britons. Sexual anger, relative poverty, racism and disgust commingle in the tirades he was sending home: 'These people, Englishmen and English women and co. actually started a Vice Committee . . . They are the greatest hypocrites on earth outside British India and Hong Kong.' 'I wish I was American. They are the only people who get paid real wages.' 'Sometimes I hate British people. You have free and compulsory education and turn out the most prejudiced, uneducated, ignorant people in the world, at least more so than any other White race.' He was angry with the Chinese. Time was running out for the British China establishment, and Tinkler sensed it. 'Getting the better of' the 'Chinaman or the Jap' was no longer a case of savvy quick thinking in a haggle over silk. After the Zhejiang-Jiangsu war the stakes were much, much higher. 'They are treated too kindly nowadays', he announced as early as 1921, 'and do not respect the whites as they did in the old days when "might was right".'

*

The politics of his work was hotting up, but how does this policeman's lot square with mythic Shanghai? In some ways it seems far removed. These men lived and worked close to the Shanghai streets. The charge room sergeants sat out their shifts in the stations, tied to the desk, with little passing foreign company, filling in the books. But most men left the police compounds every day, and saw more of the city than most of the foreign community. They walked strange streets, far from the familiar thoroughfares used by expatriate residents. Here in the steamy heat of the summer's day they were surrounded by the din of the Shanghai street life. The streets were crowded, pedestrians thronged pavements and roadways, beggars and vagrants abounded. Always there was talk and shouting, streetside arguments, spitting and yelling and loud life lived on the streets. The air was foul. Close by the Bund, launches and tenders at the jetties and pontoons belched out 'dense volumes of smoke', and their whistles rent the air throughout the day.[88] This was the beat life, day in day out, regulating the traffic, saluting members of the Council when encountered, keeping the Chinese constables working, watching the Sikhs. Most men worked quiet, dutiful lives, but there were other sides as well, and mythic Shanghai intruded. Some men played small roles in the large morass caused by the opium prohibition, gambling or prostitution. Some got away with it, others didn't. And Tinkler wasn't alone in playing up the tough guy. Dan Cormie's racy memoirs talk up a gung-ho toughness in which men piled out of their stations when the alarm bell rang, heading for the action, guns ready and danger lived with. Always after the shooting there was the squabble for recognition: who was in first, who brought the man down, who gets the cash reward, who gets the four months' seniority (and so a quicker promotion). Others were not so pushy. Sam Sherlock worried about going out on patrol – but it was meningitis that got him. This was the world of Maurice Tinkler, Shanghai policeman, Shanghai detective; now what about Tinkler the man, what did it do to him? Why did it make him so very angry with the world?

6

'Learning to be a man'

By 1923 Maurice Tinkler was feeling like an 'old-timer'. The city was changing swiftly, new buildings 'shooting up like mushrooms'. 'Shanghai has altered me too,' he'd written earlier, 'Wonder what Lily would think if she knew.' Before October 1919, when he left the Depot, Tinkler had mostly spent his life in institutions, in the school or the army. The SMP would continue to regulate his life on and off duty, but here in Shanghai he could set about making a life for himself. He was also, self-consciously, growing up. He told Edith all about it in long letters less concerned with work than with what Shanghai offered, and what Tinkler took. He was handsome and confident, cocky even, and he could obviously charm, and he was a long way from home – and anyway home was no longer really a place; Edith and his Aunt Florence were almost the only home he had left outside Shanghai, and his sweetheart Lily Wilson. For Tinkler and for his fellow recruits Shanghai was a place in which were laid out for the taking opportunities unimaginable in Lancashire, or the quiet shires and suburbs from which they came. They were servants of empire in Shanghai, working under King's Regulations and faced with the patronizing snobbery of the expatriate elites, but they steadily made their own way through this empire world, regardless. Sometimes the discipline or the city broke them, but for the most part they evaded or accommodated its constraints.

They mostly made their way together. The journey out and Gordon Road were bonding experiences and were meant as such. By the time they left the Depot the recruits had been living on top of each other for almost four months. They had shared the novelties of the voyage, and of arrival in the electric city awaiting them, that first cup of (real

China) tea in the morning, that rickshaw ride, that strange sensation of having arrived at empire good life. They explored Shanghai together, learnt police duties together, drank together, covered up for each other, and hunted together for women. They knew each other well, too well probably in some cases. Close-quarters confinement might have made some eager to get out into routine working life. But despite their dispersal to the stations of the settlement, the draft a man arrived in remained a part of his identity. Length of service remained a key ingredient in promotion, so men would be able to gauge each other's progress – or lack of it – celebrating joint promotions, or commiserating with each for not getting on. Men formed close friendships: they witnessed each other's weddings; they even married each other's sisters. They went on leave, played rugby or cricket, took excursions out of the city, and looked up each other's families at home. They acted as pall-bearers at the funerals. When Stanley Wyles killed himself in 1927 six of his 1919 contemporaries carried him to his grave in Hungjao (Hongqiao) cemetery. William Pike gave evidence to the inquest as 'a friend of his; they came from home together'. Wyles 'was inclined to worry over small things', reported the man who knew him, and knew his worries.[1] When Cyril 'Busty' Bishop died in 1938 a different six carried him to his grave. Tinkler doesn't show up in such records, he doesn't seem to have stood best man. He doesn't name any friends in his letters home. There are plenty of women, and men unnamed surround him as competitors, companions, colleagues, but not as friends.

It's not as if he didn't take part in the ordinary leisure life of the force, and his photograph albums show that for a while this involved groups of his fellow recruits and colleagues. On 15 September 1920 he travelled by train ('First Class', he pointed out), motor launch and sedan-chair up to the mountain resort of Mokanshan (Moganshan), south-west of Shanghai. The SMC ran a sanatorium here, with bungalows for hire to employees. Such hill stations were as much a feature of colonial life in China as in India or Africa. They brought a little touch of authenticity, of Simla and the Cameron Highlands to China. And really, 'The clean mountain air is splendid after Shanghai . . . being amongst the hills is like going to another land'. Tinkler photographed it all, the trains and the view from them, snapping pagodas and rice fields, the terrain, the mulberry and bamboo groves, the bungalows dotting the steep slopes. This is a beautiful highland spot, and at dawn on 21 September he shot the sea of clouds revealed 1,000 feet below his lookout. Landscape held his attention. He photographed it well, and described it well, noting trees and flowers with an easy familiarity. He was not yet an urbanized man. He posed for shots himself, puffing a pipe against a mountain backdrop, sitting on a tussock with some men and women. At least one of the men Tinkler spent this month's short leave with was fellow draftee Bert Munson. They teased missionary vacationers with a spot of graffiti at the site of the new church, pointing the way to 'Hell Fire Corner'. From Mokanshan they sallied out on a shooting trip. Gabbutt was on this jaunt, and appears in more shots taken in 1921. On the way back down Tinkler snapped the chairs (carried by two men with 12-foot-long poles) and frightened a young farmer, who 'ran, screaming for his life' when the camera emerged. After Shanghai this really was 'another land', China even: the China that men like this would have known of, a landscape of pagodas, walled cities, 'joss houses' (temples) and bamboo.

This wasn't bad: a month's paid leave, a swimming pool to hand, and much tramping up to the peaks overlooking the resort – 'I'm much fitter now and sunburnt,' he wrote. The luxury of paid leave was one of the new perks of empire life for lower-class men. He had a month a year to learn how to use, and he'd have to learn to spend it outside Shanghai, as the men were required to leave the city. This was partly to get them out somewhere healthier, especially in the humid summer, but it also stopped them getting up to mischief in Shanghai's cabarets, or mooching about the barracks. Tinkler's personnel file is incomplete, and the details of his leaves have not survived. But we can piece together some of the details from the albums and letters. There were at least three more group jaunts between 1922 and 1925. Towards the end of 1922 he went on a shooting trip with some colleagues, hiring one of the three houseboats owned by the Police Recreation Fund, and heading out along the networks of waterways that surrounded the flat lands west of Shanghai. One photo survives showing Tinkler and three others, guns in hand, the last traces of the season's snow at their feet. 'Unless something is done soon, gamebirds will be extinct,' the Revd Darwent had warned, and he bowed to the expert's opinion that 'Few large places can boast of better shooting than Shanghai'.[2] It was a popular pastime, and was one of the things that had appealed to Fred West, for example, when he was deciding whether to apply in 1921. Maurice Springfield had his own favourite patch near Wuhu on the Yangtsze and lamented that after 1921 commercial shooting denuded the countryside.[3] Still, nature got its own back on this trip, and Tinkler ended up in hospital for a month with an infection. In mid-November 1923 he went out again for a month, this time along the Grand Canal with six others (and two pigs for an early Christmas feast), passing Suzhou and Wuxi and reaching Anhui province. There are more photographs of this trip, of Suzhou's leaning pagoda, and its great walls: 28 feet high, 18 feet thick and 12 miles long. There are two snaps of the men, not all of whom were police, and one shot of Tinkler, standing in a field, aiming a pistol out into the Chinese winter, firing out into the Chinese countryside. It's a telling pose.

The photographs evidence other travels. Here he is at the Lunghwa (Longhua) pagoda south of Shanghai with Albert Balchin, in July 1921. Here are two European women at Songjiang railway station in May that year. Here he makes a weekend trip to Hangzhou, to the West Lake and then south by boat to watch the famous Bore on 18 September 1921. He's probably not alone, but there's no way to identify the company. These are all easy jaunts out from the city. For his annual leave in December 1921 he made a much more unusual journey with an unnamed colleague, sailing to Taiwan, then a Japanese colony, and on Christmas Day sailed on, alone now, to Japan for a few days in Kobe and Tokyo. He kept a diary of the tour starting with the departure of the SS *Kohoku Maru* on 5 December. They travelled first class ('better than expected') down past a coast 'ragged and strewn with islets', the water 'glorious green with rolling white crests. Blue sky flecked with long rags of white cloud.' They called at Fuzhou where it was 'good to see a few hills and rocks after a few years in Shanghai'. He noted the Chinese Naval College ('a typical air of Chinese neglect: resembles a scrapheap'). As an old hand of all of two years' standing he can of course now spot the 'typical' in China. There were several foreign-style buildings but he thought most of the foreign businesses 'dark gloomy places semi Chinese and nothing like 1921'. Shanghai, obviously, was much more '1921'; more so than home as well. In Taiwan, Tinkler and his companion worked their way down through the provincial capital Taihoku (Taibei) to Tainan, visiting sights still standard eighty years later: Sun Moon Lake, Arisan mountain resort (Alishan), the big tree (and Taipei prison, not quite the norm now). They spent mornings photographing in the public gardens and looking up the museums, called on the local police wherever they went, and were treated with gratifying respect: 'Police Chief meets us', 'Inspector of Police visits', 'Police very good'. The diary stops as his journey continues to Kobe. What a triumphant progress. He had himself snapped in the posh lounges of the hotels, photographing the exteriors in addition, just to complete the picture.

In December 1925 he made a weekend trip to Chinkiang (Zhenjiang), 'a dying port on the Yangtszekiang', with a tiny British concession. He was there to attend the Lodge installation. Tinkler had complained more than once about the effective freemasonry of place in the SMP, and about the Scottish presence in the force, claiming that the Scots favoured each other: but he chose formal Freemasonry to aid his entry into the Shanghai world. Obviously, as well as their shared journey out, shared regional origins drew men together. Sometimes the links were in place already: friends, neighbours and distant relatives suggested the force as an option. In the army, Tinkler seems to have sought out men from his own locality, and he may have done the same in Shanghai (he recorded the send-off for a fellow Lancastrian sailing home on long leave) although his developing antipathy to home suggests otherwise. Shanghai's social institutions reinforced some of these connections and identities, however. The Royal Society of St George (membership 523 on St George's Day 1919), and the St Andrew's (700), St David's and St Patrick's societies in particular held annual balls (and helped fellow nationals in distress). Chief Inspector Eugene Hugh Lynch was a stalwart of the latter society's committee in the early 1920s. Dubliner Barney Wall had his mother send him shamrock to help deck out the ballroom hall. Through the organizing committees and festivities men made new connections outside the police force, and the societies added yet more events to a crowded calendar. Another route was through a club (Tinkler certainly joined one on arrival, but I have not been able to discover which), or an ex-servicemen's organization (Tinkler joined the United Services Club), or the Freemasons. The elite Shanghai clubs were beyond the pockets of the rank and file of the SMP – men in no position to scrape together joining fees which were greater than a month's salary – and they would probably have declined to admit them anyway. Masonry – although lodges could still be socially differentiated – was more effective, and more cosmopolitan.

Tinkler was initiated on 19 June 1921 into an Irish lodge, Lodge Erin No. 463, founded in Shanghai in 1919. It wasn't particularly Irish; anyway he 'just liked this one the best' and kept an ironic distance from the ceremonial: 'I am through my third now,' he wrote in November that year, 'and fully entitled to run around town with a trowel and a handful of cement. You'd laugh if you could see me hopping round in a long-tailed dress suit.' He joined it because 'Masonry is a great thing in Shanghai, particularly amongst Americans' – the Americans again – and it also gave him useful access to the Masonic Club, which was 'way ahead' of the one he had already joined. There were a few policemen already in the lodge: two of them had helped found it, notably Inspector Young, who had commanded Gordon Road Depot when Tinkler was training and ran Central station when he was there in 1924. Two other founders were former policemen. So it couldn't hurt: they were older, more senior men and it was another way to get noticed. Four of the 1919 draft joined this lodge. Many of the Scots police joined Lodge Saltoun. Through the 1930s Lodge Erin gained an even greater police presence. Tinkler got on fast here. Acting Secretary in 1923/24, he was elected Worshipful Master for 1925/26, 'dreading the speeches' at the Astor House Hotel banquet which followed his installation on 1 December 1925. He was, he boasted proudly, 'the youngest master in China', and Masonry remained one nominal constant in his life down to his death. Tinkler was secretary of the lodge from 1928 to 1930 and, barring 1931 when he was listed as an absent member, he seems to have kept it up until 1939. The lodge notices, in fact, turned out to be important clues to his whereabouts in the early 1930s. Freemasonry truly was big in Shanghai; a significant proportion of expatriate men were members of lodges, and there they made different connections, finding different routes into Shanghai life.

Tinkler stands out from his peers. He was comparatively well educated, and had interests beyond the station canteen, the cabarets or sport. Other men threw themselves into Shanghai sporting life: the SMP rugby team, the cricket eleven, football. There was a Shanghai Rugby Football club, which played matches against teams from other treaty ports, at Hankow and even at Hong Kong. Ivo Barrett, Commissioner of Police from 1925 to 1928, played a central role in the Shanghai Cricket Club. The force's own recreation club had a modest budget, but sport was a central feature in expatriate life. It kept men fit, and was also seen – notions of healthy bodies linked ever-hopefully with healthy minds – as good for discipline and morale. One group of policemen took judo lessons under the guidance of W. E. Fairbairn. But Tinkler was no sportsman (although he sometimes wrote reports of police matches for the press in 1922). He read, attended the odd public lecture, played a bit of tennis, prowled the city in 1920 and 1921 taking photographs, and he collected stamps. Unusually for a Shanghai policeman, in the winter of 1920/21 he took French evening classes at the École Municipale Française. This didn't just involve a trip south to Frenchtown, it took him into a different world and direct contact with the other Shanghai that so dazzled at a distance. 'It's a rather swagger class we have there,' he told his aunt, 'I am the *only* one that didn't come in a motor-car.' He played the bad boy, delighting in shocking some of the 'awful prigs' there – which he could do simply enough by telling them about his job, as 'People here get deceived with me, and seem quite astonished when I turn out to be a policeman'. He moved into a senior class in late 1921, studying with some of his Shanghai social betters, among them a former US judge, and a British consular official.

Part of the night school fun was a 'peach of a girl', a Danish-American class-mate. He obviously found her attractive; and her wealth as attractive too as it plainly limited his freedom of action: 'She doesn't own that motor-car after all,' he wrote in January 1921, 'but she rides ponies and heaven knows what else so there's no possibility of my going ahead very far. She got an awful shock when I told her I was a policeman.' Tinkler might have been 'awful keen to go to the French class' as a result ('she's a darling and American') and he gave her his best opium pipe, but his letters over the next two years start displaying a charged sexual anger, in which the women of the foreign community – as he saw them rich, attractive and therefore so very unavailable – were assailed with growing bitterness. 'White women have an inflated value here, because of the fact that the greater part of the population consists of males and, if a woman with any looks whatever leaves the narrow path of virtue, you bet your life she lives with about $500 a month, with automobiles, jazz and everything'; 'They are too damned expensive in this country. Can't go anyplace without a spanking big automobile. All the white women are the same, from stenographers to millionaires' wives.' The novelty of his ability to shock through lowly position wore off, and constraint became more evident the longer he stayed in Shanghai. Life might seem peach-fresh, and awash with opportunity, and he might attend night classes and the like, but he was still only a Shanghai policeman, still beyond the social pale: the cars and the women were above him. But in 1921 his mood was still up, and his classmate, he told Edith, was still 'nearly as nice as Lily'. He told Lily Wilson about her too, 'just to make her jealous 'cause she's apt to get a little swell-headed at times'.

At the start of these Shanghai years Tinkler's sense of self was still intertwined with Grange, Ulverston and home, with school friends, neighbours and family, and with his sweetheart Lily. In the pages of the commonplace book 'swell-headed' Lily Wilson opened in January

1919 lie small clues to the progress of their relationship. She copied into this book stanzas, poems, prose, and later on songs and quips from university days, and was still annotating it in the late 1970s. It is a window into a life lived with regret – in private at least. Her nephew found the book in his attic, and combined with Tinkler's sparse comments in his own letters it helps sketch the trajectory of a failing relationship. The volume almost opens with the drawing by Tinkler of soldiers carrying a dead comrade, the fruit of the pencilling he amused himself with in quiet moments at the front. But what is more germane is the fact that his imminent departure for China was noted by her on 14 June 1919 with pointed verses from Ella Wheeler Wilcox, a then-popular American poet:

The day is drawing near my dear
When you & I must sever;
Yet whether near or far we are,
Our hearts will love forever,
Our hearts will love forever.

O sweet, I will be true, and you
Must never fail or falter;
I hold a love like mine divine,
And yours – it must not alter,
O, swear it will not alter.

Fifty-eight years later she noted by the side: 'Maurice Went'. The poem's title is 'Love'. Another Wilcox effort, 'Threefold', was inserted on 14 June 1921 with the added note 'R.M.T. went to China July 1919'; then, on the last day of August, when Tinkler was already in Shanghai:

All said & done life's sum total is this –
Summer & you – and a remembered kiss!

There hadn't been that much time together, but there had been a courting, a consolidation of the intermittent meetings snatched on leave in Leeds, building on friendship from school, 'days of early 1914' (as she later wrote). He was discharged from the army at the end of January; she had her university final examinations to prepare for and graduated on 7 July. There had been enough time for a declaration, and perhaps that kiss was no metaphor. They considered themselves engaged, they even talked about children. Tinkler kept up a furious correspondence from Shanghai, and drawing too. Lily gave him a photograph of herself, taken in Scrimshaw's Photographic Studio in Leeds, minus the cap and gown of the graduation pose she gave her parents at the same time. He drew a copy, and mailed it back, labelling the somewhat idealized portrait of her neck and eyes 'Pensive maiden after Scrimshaw'. She stored it in the book. But months before Tinkler joshed her from Shanghai, Lily had already copied out a poem written for her by 'G.R.B.', the subject also, the following year, of an excerpt of a Browning love poem. She married George Richard Benson, a 33-year-old fellow schoolteacher, in August 1923.

What was broken was not just a tentative understanding between two young people, but for him a tie to home, and to an old identity. The decision was most likely hers. 'O sweet, I will be true,' Lily wrote in June 1919, 'But Alas! I was not,' was added in September 1977. With a suitor pressing, she may have given Tinkler an ultimatum, return from China, or else. There is a hint of a deadline in a November 1921 letter of his, and he wrote of getting a 'sort of farewell present for Lily' in Tokyo. But he couldn't marry in his first term's service – and even permission to marry was limited until 1934 to a third of the sergeants at any one time, to limit pressure on married quarters and to limit expenses – and he wasn't due long leave until at least 1924. He couldn't even leave until mid-1922 without forfeiting his passage money, and probably half of his superannuation, and he had no savings. He would have left with almost nothing. Even if Tinkler had risked the return there were no prospects in Britain. Unless he attempted to continue his education – and there were no funds available for that – he was qualified for nothing other than police or military work, and Shanghai was spoiling him for home. The dislocation from Ulverston, from his friends, and the remains of his family, was compounded by his new life and its opportunities. And for Lily to have waited, and gone out to Shanghai as a policeman's wife in 1924 or so, might have seemed increasingly unthinkable as her career progressed. Openings may have arisen in SMC schools, and she might have applied from England, but she was already off to a good start in Easingwold, Yorkshire, and there was little logic to any move, other than two hearts loving forever. She'd gone to university in wartime at great financial cost to the family, and at the expense, in family legend, of her fighting brother, some of whose meagre army pay went to support her. So there may also have been family pressure on her to forget the distant boyfriend. Small wonder, then, that it all buckled.

Others waited. Bertha Smith waited in Pontypridd for Tinkler's fellow recruit Walter Hotchkiss, marrying him early in his first long leave in 1923. Waiting was after all a root fact of empire life, as men worked out their first contracts in trading companies, banks, civil services and elsewhere, or served their time awaiting promotion into positions which supported married men. Our great-grandparents were more patient, and financially and socially constrained too, as there were few employment opportunities for married women in the empire world. But in June 1922 Wilson slipped into her book some lines from Tennyson:

> . . . More things are wrought by prayer
> Than this world dreams of, therefore
> Let thy voice rise like a fountain for me
> Day and night.

She underlined the date, and added the bracketed initials 'R.M.T.' Perhaps she wrote asking him to decide (perhaps extending that hinted-at deadline), to raise his voice against George Richard Benson's. But it's also possible that she'd sent off the dismissal, the 'Dear John' letter. Tinkler hints that she had wanted to stay in contact, but that he refused. We shall never know, but the lines of verse marked a significant moment in the relationship and Tinkler's confident teasing in early 1921 gave way to bitterness in October 1922: 'La donna e mobile. I'll say she is,' he wrote to Edith. There is a letter missing from the collection from earlier in 1922, in which he let his guard down in an 'outburst of sob stuff' that he later told Edith to ignore. 'And say, I don't want you to think I'm mush headed . . . It's all no account anyway.' After this break, bitterness and rage grew; against Lily, against the Chinese, against the British, against God, against everything and everyone. 'I never had any "pals",' he later wrote bitterly, '$ are the only ones you can rely on.' He used 'pals' in the romantic pulp-fiction argot of the time; a pal was a soulmate, a sweetheart. This was not true. He'd had Lily, but had her no longer. He kept one photograph only, stuck in an album, with nothing to identify her, no date given, no name. If I hadn't found her own relatives and papers, I wouldn't have known it was her. He didn't keep anybody's letters (at least, almost none survive): 'It's all no account anyway.' But she kept every single letter he ever wrote to her.

The year 1921 had been a good one, at work and out of it. He was getting on and getting about. There were many letters and many photographs. But 1922 is different, with a long break in the correspondence with home, no dated photos, and coming to the fore a violent, tough-guy style. The break with Lily Wilson was important. He may have been broken-hearted, he was certainly very upset; he may also have been affronted, unmanned, ambushed. It was for him to tease and flirt. 'Women are a nuisance to me but I can't leave them alone, if they like me (and they usually do). Sometimes they won't leave me alone. It makes me very conceited too and is spoiling me.' From here on Richard Maurice Tinkler called the shots. 'I have a sort of reputation to keep up with two other fellows as a "breaker of hearts" and a "wrecker of homes",' he wrote in 1924. (There was always an audience.) The jealousy at the mores of wealthy, untouchable Shanghai, and the shock of an emotional betrayal fused with the American-flavoured tough-guy masculinity saturates his later letters home.

One reason for feeling trapped in Shanghai was money, and the reason Tinkler was short of money was that he was spending it. 'I want to save money but it's very hard,' he wrote in September 1921. Keeping up with '1921', with those expensive 'dames', and standing his round in the masculine social culture of the city took their toll, especially when 'prices here are outrageous'. Even if he had savings the changing exchange rate was working against him; his Shanghai earnings amounted over the years to less and less in pounds sterling. Still, he was in at the start of the Shanghai spree, and as a detective he had to get out and about, and he did so with gusto. He lived in public. He needed to kit himself out, and it is clear from his photographs that clothes mattered now as much as they did in the army. 'I was going along to see a girl,' he wrote in November 1921, 'wearing some very swagger white serge trousers and a new sun-proof', and 'a pair of those American tortoise-shell-rimmed glasses'. Shanghai offered him reinvention, and for that the sooner he cut Penrith, Ulverston, Grange, the better. The break with Lily was a part of this, but he'd really said goodbye to all that in 1915, when he joined up. He grew less and less interested in home, Grange 'sounds quite awfully medieval', and Shanghai of course was 1921. He reinvented his speech, piling up the Americanisms (note how 'cars' became 'automobiles'); he cast off class inhibitions as he strutted about this Shanghai stage, its hotels and bars, mixing with society, judges and diplomats, 'getting cheekier now'. He had to cast off other inhibitions too: 'One day I'll have enough courage to join a real dancing class. But it's fearful expensive jaunting around the Cafés and hotels in town (they all have ball-rooms and are more mad here over dancing than anywhere).' And the dancing was 'different from that they have in England. It's more up to date.' 'You may smile at that if you like,' he added, 'but it's true.' The dance craze swept Britain too after 1919, when the Hammersmith Palais opened, but it was Anglicized.[4] In Shanghai it was raw American, direct from across the ocean. And 'all the dames here are crazy for dancing'.

He was self-consciously making a more up-to-date modern life for himself in this modern city, even allowing for the boasting tone of his letters to Edith. And it wasn't all Astor House swank. He could trawl through the cabarets with the worst of them. 'I'm feeling,' he wrote from Louza station in October 1922, 'at least I suppose I am – remorseful after a little jag last night and this morning (I was home before breakfast though) at the Carlton, Del Monte, Crest and Royal cocktail foundries.' He'd been out to the cinema and then 'met a bird with a jagged disposition at the Masonic club', and out they went. 'Well that's just Shanghai. I don't say this in boastfulness, and I've been very quiet for a month.' Empire culture was sociable, fuelled by drink the globe over and on the ships that linked it. Police culture was perhaps even more so. We know what other men got up to from the debts outstanding at their deaths. Detective James Douglas, who sailed with the second 1919 draft, left unpaid bills for tailors, his shoemakers, bars (police canteens, Engley's, Eddie's Café, Shepherd's Hostel ('High class catering a speciality'), and La Gaîté (one of the seedier 'Trenches' bars), a watchmaker, and car chits (there was little point in swaggering out in a rickshaw). He lived out and about, then, spending on his appearance, his shoes, a new watch perhaps (or was it a gift for his fiancée?), nights out and the odd few drinks in the station bar. George Sale had also drunk at Shepherd's, as well as the Victoria bar, and station canteens. Stan Bailey spent his way out of his job in 1924, by accumulating unpayable debts at Eddie's, Shepherd's, his tailors and various garages.[5] Harold Gill's notes for a lecture on his Shanghai days included: 'Relaxation: Clubs. Social Life. Receptions. ADC. Light opera. Night clubs. Artistes from the USA making the Grand

Tour. Cabarets. Bars – doubtful reputation. Fights. Susie Wong.' Shanghai he noted was 'truly a bachelor's paradise'.[6]

And there was that breaking of hearts. Tinkler upset Edith in October 1922 with a long, pugnacious account of his affair with 'Elise', a White Russian refugee he had met in a cabaret. She lived on the edge, at least, of the world of Shanghai prostitution. Eastern Europeans and American women had staffed Shanghai brothels until the huge refugee flow caused by the defeat of the White Russian Armies in Siberia. As the International Settlement closed its brothels, many of the Madams simply set up shop in the French Concession; others responded by finding new ways of contacting their public. The position of the White Russians became the stuff of League of Nations' reports, and salacious reportage; and it was the stuff of the lives of these Shanghai policemen, at least forty of whom married Russians down to 1942, and of Tinkler's life, too. Between 1915 and 1920 the Russian population in the International Settlement alone rose from 361 to 1,266; by 1930 it stood at 3,487, 1,300 of whom were adult women. Some 10,454 Russians arrived in the city between 1922 and 1929; another 10,572 had arrived by the end of 1936. In 1934 there were 8,000 living in Frenchtown and 13,000 in Chinese-controlled districts, after a second wave of migration from the Japanese-occupied north-east.[7] They came initially from the former Russian sphere of influence, Manchuria, from the cities and communities established there in the shadow of the Russian-controlled Chinese Eastern Railway, and they migrated south in search of better employment. Otherwise they came directly from Russia, trickling out or fleeing in groups as the civil war turned in the Bolsheviks' favour. Fifteen ships from Vladivostok arrived off Wusong in December 1922. The 1,500 people on board were 'practically destitute', but 80 disembarked on 9 December, 'a good type of people well dressed and clean'.[8] The overriding fact is that refugee poverty, however 'well dressed and clean', deracinated the Russians in Shanghailander eyes. They were not in Shanghai by choice, but by necessity. They were not settlers. Stateless, lacking extraterritorial rights, subject to Chinese law, and in a poor financial position, the Russians were seen as Asiatics.

In April 1922, as he told Edith – and the letter reads like a telling, like an essay into fiction ('Well it won't make you feel good if I talk about work,' he typed, 'so I'll talk, or write (or do one finger exercises on this Oliver) about play, etc. to start with') – he saw Elise in the cabaret where she worked, sitting amongst some others: 'I liked her and told the boy to ask her to come over to my table. "Dance with me . . . Buy me a bottle of 'Vine'" (fake champagne)'. 'Talk talk part in English part in French . . . my friend meantime throwing choice remarks in Chinese across the table which the girl does not understand.' She was 19. Her father, an ex-Tsarist officer living in Harbin, had managed to send her to a French convent school in Tokyo. Afterwards, trained as a stenographer, she had come to Shanghai. The employment prospects of the Russians were very poor, however well qualified they were. Chinese were cheaper, and usually spoke and typed better English. Like many others Elise wandered into mercenary life. 'I think', wrote Tinkler, 'Shanghai must be one of the worst places on earth to be broke in.' She became, he reported, the mistress of a 'wealthy American-Jew', but the man broke with her when he caught her dancing with another man. She wanted to be Tinkler's 'temporary wife', she wanted him to set her up as his mistress. If he could have afforded to, he wrote bluntly, he would have done so (although it was against regulations). They had an affair, nonetheless. 'She used to go to dinners with me and movie shows and automobile rides, and sometimes I used to go to her room.' 'Wonder what Lily would think if she knew,' he mused, 'still, I suppose all this is a necessary part of the process of learning to be a man.' For Tinkler, Shanghai and empire manliness was concerned with this home- and heart-breaking toughness. In his narrative of the affair he adopted the same stance: emotionally controlled, knowing, directing, distanced. It may have begun before he and Lily 'ceased being in love' (his phrase), although he acknowledged a similar fling in 1920, but it seems likely that his style derived in equal measure from a Shanghaied masculinity (the 'choice remarks in Chinese') and from the break with Lily. He'd been much in the company of men since he joined the army. As in France, so in Shanghai he was surrounded by men whose expectations of his behaviour he grew all too complicitly conscious of, keeping up that 'sort of reputation'. He knew what women wanted – 'automobiles', money, 'jazz' ('Shanghai is nothing but jazz') – he knew what to say, and when. 'I had already told her a thousand times that I loved her. I tell that to all of them.'

Tinkler and Elise split up, he wrote, because she had had to earn a living and had returned to prostitution, to his distress, and her decline. Now 'she's getting like the rest – powdered up – money – "snow" (morphine and cocaine) then Finis'. Note the capitalized, sensationalized, 'F'. And that, he concluded tendentiously, 'is what Shanghai has done and is doing to hundreds of splendid girls. And men who Know the Orient all wonder if any woman is worthwhile.' Such was the world-weariness of the 24-year-old detective, old enough now, man enough now, to Know the Orient. He saw Elise again in 1924, after she'd spent a year in Bangkok, but there was nothing romantic to rekindle. Tinkler was writing in 1922, some years before the publication of such salacious, sub-pornographic exposés as Hendrik de Leeuw's *Cities of Sin* (1934) or Henri Champly's *The Road to Shanghai: White Slave Traffic in Asia* (1934), which told the Russians' tales in styles at times not far removed from his. But even if the solid identification of White Russian women with Shanghai prostitution, and the all-too-public *demi-monde*, can be overstated, it is true that the influx of these European migrants far outnumbered the opportunities available for employment. The men sold their bodies as soldiers or bodyguards. For women there was dressmaking or millinery, but certainly not enough to go around, and there was a big market for sex. Dancing, hostessing and the sex trade formed a continuum, and a kept mistress was working out a form of regularized prostitution. So Maurice Tinkler's Shanghai was a world of sexual opportunity: a feast of women.

Maurice might hope for the Americans, but it was mostly the Russians he dated. Shura, however, was certainly different from Elise, older, more settled and more respectable. This affair lasted at least five years and talk of marriage replaced macho bragging. 'This is the only serious heart attack that I have had in my life,' he wrote in 1925. 'I am always afraid that we are too happy for it to last long'; 'She's clever and much better brought up than I am . . . and I love her.' Alexandra, or Shura, whom he knew as 'Sonnie', refused to call him Maurice. She 'likes Dick, which I don't'. (But he was 'Richard M. Tinkler' on that calling card.) She had Italian citizenship, through a

marriage which was in the process of being formally dissolved when they met in the autumn of 1923. 'If we don't quarrel', he announced, '(we have several times already), I may stay in Shanghai a long time yet before I go on leave to Europe and get married. (Must get some money first though.)' In the meantime, he told Edith, Shura wanted '(you mustn't laugh at me) a photograph of me when I was a kiddie'. Please send a copy, he wrote, of the one of 'me sitting on a table at the age of 4 or so'. He did not take long leave (which was due in 1924–5) until three years after this was written, in 1928 when it was already long overdue. There is little more in his letters about the relationship. He wrote to Edith hoping that she wouldn't be prejudiced against a divorcee, but perhaps he felt she was, or that as the years passed by with no development perhaps it became too awkward a topic. There are glimpses. They swam together at the open-air pool. In October 1925 they were seeing each other every two or three days. She went shooting with him one rainy Sunday, on a 17-mile ramble with no tiffin. They planned to dine together on New Year's Eve 1925/26 at the Plaza Hotel. One of their quarrels was probably about the 19-year-old Russo-French daughter of a French Concession detective he was 'seeing' in February 1924. A familiar and transparently insincere litany was occasioned: 'I wish I had some money then I would marry her, if she'd let me.'

We don't know Shura's surname. But we do know what she looked like. One of his photo albums was devoted to her (not to them, for there is only one shot of the two together and that also included another man). Brief captions to some of the shots give the locations as the seaside resort at the former German-leased territory of Tsingtao (Qingdao), a popular summer holiday destination for Shanghailanders; Mogi, Japan, in July–August 1927 when he was on a month's sick leave in the small fishing port near Nagasaki; and the hot spring at Unzen, Japan, in April 1928. In the Tsingtao photographs she poses for him in the season's finest Jantzen beachwear, elegantly accessorized to the minute, relaxed and good-humoured. Another of the photographs is dedicated 'To my loved one/from loving Kitten/Shou/July 12th 1927/Mogi Japan'. This is the only direct trace, perhaps, that this unsurnamed woman has left to posterity. Tinkler mentions her in his letters as late as 1926, but thereafter there is nothing. He mentions the sick leave at Inagi, but actually writes as if he was alone on a 'disappointing holiday', where he swam in the bay in the mornings and fished in the afternoons. The 1928 trip was taken at the start of that delayed long leave when the pair must have travelled together to Japan where he spent ten days. He didn't take her to Europe, that fantasy of waiting for marriage seemingly remaining unrealized. There are only a few letters for 1928 – when he was on leave from April to December – 1929 and 1930, and Shura is not mentioned in these. Edith wondered at his death if there had been a marriage, but there is no record of one. He certainly still had no savings by January 1929, when he was living hand to mouth after arriving back in Shanghai after his travels. We don't know what Shura did for a living, whether he kept her as his 'temporary wife' or not. Given his repeated observations on the role of women in Shanghai relationships – passive recipients of male largesse – it might have suited his nature and controlling role to be playing benefactor.

Marriage becomes a recurring theme in his letters, perhaps to reassure Edith about his morals. There might be something, as he put it, in the Shanghai 'climate that would take the morality out of the Archangel Blondin', but he was conscious that his choices were not wholly his, that Edith's feelings and beliefs had to be negotiated. 'I wasn't offended at your letter,' he wrote in June 1923 after his tale of Elise had garnered strong reproof. 'I'm not angry or anything as I guess I deserved what you said.' Always the barrier to marriage is said to be money. But he was also getting choosy, and his choice of lovers was self-consciously a Shanghai choice, a 1921 choice: 'I feel I could never settle down married to an English girl.' He liked Shanghai's 'cosmopolitan atmosphere' too much. But settling the men down with homeside wives was the SMP's preference, although in Shanghai his former Depot commander's wife, Elizabeth Young, tried to engineer marriages for the men with governesses or probationer hospital nurses, by bringing likely candidates together at dinner parties. 'By *now*,' he wrote in 1924, 'Mrs Young recognises me as an extremely hard-boiled egg.' There weren't many other British women in Shanghai who would think of marrying a policeman. And Tinkler's characteristic response was that half of those who married locally contracted such unions and 'It's frightful because they are so "regimented" and ugly'. In 1928 the British Women's Association planned monthly dances for the SMP with similar aims.[9] In reply, Tinkler and his friends flaunted their 'Russian lady friends of the doubtful variety', aiming to 'disgust' such do-gooders. For many Shanghailanders, all Russians were suspect because so precariously marginal. They had no secure European status, and they were not considered 'white'. A further problem for the SMP was that many Russian women, such as – it seems – Elise, had compromised themselves too much to make suitable wives for policemen. There was also a distrust of motive, and women were seen as passport-hungry gold-diggers, ensnaring impressionable young men who found themselves responsible for their in-laws as well as their wives. Shanghailander women 'ripped their morals to pieces', into the bargain, Maurice reported, because the Russians were prettier and men 'flocked' to them.

White Russians like Elise and Shura provided both new solutions and complications to an old problem: who were the men of the SMP to marry? Marry they should: a married man was felt to be more efficient, more ambitious (he needed advancement more, he had some-one pushing him more), more likely to stay on longer. But this was only felt to be true of the properly married man, who had bagged himself a woman of his class, background and 'race'. The big worry was that men would marry Chinese. 'Thank God,' Tinkler wrote in 1923, 'I have kept clear of the Asiatic ones and have retained some self-respect.' By the First World War, the latitude once given to the administrators and servants of British empire in matters of sex and marriage was fast disappearing. New-style racism powered social and official intolerance of practices, such as concubinage with local women, which had previously been encouraged in the interests of the overall health of empire administrators.[10] Greater leeway might be given to lower-class sexuality, to men who were unlikely to mix in settler society more generally. The British army was pragmatic. Chinese prostitutes were offered to the British troops of the Shanghai Defence Force in 1927 in brothels established outside the Settlement, and from 1932 onwards what was described as a 'Regimental Brothel' employed seven Russians at 108 Weihaiwei Road.[11] The SMP was not alone in censuring and attempting to prevent relationships and marriages with 'natives'. For the trading houses, transnationals and banks operating in Shanghai, 'Foreign, native, half-caste' were 'definitely taboo' as marriage partners for their middle-class staff.[12] In January 1927 the Commissioner and the Watch Committee both agreed that 'as a general rule mixed marriages were not in the interests of the force', although there was no prohibition as such in the 'Terms of Service'.[13] Some men had been given permission to marry Chinese before. Edward William Everson had married May Poon in 1920; her sister married Reg Conduit; Sub-Inspector Whiting married a Chinese woman in 1919 on his promotion to Sub-Inspector, but was refused marriage benefits by the Commissioner for another four years. In 1927 Commissioner Barrett recommended non-renewal of Sergeant William Parker's contract, after he had asked permission to marry a Chinese woman recognized by the Commissioner as being of 'respectable parentage'. As Parker was 'unlikely to rise to the more senior ranks of the Force', the Watch Committee overruled him, 'provided his services in the Force do not deteriorate as a result'.[14] The SMP worried about the potential corruptions of such personal links with Chinese society, of men buckling to their new family's social obligations. It also recognized the effective ostracism that men might meet with from their peers, or from Shanghailander society, or the awkwardness of social relations in such contexts, and the likelihood of men's service 'deteriorating'. Relationships of any sort with Chinese were not liked, even though they might be useful for giving men language experience. Dan Cormie claimed that many men set Chinese women up in a room and kept them, 'so the young man had always somewhere to go on his off duty hours'. They were 'good companions'.[15] This was against regulations, but if the force found it difficult to police such behaviour or turned a blind eye to it, at least it could rely on racism – on Tinkler's sense of 'self respect' – to keep men away from legalized commitments to Chinese women.

These prejudices changed dramatically in the 1930s, but even in the early 1920s some men had no qualms, and – as throughout the British Asian empire – Japanese were popular. Sergeant Dow's first term of service was undermined in the eyes of his superiors by his being 'mixed up' with a Japanese woman. Sergeant Barnes was very friendly with Matcha, a taxi-dancer (a paid dancing partner) at the Venus Café. E. W. Peters dedicated his book to 'Sumiko' whom, he announced, he fully intended to marry when circumstances permitted, a promise he did not keep. Like other Shanghailander men, many officers took short leave in Japan, especially at Obama, effectively taking sex holidays. As Dan Cormie noted, at the hotels they chose the girls 'went along with the rooms'.[16] One or two even retired there. In the hierarchy of sexual acceptability then current, Japanese women came somewhere between Russians and Chinese, the latter considered unattractive by most in the 1920s. But the Japanese were also considered to be 'cleaner' than both. Recreation was one thing, marriage was different; although the privacy of a consulate marriage in Shanghai or abroad might help discretion. I found evidence of only one marriage to a Japanese woman, and that came to light in 1928 only because the man concerned was retiring from the force and was planning to abandon Matsuda Mitsu (having married her secretly in Japan three years before) and contract a bigamous marriage with a British woman. He was ordered to resign on the spot and a large cheque was extracted for her support.[17] Of course, Shanghailander sex taboos were often ignored. A masculine settler culture, a meeting in Japan, for example, with its different sexual mores, or even in Shanghai, with its heavily sexualized entertainment culture, might prompt men to shed prejudice in the anonymity of the hotel, the brothel or the quiet room in a clean back street. Abroad, for the British, had always been about seeking sexual opportunity. But returning home was another matter. Matsuda Mitsu was not the only woman abandoned, while other wives seem to have decided against the pains of migration from China. Some men found themselves unable to return home with their new families, fearing ostracism from their people, or the censure of neighbours or strangers. Sub-Inspector Whiting did not take his wife back on his long leave.

Tinkler was not alone in staying unmarried, but the great majority of his peers who were still in the police or gaol service in early 1941 were married. At least twenty men from the 1919 drafts had wed, and, of the nationalities identifiable, ten women were British, three Russian and two American. Fourteen of the weddings took place in Shanghai, mostly to locally met women. Robert Norton married Ada Lewis in February 1921, barely eighteen months into the job. He was dismissed nine days later, probably as a result. We don't always know their occupations, but many of those married in Shanghai were SMC nurses (who had to resign six months after the wedding), or stenographers, sometimes the daughters of Shanghailander households. The force permitted marriages out East only after the men had had their first long leave so that they could explore 'the marriage market at home' and not rush into 'undesirable marriages' in Shanghai, or in Hong Kong or Japan on the way to Britain.[18] Men routinely asked permission to marry at home on long leave, often just in case. They went back on that first long leave often intending to wed a waiting woman, look up an old flame, or just scout about. The prospect of solitude in the years to come might pall. They had to scurry. If they didn't get the woman up the aisle or into the registrar's before leave ended they'd be paying her passage out themselves. Sometimes to Shanghai came letters from fathers, unsure of the status of the SMP: 'Would you marry your own daughter to him? Does he have the money to support a wife (and possibly a family) as an English lady should live in Shanghai?' (Yes, was the answer, at least to this particular enquiry.) Women in Shanghai were vetted, eventually by the force's

Special Branch. George Craik, a recruit of 1919, asked permission in 1929 to marry a nurse at the Council's Victoria Nursing Home who was, as he noted on the form, '(Eurasian)'. 'Await report from CPH [Commissioner of Public Health]' was scribbled on the application; 'CPH reports lady O.K.' was the laconic reply. In some cases the lady was not 'O.K.' One sergeant was refused permission by Commissioner Barrett in October 1926 to marry a woman allegedly of 'very indifferent character who had at one time been the inmate of a foreign brothel, and who had also been an in-patient in the mental ward. She was in point of fact at one time a notorious character well known in Shanghai.' He married her anyway. Marriage allowance was refused and, failing to make ends meet, he resigned, asking for passages for them to join his father in Canada. Instead, his superannuation fund was docked the contributions made by the SMC and, in a last twist, he was issued a single passage to Britain. He never made the journey, dying in a hospital in Shanghai in November 1938.[19] A 1921 recruit, Londoner E. P. Malone applied to marry at home on long leave in 1927. Barrett objected that it was wrong for the Council to 'assist him to start his married life seriously in debt'. Men did apply to marry 'off the strength', with no allowance or quarters, but this might sometimes lead to 'financial hardship and continual temptation' in the eyes of the Council. Sometimes they married through necessity, and the force was grudgingly amenable and didn't always tell their folks at home. Marriages to Russians began to take place at the very end of the 1920s, and to Chinese at the end of the 1930s.

The empire world was changing, and these men were changing it, straining against the rules, evading them, and making their own lives in the world they found themselves in. They were recruited as servants of empire, whose task was to maintain the Shanghai status quo, to protect the foreign community. Protecting that community also meant protecting its good name, and this meant accepting its mores and taboos, knowing their place and marrying within it. But as the SMC used the men of the force, so the men used the opportunities Shanghai provided. Some felt they had little choice. The barracks were institutional, closed up, dreary, and for someone like Tinkler almost demeaning. 'This place gives me the jim-jams,' he wrote of Hongkew Station in 1924, 'and makes me go out at nights.' So out they went, spending or saving, playing on the sports field or in the cabaret, squiring a nurse from the Victoria Nursing Home or setting up a Chinese woman somewhere in a discreet little room. Abroad was also about different sex. New Zealander Rewi Alley found the Shanghai Fire Service an amenable billet from which to enjoy what he found to be a more tolerant Chinese cultural attitude towards homosexuality. Its illegality obscures practice in the SMP, only highlighting a couple of men who made unwanted advances to Chinese subordinates.[20] But there was opportunity enough in Shanghai for both heterosexual and homosexual exploitation of participants in the commercial sex-trade. These Shanghai policemen were obliged when single to live in the barracks, their behaviour on and off duty was regulated, and a tyrannical regime allowed or prohibited their marriages, and sometimes hounded out defaulters. But the servants of empire acted as free agents, and their superiors knew it. 'If he is found taking a woman into his quarters he will be severely dealt with – as a Sub-Inspector I rely upon him to play the game and avoid scandal,' warned Commissioner Barrett of another 1919 high-flyer, Reginald Beer, whose private life was garnering complaint. Playing the game and maintaining appearances was important, but at the same time Barrett had also effectively ordered him to 'wed the lady' if need be.[21] These Shanghai policemen learnt their way around, reckoning up the pros and cons of the police life. Some chose Shanghai without the police, as Beer eventually did. Other men chose to leave, looking to better themselves elsewhere. They encountered a city in flux, and they set out to remould it to their own image and desires.

For Tinkler, this was a good life. True, he was often low on cash. He spent on things – piling up a collection of curios and other items in his station room – and he spent on appearances, on travel and on getting out, but he seems to have escaped the problems of debt. Debt was probably a factor in one or two suicides, and certainly occasioned dismissals and resignations, and the odd bit of peculation. Here is an inspector – 'a disgrace to my family and self', according to his widow – who had been 'borrowing' from the Poor Box fund at the Mixed Court before his sudden death. Here is a 1936 recruit, 'heavily in debt to an extent which is prejudicial'; another man, dunned for two months' pay by a Sikh money-lender, resignation requested by the

Commissioner. Here is Stan Bailey, 'heavily in debt, chiefly for clothes, liquor and motor cars'; another man, 'Hopelessly in debt' (a marriage, possibly off the strength, wouldn't have helped).[22] Men borrowed from Sikhs, or from their Chinese colleagues. They might get a 'severe reprimand' on file if caught out, if not a worse punishment. They asked for advances from their superannuation, and didn't always get it. 'Devotes too much time to pleasure and is heavily in debt' (to the tune, eventually, of $1,440 owed to five Sikhs: services terminated, reads one report). Tinkler does not seem the type to have borrowed from the Sikhs, or from Chinese. His racism and his sense of self would have prevented that. But we know that after almost ten years' service he had no savings. He had his superannuation accumulating with the SMC's contributions doubling its value, and by the time he left this was a sizeable sum. But otherwise he was spending as he was getting. This was the way he lived.

Tinkler returned home once only, and was plainly lost. The late summer and autumn of 1928 showed how far removed he was from the lives of his family. For his young stepbrother he seemed an uncomfortable figure, out of place. He was clearly estranged from English life, undone and spoilt by empire living. Tinkler was not alone in delaying his first long leave as late as he did, but the first of his fellow recruits had gone back on leave in late 1923. CID was short-staffed and the detectives could not be spared early, but perhaps he also felt like his fellow recruit Frederick Carnell, who deferred leave in 1931 because 'he has no one he wants to see in England and does not wish to visit any other countries at present'. Altogether, the delay was probably down to a combination of indifference and lack of cash. This first trip home was for many men the opportunity for triumphant progress. Tinkler was no different. Men often took leave together. John Weeks applied to take his leave especially in 1934, wanting to go on leave with three of the friends he came out with. Dan Cormie travelled back with fellow 1926 recruit Louie Stewart, a former railwayman, 'bound for Scotland via Japan, Honolulu and the United States, two young men with about 200 pound sterling in our pockets just to spend on ourselves in having a good time'.[23] Cormie bought himself a car, visited friends and relations and drove from one end of the British Isles to the other. Tinkler sailed from Kobe on 27 April, presumably leaving Shura there to return to Shanghai. The vessel sailed to Honolulu, San Francisco and Los Angeles, then to the Panama Canal Zone where after a few days he embarked on another ship which sailed via Colombia, Venezuela, Trinidad and the French West Indies to Plymouth, arriving on 4 July, his leave almost half over. He spent a few days in London, and then stayed at his stepmother's house in Scarborough, where his young stepbrother John remembered him as an exotic, lost in the Yorkshire seaside town, standing out and distant. He revisited Grange and Penrith. He made a trip to Paris at the end of his stay, flying over – flying was modern indeed for 1929 – and burning cash as he did so. The Imperial Airways Argosy from Croydon would have cost him about £8, a hefty part of a month's pay. He may have revisited the wartime battlefields; he certainly bought some postcards of them. On his last day in France he lost most of his remaining money. It can't have been stolen, he argued in a letter to his stepmother, but it seems likely rather that the Shanghai detective, all smart suit and flash American glasses, had had his pocket well and truly French-picked.

'There is nothing for you here,' concluded his stepmother. Postcards of Scarborough, the Lake District and Paris were pasted into an album, but otherwise this was a defining visit. He had talked himself out of England in his letters over the years, lambasting the stupidity and ugliness of the English (and Scottish, and others), and the virtues of America – the 'other place' in the English imagination, and in his. 'If I had enough money to take up residence in the United States,' he wrote in 1925, 'I would change my nationality. The British are a nation of snobs and hypocrites.' He had the *North China Herald* delivered while he was in Britain, so as to keep up. He looked to Shanghai while away on leave, and he was not alone in not looking back to Britain on his return. Even before the Second World War many men moved on retirement to Australia, or Canada. Sometimes climate was a factor, at other times they joined up with family members who had already moved there. Ireland had changed too much for many of the Shanghai Irish in the early 1920s. Often, however, men moved on because Shanghai had spoiled them for life in Britain. They'd moved on, and moved up, and a return to the certainties of British life and society would have cramped men who had lived well in China.

The view west from the Huangpu could be disturbing. Britain in the early 1920s, struggling with the post-war economy and an active labour movement, hardly appealed. 'England seems to be an awful place from our newspapers and I'm glad I'm not there,' wrote Tinkler in 1921. Instead, Shanghai often delivered a good life, and it pointed the way to empire good life elsewhere. It is curious that Tinkler didn't take the overland US route home. Cormie sailed via Japan to the United States, took train to New York and sailed on from there. But Tinkler was a wanderer, and the longer, more varied route probably appealed, and delayed his arrival in Britain.

Perhaps the most painful estrangement was the gradual distancing from his sister Edith. She had had cause to grumble at the picture he was painting in his letters of his life and thought. When she mentioned in 1921 that she had been to a 'Chop Suey house' in London with a Japanese man he reacted violently:

It is a great pity that people in England don't have more sense. If you went with an Asiatic in Shanghai you would never live it down. With a man it is different. I don't want a sister of mine doing things like that ... People in England are terribly ignorant in dealing with foreigners who should only be treated as the animals they are. The Japanese are only the best of a bad bunch.

She castigated his louche way of life, watching him turn from a man described by Ulverston's curate-in-charge as a 'fine, clean-minded and intelligent fellow', into a virulent racist atheist with a taste for Russian women. He made a point of disavowing religion. In 1923 SMP Central Registry eyebrows were raised and questions asked when he entered 'Nil' to a question on religious affiliation on a biographical form. 'Sir, Shall we accept this please?', asked the officer in charge. 'Yes,' answered the Deputy Commissioner. Tinkler was also not alone in attacking the image of China publicized by missionaries in Britain, nor alone in blaming them in large part for the nationalist upsurge in the 1920s. It was a common settler refrain, but his language was more violent than many. Missionaries, he ranted in June 1925, 'ruin every country in which they set foot ... selfish, illiterate fanatics whose proper place is the lethal chamber. Some day I will start a fund for the purpose of assisting missionaries to reach the kingdom of heaven (with cyanide of potassium).' Christianity 'started this damn nonsense in China . . . one of the greatest curses of "civilisation" . . . it would be better far to sow cholera germs than let missionaries loose in this country' (1927). Such hate must have been difficult to read. It wasn't wholly new – we remember those wartime strikers – but it becomes more generalized.

Thirty-six letters home were originally deposited in the Imperial War Museum. His aunt received nine of these, and Edith twenty-seven, but they are unevenly spread (apologizing for not writing, or more often noting his neglect, is a constant theme). After 1925 there is barely a letter a year. One year – 1921 – accounts for almost a third of the correspondence (thirteen), but from 1922 only one letter survives. Twice, the long early breaks (nine months in 1921, eight months in 1922–3) were deliberate. After her letter castigating his January 1921 account of his apparent connivance in extortion he kept mum: 'Surely you didn't expect I would write for a dickens of a long time after receiving it?' he wrote in surly mood in September. After his comments in his October 1922 'one finger exercise' about 'play, etc.', and about Elise, Edith told him off again. 'I wasn't offended at your letter,' he wrote the following June, 'at least not enough to cause me to stop writing.' We don't know what she said, as he didn't keep her letters, but it obviously was not an easy relationship and he plainly begrudged her long-distance assumption of a right to rebuke. Edith also questioned, it seems, his own jaundiced picture of Chinese politics and the required British solutions (war, war, war at all costs). Opening a letter in late March 1927, he asserted that it was 'apparently useless for any of us here to try to explain the "Chinese situation" that you ask about to the people at home'. Their 'ignorance is appalling', he added, and he was including her in this. The letters are often quite impersonal, and sometimes read as exercises in factual journalism, if not reportage, and in 1920/21 he dabbled in journalism in a slightly more serious way, by sending letters to the *China Press* – although 'the chiefs of police don't like that sort of thing' – even though the Shanghai tradition was for writers to send their card, but use a *nom de plume*. Quite what Edith made of the arrival of yet another four-page, single-spaced typed account of Chinese civil strife is hard to imagine; it was a letter, but it wasn't really communication.

In 1923 Edith had also written asking Maurice about the chances of employment for her in Shanghai. 'Yes, I could get you a job here, I guess, but I wouldn't,' he replied. The woman who ran the

swellest millinery store here is quite friendly with me, unfortunately she is the reformed proprietress of a snow white 'girl house' that was famous throughout half of China. Anyhow, working for wages here at your trade would be useless, there are so many Russian women who must work for pitifully low wages. And a lot of these concerns are run by Jews.

The empire world thrived on networks, the gentlemanly financiers who schooled and clubbed together, the Ulster neighbours for whose sons Sir Robert Hart found billets in the Chinese Maritime Customs Service, the Shanghailander oligarchs found a niche here, or even a senior police post there. In 1926, the appointment as an assistant commissioner of an insurance agent, a cricket-playing chum of Barrett's who had no police experience (and no Chinese), was a minor scandal in the press and amongst the rank and file.[24] Lodge life hummed with networking, and provided introductions for newcomers into almost any China community. But the servant classes, too, took hints and sought introductions using family or other connections to get on. Older men sought billets in the force or the Council's other services for sons and daughters. Fred West thought of China only at the suggestion of an aunt, working in Shanghai as a nanny, who had married a policeman and who came home on leave in 1921. 'What are you doing Fred? Why not try the police. They're recruiting in a couple of months.'[25] Once there, once settled with the lie of the land checked out, they summoned out sisters or other relations. James Douglas's sister married well, netting a senior man in the Public Works Department. Other sisters married into the force itself. They may have met men on leave in Britain, or else were pointed to openings as nurses or in other departments of the SMC. (The record holders were the Shanghai-born sisters Crank, who married five officers, and two of their brothers joined up.) Tinkler was having none of this. He didn't much rate the position and prospects of women in Shanghai, nor women in Shanghai. And it might cramp his style having a sister about. He'd have felt responsible, as well, for what might also be an unwelcome and unpredictable burden (unpredictable because, as we have seen, he had good cause to doubt her agreement with his race views). Perhaps, most of all, she would be a reminder of home, of dead-slow Ulverston. The anti-Semitism was an offensive flourish, but no sister of this 'White man' was going to work for 'Jews' in Shanghai.

Most men who landed in Shanghai were still tied into family networks. They might be sending money back to parents: 'He told me he had arranged to send £4 per month,' wrote one widowed mother with two children to support and a year's rent to pay. She'd not heard from her son for four years. W. E. Fairbairn withdrew some of his superannuation in 1920 to buy a home for relations. T. P. Givens withdrew from his to pay his brother for a farm in Tipperary. M. Ganly invested in his brother's building business in Dublin. In 1933 Dermot O'Neil was supporting his mother in Ireland and a brother in Shanghai who'd come to try his luck after Australia. Family might call them back, although they didn't always go. Fred West surrendered to family entreaty on his first long leave in 1925, and resigned to help out in his father's pub. But after a few weeks cleaning the pipes and serving the public he wrote off again to the force asking to rejoin: 'I thought I'd rather be waited on myself than serve somebody else.' Shanghai had spoiled him. Ex-soldier Alexander Hindson resigned after three years' service as 'his people at home', who had not seen him for six years, 'wanted him so much to come home'. After second thoughts he stayed on.

Tinkler wasn't much interested in family by the end of the decade. There were no real ties. His parents were dead, and he seems to have been drifting away from Edith, who was making her own way in business. Scarborough would have been a vision of the end of his English life. He wrote less frequently, and after 18 January 1930 did not write again. It may have partly been shame, for his thus far stellar career was to take twists which would have been difficult to report home after the loud boasting years. But it was mostly that he had found a place for himself in Shanghai, and in the empire world. There was no going back.

Maurice Tinkler arrived in Shanghai, 21 years old, schooled by war but still fresh, open and young. The sights he saw on the journey out were still 'ripping' and 'jolly'. But in Shanghai he re-learnt how to speak, picking up the necessary pidgin English ('I'll break out bime-by') but concentrating on the Yankee patter, and he learnt, self-consciously, to 'be a man', and to be a man alone ('I never had any "pals"'). He wrote tenderly about Shura, at the same time still chippily noting that 'we have a Russian lady translator in this office, but she's not very interesting and she knows my proper one [Shura] so could not flirt with her. One across the corridor is O.K. though.' There was always an audience: the 'two other fellows' to show off to about his love-life, the prigs in the French class, Elizabeth Young, Edith Tinkler, probably Lily Wilson too, treated to his accounts of the Danish-American attractions of studying French. Empire life was in large part a life of appearances: the appearance of strength, of virtue, superiority, confidence in the face of the subordinate. The appearance of solidarity, fitting in with one's peers, with not letting the side down, playing the game. Tinkler's own masculinity added to this, with his sensitivity to appearance, and to that self-respect of his. He dressed for the parts he chose, and lived them. Men like him were concerned in their most public and in their most intimate moments with the boundaries of empire, watching how they appeared in front of Chinese in public, aware of imperial duties and taboos even as they transgressed them in private. It could lead so very easily to physical violence. And it led quite directly to violence of language and thought. Some of this was bluster and boast, but Tinkler wrote, spoke and acted violently. Empire manliness was about sport, hard work, and hard play. For him it was also that tough-guy thing, soused in detective sauce. 'I didn't get on well with him,' remembered Fred West, who ran Central station when Tinkler had charge of the CID there. He was a 'funny cuss', a 'nasty bit of work' who 'lost his temper very quickly'. 'I had some trouble with him, he used to try and push you around, knocked my cap off . . . I used to keep out of his way . . . very easy to get into a fight with him.' This wasn't the man who sailed to Shanghai, but the man who knew that the city was altering him. Maurice Tinkler made and unmade himself. His choices were his to make, but like Elise and like Shura he was also made and unmade by Shanghai.

7

The End of the 'Good Old China'

On his Masonic jaunt to Chinkiang (Zhenjiang) in December 1925 Maurice enthused about the tiny British Concession: 'It is (like Foochow) a glimpse of the "good old China" of the earlier white men, when hospitality was the keynote of everything. In olden days in ports like this the foreigner did very little work (he still does at Chinkiang) made money easily and spent it easily.' The 'uncrowned King' of the place, U. J. Kelly, was 'secretary of the Doric Lodge, Chief of Police, Fire Department, Secretary of the British Municipal Council and of all the Clubs', and even that meant 'very little work', claimed Tinkler. He supervised thirty Chinese policemen, who locked up the British Concession every night. Such was the good old China. It wasn't really 1921, but it wasn't bad, even so. 'You walk into other people's houses without ringing the bell,' wrote Tinkler, 'and just order your drinks.' British diplomats had a less romantic view. Chinkiang was the 'reductio ad absurdum of the object of holding concessions in China'. It served no purpose other than to provide a steady income for a series of absentee landlords, and, of course, for men like U. J. Kelly.[1] It couldn't last. It didn't. Tinkler's nostalgic sketch was penned at the end of a year which had seen an unprecedented assault on the British position in China. The assault began in and because of Shanghai, and Maurice Tinkler was in the thick of it.

In testimony to the Mixed Court on 2 June, at the trial of fourteen men charged with rioting and distributing illegal pamphlets, Inspector Edward Everson, a softly spoken Welshman, began to give his version of the events that sparked the assault. 'At about 12.40 p.m., on Saturday, May 30th, a telephone message was received from the Commissioner of Police, to the effect that students were organising meetings and distributing leaflets outside the Settlement and that Inspectors in charge of districts were to take special steps to stop them from spreading into the Settlement.'[2] Everson commanded the Louza police station. An hour and a quarter after the warning word came in that students were holding meetings nearby on Nanking Road. He took Sub-Inspector Shellswell and two detectives out, broke up a small meeting and arrested three or four men, bringing them back to the station for questioning. They were followed in by fifteen more.

I asked the first man, who was making the speech, through an interpreter: 'What is the nature of your speech.' He said it was anti-Japanese. He said it was a protest by the students against the killing of a Chinese workman in a Japanese mill in the Pooto Road district ... I also asked them through an interpreter: 'Do you know that you cannot do that in the Settlement?' They said they could not help it, but they had to carry out the instructions of [the Students' Union]. I then picked out three of the ringleaders, and said: 'Very well, I am going to lock you up, and charge you with this offence.' I advised the remainder to go away, outside the Settlement and not make any trouble in the Settlement.

All insisted on being jailed together, and Everson obliged. But more reports were coming in of impromptu meetings in nearby streets, and over the next forty-five minutes Everson and his men were kept busy, sallying out to break them up and bring back 'ringleaders'. At 2.45 a 'huge crowd of hundreds' followed one of these parties back to the station, and forced their way into the charge-room. For the next twenty minutes Everson and six colleagues struggled to push them back out onto Nanking Road, and eastwards past the Town Hall. 'At that time I thought ... that we had the upper hand of things,' he continued. The crowd came to a standstill.

Everson locked up the station's back gate, and posted an armed guard just inside the front one, 'ready for any eventualities', and went to watch the crowd from the centre of the road.

I could see the flags and leaflets being thrown up in the air as ... crowds came round from Chekiang Road to join those in Nanking Road. This appeared to put new heart into the crowd ... and they started surging west ... towards the Police Station, pushing the Police before them . . . Every minute the crowd appeared to get denser and the cries became worse.

'Did you hear what they said?' the prosecutor asked.

In the last five minutes, before they made a mad rush, I could distinctly hear, in English: 'Kill the foreigners.' This was shouted in English and in Chinese . . . One continuous shout of 'Kill the foreigners.' I saw all the Policemen who were attempting to keep them back assaulted . . . They of course were using their batons and sticks . . . Tram cars and motor cars were all in a jam, and the crowd was jammed up with them. I shouted to the Police to get to one side quickly. As soon as some of the Police ran to the side of the street, against the wall for shelter, and others to the armed guard, inside the gate, I pulled out my pistol. I knew it was useless and pointed it here and there in the crowd . . . when the Police got into the Station behind the guard, the crowd made one blind rush for the last 10, 15 or 20 yards, one blind rush to the Station gate. Just as they were 6 feet or less from the Station gate, the order to fire was given.

'Ding, veh ding-ts-meh iau tang-sah,' he had been shouting, 'Stop, if you do not stop I will shoot.' He could barely be heard in the court-room, even, and 'thought I was shouting loud, but I had been shouting from 1.55. I thought I was making an awful noise.' About ten seconds later, at 3.37, Everson gave the order to fire. Nobody heard, so he snatched a rifle from one of the men and fired the first shot himself. His squad of eleven Sikh and a dozen Chinese police then fired two ragged close-quarter volleys with their carbines. Shellswell fired his pistol. 'Yes, certainly I fired to kill,' he said in his own testimony. 'In the event of danger to life and property, the order is to shoot to kill.' 'Those are my instructions,' added Everson, 'and I must obey them.' 'If I had not given the order at that time,' he concluded, 'The station would have gone, without a doubt.'

'I thought they would get my station,' he said to McEuen when the latter turned up, still kitted out in his race-day blazer and panama. No threat of demonstrations was going to keep McEuen from the races. He claimed to have passed the scene about twenty minutes before the firing, not noticing anything untoward. Few believed him.

Forty-four shots had cleared the street ('like magic', sneered Tinkler), but four young men lay dead outside the station gate. Another eight died later. Those in the front ranks of the crowd had stood no chance. Despite the portrayal of a bloodthirsty anti-foreign mob, all witnesses agreed that the crowd had been good-humoured almost up to the last. Why were there no other shootings when the demonstrations were taking place all over the Settlement, Everson was asked in court. He responded with a backhanded compliment to the dead. 'It must have been the bravest spirits amongst them who would go up, right up against the station gate, to start a meeting, and the people in that crowd were probably very much braver than the others. That is my opinion.' The Chinese Ministry of Foreign Affairs collated photographs of the wounded and the dead, preparing a dossier of their names and wounds. Ghostly photographs were taken of the white shirts worn by two of the men, to show that they had been shot in the back.[3] 'About twenty-five of the swines were killed or wounded,' gloated Tinkler, who spent the day arresting demonstrators near the Central Police Station. The events of 30 May brought out the worst in him. The crowd was 'shouting in such a frenzy as is only possible amongst hysterical Asiatics', 'The Sikhs love to fire . . . although they are a better race, the Chinese treat them with contempt for being a beaten nation and slaves of the British . . . One of the birds who bared his chest I am told, attracted so much attention that he was riddled.' It was not the first time the SMP had cleared a crowd like this. In April 1918 two men were killed when police 'quelled' a riot of rickshawmen. One marcher had been killed when May Fourth protesters had tried to march into the Settlement.[4] But those days were now over.

The May Thirtieth incident was instantly portrayed as a 'British' imperialist crime, but it was a China killing. Sikh and Chinese policemen made up the firing squad, and of the two Europeans who fired, one was married to a Chinese woman. Settler politics hindered resolution of the crisis, but the British empire took the flak. May Thirtieth was Britain's single biggest disaster in China, and it was the SMP's fault. Everson testified that there had been no time to send for reinforcements, and there was no riot squad. Anyway, it would have taken '3 minutes to explain what I wanted to a Sikh and then, probably,

it would not have been done correctly'. Everson, in private life a 'strict disciplinarian' who 'wouldn't stand any nonsense', ordered the firing because he believed that he would lose his station.[5] For some thirty minutes the handful of officers had been scuffling with the demonstrators, battling them out of the charge-room using anything which came to hand – sticks, stools, chairs. The closest body lay barely six yards from the alleyway entrance onto Nanking Road. Everson had a point, perhaps. This was not Amritsar, where six years earlier General Dyer had calmly set up his killing squads and gunned down hundreds of Indian protesters.[6] The Louza killings happened *in extremis*, although the Indian massacre echoed loudly in protests about May Thirtieth. The SMP should have been ready, however. In March 1922 Deputy Commissioner Hilton-Johnson had updated his 1919 assessment of potential threats facing the SMC, especially looking at lessons to be learnt from the recent Hong Kong seamen's strike.[7] This, he argued, had shown the need for the authorities to urge businesses to treat labour demands sympathetically, to support conciliation, and to avoid 'bombastic utterances in official proclamations and documents'. 'The days of "tremble and obey" among the Chinese masses have gone for good,' he continued, referring to the language of the old-style official proclamations pasted up by Chinese authorities and copied by the SMC. The slickness of the labour activism had shocked observers. He had recently 'considerably expanded' the police intelligence service, so the SMC should always have 'ample forewarning', and should be able to put into effect emergency plans to protect essential services (food, water, fuel, light, communications and – of course – 'domestic services, household servants' amongst others). As a result the Council updated and upgraded its 1920 state of emergency plans, and Hilton-Johnson was given another tranche of cash to take 'extra measures' to get political intelligence.

But despite this, despite a month of tension, despite the warnings from the Zhejiang-Jiangsu war crisis which was still being played out in the region, despite the warnings from the outcry over the Gabbutt torture case and the Dunne manslaughter trial, and despite the growing organized nationalism evident in the city since the May Fourth Movement and the communal clashes in Hongkew in 1918, the SMP was wholly unprepared on 30 May. There were no extra men on duty.

(And at Louza, out of 318 policemen, only about 20 were present at 3.37 p.m.) Language limited their capability in any case, as Everson showed in his evidence about communicating with his Sikhs and questioning prisoners. And the force had warning enough, as the American Chief Justice on the Commission of Inquiry pointed out, after reading the Police Daily Reports for the six months up to 30 May. Agitation over the treatment of Chinese workers in Japanese-owned mills had begun in February, and had re-ignited in mid-May. The killing of a factory worker by a Japanese foreman on 15 May had worsened the situation and galvanized activism. A memorial meeting for the victim was held on 24 May at which student and labour activists called for anti-Japanese agitation. Students' union meetings on 27 May called for a day of action on 30 May. They got one. Astute political analysis could see an explosion coming, and local political intelligence gathering should have better prepared the SMP for its black Saturday. The politics of industrial disputes had intermittently engaged the Council and Commissioner, as they deliberated the extent to which the SMP should stay out of disputes, caught as it was between labour, employers, local political authorities and foreign diplomats. But for Tinkler this was about the politics of hate. 'Soviet propaganda' had certainly been doing its work, but for him it was more visceral than that. The Chinese, 'cruellest and most cowardly race on earth', were 'against all progress introduced by foreigners', and 'one of the most filthy peoples in existence'. They hated Westerners, and they hated the Japanese, he claimed. And he hated them.

The day following the Nanking Road shootings Chinese merchants and students issued calls for a general strike, and on 1 June storekeepers shut up shop, while industrial workers downed tools. A triple strike of workers, students and merchants was announced, co-ordinated by a Federation of Labour, Commerce and Education. The Chinese Communist Party founded a General Labour Union on 31 May that co-ordinated the strike until it was suppressed in September. The SMC declared a formal 'State of Emergency', banning public meetings and any activity which might 'stir up animosity, foment trouble, cause public alarm or incite to a breach of the peace'. It placarded the Settlement with a manifesto justifying its actions, concluding still with outdated sternness: 'Warning is duly given. Let all Obey'. The Shanghai Volunteers Corps was called out and stayed on duty for thirteen weeks. By 4 June, 74,000 workers were on strike, including staff at the municipal power stations and waterworks, the telephone company, tramways, nearly all British and Japanese mills, foreign newspapers and others, including that feared walkout of domestic servants. The SMC had few Chinese friends at that moment. Demands presented to the Council ranged from punishment of those responsible, to an apology and indemnities, but also included broader issues. The Mixed Court should be returned and the SMC's still active expansionist plans reined in. The SMC had also upset friends and enemies alike by proposing to introduce new by-laws to license the press and so – it was claimed, probably rightly given the Dunne affair in 1924 – muzzle radical journalism. It outraged commercial opinion by seeking to bring in regulations to limit the employment of child labour in Chinese enterprises. Such regulations were seen as infringing Chinese sovereignty, undermining her economic competitiveness and punishing poorer families who relied on such income. The foreigners saw the hand of the Bolshevik and the Comintern's silver behind it all; they saw the new nationalism as merely the old 'antiforeignism' relabelled, and misunderstood the saliency of their little local difficulties. The SMP was mobilized from 30 May until 16 September; throughout June and July all leave was cancelled, and the men spent the hot humid summer confined to barracks. It hardly helped their tempers.

Violence was constant at the start. On 1 June a crowd attempted to burn some tramcars at the junction of Nanking and Chekiang Road, outside the Wing On store. On 2 June Tinkler was having tea with a Russian detective in an American café on Nanking Road when they heard firing from the New World amusement centre. A mounted detachment of the American company of the Shanghai Volunteer Corps had been ambushed. Both men rushed over, but were 'too late to use our pistols as the firing had stopped'. About '350 rounds were fired officially,' he noted, 'but a lot of birds fired scores of rounds of their own private stock.' 'Only war can now make it possible for whites to live in China,' he claimed, and he was eager for war. 'I have been longing for an opportunity to kill a bunch but have had no chance of firing yet.' So he took his own revenge instead on about 1 June.

I had a student of the patriotic 'dare to die' type in a cell at Central Station. He had been trying to tear down a Municipal Proclamation . . . Just for a joke I told him that he would be shot at 6 a.m. next day. As soon as he savvied the meaning of the different dialect he was screaming and crawling about the floor of the cell, begging for mercy and trying to lick our boots. This is typical of the whole Chinese 'nation'.

It is no surprise that he was so cheerily belligerent and unsympathetic. His earliest political comment was tart. On the voyage to Taiwan in 1921 he met three Fujianese students studying at an American-run college. 'What did [he] think of the Peace Conference in Washington?' they asked. 'Not much,' he replied. The Washington Naval Conference mapped out a balance of power for the Pacific that aimed to hem in the Japanese. But the powers with interests in China also undertook to respect the sovereignty and integrity of China, and to re-examine extraterritoriality and other aspects of the treaty system. Tinkler knew what was happening, but unlike many observers had no sympathy whatsoever with Chinese aspirations. Empire made him what he was. Without it he was nobody. So there was no ground for respect, or re-examination; that was surrender. Tinkler was fighting for his life.

In all, at least twenty-two Chinese were killed during what became known as the May Thirtieth Movement, which galvanized radical politics nationally. In Peking caricatures appeared on the city walls showing helmeted SMP men gloating over bleeding Chinese corpses, captioned 'SHOOT TO KILL'.[8] The SMC counter-attacked by issuing two dozen pamphlets on such topics as 'What happens under Bolshevism', and 'The Soviet: China's enemy'. It plastered caricatures of 'The Agitator' on telegraph poles and hoardings, posted out its versions of the events, broadcast others on the Settlement's new radio stations and prepared propaganda slides for film theatres. But appeals 'To the peaceable Chinese of Shanghai' cut little ice.[9] Membership of the Chinese Communist Party leapt from about 1,000 in May 1925 to 11,250 a year later.[10] Quiet Inspector Everson was its most effective recruiter. The Mixed Court thought little of the charges he presented against the accused, and imposed only token punishments. The Diplomatic Body in Peking dispatched a delegation to negotiate a solution, based on its investigation of events. The SMC rejected the report. McEuen was 'one of the oldest and most valued servants' of the SMC, claimed Chairman Sterling Fessenden in a letter expressing the Council's categorical dissent from the censure of the Commissioner and Council by the Consular Body, rooting its objection in its claim to be responsible only to the Shanghai landrenters.[11] A Judicial Commission of Inquiry was then established to break the impasse, but the Chinese boycotted it. The Commission failed to agree a report, but the American judge demanded McEuen's head, and located the events of 30 May wholly within a rotten and explosive political context that had resisted any recognition of Chinese political and national evolution. At the tail end of the year Everson and McEuen were forced to resign, 'under conditions mutually agreed upon', as McEuen noted – which meant a very fat pension.[12] Fessenden later described both the Commission and the scapegoating as 'camouflage'. The SMP hardly tried to stay in hiding. One thousand police gave McEuen an allegedly unofficial and 'stirring' farewell at the quayside.[13] He was 'easygoing', noted Tinkler to Edith, 'but otherwise of little use'. McEuen took his pension off to Obama, Japan. Everson took his stipend and family back to Machin, near Gloucester. 'There is no suggestion', went a letter of appreciation to him, 'that you failed in or exceeded your duty as a responsible police officer in any respect whatever.' 'No blame whatever attached to me,' he wrote carefully in his diary.[14]

Tinkler was transferred to the CID's Intelligence Office (IO) in early

O.C. 11 : 17   **FRI., JAN. 1**

Result of Judicial Inquiry into riots of May 30th published & no blame whatever attached to me

June to replace a man who had gone on long leave. Given his comments on May Thirtieth, a shift to a more deskbound job was probably just as well. Later renamed Special Branch, the IO dealt with political issues very broadly defined indeed, and had grown out of the appointment of an Intelligence Officer in 1898 to report 'on any matters with regard to the Chinese that the Council may wish to be enlightened on', and to assist detective work.[15] 'I have to know everything that happens in connection with the various strikes and write a report covering the whole lot daily,' he boasted to Edith, 'I am very popular with the newspaper men and can't get rid of them,' he continued, happily hooking up with the hacks once more. One of his daily reports survives in the Special Branch papers in the US National Archives, a competent summary of the 'General Situation' over the twenty-four hours preceding 10 June 1925.[16] Tinkler would have been a prime candidate for shoring up the IO personnel – especially given his language aptitude and his intelligence work in 1924 – and the temporary shift would have been made with an eye to testing him for a formal transfer. To Edith he boasted of a central role: 'I prosecute seditious magazines, gramophone records etc., arrest deported Bolsheviks (Chinese) from Java and Hong Kong etc., etc., take a look at the Arsenal or Lunghwa military yamen [headquarters] once in a while or write reports on whether or not the Chinese Branch ought to have a rise' (the latter file sits on record in Shanghai). He also read the foreign press. Well, perhaps he did all this, perhaps not. Tinkler's list touches on most of the concerns of this key unit, run by a Tipperary man, T. P. Givens, which was quickly developing into an important political policing resource, especially in the battle against communism in the city and beyond, and against other perceived threats to the settlement and to the culture of colonialism: Indian nationalism, *Lady Chatterley's Lover*, the visit to Shanghai of George Bernard Shaw, pornography featuring European women, Korean independence groups and the many other subjects of the twenty thousand separate files created between 1916 and 1941. It followed up leads and queries from friendly diplomats and intelligence agencies, prepared and circulated a daily report and press translations to the SMC, newspapers, utility companies and diplomats. Tinkler claimed in late December 1925 to have 'hated the IO'. It suited his politics, but would not have suited his temperament. Access to a car and a roving commission was probably fun, but much of the work was deskbound and clerical. He wasn't much interested in knowing: doing was all.

From May 1925 the balance of the content of Tinkler's letters shifts towards long political tirades. The China crisis was a major international news story, and Shanghailanders came off badly. Arthur Ransome's articles for the *Manchester Guardian* gave best form to this picture of the settler die-hard, living in the 'Ulster of the East'.[17] Tinkler picked up on some of this, blasting some 'socialist swine who described us as 17,000 shady characters' in 1927. The diplomats in Peking and at home were turning against the SMC. They had been happy to leave things be as long as the International Settlement fulfilled its role as Britain's trade bridgehead in China. But after 1925 it became apparent that there really was a 'Shanghai problem', and that the problem was the fact of settlement and settler power. May Thirtieth had caused China-wide anti-British agitation. A massive seamen's strike in Hong Kong crippled the colony's trade until well into 1926. The SMC and the SMP were no longer part of the solution to the problem of British trade in China. As historically presented, the self-regulation of extraterritoriality and the concessions saved Britons from cruel and haphazard Chinese justice. Shanghailanders reinforced the point in letters home. 'Less than a year ago a number of public executions took place,' Tinkler wrote in July 1926, 'the heads of the victims being displayed in cages of bamboo hung on telegraph poles.' If extraterritoriality was abandoned then 'foreigners will soon be treated likewise by a cowardly and merciless horde of savages'.

Murderous 'xenophobia', of the type exemplified for foreigners by the 1900 Boxer uprising, would be the norm. But Maurice Tinkler and his colleagues were now the problem, not the solution. Everson ordered the shooting, claimed the former Shanghai Consul-General Sir John Pratt, because it was the 'simplest and most efficient way of restoring order'.[18] 'Who is the Boxer?' asked a Chinese poster, answering its own query with a caricatured bayonet-wielding Shanghai policeman.[19]

Tinkler hoped that an outsider would be brought in to run the force. None of the force's officer corps was 'fit to handle it properly', he told Edith in December 1925. 'I hope we get an up-to-date American. Some of the Britishers round here think it is 1825 not 1925 and nearly 1926.' May Thirtieth led to a sustained public exploration of the workings of the International Settlement regime, and few liked what they saw. But it was a Britisher, Ivo Barrett, who took over as Commissioner of Police, although this was merely delaying effective reform. As Commissioner he did not shine. Council Chairman, later Secretary-General, Sterling Fessenden battled with him over matters of style and priority. Hypersensitive to press criticism, a petty tyrant when dealing with men, especially over marriage issues, Barrett attempted the wholesale politicization of policing in the Settlement. 'The policy of arbitrary and often harsh discrimination against the Chinese is in great measure responsible for the present troubles in the settlement,' thundered Fessenden in 1928, referring to what he saw as SMP inconsistency in suppressing Chinese gambling, but ignoring that 'carried on by foreigners on a colossal scale'.[20] The force used highly restrictive licensing laws to limit and police Chinese clubs and associations, while foreign clubs needed no licensing. Little latitude was given to any actions which smacked of political agitation. But Chinese politics gave the SMP no let-up. In the aftermath of the mass activism of the May Thirtieth Movement, the Chinese nationalist party of the late Sun Yat-sen, the Guomindang, in alliance with the Chinese Communist Party, planned a northern expedition from its south China Canton base, to clean up the warlord shambles and re-unify the country.[21] The alliance was the price Sun paid for Soviet and Comintern advisers and material support, but it proved to be an uneasy and factious relationship. In June 1926, now led by Chiang Kai-shek, the party's National Revolutionary Army moved north, with Shanghai as its prime target. The military thrust was accompanied by sustained mass mobilization, largely developed by CCP activists, of labourers, farmers and students in particular. The intertwined twin evils of 'warlordism' and 'imperialism' became the focus of the huge propaganda campaigns. In Hunan province, one rising CCP activist, Mao Zedong, watched young children playing: 'If one gets angry with another, if he glares, stamps his foot and shakes his fist,' he wrote, 'you will then immediately hear from the other the shrill cry of "Down with imperialism!".'[22] In Shanghai the 'warlords' – in the shape of Sun Chuanfang, with whose agents SMP relations were 'most cordial'[23] – and the 'imperialists' sat side by side.

Normal policing continued, of course, but sustained political activism entered the equation. The fallout from the 1924–5 Zhejiang-Jiangsu war – the abundance of weapons, the deserters, the defeated and demobbed soldiers – fuelled another armed crime wave. There were 109 reported armed robberies in 1923, and 448 in 1926. Nine Chinese policemen were killed on duty in 1926, while none had been killed in 1923. Underground work by Guomindang and Chinese Communist Party activists added to the workload, and the new confidence of nationalism saw major challenges to the SMP's policing sovereignty in the outside roads when the Chinese authorities placed patrols of their own on some of them. 'Instead of ordering us to fire on them,' Tinkler wrote to Edith in July 1926, 'the Council and higher authorities have simply written feeble letters of protest against these outrages.' His letters show how expatriate life took the crisis in its stride. He raged but was soon back at play, as they all were. Serving as Master of the Lodge Erin, he attended a rich series of installation meetings and banquets at the Astor House, the Masonic club and the Shanghai Club. Vacations continued up country. Improvements in pay and conditions became a hot issue in the force, although his own appointment to Sub-Inspector helped. But he still wanted war: 'The way the foreign powers are "crawling" to these damned yellow pigs is nauseating. Unless there is war quickly, life will soon be impossible for foreigners in China,' he claimed in July 1926.

War, of a sort, came. By November 1926 National Revolutionary Army forces had captured the Yangtsze cities of Wuhan and Kiukiang

(Jiujiang). Sustained activism led to the evacuation of the British concessions in those ports. Foreign refugees poured into Shanghai and other coastal treaty ports from the interior. The British Foreign Secretary announced important shifts in China policy in a bid to deflect the anti-British focus of the agitation, but also dispatched 20,000 British empire troops as a Shanghai Defence Force ('Shaforce'), while the Royal Navy's China Station was reinforced. Tinkler was not alone in believing that war was imminent, and that China was the chosen ground on which Soviet communism was to be blocked and then rolled back. It looked to many sailing eastwards as if Cold War One had turned hot at last. British empire was under attack at home: Ireland had been severed, and now there was the Labour government of 1924 – 'exposed' as a Comintern tool by the *Daily Mail's* publication of the forged Zinoviev letter – and the General Strike of 1926. Empire was under attack abroad, in India, Egypt and now in China. The British and other anti-Bolsheviks conspired and acted together where appropriate. But in the meantime how lucky was settler Shanghai. The city was chock-full of smart young officers who needed entertaining, and solid military bands to entertain them. Shaforce units camped out on the racecourse, and went on route marches about the Settlement: 'nothing has enthused Shanghai more', gushed the *North China Daily News*.[24] They added real martial empire class to receptions and national day balls, and Shanghailanders truly felt themselves in the empire mainstream, if not its front line. Tinkler was not too impressed. 'Our men looked shabby and badly dressed', especially – but of course – 'beside the US Marines'. Such things were important to the Chinese, he claimed. After all, appearance and face mattered to them. Not all visitors liked what they saw either: 'A thoroughly suburban-commercial population', sniffed one naval visitor. 'I can't stand the local people,' wrote a young officer in the Suffolks. Shanghailanders, for all their empire enthusiasm, were more often than not derided by empire's agents.[25]

Tinkler had been enjoying himself hugely through all of this. Hilton-Johnson plucked him out again and sent him off to do military intelligence work in the Shanghai region, reporting on the military situation. It was 'done for the British government and not particularly for the International Settlement', he noted. It was the sort of favour that

earned Hilton-Johnson a stout consular recommendation for his CMG in 1928.[26] A rather nice motor launch was provided and Tinkler, one British colleague, and two Chinese assistants headed out of the concession to keep tabs on the forces of Marshall Sun Chuan-fang. Sun had run the Shanghai region since the 1924 war, laying claim to the five eastern provinces. But his forces were being pushed north by the NRA, and when Tinkler first made contact with them were in 'full flight' from Hangzhou, which fell to the nationalists on 18 February 1927. Tinkler's boat, the *Pursuit*, motored up the Huangpu and along the creeks to watch Nationalist forces take Kash-ing on 23 February. After returning to load up with stores the party sailed to Songjiang, now headquarters of Sun's Third Army Corps, where they spent a fortnight. There they entertained visiting British officers ('Brigadier Generals, staff Colonels etc.'), and escorted them up to the front line, sometimes on foot, sometimes on one of Sun's three armoured trains. From the photographs it looks more like a holiday than a trip to a war zone, and the snapshots were slotted into an album between his 1923 houseboat trip and postcards of his ocean voyages. From 12 March, as Sun's forces moved back, Tinkler was making daily sallies out by train or by car to watch the situation, latterly with a young British military intelligence officer from Shaforce. On 20 March they were cut off by the nationalist advance, and lost the car, facing a 20-mile walk back to the Settlement. No entry was made on his record about this work, but the SMC gave him a parchment scroll thanking him for his services; it was marked 'SECRET'.

On 22 March the nationalist forces entered Chinese-controlled Shanghai. Their communist allies had launched a general strike to undermine Sun Chuanfang's position on 19 February, but it had been violently suppressed: a few beheadings worked wonders. For its part the SMP 'arrested all persons found intimidating loyal workers and distributing inflammatory literature' and closed 'bases of agitation'.[27] But buoyed by the rapid advance of the NRA the communist General Labour Union called another strike on 21 March, one day before the army's arrival, and the Workers' Supervisory Corps launched an armed uprising that captured all police stations and government offices in Chinese territory. On occasions the defeated troops rushed the

Settlement defences seeking sanctuary; such was the panic at times that the foreign defence forces joined combat with them, but many were disarmed and allowed in. The 21 March uprising was an audacious CCP flanking movement aiming to seize the Shanghai prize from Chiang Kai-shek. But Chiang had been preparing for just such a Shanghai problem for some months. He had already bloodied leftist noses in Canton in March 1926 in an internal coup which aimed to restrict communist influence. He was ready to act now. An informal alliance of Shanghai capitalists, gangsters, Guomindang rightists and the concession authorities went into action in the early morning of 12 April, when the foreign defence forces closed tight their perimeter, having been 'secretly made cognisant of the events which were to take place in the morning'.[28] Armed squads of Green Gang members disguised as labour militants were transported through the concessions into position for a general assault on labour and communist strongpoints. NRA units feigned neutrality but disarmed the workers. By the end of the day their organizations were broken, and hundreds of their activists were dead. The following day protest demonstrations were fired on by NRA troops, to bloody effect far outstripping that of the SMP in 1925. The CCP–Guomindang alliance was in bloody tatters.

Despite the passing of time, and despite the turn against Stalinism and the revolutions of 1989, the men and women of the Chinese Communist Party are still cast as those in the right, fighting black forces of oppression. Theirs is the just cause. The April coup is entrenched in the mythology of this righteous struggle through André Malraux's 1933 novel *La Condition humaine* (usually translated as *Man's Fate*), which takes as its focus the activities on 21 March and 11–12 April of a cast of communists heading towards mostly grisly ends. But for the men of empire these romantic revolutionaries were a real threat to Christian civilization. 'War with Soviet Russia and China is absolutely necessary for the continued existence of the British Empire,' wrote Tinkler. Foreigners on the spot, who knew, as those in cosy England could not, the dangers of inaction, would provoke that conflict themselves if necessary. The political analysis was a race analysis: 'if we admit that any of the yellow or black races are our "brother workers" and such tripe (when nearly all of them are only a shade above the animals),' he sneered at Edith, 'we are admitting our eclipse as they outnumber us fifty to one.' Race thinking and anti-communism blended imperceptibly, and they were close to the heart of mainstream politics. If the concessions at Hankow or Kiukiang were not retaken, Tinkler claimed, then 'the Empire will deteriorate to a tenth-rate power in a few years (it is already a second-rate one)'. But empire adapted. The Foreign Office did not heed the settler demand, and did not listen to the China hands. The British didn't storm the lost Yangtsze ports, and worked instead to counter the underlying threat from the USSR by developing a conciliatory China policy.

The hysteria of early 1927 soon subsided. Once dubbed the 'red general', Chiang Kai-shek revealed himself to be a reliable anti-communist, even a Christian, marrying Song Meiling in a Methodist ceremony. Missionary hearts were all a flutter, and probably so forgot themselves as to swing to the jazz tunes played at the reception by Whitey Smith's band. Chiang's regime set about consolidating its rule, knocking out its remaining leftist opponents, launching a further strike north to defeat or suborn its remaining enemies, and, disturbingly, touching off a short vicious battle in Shandong province with Japanese forces, who trounced the Chinese. With a new, well-organized anti-communist neighbour in place in the shape of the Chinese 'Special Municipality of Greater Shanghai', and its police, the Public Security Bureau (PSB), the SMP could work systematically to fight communism. A 1928 file shows the dirty work being done. On 17 April 1927 a letter from the new military authorities to Commissioner Barrett requested the arrest of eighteen communists, allegedly 'residing within the British settlement'. One of these was Luo Yinong, on whose head was placed a $1,000 reward. At the age of 27 Luo was already a key figure in the CCP. Radicalized by the May Fourth Movement in Shanghai, he had joined the party in 1921, spent four years studying in Moscow and played a key role in the Shanghai uprisings of 1926–7. On 15 April 1928 an informer set the SMP Special Branch onto him. Luo was seized at a house on Gordon Road, taken before the Provisional Court on 18 April and then handed over to representatives of the Nationalist Defence Commissioner. He was executed three days later, leaving his possessions to charity and urging that his comrades 'be not discouraged by his execution'. The informer was paid his handsome $1,000 – 'quietly for obvious reasons' – by T. P. Givens, in the presence of another senior officer and an interpreter.[29] Over the next decade Special Branch played a key role in driving the Chinese Communist Party out of the city, arresting hundreds of activists, many of whom were handed over to the PSB, and many of whom were executed. And it successfully frustrated Comintern activities, most notably in the summer of 1931 by shutting down its local 'Department for International Liaison' – which serviced its Far Eastern Bureau and other organs – with the arrest of Russian co-ordinators Yakov Rudnik, known in Shanghai amongst other names as Hilaire Noulens, and his wife Tatyana Moiseenko.[30] The SMP liaised closely with the PSB, and with MI6 and colonial special branches. The Noulens arrests were triggered by evidence found with the arrest of a Comintern agent in Singapore. The voluminous documentation seized was shared with MI6, and so with the British domestic Security Service, MI5, for whom it was hugely enlightening.[31] Empire was a community of shared ideals, and information; anti-communism became one of those ideals.

But, as with other recent political upheavals, 1927 brought with it a sharp increase in crime, and crime was the SMP's central concern.

Armed robbery and kidnapping spiralled: here was sustained and systematic political terrorism. After spring 1927 the Guomindang used kidnapping to raise funds and to intimidate Shanghai business circles. Reported abductions rose to 27 that year from 5 in 1926, but the figure grossly understated the problem, as even in these cases 'little or no cooperation is received by the Police', or the police were 'hoodwinked' by families to throw them off the scent.[32] Most cases were simply not reported. Violence became more routine. There were 1,458 reported cases of armed robbery in 1927, up threefold on 1926. Fourteen members of the force, and one police special were killed in 126 shooting incidents. In 1928 reported armed robberies fell to 981, but police casualties stood at 9 dead; in 1929 there were 707 armed robberies, and 2 dead SMP. Although the level of violence subsided the police plainly could not cope on their own. Shaforce provided military back-up, mounting curfew enforcement and anti-kidnapping patrols. The SMC then acquired its own small mercenary army, the eventually 430-strong SVC Russian Unit (later 'Russian Regiment').[33] The Russians provided back-up for police search parties, and for serious incidents. Relations between Shanghai policemen and the Russians were not good, as the Russians were accorded little respect. 'You don't need to salute these bloody people,' shouted Sergeant Young boozily at an army colleague who attempted to salute the Russian Unit's commander in April 1927. (Actually he did, and to reinforce the point Young was reduced in rank.) Russian recruitment into the permanent ranks of the SMP after 1926 (they were first recruited temporarily in 1923) worried the rank and file. A 1927 memo lauded their keenness, discipline and aptitude, but claimed that their Chinese colleagues had no respect for them, that their stateless status would lead to problems with the Chinese authorities, and that if there was any royalist revival in Russia they would probably abandon their posts.[34] Large-scale recruitment ceased the following year, although the Russian Regiment was maintained up to 1941 when it was merged into the SMP as the Russian Auxiliary Detachment.

The SMC also had to adapt to the nationalism that it had once vilified. The Guomindang established a national government in Nanjing under the effective control of Chiang Kai-shek. Its anti-imperialism was certainly watered down, closely associated as it was with the now-banned Chinese Communist Party, and the political radicals now heavily distrusted by Chiang and his rightist allies. But the new government still followed a specifically nationalist agenda, opening negotiations to rework existing treaties, and to reclaim Chinese sovereignty over such areas as the tariff autonomy, control of the Chinese Maritime Customs and other foreign-dominated agencies. The British were drawn into negotiations over their redundant concessions, such as sleepy Chinkiang, which was surrendered in 1930. In 1931 talks on the repeal of extraterritoriality and the surrender of the International Settlement reached an advanced stage before the Japanese invasion of Manchuria that September prompted the National Government to shelve such moves. But in Shanghai there was a sustained campaign to remodel the Settlement regime. Small details of colonial rule which loomed so disastrously large in foreign and Chinese press opinion were revised. The gates of most of the Settlement's parks were opened to Chinese. Stalled initiatives to introduce Chinese members onto the SMC were pushed through in 1928. The Council set about repairing its past neglect of such issues as Chinese education in the Settlement, and employment of Chinese in substantive positions in the administration and its services. It attempted to co-opt new allies and preserve a foreign core to the administration that might just manage to survive in the new order. But the SMC and the SMP also faced a flanking manœuvre as Chiang Kai-shek established the new Special Municipality and police force. The SMC had had little competition in the past two decades from local Chinese authority, but the new city government aimed to out-model the SMC, in preparation for assuming control of the settlements, and meanwhile it set out to roll back foreign power from areas outside them.[35]

The policing context was changing sharply. The Chinese regained sovereignty over the old Mixed Court, where Tinkler had worked in 1920. A new Shanghai Provisional Court was established in January 1927. There followed a marked decrease in the ability of the police to make prosecutions stick, as they saw it. It even, for a brief period in 1927, saw the abandonment of the death penalty for crimes of violence. Barrett showered the Council with letters of complaint about inadequate sentences. At the peak of the 1927 crisis on 19 March he had even demanded authority to hand over to Sun Chuanfang's military authorities 'any person found in possession of arms without a licence or charged with armed robbery, crimes of violence, and offences connected with labour unrest'.[36] Barrett wanted the SMP itself to act as hanging judge. He didn't get the chance, but the new court began to work (helped by the sacking of the 'grossly inefficient' SMC prosecuting solicitors), and the SMP and the PSB found that they could easily reconcile some of their differences over a wide range of issues. Besides, as Fessenden argued in 1930, the SMC's position regarding the refusal to allow Chinese government agencies to operate in the International Settlement could not be defended 'on legal grounds alone'. The Council had prevented the collection of taxes from Chinese citizens 'through the exercise of police power', not by treaty, and as a result of 'sound considerations of political and practical expediency rather than abstract right'.[37] Expediency now suggested that the Council develop a much more flexible relationship with Chinese power.

Reform of the SMP was now overdue. A twenty-two-year veteran of the Lahore Police, W. G. Clarke was appointed as an Assistant Commissioner to replace Barrett as commander of the Sikh Branch in 1925. The political situation in India required 'an increasingly minute supervision of both Sikh police and Mohammedan warders' in Shanghai. Clarke's relatively brief career in the SMP was significant for the supervision he gave to the CID, and then the force as a whole. Barrett pushed for Clarke's appointment as CID chief as early as 1926. There were sound reasons for placing an outsider in the post, and an outsider with police rather than military experience. The 'general reputation and integrity of the personnel' was felt to be lacking, and the department needed modernizing. Clarke set about the task with gusto and by June 1928 Barrett was reporting that CID was 'obtaining results never before obtained in its history'.[38] Large numbers of men were drafted in, the branch was reorganized and the shadow organization of Chinese operatives incorporated into the structure of the force. In particular, resources and systems were put in place to facilitate political work. The Intelligence Office was reorganized and new record systems put in place. By September 1928 Clarke was engaged by Fessenden to produce a full-scale inquiry into the SMP. The Council was trying to rehabilitate the force in private, keeping its dirty laundry

out of the public eye when every fault might have political consequences. The armed robbery boom and the kidnapping wave were
spectacularly undermining public confidence. The events of May
Thirtieth 'shook the confidence of the public in the Police, not only in
Shanghai but throughout China', Fessenden claimed in October 1928,
and 'there have been constant rumours that "all is not well" with
the Police Department'. 'To say nothing', he concluded, 'of outspoken
criticism in the public press.'[39] The force had been run for too long as
a 'watertight compartment', the systems in place not only 'contributed
to the causes which gave rise to the May 30th affair, but failed the
community in the most critical moment of its existence'. The 'same
system rendered possible the disgraceful conditions disclosed by the
Gabbutt case and other incidents'. The 'fetish of military discipline
pure and unadulterated' was hampering reform.[40] Barrett retaliated
by rallying his fellow insiders, 'intriguing' against Clarke (a 'Lahore
Irishman' he sneered) – to such an extent that the CID chief was 'on the
verge of a breakdown' before taking leave in January 1929. The internal
inquiry foundered. Before leaving, Clarke made very serious allegations about Barrett to the SMC (but the details remain obscure). The
Council swiftly called on the British Minister in Peking to help them
find an Indian police officer to reorganize the force. Frederick Wernham
Gerrard arrived from the Bombay police in May 1929.[41] Barrett had
taken long leave. Gerrard 'will not teach us much', he wrote to
Fessenden from London, idling away his time at a colonial police
senior officers' course and misjudging his moment and correspondent.
'We have very little to learn from the London police,' he also told
Fessenden, who had him at last. Both Clarke and Barrett were sacked.[42]
Gerrard was appointed Commissioner in October 1929 in order to
put his reorganization into place, but then stayed on until 1938.

Tinkler, like all his colleagues, was heavily involved in this new
drive to restore confidence in the SMP and the SMC. CID launched
an anti-kidnapping and armed robbery campaign in 1928–9 – and as
we saw in Chapter 5 – Tinkler worked from Central station on the
type of well-publicized raid that made some difference, at least to
public confidence. The new political complexion to the SMC saw it
move sharply against both foreign and Chinese gambling, and it moved
back from Barrett's flirtation with allies of the Green Gang asking to

establish a Settlement opium monopoly.[43] Part of the SMC's overhaul was implicitly concerned with demonstrating that it was not in hock to gangsters. After almost three years of uncertainty, the crushing of the left and the establishment of a new stable-looking local and national regime was a huge relief. 'The future of Shanghai is a glowing one,' noted Indian tycoon Sir Victor Sassoon in January 1928. He was backing his confidence with his money, and was publicizing plans for what was to become a new landmark on the Bund, Sassoon House and the towering Cathay Hotel. Confidence was expressed in stone elsewhere. The Masonic club moved into new premises with wholesome facilities aimed at diverting 'younger masons' from seeking 'relaxation in less favourable places'. Barrett had even inaugurated an annual Police Ball in February 1928.[44] It cannot have convinced his critics that his mind was fully on policing. Sassoon also invested in dogs. A new scam had surfaced for the police in 1927, when a syndicate which included once and former SMC councillors, among them sometime chairmen H. E. Arnhold and Brigadier E. B. MacNaghten, sounded the Council out about the establishment of a greyhound racing club. The syndicate became a company and opened Luna Park in May 1929, which faced competition in Frenchtown from the Canidrome. This was, remarked Fessenden, purely 'a medium for Chinese gambling', and a 'public nuisance'. But this did not stop Assistant Commissioner Martin making a useful profit on Luna Park shares, nor Maurice Springfield investing in a dozen dogs. This was industrialized gambling, with Shanghai's legal peculiarities brazenly exploited on a vast scale. 'Saturday nights', claimed John Pal, 'were "Luna Park nights".'[45] The Shanghai of 1919 was going, that city where the Kalgan Livery Stables on Chaufoong Road still hired out broughams and victorias with pony or horse ('*much* cheaper than motor-cars when you want a vehicle to *wait* for you a long time,' noted the Revd Darwent[46]). Four and a half thousand of the automobiles that so obsessed Tinkler were licensed in the Settlement alone by 1930, up from only 209 on his arrival in 1919. The Bund skyline was changing. Social change followed in the wake of political compromise; Chinese and foreign elites were beginning to interact more often, and began genuinely to get along. They had many interests in common, not least hostility to the left.

This new Shanghai was a minefield for an 'old-timer' like Tinkler, and this is where he starts to come unstuck, shortly after his return from long leave on Christmas Day 1928. In May 1929 his aggressive individualism was sharply checked. On the night of 2/3 May the Chinese caterer to both the American Club and the Canidrome (the greyhound stadium in Frenchtown), was kidnapped from his home. Feng Yixiang (Y. C. Vong) returned from the stadium after the evening's racing was done, and was dropped off by his driver at the alleyway entrance to the building, behind the American Club, to which he'd recently moved in the face of new kidnapping threats (having escaped a previous abduction a year earlier). Three men were waiting for him in the Honan Road alleyway, and forced him out along the street to a waiting car.[47] He was within fifty yards of the Central police station, as even the *North China Daily News* had to point out, and Tinkler was duty detective. There was a board of inquiry. The full file has not resurfaced, but Tinkler was found guilty of gross neglect of duty for failing to 'promptly and diligently inquire' into the report of the kidnapping. What happened was described in exquisite detail in the outraged pages of the new American-owned *Shanghai Evening Post*, reproduced with glee in J. B. Powell's *China Weekly Review*. Both printed at length the statement of Kao Veng-mieu, a waiter at the Club, who, with a colleague, Yung Foo, went to Central police station at about 2 a.m. to report the abduction. The uniformed sergeants in the charge-room called for the duty detective, who at the third request demanded that the men be brought to his room. 'We went upstairs', reported Kao,

and found a big tall foreigner, wearing street-clothes but without any collar or tie, in the room. He was wearing slippers.

When our report was being interpreted, the foreigner interrupted and called Yung Foo and myself 'brainless coolies' and refused to listen to our story. He then ordered Wong, a Chinese detective, called. He refused to listen again when Wong started to tell him of the kidnapping. He refused Wong's request that a report be made, then sat down, wrote a few words on a piece of paper, stopped and then tore up the report.

With this he got up and came over to Yung Foo and seized both of us by our collar and knocked our heads together. He declared that our report was false and ordered us out of the room and pushed us towards the stairs.

The 'big foreigner' – Tinkler of course – ordered the men to be detained in a cell until the morning, and retired to sleep.

'The implication of this report', noted the *China Weekly Review*, 'is that the foreign police officer referred to was intoxicated', and had had the men detained until he 'could become sufficiently sober to resume his duties'. The drink charge is not reflected in Tinkler's punishment (but there would have been little evidence by the time he surfaced that morning). Presumably he spun the line to his superiors that the two men were making little sense, were incoherent and 'excitable' (a common racist shorthand), and were perhaps covering something up. Servants were suspect, and Yung Foo had witnessed the actual abduction. Perhaps a little time cooling off in the station cells would help focus their minds, or perhaps he claimed that he thought it might sweat a little truth out of them, or at least calm them down. Barrett had articulated the long-held police prejudice in 1928, that, in kidnapping, servants were 'often the organisers of the crime'.[48] And we have seen how other policemen dealt with servants. Five nights later Feng Yixiang was rescued from a small boat moored in a creek just outside the Settlement by a party led by DSI Henry. Twelve men were eventually arrested, but on 10 May the inquiry board met and censured Tinkler. He really had banged the wrong heads. Perhaps that old boy network that he had noted long ago did for him here. The SMP was certainly battling to regain the trust of the Chinese elites who, together with their children, were the main targets of such crime. But the real issue was the American criticism. Feng was well connected to the American Club, the social centre of the American community. The Club Vice-President was Carl Crow, veteran China coast hack and founder editor of the *Shanghai Evening Post*. The kidnapping, the detentions and the obvious lack of any immediate effective follow-up were far too close to home and got far too much press coverage (although the *North China Daily News* was silent on the treatment of the waiters). The *China Weekly Review* was often dismissed as 'anti-British' and especially anti-SMP, but the events in the station outraged the mainstream American community. The Council acted. A notification was prepared threatening instant dismissal, to start with, for men who ill-treated prisoners in future. Compensation was offered to Kao and Yung Foo, and the board recommended that

Tinkler personally foot a quarter of the bill. The Secretary of the American Club indicated his approval of the settlement. So Tinkler's earlier claim that 'half the wealthy residents in town could cause the Commissioner to lose his job if he annoyed them' came back to haunt him in quite a different way. It was not only the Commissioner who was vulnerable. Tinkler was deprived of six months' seniority, and he was booted out of CID.

So, from 4 June 1929, after almost nine years as a detective, Maurice Tinkler was back in the straitjacket, and back in police uniform. A man in uniform couldn't make his own life: he was part of a system. For all of Tinkler's complaints about CID he was much more his own man there. At Central, Tinkler's reputation was as a tough guy, but as a lazy one, too. He was 'a good detective in his way,' remembered Fred West, but 'never liked to be told anything.' Given a task he'd delegate it.[49] (Given Feng's kidnapping he had also ordered, before turning in himself, that a Chinese detective be roused from his home to question the Club 'boys'.) A Sub-Inspector's uniform role was hardly glamorous. This wouldn't do, and fairly swiftly he badgered his old Training Depot Sergeant-Major, W. E. Fairbairn, now Superintendent, to take him on in the Reserve Unit (RU). He couldn't play at detective sophistication here; the Reserve Unit was about speed and force, but it wasn't ordinary policing. While the SMC blustered publicly throughout late 1925, moves had been made to ensure that the Louza shootings would never happen again. An August 1925 proposal called for the creation of a 'Rapid Fire Riot Division', an 'organisation of capable, loyal and self-sacrificing men willing to deal with any situation or emergency which might arise from strikes, or other local disturbances'. The chosen weapon would be the Thompson sub-machine gun, using shot-gun cartridges, which would lessen the risk of fatalities and serious wounds. It was also felt 'more likely' that the police would in future 'have to face street fighting and well-armed opposition'.[50] The SMP was preparing – after the event – for effective riot handling, but also for semi-military defensive operations. Fairbairn was the key figure in the development of this squad, eventually based in two depots, equipped with custom-made 'Red Maria' transport vans – the 'Bloody Marys' – 'under the command', sneered a local foreign-owned radical journal, 'of British experts in the murder of working class rebels'.[51] The unit operated stop-and-search parties, turned out to face demonstrations, and provided fast back-up for ordinary police work, especially armed robberies. Members were also available for hire, to transport cash, for example.[52] Tinkler was deputy commander of the unit, with a small monthly allowance, far less than his CID bonus. Service in the RU was popular, a contemporary press account reported, 'as the work is more varied, and generally more pleasant than the routine work of an ordinary Police Station'. But it went on to state the obvious: 'its efficiency depends upon the maintenance of a high standard of discipline.'[53] Fairbairn had risen through the ranks, so it is perhaps not surprising that he was at once fiercely loyal to his men, arguing for rewards after shootings and protecting those who'd got into debt, and that he was prickly and quick to see slights.

A typical RU operation, one of thirteen such in 1929, took place on 22 February. Less than four minutes after receiving a report that armed robbers were in the house of a Japanese businessman, an RU squad was on the spot. Police were already there and had killed one robber, and wounded another who was still in the house. The residents were evacuated and a machine-gun party wearing steel vests and with shields 'took up a formation' and entered the building with instructions to shoot to kill. ('My reason for giving this order', reported Fairbairn, 'was that I had been informed that the robbers had fired on one of the Japanese women.') They met no resistance inside but still killed one man on the stairs, and another in the attic.[54]

Tinkler was possibly involved in the SMC's long overdue and high-profile crackdown on public gambling in which the RU played its part. On the night of 26 May the Red Maria left Yangtszepoo station with Fairbairn and squad on board. Seventeen minutes into the journey, reported the press, presumably on the basis of a copy of the police report, Fairbairn revealed their destination – Carlos Garcia's 'Wheel' on Bubbling Well Road. An SMP Special Policeman had already entered the club in mufti to mingle amongst the 200 guests and confirm that gambling was taking place (it was and he did rather well himself). The Red Maria's arrival was timed to coincide with that of a truck carrying barbed wire, which was strung across all exits to the building. Between 1 a.m. and 4 a.m., having collected their winnings and the coats, the guests were allowed to leave one by one. Their names and addresses were taken in the glare of the RU spotlight ('You know me well enough, I will not give you my name,' barked one man, but the police had the latest Shanghai residents' directory to hand). All were later bound over in court for 'haunting and resorting to a common gaming house'. Tinkler may well have been involved in this 'New Saturday Night Thrill' as the bemused *North China Daily News* labelled it. Either way, we know he'd have enjoyed it. Garcia and his partner were jailed for two years after the Mexican Consul – Norwood Allman bowing to the inevitable – withdrew recognition, and extra-territorial protection. On 21 June the RU raided a second joint on Yates Road. The same tactics that shut the Wheel were used, belatedly, against Luna Park in February 1931.[55] Otherwise, RU work could be fairly routine. The units stood by forty-five times that year, mostly on the political anniversaries that came to pepper the calendar (May Thirtieth became a hot one). On 26 July the unit broke up a pro-communist demonstration protesting against a French Concession crackdown, and it stood ready, hidden in the Drill Hall of the Foochow Road Municipal Building on 1 August, 'International Red Day'.[56]

The Eastern Depot of the unit was on a desolate corner in the Yangshupu district, far from the city centre buzz that Tinkler thrived on, bordering the mill area. The accommodation he occupied – 'fully modern with central heating and modern plumbing' – was claimed to be 'the envy of the remainder of the force', but it was surrounded by 'hovels and shacks'.[57] There was no parading in the hotel lounges here. It was 'miles out in no-man's land', remembered Dan Cormie, and the men 'could not go out on the town, felt cooped up and unable to enjoy any normal activity'. As a result they were 'somewhat wild . . . living it up and drinking excessively' in the Depot canteen.[58] And the station canteen was, of course, the station bar. It wasn't Shanghai; it was the SMP's Siberia, and Tinkler was in close quarters living with a small group of British and Russian sergeants. If Hongkew gave him the 'jim-jams', Yangtszepoo station would be wholly unbearable. An uncompleted transfer request, dated 25 September 1929, is lodged in his file, but he got that transfer, and a reprimand for disorderly conduct into the bargain, only a week later.[59] The night duty sergeant reported on 1 October that Tinkler had wandered into the Guard Room for a chat at about 1.30 a.m., returning later with a bundle of firecrackers which he set off in the compound and then threw into the rooms of various sleeping men. He was 'quite sober', reported Fairbairn (although Tinkler later admitted that he had been drinking) and claimed to be 'only playing a joke' when cornered in a room by his furious commander. 'You are a damned disgrace to the rank of Sub-Inspector,' Fairbairn told him the next morning, 'and I consider that you were trying to insult me. You who are supposed to be No. 2 of the unit, you are not fit to be a Sub-Inspector. This is the way you support me after I went out of my way to have you transferred to the Unit and this is the way you repay me.' Tinkler was ordered to hand over command to one of the ex-navy men he so hated, and Fairbairn sent him on a charge to Central station. 'I am of the opinion you ought to be put under observation to see if you are safe to be at large.'

He was transferred and reprimanded. The reprimand was a formal punishment, lodged in his file, but the bigger issue for him was that he was now firmly back in uniform and back on the Shanghai beat. At least he was out of the dreary Eastern District, and the defaults in the file didn't prevent his promotion to Inspector (on probation) in February 1930. This had required another examination, and he had been placed first, he understood, when 'all the other candidates were much senior men'. He was one of eleven men promoted to Inspector that year. Four of his 1919 peers had got their promotions in 1929, and without that six-month loss of seniority he would have joined them. The reorganized force desperately needed more experienced men at senior levels, especially as there was a large influx of recruits to accommodate. Men appointed Inspector between 1921 and 1925 had usually served almost seventeen years in the force. Between 1926 and 1930 they had waited for almost fifteen years on average. Tinkler and his peers had got their promotion in under eleven years. But this was small consolation for the fact that, as far as he was concerned, there wasn't very much at all for him to do. There was also, as he saw it, resentment from more senior colleagues. Any indication of ability incurred 'an astonishing amount of pettiness from candidates of senior rank'. So here he was in the uniform branch, attached to Louza station, where most of his time 'was devoted to patrol chiefly on which I did much the same work and was given no more responsibility than I exercised as a Constable ten years ago'.[60] The lack of responsibility rankled; and so did the embarrassment of it.

Tinkler took himself out of the city in December 1929, spending his annual short leave on a meandering journey along the China coast, touching at Amoy (Xiamen) and Hong Kong, sailing up to look at Macau and Canton (where his movements were restricted by 'another Chinese civil war'), and then on to Haiphong and Hanoi in French Indo-China. He liked Macau, with its 'dapper little hotel haunting [Portuguese] officers', and the way the moonlight played through the banyan trees on the waterfront Praya Grande. He was also impressed with the French (except for their 'uncomfortable' steamers and 'uncouth' immigration officials). 'They are obviously trying to keep [the Tonkinese] as backward as possible,' he claimed, 'In this case I think we should take a leaf out of their book.' His style is fluent and engaging in this letter to Edith, at least when he doesn't touch on politics. It wasn't the usual short-leave break, and the inquisitive, ruminative wandering probably indicates that this was a solo journey (and he had enough time on his hands for typing). He couldn't get much further away from Shanghai on short leave, and probably felt the need to get some distance on a year that hadn't gone too well. As ever, it wasn't China which interested Tinkler, but Britain in China, and the achievements of the foreign enterprise of which he so consciously saw himself a part. 'Amoy', he wrote, is a 'quaint little old-world place'. There was a tiny international settlement there (which modelled itself on Shanghai), and a small British concession as well. Like Fuzhou and Swatow (Shantou) 'you can still see how the foreigners lived in the old sailing days. The inscriptions in the old gravestones in [Amoy] ... are full of romance.' He had a modern man's sense of nostalgia, and of the place of the past. The British communities in China, as elsewhere over the seas, wrote their history, finding within it elements that justified their present position, and which also linked them tightly to the greater imperial enterprise. India was the real model for the south-east and eastern outposts of British empire. Britain in China had more than a fair share of Raj style. It spoke a pidgin English peppered with Anglo-Indian terms (bund, tiffin, shroff), and it imported Sikhs as policemen (even in tiny Amoy) and to provide 'spectacular' colour at its all-too-frequent ceremonial.[61] It constructed its own history on British India terms, and so to legitimize its essentially free-lance informal imperialism by making *pukka* sahibs out of China coasters. The Boxer year, 1900, was its 'mutiny' (and May Thirtieth, then, really was its Amritsar). As the threat of being disowned grew, as the British diplomats and 'socialist swine' reworked British China policy and planned the dismantling of the treaty system, this history and its meanings became even more important. Wandering the old cemeteries was the act of a tourist, as he himself acknowledged, but it was also reinforcing an identity. And there was also, for Tinkler, perhaps an element of regret, of having come too late for this easy life, especially as his own smooth progress had been rocky of late.

This was the last letter he wrote to Edith that survives, and probably the last he ever wrote to her. Tinkler claimed in September 1930 that 'since I was reverted to uniform . . . I have found it increasingly difficult to work harmoniously with some of the older men'. They aimed, he said, to 'put any petty obstacles in my way', and to prevent him from making a 'come back'. 'I have frequently been told by senior officers that I have "ability" but in my case this was never required for use by the uniform branch.'[62] In August 1930 he was up again on a charge before M. O. Springfield. 'The prosecutors', he later claimed, 'seized the looked for opportunity with avidity.' And on 13 August he was demoted to Sergeant, back down to 1921, back down to the beat, down to a reduced salary, a cramped room, down, down to servants' quarters. He hadn't mentioned to Edith in January that he'd left CID, or that he'd been in any other trouble. He never wrote to tell her about the demotion.

His disaster, his comeuppance, occurred because on the hot summer evening of Saturday, 9 August the commander at Louza station, Chief Inspector Crouch, decided that the duty Charge-Room Sub-Inspector, E. P. Malone, had been drinking. Tinkler was in command that evening, although he wasn't actually aware of the fact (and the disciplinary board accepted this and dropped that charge), and he was found in his clothes 'asleep on his bed on the verandah'. 'I tried to wake him,' reported Crouch, 'but found that he too had been drinking and I could not get any sense out of him.' The Divisional Officer E. C. Baker, that cricketing crony of Barrett's, was called in, and then the police surgeon, who certified that Tinkler was 'drunk and incapable of doing his duty'. Still attached to the file is a Lodge Erin envelope, in which Tinkler's usually confident florid signature is written in a shaky hand, a moment of unsteadiness caught on paper. He paraded for the disciplinary board the next morning. After working as General Duty Inspector from 5 a.m. to 10.30 he'd spent the day mostly in his room, he said. He knew he was in charge on Sunday, but didn't know that Sunday leaves at Louza ran from 6 p.m. on Saturday to 6 p.m. the following day. He was found guilty of being 'drunk and unfit for duty' in what he granted was a 'fair and satisfactory' hearing, although he pleaded 'Not guilty'. He was ordered to attend the Commissioner's office. There he 'stated that he had had a drink, but was not outrageously drunk', and that if he'd left the station 'he would not have been available had he been wanted'. Just because he lived in, and had stayed in, he was caught. It was pretty bad luck all round in that case, surely. But Gerrard found him guilty of the offence, which was aggravated by his seniority. 'It is extremely dangerous to the Settlement that an officer in his position in one of the most important Police Stations should at any time be in such a state as to be unfit for duty.' Gerrard wasn't having his men drunk on duty or off it. And Louza, of course, was a station with too sensitive a history.

Police Order No. 5912, dated 15 August 1930, was circulated to every station, and to every administrative unit. All 500 European members of the force would have seen it, as would the Asians who could read English. 'Probationary Inspector R. M. Tinkler is reduced to the rank of Sergeant with effect from August 14, 1930.' The audience this time was his largest ever, and reached in the worst way possible. The story would have circulated pretty swiftly in gossipy charge-rooms and canteens. (The word there, according to Frank Peasgood, was that Tinkler had persuaded Malone to go out drinking with him, leaving a Chinese clerk to cover the charge-room, but this could not be proved.[63]) How could he stomach work as a sergeant, and in uniform too? He'd be back on the beat, in full view. The journalists he'd joshed with would know. It would be a humiliation for a man who'd hobnobbed with Brigadier-Generals, swanked his way around town, and who was still lodge Secretary. Tinkler took annual leave, and on his return to Shanghai a month later lodged a somewhat leisurely appeal from Wayside station – the transfer there would have felt like punishment, too, as also were the more cramped sergeants' quarters. This document (which he headed 'CONFIDEN-TIAL') is part apologia, and part claim that the punishment was in fact designed to secure his resignation, and also that older colleagues had influenced the decision against him.[64] Crouch had told him, he said, that Gerrard hadn't dismissed either Tinkler or Malone (who was reduced to Sergeant as well) so as not to affect their superannuation, but that the Commissioner had said that they had 'better resign', and that the 'severe punishment' was 'deliberately inflicted on us as a powerful incentive to resign'. Gerrard gave all of this short shrift in his covering note to the Watch Committee which was to hear the appeal. 'Had I wished for his resignation, I should have passed an order, requiring it,' he said, 'The punishment will have no far reaching consequences to the Appellant, if he cares to mend his ways, suffer his punishment and show that he is again fit to hold a rank more senior than that of Sergeant.'

'I started my work in the Police in a keen and conscientious endeav-our to serve the SMC and the public,' wrote Tinkler, before giving a resumé of his career to date, noting his rapid promotion, the fact that he had 'frequently done extra work not called for by the terms of my contract with all willingness', especially in 1924, 'when on occasion I was under rifle, shell and machine gun fire miles from the Settlement'. Perhaps this good work, not all of it on record of course, 'may offset some of the misconduct I have been punished for'. Demotion 'will have a further reaching effect on my future than [it] would in the case of an ordinary individual inebriated on a Saturday night'.[65] Gerrard was unimpressed here too. '"Saturday night inebri-ation" on the part of the senior officers of an important Police station like Louza cannot be tolerated in a disciplined and efficient Police Force.' In the circumstances, he added, the punishment was hardly severe. Tinkler claimed that it was hardly a unique offence, everybody could name names, and point to senior men who'd done worse, who had been out of action for days. But this was obviously partly the point. Gerrard's brief had been to reform the SMP, and to purge it of old inefficiency and corruptions. The new recruits of 1928/29, especially the ex-army men recruited direct from Shaforce, had been as truculent as Tinkler's intake. They boozed, and they were sacked. The force was being purged of those who might hinder its reputation and efficiency in the new political world of nationalist China. The Watch Committee swiftly confirmed the punishment, and Tinkler handed in his resignation as from 1 October 1930. A copy of his discharge certificate, issued on 3 October, is placed at the front of the file. Reason for discharge: 'Resigned'; Conduct: 'Very good until the last 18 months.' The kidnapping case, the fireworks at Yulin Road, the Louza debacle were the cause of the latter judgement. Superannuation was issued in full, including the Council's contributions, and Extra-Commissioner Martin penned a frank but solid letter of reference incorporating the discharge verdict on conduct, but adding that he had been 'frequently detailed for military intelligence work which he carried out with distinction'. There had been recent serious breaches of discipline but these were disciplinary offences only, 'and in no way affected his honesty'.

Why did he resign from a secure job, when the world economy was a year into the Great Depression? Tinkler might have calculated that it would be better to get his superannuation out and converted into sterling: in 1929 the Chinese dollar ranged in value from 1s.10d. to 1s. 6d., in 1930 from 1s. 5d. to 1s. Back in 1920 it had swung between an unusual high of 6s. 8d. and 2s. 9d, and through the early 1920s was reasonably stable at 2s. 2d. to 2s. 7d. He might have been earning more throughout the 1920s, but it was suddenly worth less and less, and the reduction in salary looked as if it would hit him hard. But I am not convinced he had the patience to think that through. And he might have stayed on, others did. Dan Cormie relates one story of a man busted from Sub-Inspector to Sergeant, as Malone was, for being drunk on duty. He 'persisted' and within a year was back to his former rank, eventually rising to Inspector. But Cormie also wrote that it would have been 'an awful blow', even for a Sub-Inspector. The Chinese, especially, 'would look upon it as a loss of face' for the man involved.[66] Empire was always a matter of bluff. The resources available for effective and sustained repression were always overstretched and the ideological quirks of imperial living so very central to its success and persistence. The agents of empire created or adapted baroque rituals to make manifest – and exaggerate – their strength, confidence, power. They created codes of conduct, and deportment, and rules for engagement with and distancing from native power, and native individuals. These were often affirmed in the breaking, of course, but such was the power and privilege of the imperial agent. Laws as well as social codes aimed to protect 'prestige', whether they threatened dismissal for men mis-marrying, or prosecuted the sellers of art books which laid too great an emphasis on the naked European female. In China, such ideological imperatives were also subsumed into Chinese social concerns with 'face', with protecting personal reputation in front of Chinese subordinates and spectators. 'Face' played a key role in the notions of the 'Chinese character' that were peddled in crude sociological fashion by commentators in reference books and polemics alike, and which were passed on to newcomers by 'China hands' in club bars and station canteens. Shanghailanders were keen about face, policemen no less so; recall Gabbutt, Dunne. 'The command was given in the presence of gatemen who were laughing at my discomfiture,' claimed a Sergeant on a charge of insubordination. A Probationary Sergeant was charged with beating a hawker (with 'unnecessary violence') who, on being asked to move along, 'even laughed at me'. The same man defended a stream of foul abuse thrown at a Chinese police clerk, he 'thought Clerk Li's attitude was sufficient justification'. He was eventually dismissed. Such men slapped the faces of others to save their own. Tinkler was a man sensitive to his place on the Shanghai stage and streets. He'd made enough enemies in the police force – people were 'very pleased' that he'd left, claimed Fred West – to have made accepting the demotion an unthinkable option. And we can readily see that he would have felt it viscerally demeaning to work again as a Sergeant, in front of Chinese and Sikh colleagues. He'd lived the life of empire too far for that.

What went wrong? We might think of a number of interpretations of the events of 1929–30. He had been on long leave. Perhaps his return to Britain had unsettled him; perhaps he had missed a significant shift in the Shanghai atmosphere. But the laconic (if not lazy) tough-guy attitude that infused Tinkler's sense of self led him to overstep the mark perhaps one time too many with the Feng kidnapping case. His own inability to handle the return to uniform did the rest, conceit and pride helped by a fair bit of bad luck. 'For some time past,' he wrote in his appeal, 'I appear to have been regarded by many of my seniors of the Uniform Branch as something between a dangerous anarchist and an irresponsible school-boy which has had a very detrimental effect generally.' The freewheeling CID style hardly translated into the highly trained and tightly designed procedures of the Reserve Unit or the orderly routine of the Settlement stations, and so neither did he. This was also the end of his good old China. Another scenario might be that his style of policing could survive only when the challenge to colonialism was contained. With the body blow the SMC took in 1925 the old certainties were shaken. Every 'incident' threatened a new May Thirtieth. Tinkler, still so new to Shanghai but feeling like an 'old-timer', was stuck in his good old China of the unchallenged and unconstrained good life. Had he just taken the low road of the Shanghai policeman and turned to booze? (Was it related to the possible end of the relationship with Shura?) Both incidents were drink related but I am not convinced. Nothing in the files suggests a problem extending beyond the actual incidents themselves, and he was given a fairly clean discharge certificate and references, and full superannuation. Overall, we can't really know, and chance played a major role. But one thing which does strike one is that Maurice Tinkler took empire too seriously. In *The Road to Wigan Pier*, former imperial policeman George Orwell wrote about the fact that every imperialist knew that the rhetoric of empire was all airy bluff at heart, and that empire was the brute fact of power. 'From the most unexpected people, from gin-pickled old scoundrels high up in the [Indian] Government service, I have heard some such remark as: "Of course we've no right in this blasted country at all. Only now we're here for God's sake let's stay here".' Empire was despotism, and in the police 'you see the dirty work of Empire at close quarters'.[67] Tinkler had no problem with empire's dirty work, but no sense of perspective about it. There were no midnight doubts. For Tinkler it wasn't merely that empire was the geopolitical status quo, or functionally useful to British trade: empire was a serious, necessary business close to the heart of civilization. Empire ascendant could contain such loyalty, but empire challenged needed a defter touch. There was a purging of the China-ranks, of old-time missionaries, die-hard customs officials and undiplomatic consuls, as well as irreconcilables in business, in the SMC and in the SMP. Out went McEuen, Barrett and Clarke. Out went 'Richard M. Tinkler, C.I.D.'

8

What We Can't Know

Once the servants of empire were no longer being used, it was felt best that they pack quietly and head home. Shanghailanders should sail back with their pensions and payoffs and their knick-knacks, their lacquerware and curios, a scroll or two, an opium pipe. With the exceptions of the settler colonies (Rhodesia, Kenya), British colonial authorities in Asia and Africa worked to prevent the emergence of a permanent 'non-official' community. Settlers blurred imperial boundaries, made awkward demands and entailed unwanted responsibilities. And they might not do what they were told. People did stay, of course. They retired to hill stations, opened hotels or other businesses, trying to fill in some niche they'd spotted when in service. But this was the minority; most returned to Britain (or went somewhere warmer, seduced by the advertisements in their Shanghai magazines: 'An Ideal Home', one read, 'for anyone retiring from China or going on long leave. Perfect climate'[1]). Discharge from the SMP was no different. The consuls did not want unemployed Britons in the city. They were likely to end up as a charge to public funds, especially ex-police and ex-military men who had few skills that could not now be more cheaply hired from Russians. The SMC could not force ex-employees to leave, but it penalized them by refusing to pay passages home if they stayed on longer than one month after they left its service. For men whose Shanghai sojourn had been short this was a significant sum, and most calculated that it would be best to leave. The SMP believed that men who stayed on were likely to get into trouble, although not necessarily through any fault of their own. They were a potential embarrassment. They might go to the bad in other ways, poverty and necessity leading to transgressions of settler taboos. Some-

times Special Branch drew up a list of ex-police still in the city, although the number who actually got into trouble with the law was quite small. So Maurice Tinkler was offered a sergeant's second-class return to Britain which obviously did not appeal (an Inspector would have gone first class), while the lure of America was strong. He proposed an alternative, asking for a passage to Seattle, as he intended 'to remain in the United States for a few months then continue to Caribbean countries (or elsewhere if I discover prospects of employment)'.[2] Could the balance of the £76 cost of the passage to Britain, once the fare to Seattle was deducted, be issued to him in travel coupons on Thomas Cook's San Francisco office? The plan was agreed, as long as the coupons were not cashed in. A letter of introduction was produced for the American Consulate-General's Passport Office. Commissioner Martin had 'no hesitation in vouching for his honesty and integrity', and supported Tinkler's application for a six-month visit. On 25 October 1930 Tinkler sailed for Seattle via Japanese ports on the NYK vessel *Hiye Maru*. There is a postcard of it stuck into the back of one of his albums. A passenger list printed in the *North China Herald* on 28 October recorded, with a small inaccuracy he would never have seen, the departure on that service of 'R. N. Tinkler'.

He arrived in Seattle on 12 November 1930. At immigration, Tinkler declared that he was heading for London via New York after visiting San Francisco. He had US$1,600, and listed himself as a 'Retired Police Officer'.[3] He was given four months to make his way out. If he really was looking for work it wasn't the best time to be scouting for it in the United States (and he did not have the proper visa). The Great Depression was hitting the country hard. Unemployment, which rose from 1,550,000 in 1929 to 4,340,000 in 1930, would almost double in the coming year, to just under 24 per cent of the labour force. It was a time, in fact, when some young Americans were heading in exactly the opposite direction, setting out like journalist Helen Foster Snow for Shanghai, where their US dollar savings went ridiculously far.[4] Tinkler's optimism partly suggests something of the parochialism of the Shanghailander world and its narrow horizons. It also suggests again the power of his mythic, idealized America. He got nowhere near the Caribbean, which was surely a feint (and was not mentioned at immigration). At his death it was suggested that Tinkler had left 'for the United States where he went into business of his own, returning to Shanghai some years later'. Another account claimed that he had travelled in the United States for six months.[5] But the immigration manifest shows that he left San Francisco on 22 December, barely six weeks after arriving. He was heading for Canada, and he was not there for long. The sole record he kept of his next and last voyage is another one of those postcards, the final item in the album, its itinerary scribbled beneath it. The NYK line's *Hikawa Maru* sailed from Seattle on 6 January; Tinkler joined it at Vancouver. After sailing via Yokohama and Kobe it docked, on 28 January 1931, in Shanghai. He had pulled a fast one on the SMP: he came straight back.

But here we have to stop the chapter. The confident recital of contextualized facts dries. Nothing more is known until February 1934 except that the roll of members of Lodge Erin records Tinkler as an absent member in March 1931, and as active in September 1933.[6] He was based in Shanghai at least from that latter point on, but was probably there from much earlier, although no lodge lists between the two dates could be checked. Overall, between January 1931 and February 1934 nothing has surfaced to confirm Maurice Tinkler's whereabouts or activities. He is lost to sight. Factual narrative will resume with his departure from Shanghai on 2 February 1934 for the inland city of Nanchang, almost three years to the day after his return. Between these two dates there is only silence and specu-lation: his silence, and my speculation. For all that I have managed, for the eleven years of Tinkler's Shanghai sojourn, to augment his thirty-six chatty letters with direct and indirect documentation from the SMP files, his colleagues, newspapers and memoirs, I have failed to find anything for these years. His family knew nothing at the time, or in retrospect, and nothing that deals with his subsequent Shanghai activities throws light backwards to the facts of this period. There are no photographs which look as if they date from this period. Perhaps there is an album missing. But the inventory of Tinkler's possessions at his death in 1939 lists five photograph albums, and that is what his relations now have. Tinkler may well have lost the inclination to photograph; if he did so, it seems to have happened before he went on leave because there are no snapshots of the United States, Panama, France, or of his 1929 trip to French Indo-China. He possessed no camera at his death. For this chapter of Tinkler's life, three years out of the forty he was to live, three years out of the twenty he spent in Shanghai, only these two slight Masonic details survive. There are certainly still questions that can be asked – such as why might he have returned, and what might he have done by way of employment, and was he actually there after all – and speculative answers can be offered to these that might help an understanding of the world Tinkler found himself in, and the choices he may then have made. It is not always necessary for Maurice Tinkler to speak for us to understand the position he was in.

By way of context, we know that financially he wasn't badly off to start with. Superannuation was issued in full in the shape of a cheque for 6,707.39 taels on 7 October.[7] His monthly salary before the demotion was 245 taels, with an extra 24 taels as a language bonus and a temporary cost-of-living allowance, just introduced, of 45 taels: altogether, an annual salary for 1930 of 3,768 taels reduced to 3,108 taels after deductions for quarters, light and fuel. (If he'd still been in CID he would have had another 40 taels a month as a detective bonus.) So the superannuation represented – simplistically – about 21 months' salary. But this is not the full picture because he'd also lost his medical benefits, his subsidized housing and canteens, and he'd now have to do his own saving (and work out his own future pension).

Maurice had also, presumably, been spending in North America, with an unfavourable rate of exchange, and he had probably paid his own way back. He could live on what was left for perhaps one comfortable year, a bit longer if he skimped, but the general cost of living in Shanghai was also still rising, up by over a quarter on 1926 levels when he resigned. As a result, the SMC had introduced an additional temporary cost-of-living allowance in August 1928 for married employees, and in 1930 introduced a general temporary allowance for all staff equal in value almost to 20 per cent of his final salary. Rents in particular were getting more expensive, and they were not going to get any cheaper in the 1930s. The *North China Daily News* classifieds in late January 1931 offered full board from 100 taels a month ('cosy attic room') to a luxury 175 taels ('suitable for business gentleman'). There were unfurnished rooms starting at 75 taels (Western District); a three-roomed apartment in the Concession for 110 taels, and a two-bed flat on Bubbling Well Road (75 taels all in). There were certainly cheaper rooms available which might still suit a respectable foreign pocket (and there was always board and lodging at the navy YMCA at $3.50 a day), but living outside the police was going to be increasingly expensive. By October 1931 the foreign cost of living had risen 75 per cent in three years. A bottle of Allsops beer cost $3.75 in 1928, and $9 in 1931, a tin of Lipton's tea rose in price by 132 per cent in the same period, Lea and Perrin's Worcester Sauce – the staple of the expatriate mess table – had also more than doubled in price. Smokes and drinks and a night out at a cabaret were also getting pricier.[8] He would also have to pay for a servant, about $25–$35 a month. A 1934 United States Consulate guide to living in Shanghai argued strongly that foreign residents had to pay over the odds for their accommodation, and maintain what might be thought an extravagant lifestyle, otherwise they would be 'lacking "face"' and would 'incur the contempt of all classes of Chinese people (as well as a large section of the foreign community)'.[9] We know that Tinkler did not live cheaply. He had no other savings, and he had appearances to keep up. He had enough to make a start, to take the risk of returning and waiting while he looked for something else, but he really needed that something else.

But really, why return? Why didn't he cut his losses and start afresh somewhere else? The empire world was fluid, and getting even more so in the 1930s. Men who worked in one colony might decide to follow up better opportunities elsewhere in the same world of empire service and opportunity. Constable Ritchie, dismissed for drinking in 1924, was indulged a passage to Colombo, Ceylon, to seek a position through relatives there; 1919 recruit Charles Macdonald left in 1925 to seek work in New Zealand to 'better myself' (but left the ship in Singapore with a colleague who had been dismissed); Hugh King, dismissed in 1929, 'made good' in Canada ('so you will see I had all the faults of youth,' he explained of his Shanghai years), acquiring a civil service position after work on the railways, as a lumberjack and as a seaman; Jack Darby left the SMP for a planter's job in New Guinea.[10] So why didn't Tinkler follow this course? He was still young, spending his thirty-second birthday at sea on the way to Seattle, and there were no family connections. He could have moved on to 'better' himself, or to start with a clean slate and 'make good', thoroughly respectable and ordinary motivations. Something drew him back, and we can profitably run through some of the possibilities. It may just have been plain laziness. Moving on would be difficult, a whole new business of searching, locating, understanding – and he'd be a newcomer, an immigrant, not in control, not master of the situation. Immigration would surely be a humiliating business anyway, filling forms, giving an account of himself and his finances, undergoing tests. Perhaps he just couldn't face it, wasn't strong enough to risk such a jump into the dark, especially as he was an old-timer in Shanghai terms. He might simply have returned because of Shura, who was last noted on their trip together to Japan in April 1928 at the start of his long leave, although the letters home don't mention her after December 1925. If Shura still had Italian nationality after her divorce (assuming that it came through), she would have been able to travel more easily than other White Russians, effectively trapped in Shanghai because they were stateless. But presuming that she had employment, and wasn't set up as his 'temporary wife', it would have been too risky for them both to leave the city and their jobs. Tinkler may indeed have set her up like this, and so had a home of sorts to return to. But his solitary off-duty nights in barracks on the occasions he got into trouble in 1929 suggest otherwise. He doesn't seem by then to have been in a relationship. After his resignation he wrote to Commissioner Martin from an unusual address, 26 Carter Road, a few doors down from the Carter Road police flats. But this seems more red herring than clue. Shura may have been a reason, but she may have been history. Either way, all that remains of her for now is an album of photos and that solitary dedication in her own hand, 'To my loved one'. The 'serious heart attack' was over.

Perhaps he returned because someone had made him a firm offer of employment. In that case why leave Shanghai at all, unless to take a North American break at the expense of the SMC? That's not unlikely – he would have enjoyed pulling that one – but Tinkler is not listed in any published Shanghai directory after 1930 (when he's listed in the SMP) until 1935. The *China Hong List*, published by the *North China Daily News*, was a voluminous annual directory of the foreign China establishment. Arranged in three sections – a building-by-building street directory, a business listing, and a residents' directory – it provides a comprehensive, and pretty reliable survey of those working and living in Shanghai. The lack of a listing initially suggested that he wasn't there at all, but as we now know that he was, it suggests instead that he was unemployed, or underemployed and perhaps working in an *ad hoc* fashion. In the time Tinkler had before leaving the city, he took one month's leave, and then the best part of a further month passed as he got ready to go. It's not clear that he had the time in which to sort out any firm offer of work before his voyage to North America. And there was not much on offer in the *North China Daily News*. Its 'Positions Vacant' columns for the days immediately following the arrival of the *Hikawa Maru* offered secretarial work, openings for a qualified bookkeeper, an assistant architect, a wood-working expert and a travelling companion. The posts were mostly aimed at women or English-speaking Chinese, and Tinkler was not the only man looking, either. 'Young Englishman' offered 'fluent Chinese' and his experience as a car mechanic. 'Young foreigner' offered 'experience of general office routine'. From Singapore, 'Energetic Britisher' sought anything connected with sales or the motor trade. 'Not afraid of hard work', he added. The difficulty of getting an opening was highlighted in another entry: 'Young man, foreigner, with 8 years local experience, presently without employment, seeks companionship of person of social standing for assistance in obtaining position.' 'Any opportunity', he concluded, 'is greatly appreciated.' The time really didn't look right. By late 1932, 123 job seekers were registered with the British Chamber of Commerce.[11]

Unlike the 'Young man', Tinkler had some local connections outside the police through Lodge Erin, especially as he had played a crucial administrative role in it since 1928 as Secretary, and he would possibly have turned to that network first in his search. But although a few of those in the lodge in March 1931 had some 'social standing' (an insurance company manager, a company director, the owner of an import-export company), the majority of those identifiable from the China Hong List were either in council service (police, fire brigade, Public Health or Public Works departments), or worked for the Shanghai Power Company, the Chinese Maritime Customs, or in junior positions for British trading companies. This doesn't look promising, although Lodge Erin was just one among many, and men with multiple memberships could provide introductions to a broader Shanghai circle. But we also know that Tinkler was short on friends, and might guess that his arrogance had already alienated men beyond the SMP. What did other ex-policemen do? A November 1936 Special Branch report lists twenty-nine of them living in Shanghai, including Tinkler (there were others in the city, older men who had been longer out of the force).[12] Fred Barling was managing the 'Frisco Cabaret on Rue Chu Pao San, better known as 'Blood Alley', the home by then of over a dozen cabarets and a violently riotous night life. Two other men owned more respectable businesses, a photographic studio and a riding school. Seven worked for other departments of the SMC or the public utilities. Two were salesmen (soap, beer), one had joined the river police, another was an inspector for the Shanghai Society for Prevention of Cruelty to Animals. Others worked for trading companies. Three are listed as unemployed and no employment is given for another trio, which suggests that one in five of these men was without a job. For some, such as the salesmen, even these positions were insecure. Most would also be on local contracts, rather than expatriate terms of service which were more generous, especially in terms of repatriation or protection against the fall in the value of the Chinese currency against sterling. A bit of luck was needed. Tinkler's inadvertent nemesis also stayed on in Shanghai. Sub-Inspector Malone had married on his first long leave in 1927, against the wishes of Commissioner Barrett.[13] A month after he was demoted to Sergeant he resigned, again with full superannuation. In May 1933 he wrote to the Secretary of the SMC pleading for passages home for himself, his wife and their 4-year-old child. 'I did not leave [Shanghai]', he explained, 'because I believed that I would more easily obtain employment here than in England. Through no fault of my own I have failed, and am facing a future of poverty in a land not my own, nor that of my family.' Commissioner Gerrard recommended that third-class passages be granted them, as it was known, 'through Major Darby of the Salvation Army, that this family is in great need at the present time'. Malone had possibly been mostly living off his superannuation since September 1930, and now it had run out. He had to beg for a ticket home. 'I sometimes think', Tinkler had written to Edith in 1922, that 'Shanghai must be one of the worst places on earth to be broke in.'

But Shanghai was what he knew best. He didn't have family connections elsewhere in the empire world, and the global economy was against him. He spoke Shanghainese, and he knew the city. He might have sought work elsewhere in British China, in Hong Kong or Tianjin, but he had little knowledge of either place, spoke neither Cantonese nor Mandarin, and besides, there was more likelihood of opportunities arising in Shanghai. Tinkler was well educated, literate and intelligent. He may have sought work, as some ex-police did, with Clarke's Inquiry and Protection Agency, run out of two rooms on Nanjing Road by the former CID chief ('Member and Far Eastern Representative of the World Association of Detectives, British Detectives Association and International Secret Service Association'[14]). But it may have been too much like the past: that Nick Carter business was done with. In 1934, as we shall see, Tinkler worked briefly for a British-registered company and he may have had some previous business experience by then, as the job required more than brute force. But if that didn't work there were always British companies which needed security supervision pure and simple. He might have found work as others did with Swires, or Holt's Wharf. Such companies were squeezed by the downturn (Swires cut salaries by 10 per cent, and banned double-spaced typing to save paper), but they still needed supervisors. He could offer himself, as did other colleagues, as an expert in supervising 'native labour' generally, and Chinese in particular. Supervision of 'Asiatics' in the force was a primary function of the British men of the SMP, and other organizations replicated that hierarchy and structure in China and elsewhere. They needed their British supervisors. So there were sound reasons for staying put. There were also sound economic reasons for not heading to Britain, or elsewhere. Unemployment was rising sharply, from one and a quarter million in 1928 to close on two million by 1930, and rose to two and three-quarter million by 1932. Tinkler was also now wholly cut off from Britain. His parents were dead, his sister and stepmother had moved on from Ulverston, and anyway, as she had written in 1929, 'there is nothing for you here'. He had nowhere else to go, no home but the empire world, and no home within it but Shanghai. There are no further postcards of vessels he had sailed in stuck into his album. Tinkler would have pasted them in if he'd made any other major journeys. He was careful like that. He never made another ocean voyage. Tinkler was stuck to Shanghai.

What did he do there? Let us speculate and propose Tinkler's history for these missing years. It would take that single new fact, an entry in a directory, relocating him to another city or unsuspected employment, utterly to undermine it, of course. But much of this narrative so far has been speculation. After all, Maurice Tinkler's raw, direct voice has been restricted to a series of letters to members of his family – mostly Edith – a few official documents, and a few work documents. I've met and talked with only three people who as adults knew him, and two have since died. New questions are now unanswerable. What remains is rich, but it is still limited. Not as limited as some, of course. In *The Life of an Unknown*, French social historian Alain Corbin deliberately set out to chart the life of a randomly chosen individual, guided only by a focus on the region and archive that he knew best. Picking a name from the inventories, he alighted on Louis-François Pinagot, a clog-maker who lived and died in obscurity between 1798 and 1876, and who now enjoys as a result the weird memorial of a Library of Congress catalogue subheading. Corbin recovered Pinagot's world using whatever fragmentary official notes on the man and his circle of family and neighbours he could locate: court records, military service, taxation, franchise, marriages, births, deaths and so on, all of them harnessed to a survey of the history of the locale in which Pinagot lived all his long life. A biography was 'impossible' to write, but the life could still be mapped out, and it could be evoked.[15]

It is simple, on the surface, to recover Maurice Tinkler's life. To start with, there are the letters to family covering his wartime service and his years in the police. The records of the SMP provided more documentation, as did the records of the SMC; and Tinkler's death generated full files now found in four archives, newspaper comment and the bureaucratic sorting out that death requires. I know Tinkler's height (6 feet, half an inch), that he developed a taste for wearing berets (he had five at his death), that he smoked, could not eat eggs, and liked a woman's legs (his photos, his scrapbook clippings are all legs). I even know how he signed his name when he was drunk. I've talked to people who knew him directly. The relatives and descendants of others searched out vital materials. So Tinkler's voice was itself loud and candid. We have seen what he thought on a range of topics, and we know what he did, and what he looked like – even, courtesy of a Japanese newspaper – what he looked like on his deathbed. Corbin never found his subject's voice represented except once, in the form of Pinagot's illiterate mark – a 'large clumsy cross' – on a municipal document recording his opinion on a road project.[16] Most of us leave even less.

What do we need to know in order to recover a lived life? In so many ways, I myself might as well have had only that 'clumsy cross' to work on. The materials tease as much as they inform. The correspondence is one-sided, and incomplete. Some topics – Lily Wilson – are touched on as if there have been prior discussions relaying fact and information. Shura just disappears, presumably because he doesn't wish to offend his sister's sense of propriety, possibly because he cannot, will not, write of disappointment, defeat, rejection. Edith Tinkler may have decided herself to suppress some letters, but others remain which hurt her at the time and which surely would have been destroyed if that was her aim. They may after all just have been lost. Lost too, now – bar the one sketch of her that she kept in her commonplace book – is what Tinkler described to Edith in 1922 as 'that wonderful collection of art and literature', his letters to Lily and the drawings he sent with them. The SMP files, even his own personnel file, are incomplete. The items he left at his death, a few letters, the albums, certificates, and references, help and hinder in equal measure. Pulled together, the paper trail is impressive nonetheless. But in the end we really don't know very much at all. We can never know what Tinkler thought or feared, what he dreamt or wished for, whom he loved, or why he made certain choices. How much an indication of a man's beliefs are these letters, scribbled in an exuberant and often illegible hand? As for their facts, these are pretty reliable. Tinkler had a pedant's way with detail, and a hectoring, lecturing air. He liked to tell. Two Special Branch reports he mentions writing (on Chinese police pay, and on strikes in June 1925), and found by chance in different archives, suggest that while he might boast and boost, he didn't invent. The wild, vicious talk of early 1927 was clearly fairly accurately conveyed canteen shop. Tinkler wrote as he spoke and thought. But there is little independent evidence outside the family, and what there is is mostly hostile, produced by men who did not like him. Perhaps the consistency of these responses is all I need to note; perhaps it is bad luck. And I don't know, for example, what he smelt like, how he ate, how he walked, what his conversation was like, what he feared. I have been tracking him down for thirteen years, and seeking out girlfriends, sister, half-brother, colleagues and others. I know more about his whole life-story than any of these people, but in another sense he is only what I make him using the materials I have, and he remains ultimately elusive and safe from me.

Two of the intangibles can and should be drawn out for discussion: Tinkler's speech and his physical presence. He survives on paper, in print and in photographs, but this is not how he lived. And he's black and white in the photographs, of course. The US immigration officer noted that he had brown hair and eyes, a dark complexion, and a cut scar on his right cheek (how and when the scar? I can't say). It could be assumed for a start that he spoke with the broad accent native to his stretch of Lancashire, but after army service and his arrival in Shanghai started to change it. There is no hint of a patois in his writing, there are no dialect phrases or local terms. He was well educated and wrote fluent, confident standard English (written English mostly is standard English, of course). He was considered officer material in wartime, so had possibly already smoothed some rough provincial edges. In Shanghai he began to colour his prose with Americanisms, which helped disguise his background, and with that 'tough-guy' slang, as well as – although far less often – China coast terms or pidgin English. Maurice Tinkler was careful about how he looked. He was also careful about how he sounded on the page and off it. His words were deliberately chosen, up-to-date slang self-consciously repro- duced, sometimes nestling in quotation marks ('wondering how I could possibly "kid" anyone'). He practised his American. In an early letter to Edith (pointedly dated in the American style '11/27/21') he signed off cheerily with what almost amounted to a translation exer- cise, following a paragraph of plummy English with the same rendered into American slang: 'I have to go out to dinnah', 'I gotter happen along for eats', 'the beastly Chief Inspectah is using the confounded flivver, ar, don't you know', 'th' Gad-damn lootenant's gotten the whizz-wagon', 'old haricot', 'Oh Boy'. It wasn't really a joke. Tinkler presumably reworked his speech to fit his idea of a new modern self, and perhaps also further to cut free from his old native north-west, if not from his native, slow, England. He spoke Shanghainese; when he was being lazy, or dealing with the many Shanghai residents who weren't local, or who could not or would not understand his Chinese, he would have used pidgin English. He could also have used pidgin as a pointed insult ('cultured Chinese naturally dislike being addressed in that jargon,' noted a 1933 guidebook[17]). He would have had deal- ings with many English-speaking Chinese, and might have grown lazy, forgetting his police lessons – after all, many Shanghailanders never learnt a word. But his Chinese was 'pretty good' according to one native speaker. He knew his slang too.[18]

We've seen what Tinkler looked like, but how did he move, how did he stand in a crowd, how did he make his presence felt? We can see enough in photographs and in his prose to know that he swaggered. He liked a pose. Here, his face turned for profile, behind him perhaps the river, a ship passing. Here in Jessfield Park, cigar in hand. This shot placed so, on this page. This one butchered with scissors so, the uncut edges lined up with the other snaps on the page; but who sat beside him in the lost portion? Who as early as 1920 warranted cutting out of his remembered past? There is a world of meanings in the collection. Some can be drawn out, but much is aide-mémoire no longer. In four snapshots Tinkler reads: in the lounge and on the verandah at the Taihoko Railway Hôtel (he nearly always wrote 'Hôtel'), a newspaper here and again here. Alone on a Mokanshan hill top, pipe and walking stick in hand. Alone, cigar in mouth, at the Central police station. The photographs are at times vain, pompous, jokey, careful, and nicely composed. They differ from most of those that survive from the collections of Shanghai policemen. They didn't all have cameras, of course, and owning one led Tinkler to think about how to use it, what to snap, and how to present the results. And most of those still serving at the time of Pearl Harbor subsequently lost all their possessions, so the comparison is a little unequal. But even so his albums are different. Frank Peasgood sent back home a handful of shots: Frank newly arrived in uniform, lumbering in a doorway; Frank settled in now, relaxed, nattily tailored (courtesy of 'Tom' the tailor and the boy who ironed) and well shod on the station verandah, a life away from his Yorkshire miner's background; Frank and friend in rickshaws in Japan, panamas on. The message is clear: this is what I have become, this is how I've changed. Tinkler's message is for himself alone: this is what I am. He didn't send the shots home. Jack Darby snapped the Training Depot and the world of work. Here he is lined up with his fellow 1933 recruits and their trainer, Jock Smith. Most men kept a portrait of themselves in uniform. Tinkler may have thrown out such shots, but I suspect he never had any. Other men kept group photographs: the station, the soccer team, the inter-port rugger squad, the Christmas party. Tinkler wasn't a group man.

What the albums can't show is that, as well as having charm, an attractive face, and a confident, easy smile, he could also bully. He used words and he used his body. Fred West remembered him being physically intimidating, coming up too close and pushing him around. He was plainly increasingly unpleasant to work with as the Shanghai years progressed. That physicality also more and more became his most important resource. For all that, he was bright and adaptable, all he needed to offer was presence of mind, diligence, and the presence of force. Tinkler put himself at the centre of his photographs, and of any physical situation. He posed as he lived. He called the shots, and stood in the centre. It was to cause a minor diplomatic incident in

Nanchang in 1934, and it would lead to his death. He would be listened to, he would prevail. He was ineffably, arrogantly confident. Tinkler was undoubtedly brave in wartime – the DCM doesn't come easily – and would display courage again, soon, but 'he had a temper', remembered Peasgood. He 'lost his temper very quickly', said West. And if he was like this with his colleagues and superiors, we can guess what he was like with the Chinese. We know that the 'brainless coolies' had their heads banged together, that he played executioner with the frightened student in the May Thirtieth cell. Peng Hongfei worked in the same plant with Tinkler for four years, and remembered him as a 'hooligan', using a strong term – 'liumang' – that conveys utter contempt. The impact of their encounters was still strong sixty years later. Racism obliterated any remaining caution Tinkler may have displayed in his dealings with Europeans. We can speculate about the impact on men of the violence of wartime and of the violence of colonialism, but Tinkler made his own choices, and chose his own way of dealing with the colonial world he found. He took full advantage of the space it offered for violent daily confrontation with those marked as different.

He was a racist, and his viciously expressed racism challenges the patience of any reader. The letters serve as easy evidence of settler racism, but Maurice Tinkler was still exactly a man of his time and place, and places. His comments were mainstream even if his violence wasn't. But, more than just Shanghailander mainstream, they were rooted in the ideological contortions of an imperialism that dressed up might as 'racial' right, and in the popular pseudo-science peddled by such thinkers on 'race' as Lothrop-Stoddard.[19] This was articulated in China by polemicists such as American journalist Rodney Gilbert (acting editor of the *North China Daily News* for a period in 1927), and was read with glee by many ordinary Britons in 1920s China. 'That China is in a frightful mess means nothing,' thundered Gilbert, 'unless we are right and they are wrong, unless we are superior and they are inferior, unless we are entitled to rule or are elected for eventual extermination.' His inflammatory and highly popular *What's Wrong with China* (1926) was predicated on a stark choice: 'Occidentals' had either to 'control the East, or submit to Oriental standards, sooner or later, and be dominated by the East'.[20] Tinkler's violent language adds a further vicious edge to his comments, but on matters of 'race' the harshly and the softly spoken articulated the same blunt thought. Tinkler wrote as the canteen boor declaimed, his tough-guy persona doling out repulsive justice to the targets of his contempt. His comments on the British were hardly better. But unreflective racism underpinned empire living and empire ruling. It determined the structures of empire institutions, such as the SMP's hierarchy based on imputed aptitude and degrees of responsibility. Its British men expected that segregation to extend to hospitals, to shipboard life, and to all areas of their life and work, and they were mostly accommodated.

But although we don't know, and can't know, we can create an approximate truth, a writing truth. So let me here create for Maurice Tinkler a history for the period 1931 to February 1934. It's no substitute for facts, but it may have its own truth. We first need to know what happened in Shanghai while he was lost to sight. The answer is, of course, a great deal. Shanghailanders were worried in 1931 by the actions of their diplomats, who were discussing with the Chinese the renegotiation of the treaties which underpinned British trade. By midsummer they were edging towards a settlement that would lead to the abolition of extraterritoriality and a timetable for return of the concessions. The settler British responded to this – galvanized also by outrage at the disappearance and probable death at the hands of the Chinese military of a British youth, John Hay Thorburn – by setting up a British Residents' Association to campaign against such Foreign Office 'treachery'. The draft treaty was never signed, because in September 1931 junior Japanese military officers deliberately provoked a clash with Chinese forces – the Mukden incident – that escalated into a full-scale Japanese invasion of Manchuria. And by January 1932 tensions were also mounting in Shanghai.[21] An anti-Japanese boycott was already in place, launched in July 1931 after massacres of Chinese residents in Korea. Based in Shanghai, it was well organized and thorough. With a Japanese population of nearly 20,000, almost double what it had been at the time of the 1918 'Hongkew disturbances', the International Settlement was a likely spot for conflict. Japanese residents themselves were spoiling for a fight after months of boycott activism: Chinese pickets intercepted the transport of Japanese goods and confiscated them, searching shops and warehouses, and fining their owners. The city was plastered with pro-boycott posters; there were rallies and walkouts. The pressure on Japanese residents had been great, and after 18 September increased exponentially. Although the SMP worked to contain Chinese demonstrators, allowing a patriotic parade on 10 January to march through the Settlement, for example, they used the Reserve Unit's batons to make sure that they never threatened Hongkew.

But, instead, Japanese special service units actively worked to provoke a clash, and after the killing of a Japanese monk on 18 January (engineered by Japanese agents) the situation deteriorated. On 23 January the Japanese Consul-General delivered an ultimatum to the Special Municipality authorities demanding they suppress the local National Salvation Association, the prime anti-Japanese mass movement, and, although Mayor Wu Tiecheng met the demands in full, conflict erupted late on 28 January. After declaring a state of emergency from 4 p.m., the SMC implemented a defence scheme, which – incredibly – placed the responsibility for protecting the northeastern area of the Settlement, including the contested extra-Settlement Northern Roads, in the hands of one of the potential combatants, the Japanese (British troops manned a line in the west). Nobody told the Chinese. And when Japanese marines went into Chapei to man these lines, they were accompanied by civilian provocateurs and were looking to be fired on by Chinese troops, who obliged. The defence scheme therefore invited the conflict which followed, and which the Japanese waged from the Settlement regardless of repeated SMC and diplomatic protests. The Chinese Nineteenth Route army resisted stoutly, and war raged for over a month in Shanghai. This was a vicious battle. Japanese civilian irregulars were in the forefront of attacks on Chinese civilians. Chapei was ravaged. The Japanese bombed and blasted the suburb, but the Settlement was not spared either; one bomb hit the Wing On cotton mill, and shellfire and rifle-fire killed sixty-one people. The Settlement's foreign residents watched the fires at night from their rooftops, while tens of thousands of refugees poured in. But if the conflict was devastating, this was a resilient city. The Special Municipality showed its mettle in post-war reconstruction. Shanghai bounced back.

Let's imagine Maurice Tinkler's return to this city and its history. He stepped off the boat on 28 January 1931 and would have lodged

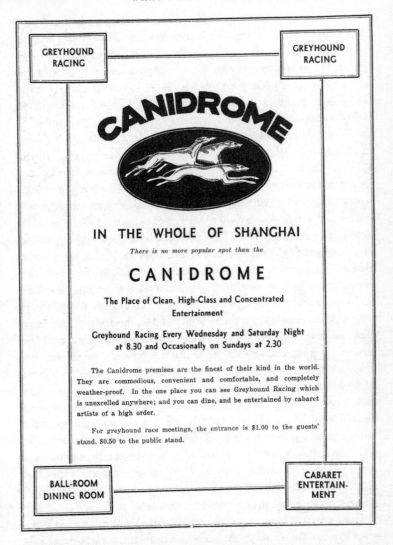
with a friend, possibly back at 26 Carter road, or with someone like G. S. Forrest – a Health Department inspector he had listed on his US immigration form as a friend – until he found modestly priced accommodation. He wasn't the lodgings type, and most likely found an apartment in the French Concession, off the usual patch, which he

shared, 'messing' – splitting the bills (rent, servants, probably a 'boy' and a cook, and food) – with someone in a similar position, or with one of his lodge acquaintances from the Shanghai Power Company or similar. He would have scanned the papers, combing page 8 of the *North China Daily News* for job ads, as well as the classifieds in the *Shanghai Evening Post and Mercury* and the *Shanghai Times*. He looked in a leisurely fashion, registering with the British Chamber of Commerce (but hoping rather to get work with a US firm) and keeping an ear out for opportunities when he went to lodge meetings or the Masonic Club. He would have met some of his former colleagues at the lodge. Perhaps his old acquaintance Assistant Commissioner S. C. Young made the odd suggestion or introduction. Tinkler wasn't broke, and he was initially too proud to take any position which opened. Of course, his reputation would have preceded him; not everybody would have been keen on a man some saw as a loud-mouth tough guy who blew his job in the police through drinking. I can't see him as a soap salesman. Instead, he took the odd job as a reliable trouble-shooter, a bit blunt perhaps at times, a little forceful and impatient, but a man who kept his word and got things done. And his 'honesty and integrity' could be easily vouched for. But what he did out of the office was his business at long last, no one else's, and this for only the second time in his adult life (the first was after his demobilization). He got by, but he wasn't saving. It was not quite hand to mouth, but it got a little more precarious as the months went on, and as his savings trickled away. He might have moved into the YMCA to cut costs. But maintaining his self-respect got more difficult. Still, he acquired some office and business experience on these jobs, which stood him in good stead when he was recruited in early 1934 by the liquidators of Tan Kah Kee Limited, a Singapore-based company, to handle the company's affairs in Nanchang, the capital of Jiangxi province.

Tinkler would have approved wholeheartedly of the war in 1932; most Britons did. Here at last, went the club talk, somebody had the guts to give the bloody Chinese the bloody nose they deserved. This is what they had expected the Shanghai Defence Force to do in 1927.[22] The Shanghailander atmosphere stank in 1931. The summer floods on the Yangtsze had prompted a nasty rash of letters to the *North China Daily News* (disowned by the paper itself) which argued that

as China wanted to rid itself of foreign settlements, then it should shift
for itself in times of trouble as foreign residents had too uncertain a
future to allow them to worry about the 'hostile' Chinese.[23] There was
the alleged 'failure' to stand up to Chinese nationalism in 1925–7,
and the tensions thereafter as the foreign position was pinned back to
the letter of the treaties. It left many Britons still spoiling for a fight,
even a proxy fight, and they cheered on the Japanese. Tinkler would
have cheered, too, even if the Japanese were only the 'best of a bad
bunch', as he put it in 1921. The Settlement needed defending during
the conflict, but he kept out of it this time. There was no scouting
behind the front lines, although there was possibly work for a man
willing to take a bit of a risk. There were British and other foreign
businesses with properties in the areas of conflict. In autumn 1937,
during the second Shanghai war, some enterprising Britons made
themselves profitably useful by entering the battle zones in the immediate aftermath of conflict to regain control of stock, records or property.
For some, this involved using their influence with the Japanese, but
others relied a bit more on presence and cheek, and extraterritoriality.
Perhaps he did some of this work.

He never wrote home. Perhaps he turned back in the United States
in late 1930 because he was unable to face the humiliation of return,
to face crossing a continent, another ocean, to report back and bring
back failure. In any case he wanted to wait until he'd got a firm
position, and could then perhaps rewrite his exit from the SMP in a
better light. After all, he'd never stopped complaining about conditions
and pay, let alone its nepotism (when it didn't benefit him) or its
powerlessness and pusillanimous political leadership. But that firm
position never quite opened up, and then silence became a habit. And
Tinkler had spent almost eight years as the Shanghai detective, glossing
his letters to give his life and work an edge of glamour. It wouldn't be
easy to find the right words to undo all that, to admit that the man of
the family couldn't even keep his own job and had lost it in such –
let's be honest – ridiculous circumstances. And he'd grown distant
from Edith over the years as well, home leave in 1928 making it clear
that he had few real ties to the country. He had been on his own
since joining up in 1915 and was on his own still. He didn't want
long-distance sympathy, and he wasn't going to take any advice. So

he got on quietly with his Shanghai life, or as much of it as he could re-create. He'd never been much of a sportsman (and he left no items of sports clothing or equipment at his death), he was more of a restless traveller and a creature of the Shanghai night. He would have dated a Russian or two, sallied out occasionally into the cabarets, but more often and alone haunted the movie theatres – the Grand, Carlton, Nanking, Lyceum, Cathay. Shanghai was all movie theatres in the 1930s, all soothing electric dreams. He turned up at the monthly meetings of Lodge Erin, keeping up with police gossip, loudly inflicting his own opinions on new police recruits who joined the lodge, damning Gerrard, damning the Scots (still in control), and of course damning the Chinese and the Western powers who acquiesced in both the boxing-in of Settlement ambition and the capitulations to the Guomindang's nationalist agenda. Disappointment and then living with such continual uncertainty coarsened him bit by bit. Police discipline had prompted him to check his tongue and think twice, most of the time anyway. Not now; now he pushed a bit harder, more insistently, sailing closer to the wind. He probably drank a bit – but who the hell in the empire world didn't? And he collected stamps, quietly sorting and ordering these small delicate objects when otherwise wholly at the mercy of fate and Shanghai circumstance.

9

Adrift in the Empire World

On 11 May 1934 Tinkler sat for a portrait in the Ho Chee photographic studio in the city of Nanchang. It's not a shot for an official pass or permit; the copy that survives sits in a card frame with stand, and was to be given or kept. It is an extraordinary image, unlike any others remaining amongst his papers, and its difference shocks. It shows a bushy-bearded man, slouched on a seat and wearing an open-necked khaki shirt, a man who has lost touch with his former self. Unlike most of his portraits, it shows Tinkler looking off to one side, not confronting the camera with a direct gaze. What prompted the man who always put his best side forward – well-groomed, well-preened, suited and shod – to commission and then preserve such an object? The act seems to speak of belligerent disdain for what others might think and see in him. But it also speaks of self-loathing. Tinkler no longer cares in the old way. 'This, after all, is what I am,' it says. Three years of fending for himself outside the SMP show in Maurice Tinkler's eyes and on his face. There are no further dated photographs among his private papers.

If this photograph shows Maurice for what he is, then what precisely was he? This book is not just the life of a Shanghai policeman whose promising career was wrecked by hubris (and a bottle). It is an exploration of a largely ignored stratum of the colonial experience. Empire life was not just about the fixed official appointment, marriage, early death or broken health of the administrative, military or business caste. But we mostly conceive the work of empire in terms of the settled, gentle rhythm of the careers of those administering it: of recruitment, a sojourn of two decades or so, punctuated by long leaves at 'home', separation from children sent back for a proper education,

concluding (usually) with retirement to Britain; re-familiarization and re-orientation to lesser, anonymous domestic states after the privileges of race and power followed.[1] But for most men and women it was a far from settled existence. There was constant movement within the world of the empire British, as they sought better opportunities, or fled mistakes, failures and even crimes. They migrated, they returned, they re-migrated or tried somewhere else. The Shanghailander world re-created in memoir and interview is mostly a place with servants, proper houses and salaries, in which families grew, and new identities were forged. But the unsettled world of empire life took in the city on the Huangpu, too, and that world is explored in this chapter of Maurice Tinkler's life. We've seen already how the experience of colonists was differentiated by class, and how misleading it is to think simply in black and white. Their experience was also about failure, about reconsideration and experimentation. In 1934 Maurice was living on his wits. He had passed through many of the differing states of the overseas empire experience. He had been recruited by a colonialist organization, had chucked in the job, had taken a look at opportunities elsewhere, returned and foraged for employment in a depression-hit world. And he almost hit rock-bottom; the Ho Chee photographer caught that squarely on 11 May in Nanchang, and framed it.

Nanchang, a city of upwards of a million souls some 400 miles from Shanghai, still possessed its city walls and was, claimed Carl Crow's 1933 *Handbook for China*, 'conservative, wealthy and proud'.[2] Crow, as we shall see, already needed updating, but his was the guide Tinkler would have had to hand when he went. (Tinkler had actually met him on the battlefield at Liuhe in 1924 – the treaty port world was small – and he had not then thought his account of the fighting very accurate.) The capital of Jiangxi province had escaped the terrible damage of the nineteenth-century Taiping rebellion, and although it was 'progressive' enough (in Crow's eyes) to have welcomed electric street lighting early, and to run an efficient health department, 'Western influence has not yet penetrated the city to any noticeable extent'. In 1921 Crow had warned that 'No one should go there except with letters of introduction to local foreigners' (about thirty of them, mostly mission-aries), but by 1933 it at least boasted a 'semi-foreign' hotel where the foreigner could perhaps be satisfied without having to send 'his white collars a hundred miles to Kiukiang to be laundered', as was apparently the case in 1921.

On 2 February 1934 Maurice Tinkler went to Nanchang, probably taking a boat to Kiukiang (Jiujiang) along the Yangtsze, and then a train south to the city. He had been sent by the liquidators of the Singapore-based rubber-goods-to-biscuits conglomerate, Tan Kah Kee & Co., and had instructions to regain control of the Nanchang branch of the firm, wind up its affairs and close it down. Tinkler was lucky to get the job; that same month Probationary Sergeant Barney Wall wrote to dissuade his unemployed brother from coming to Shanghai to try his luck: 'this is one of the worst places for employment as far as Europeans are concerned', he explained, all the big firms were laying off Europeans: 'they can get Chinese to do their clerical work for a quarter of the pay.'[3] But Tan Kah Kee needed a European in Nanchang. The firm was a south-east Asian phenomenon, built up by a Chinese immigrant into a giant producer of rubber raincoats, boots, shoes, umbrellas, tennis balls, toys and tyres at its Sumbawa Road complex in Singapore.[4] With upwards of eighty-seven foreign branches in the summer of 1933 it had decided to close them all down in the face of the worldwide collapse in rubber prices. From November 1933 onwards there had been 'deadlock' of some sort over the Nanchang store, but in February 1934 the parent company went bust and the local situation needed swift resolution. Tinkler might have done similar work for Tan Kah Kee (although none is mentioned in a letter of appreciation he received on 14 August), or else he might have done such work previously for the liquidators. Either way, in the letter it was noted that within days of his arrival on 6 February Tinkler had broken the deadlock. He had 'obtained full control of the Branch in spite of open antagonism on the part of the employees and the Authorities', and before his departure in July had 'disposed of the store on very favourable terms' and 'collected a very considerable portion of the outstanding book debts'.[5] We don't know what the problem was, but it is possible that the local employees or agents had sought official connivance in rebuffing a change in management, and the closing down of the branch. The 'foreign representative' already on the spot had been beaten by this. Tinkler had then probably thrown his weight around, presumably abusing his extraterritorial status to try and browbeat opposition, claiming that the local authorities had no right to be involved because Tan Kah Kee, as a Singaporean company, was British-protected in China. Although Nanchang was not a treaty port, extraterritoriality was deemed to follow the extra-territorial individual. Pushy British companies in the years before the reassertion of Chinese nationalism extended extraterritorial status to their Chinese employees, collaborators and agents, and even to their goods (such as British American Tobacco's cigarettes), even when in the hands of Chinese agents far from the main trading networks. Tan Kah Kee was not entitled to extraterritorial protection (and its founder, Chen Jiakang, was an ardent Chinese patriot), but by using Tinkler those closing down the firm aimed to stretch extraterritoriality to serve their needs. And after only four days Tinkler had control, and set to winding up the shop's affairs with 'energy and push'.

Nanchang certainly wasn't Shanghai. For all its 'progressive' charac-ter, foreign goods were in short supply, while 'Western methods of doing business have not been adopted by the local merchants'.[6] For a man who liked to have himself photographed in hotel lounges, staying at the shop or even at that one 'semi-foreign' hotel in Nanchang would have been a bleak prospect. There might still be those thirty foreign missionaries for company, but Tinkler wasn't company for mission-aries, and the *China Hong List* doesn't indicate any other foreign presence. And Tinkler had never much bothered with China. It was British China which he toured, the old treaty ports, the popular mountain and coastal resorts, or the houseboat country west of Shang-hai. But those forays were about blowing away Shanghai cobwebs, getting fresh air and manly exercise. He never went touring China, and wasn't alone in this, but Maurice Tinkler was particularly a Shanghai man, and nothing about Shanghai would have prepared him for provincial Nanchang. It may have been revitalizing itself, like much of urban China in these years: recent urban reform had seen the building of new wide streets, such as Zhongshan lu (Sun Yat-sen Road) where the photographer's studio was located. Yet there was nothing there for him except a job. But at least there was a job.

It was a job in a troublesome place, however, and at a troublesome time. Nanchang was no longer a sleepy provincial city; it was the key logistical base of the National Government's fifth 'Bandit Suppression Campaign', and in early 1934 it became the headquarters of a briefly frenetic social and spiritual reform drive known as the New Life Movement. So Tinkler was right in the thick of things again, and he ran foul of them. The 'bandits' were the Chinese communists. Those who had sought the sanctuary of the countryside after their Guomindang allies turned on them in 1927 had launched various uprisings in central China to little avail and much cost. Nanchang itself had been briefly held in 1927, and had repulsed a further attack in 1930. In southern Jiangxi, communist units had coalesced and established what became a 'Chinese Soviet Republic' in the highland fastnesses of the province, with a population at its peak of about five million. After 1931 they were joined by the urban leadership of the Chinese Communist Party (CCP) as it was driven out of Shanghai. Successive campaigns to extricate the soviet failed, but had succeeded in hemming it in tightly. A Nanchang Bandit Suppression Headquarters was established in 1933, and in September that year Chiang Kai-shek, taking personal command and with experienced German army advisers, launched the '5th Encirclement and Suppression Campaign' (the other four had failed). The province was laced with 1,500 miles of new roads and 14,000 manned blockhouses. Local militia were organized and half a million troops were brought in to pin down and starve out the enemy. A new aerodrome was built and bombing raids made on communist troops and positions. On 16 October 1934 the battered Red Army was to abandon the soviet and move out on what came to be known as the 'Long March' to the north-western base at Yan'an. In the meantime war was good for business in Nanchang, and presumably the demand for goods sold by Tan Kah Kee would have been high (and it may have been why liquidation was politically complicated): some two million men are estimated to have passed through the city in 1933 alone – they would have needed rubber boots and waterproofs – and refugees poured in from the conflict zones.

The New Life Movement was linked to this drive. It was formally launched in Nanchang by Chiang at a mass rally on 11 March, five weeks after Tinkler arrived in the city.[7] It aimed to revitalize troops and officials mid-campaign, but took on national significance. A haphazard mix of Confucian and Christian self-renewal ideas, flavoured with public hygiene injunctions (forbidding spitting and public urination or defecation), it aimed to reform mores and behaviour, and impose military discipline on China's anarchic civilians. 'The reason why the Chinese people were looked down upon by foreigners', claimed Chiang Kai-shek at the rally, 'was because they were physically weaker and their mode of living was not so regular and clean as that of the foreigners.'[8] This was an old refrain, long mooted by China's impatient modernizers, although Chiang welded to it Confucian ideology. But it came down to bodily basics all the same. New instructions for the masses aimed to make them regular and clean: 'Don't crowd; keep in line', 'Don't spit', 'Be neat', 'Kill flies and rats; they breed disease', 'Politeness and obedience to law smooth the way', were among the dozens of New Life injunctions. There were to be no bystanders. After the March rally 'the crowd held a big parade through the streets making suggestions and corrections of people's appearances and behaviour'. Student teams were sent out to lecture the public, and plans were laid for officials to visit every single home in Nanchang to advise on the campaign, while '1,000 citizen detectives' were recruited to watch the streets. On 18 March a spectacular lantern procession was organized through the crowded city to spread the word. The *North China Daily News* correspondent was (almost) impressed:

[S]ome of these injunctions are being carried out. The police are seeing that pedestrians keep on the sidewalk; that traffic keeps to the left; and that people keep in line at the ticket offices, public ferries and bus stations. People who appear in public with coats or collars unbuttoned are politely saluted by the police and are requested to observe the rule of neatness.[9]

Tinkler was here: in a city armed to the teeth with highly motivated nationalist soldiers, its citizens policed by sumptuary vigilantes pouncing on those with unbuttoned coats. He'd not shown much tolerance in the past for public morality campaigns; he wasn't going to change now.

'The heat has been intense with no relief at nights and hardly a breath of fresh air,' reported the senior British naval officer on the Yangtsze in his July–August report, 'and life has been most uncomfortable.'[10] On 14 July, according to a local newspaper, at about 8 o'clock in the evening in the midst of a fearfully hot spell, Tinkler took a stroll along the new boulevard named for Sun Yat-sen. He was stripped to the waist. Outside a fruit shop he bumped into a gendarmerie patrol that 'politely enlightened him' about the New Life regulations which stipulated that men should be properly clothed at all times. They asked him to dress properly in future when abroad. Without a word, apparently, he assaulted them, 'fists and feet flying'. As he was a foreigner, the patrol broke away from the confrontation as soon as it could, and reported to their superiors.[11] He may have been drunk, or drinking, his nerves may have been frayed by the struggle to regain control of the branch and to settle its affairs with no help from the authorities, but the cause was more likely to be his unrestrained quick temper. Moreover, there were few treaty port Britons who would have either taken seriously the New Life's injunctions, or felt that they would apply to them. And there were few Britons, although perhaps by 1934 there were more than in 1928, who would have taken seriously the idea of having to obey a Chinese soldier, especially over the question of the wearing of a shirt. Tinkler's troubles over Tan Kah Kee probably stemmed from local politics, but his confrontation with the local gendarmerie originated fully in the national politics and daily detail of the New Life ferment, and in his own behaviour in not observing the new 'rule of neatness'.

This was the type of incident which had long bored and exasperated British consuls, although it was getting more unusual in the aftermath of the triumph of the Guomindang. Provincial chairman Xiong Shihui had served as Shanghai Garrison Commander in 1929–31, and gave short shrift to his obstreperous visitor. He requested clearance from the British Consulate in Hankow to have Tinkler deported from the city to prevent any 'future objectionable incidents', and the Consulate agreed with alacrity, after contacting Shanghai. On 24 July, together with his interpreter Wang Youjing, Tinkler left Nanchang on a Kiukiang-bound vessel. Another report had him escorted by a squad of gendarmes to a ship on 27 July. He was transferred to a British gunboat at Kiukiang on 29 July and so finally expelled from the province.[12] The details are a little sketchy. It seems that he did not go willingly – he was 'forcibly removed on a gun-boat', remarked a British official later – and that he possibly returned after the first deportation.[13] He may have been held in some form of detention, probably house arrest or confinement in a hotel, in the intervening period. Tinkler may well have put the incident down to local harassment of his efforts to close down the Tan Kah Kee store. The *China Press* reported that local 'feeling ran high' after the incident, which suggests that the assault may have been taken up by opponents of his handling of the business closure, but equally it may have mushroomed because of the heightened nationalism of the New Life campaign in the city.[14] The small Peking legation file on the incident no longer exists, but the index survives and this shows that in a letter to diplomats dated 25 August Tinkler apparently narrated a series of 'incidents in connexion with closing of Nanchang branch' of Tan Kah Kee. The affair of the shirt was probably only one of these, and the Shanghai Consulate-General had notified the company on 18 July that it was not entitled to British protection in China.[15] 'He was a real tough guy, always looking for trouble' remembered Consul A. D. Blackburn five years later.[16] Tinkler had never liked diplomats. They didn't like him. Britons had been ordered out of the China concessions by consuls before, or spirited away to calm such situations down. Very few got a gunboat to themselves, or the publicity.

Above all, yet again, there was the humiliation of it. News of Tinkler's misadventure reached Shanghai before him. The local papers had picked up on reports in the Hankow press, as well as a Reuter's telegram, describing the misadventures of a 'Mr Dinklam' (his Chinese name was given as 'Ding-ge-lan'). 'Foreigner at Nanchang fails to keep shirt on, is deported', noted the *China Press* making fun of the affair. 'Briton removed from Nanchang', reported the *North China Daily News*.[17] Mr Dinklam's true identity would have spread swiftly in the small social world of the Shanghailander; gossiping journalists and consular staff would have helped. There would be chuckles in the police canteens, and little sympathy: Tinkler forcibly deported on a British gunboat, no surprises there. Hit a policeman, did he? Not for the first time, Fred West might have said. Back in Shanghai Tinkler presented himself at the offices of the company's liquidators in the Hongkong and Shanghai Bank's Bund headquarters. A highly complimentary reference was handed over to him on the spot. As 'the firm's branches were being liquidated, his employment is terminated', it concluded. The document has an air of tension to it. Tinkler had embarrassed the liquidators and caused difficulties with the British Consulate, and they wanted to be rid of him. He probably insisted they hand over to him a reference which fulsomely praised, as it did, his handling of the business at Nanchang. He then wrote to the Legation in Peking, aiming to put the Minister straight on the matter, probably furious that lack of diplomatic support – to put it mildly – had cost him his job. He also pitched up at the Shanghai Consulate. Former Consul-General Brenan remembered that he'd dealt with the affair personally.[18] Tinkler would have had nothing but contempt for the political excitement that coincided with his stay in Nanchang. Obviously there was stress and tension involved in his business mission, and he was also isolated from his familiar haunts in what he would have thought a dull city with few other foreigners for company. The treaty port press was itself bemusedly, but politely, derisory on the subject of New Life. Its enthusiastic correspondent in Nanchang was probably a missionary, as were most of the out-of-Shanghai correspondents, and missions saw the movement as related to their own aims for the moral uplift and physical regeneration of the Chinese. Tinkler would have sneered at the lantern parades, the prissy street preaching and the vigilante patrols. Seeing no hope for China anyway, he would have felt only the impact of the campaign's intrusive surveillance of behaviour on the streets, and he lashed out. But he was no longer in Shanghai, he was in a Chinese-administered city; and he was no longer in that good old China, where foreign prestige and might could carry a shirtless man beyond the reach of Chinese authority and the polite injunction of a patrolling gendarme. The lack of restraint boded ill.

Back to Shanghai he went, and in Shanghai he stayed, probably without work – there is no reference covering the ensuing period. The liquidators recommended him to potential employers as 'a reliable, honest and trustworthy assistant', although on the manner of his departure from Nanchang they were pointedly silent. He resurfaces with a small but telling mention in the 1935 edition of the *China Hong List*. This was compiled towards the end of 1934, and 'R. M. Tinkler' is listed as working and living at, of all places, the Salvation Army Men's Hostel, at Yang Terrace, off the city's Weihaiwei Road. This was humble pie indeed. Founded in 1929 the Shelter had facilities for some 31 men at a time by 1934, catering for 'respectable Europeans (except Russians)' – they would have swamped the facility – 'who, through various causes, found themselves Homeless in the great Port of Shanghai'. It was run by a Salvation Army Captain, David McIl-venny, and another Salvation Army couple, and usually managed on a daily basis by a man like Tinkler, responsible but perhaps also capable of handling the odd difficult situation. Run as a 'real Home from Home – providing comfortable beds and three meals per day', which for those who could pay cost about $1.50 a day, it distributed free meals and cast-off clothing, and held thrice-weekly meetings at which 'the men are urged to seek God'. By the end of the 1930s it received about 80 men a year, but 134 had come through its doors in 1932. The Depression provided a steady stream of 'stranded Euro-peans', and one of them was Maurice Tinkler. Whatever cash he had, boosted by his Nanchang earnings, had obviously been whittled down fine, for managing the hostel was hardly much better than being a homeless inmate. As the 'only credential required for their admittance into the Hostel is a genuine need of assistance', we can assume that this applied to Tinkler.[19] But Maurice Tinkler, truculent atheist, was also an anti-missionary bigot. He may have had more time for the Salvation Army, its muscular social work and low key approach to actual preaching in the hostel, but this seems unlikely. He may have had some bad luck in his missing years, but in 1934 he really hit the bottom, at least as far as his own luck went. 'To be without a job in a foreign land, and with very little prospect of ever securing one is by no means a happy position to be in,' wrote McIlvenny in November 1934, 'yet one can keep his self-respect if he feels that some one has an interest in him.'[20] Tinkler didn't want that interest, but he had to take it.

Tinkler was now in the fraught borderland between security and destitution, where control over his destiny was difficult to maintain. It was a region many Shanghailanders knew all too well. At least he wasn't the only ex-policeman who ended up working for the Salvation Army. His 1919 colleague William Slater had resigned from the force in February 1929. A former butcher and Machine Gun Corps private, he had been stuck in a sergeant's job in the Vehicle Inspection Office for eight years. An early marriage 'off the strength' hadn't helped, and by 1929 he was 'hopelessly in debt'. Slater told the force that he wanted to leave China, but instead took up a job locally with Jardines. In July 1932 that went with the Depression. After fourteen straight months without work he applied to rejoin the SMP. 'This man has had his lesson outside the Police', noted CID chief Aiers in mitigation, but there was no vacancy. By November 1936 he was managing the Salvation Army's new Men's Shelter at the former Amoy Road Gaol. This was much less of a 'home from home'. The original hostel catered 'for a little more respectable class of men', but Amoy Road was an emergency shelter for 'down and outs', for the homeless and the indigent, for ex-prisoners and men out of hospital. It catered mostly, but not wholly, for Russians. As far as we know, Tinkler never sank this far, managing to maintain at least a tenuous hold on the 'respectable'. But some ex-SMP men did sink further. Neil MacQuarrie joined from Shaforce in November 1928. In 1933 he was barrack-room Sergeant at Central, 'an easy job' according to Dan Cormie, that left him with 'a good deal of spare time on his hands', which he put to drinking. He stayed on after being sacked. Cormie 'found the poor guy on many occasions begging in the streets'. Complaints were made, he was arrested for vagrancy, and then repatriated.[21]

The Salvation Army also operated an Employment Bureau, matching employers with unemployed foreigners. There were 1,201 registrations in 1934, but only 734 were placed, and, as it pointed out in 1936, opportunities for Europeans were declining. Young Chinese, fluent in English, or Shanghai-born Eurasians were taking the available places. Many foreigners who signed on were helped to leave Shanghai altogether. Those who hung on regardless, often with few skills but domestic ties, or because after long-term residence they had 'no other home', were regarded 'because of their dissolute habits' as 'almost or entirely unemployable'.[22] This was the other side of the Shanghai experience, of the men who found themselves, like Tinkler, scraping by, failing to live the life of empire. Yang Terrace and the SMP intersected in various ways. Some of the residents were new in town. Dennis Stevens arrived in Shanghai as a seaman in June 1938, and moved into the hostel while he searched for work. In July he joined the SMP. Alexander Crighton left the Royal Navy for a job as a boxing instructor in Shanghai, but this fell through, and he applied to join the SMP from the Salvation Army home, with the stated hope 'to make good with the Force'. (A fight with a bar girl in the Tip Top Café on Blood Alley put paid to that aim five months later.) Yang

Terrace was one of the addresses resorted to by ex-soldier James Blackwood, who arrived in 1934 after the failure of his Singapore import-export business. Blackwood teamed up with former SMP Sergeant C. J. Capes, dismissed for poor discipline in 1929, and started up a similar business. Capes caught his new associate spending the firm's money 'on various lady friends', one of whom introduced him to a drug smuggler on whose behalf he had readied the firm to serve as legitimate cover. The firm was liquidated shortly thereafter, and Blackwood later tried to join the SMP. He 'has had many opportunities during his stay in the Far East to make good', concluded a report rejecting his application, but his behaviour and choice of associates told against him.[23] Other residents were out of work, not keen on leaving, and trying to make their way through an increasingly difficult city. Hugh Joseph Connolly had joined the SMP from Shaforce in Shanghai after nine years in the army, but was dismissed in 1931 and charged with aiding and abetting a robbery. The charge didn't quite stick in court, although his alleged confederates, four Chinese constables, were jailed. Connolly passed up the available passage to Britain and stayed on. During the 1932 war he joined the SVC where 'he was suspected of being concerned in the larceny of jewellery', but again nothing could be proved. He lent his name to Chinese interests in order to acquire boarding-house and restaurant licences in return for free board and lodging, and claimed to have also tried to work as a vacuum-cleaner salesman. Connolly applied through the Salvation Army for a belated indulgence passage in January 1936, but failed to take advantage of it, staying on in the city, in debt, and without legitimate employment.[24] Another man's stay was briefer: dismissed for misconduct in late June 1931 after a year's service, he tried to stay on, but was later detained in the mental ward at the Victoria Nursing Home on the instructions of the Consulate; penniless on leaving, this unfortunate stayed in the hostel before the SMC indulged him a steerage passage home.[25] Tinkler would once have considered himself above such company, and probably still did, but he shared their predicament and would have been seen by others as just another one of these grifting chancers.

A network of organizations existed, as it did in every treaty port and in every colony, to deal with such men. White indigence on the streets of a colonial possession was bad for 'race prestige'. The consuls did not have the power to eject Britons from the city, or prevent entry (although in the case of a man like MacQuarrie concerted communal effort could get rid of them). So provision had to be made to help out those who turned up, and those down on their luck. The United Services Association worked specifically with ex-servicemen (two senior SMP representatives sat on its committee in 1928). The Thomas Hanbury Institute, a sailors' home in Hongkew's Broadway, provided eighty beds, a number of which were permanently reserved by the British Consulate-General for 'Distressed British Subjects', and ten of which were so used at any one time in 1928.[26] The public balls of the British national societies raised funds to give such men a chance, or to pack them off home, steerage or third class. Some men resorted to these institutions *in extremis*, while others just managed to scrape by between jobs. Four months after his dismissal in June 1924 John Ritchie was living, destitute, in the Hanbury Institute through the charity of the St Andrews Society. Off he was shipped, third class. Young Stan Bailey had resigned after three years' service the same year, because of heavy debts. Too ashamed to return home or tell his family of his problems, he stayed in Shanghai, although without success and his requests five months later for passage to South Africa or Canada were vetoed by Commissioner Barrett. Bailey moved to Hankow to try his luck but was soon back, penniless and living in the Hanbury Institute courtesy of the United Services Association. 'We hear awful rumours from China of his doings,' wrote his sister begging for news in November 1925, 'One friend told us he had taken a lot of money and spent it on Russian women. Another told us that he was in prison for his evil doings.' Barrett relented, and sent him home to his family, third class.[27] John Thomas joined the SMP after five years in the army and a year in the Chinese Maritime Customs. Dismissed for 'Gross Misconduct' in December 1929, he spent seven months unemployed in Shanghai before persuading the SMC to book himself and C. J. Capes a passage to Brazil. Instead, he skipped town to join former treaty port journalist Bertram Lenox-Simpson, who had seized the Tianjin customs on behalf of an insurrectionary coalition of northern militarists. The coalition was defeated and Lenox-Simpson assassinated. Finding no other work in Tianjin, Thomas returned to

Shanghai, where he punctuated his unemployment over the next three years with bouts of work as a refrigerator salesman and on behalf of the National Flood Relief Commission in Kiukiang, but was often 'verging on a state of destitution' although '*fully determined to make good*'. He begged a post in the gaol service in late 1932, but was rejected. By 1933 he was 'at the end of my financial resources and completely without resources in this jobless town'. Something came through, and he is last listed as an Inspector for the Shanghai Society for the Prevention of Cruelty to Animals in November 1936.[28] Such a pattern of work and unemployment reinforces my assumptions about Tinkler's missing years, except that he had more savings to start with, no previous China experience to take advantage of, and was certainly no salesman.

Actual destitution was unusual. Few men followed Neil MacQuarrie in falling so far through the network of relief agencies that dealt with the 'D. B. S.' – the Distressed British Subject. But there was always an indigent Briton or two, seamen thrown up on the shore and the like. There is even one cheery account of drink-fuelled indigence in China, published in 1935. Bob Moore's *Don't Call Me a Crook* is a sensationalist and by no means reliable read, but it conveys the flavour of the fight, and the collapse. A Glaswegian seaman, Moore claimed to have worked for the Asiatic Petroleum Company on the Yangtsze in the 1920s and describes a six-month binge in Shanghai, before repatriation as a 'D. B. S.' For him, the highlight of the Bund was the Hongkong and Shanghai Bank building; it was 'the coolest place in Shanghai', although 'they used to put me outside': 'All Shanghai knew about me. All the rickshaw boys knew me. All the men at the bars knew me.' From the gutter, he was arrested by the police, but 'I could not allow that as the policemen were Sikhs. They are meant only for keeping coolies in order, so I said they must get a white policeman.'[29] But British indigence paled in comparison with the Russian predicament. Poor employment prospects in the city were compounded by low social status. Older men, and those with poor language skills, and women in search of a respectable trade were in a weak position. A 1937 survey found almost 55 per cent unemployment in such selected occupations as clerks, teachers, and chauffeurs.[30] The SMC was no charity. The Russians went to Amoy Road, and to the

Salvation Army. And into the mental ward came the worst cases from the streets. Anatol Kalganoff, found wandering the Settlement in June 1935, 'mentally deranged, undernourished and very poorly clothed'; Ivan Silaeff, discovered by the SMP in December 1934 in an 'emaciated condition, mentally confused and absolutely destitute'; Mrs S. Biza, found that same month by a district nurse 'living under deplorable conditions – mentally deranged, undernourished and poorly clothed'.[31] Indigent Britons could at least eventually be removed, such as J. G. Warren, his health 'more or less shattered' after years in Shanghai as a tea-taster, unemployed after 1924, in debt and then in the mental ward for ten months, before consular repatriation for himself and another Briton was arranged on a British troopship.[32] The availability of even a modest number of places for indigent Russians worried the SMC; it assumed that if word got around every Russian vagrant in China would be heading to Shanghai. The indigent Russian evidenced the nightmare of empire failure, of the 'white' man sunk low in the Oriental gutter.

Men like Thomas and Bailey played the system (one lost, one scraped through), but all those leaving the force faced the choice of staying or going. Most ex-policemen went home within the prescribed month, but why did any stay on at all when the odds were so stacked

against them? 'Why not?' might be one answer. Some were optimistic; some just happy-go-lucky. Others reckoned up the odds and decided that even if employment in Shanghai was chancy, under- or unemployment in the city was a tastier prospect than returning to Britain. Others didn't think twice or reckon once. The living could be cheaper; the drinking could be very cheap indeed. Charles Causley articulates this view in his poem 'Able Seaman Hodge Remembers Ceylon', where Hodge pines for the soft, warm, easy life: 'O the pineapple salads of Colombo/The wine-bar at Trincomali/My bonnie lies over the ocean:/The brilliant Arabian sea.'[33] We can assume too that it was the itch portrayed in Kipling's 'Mandalay' ('If you've 'eard the East a-callin', you won't never 'eed naught else'), as the 'neater, sweeter maiden in a cleaner, greener land!' was a cheaper maiden too. But Shanghai wasn't Colombo or Mandalay. The streets of the city were as 'gritty', and the climate as 'blasted' as anything London could offer Kipling's forlornly exiled British soldier. But there was always the likelihood of a passage back to Britain if things went wrong. Some men were too ashamed, while others just felt stuck. The list of twenty-nine ex-police who were resident in Shanghai in November 1936 shows no obvious pattern. Five of the men were ex-Shaforce, but although six of them were from the 1919 cohort most of the twenty-nine had left the SMP within the previous eight years, and one would soon rejoin. The force did take men back. Harry Diprose rejoined after almost two years out, W. W. Selvey after closer to three. Sergeant Duffy spent fifteen months out from 1931 to 1932, Buster Davies endured life outside for nine months in 1930, and ex-soldier E. L. Gibson took only four months to change his mind.[34] All too often the request to rejoin came from men who were desperate, and all too often from men who were no longer wanted.

In their book *Bad Colonists*, anthropologists Nicholas Thomas and Richard Eves set out to present the underside of colonial life through the letters of two nineteenth-century South Seas colonists.[35] One of these, Vernon Lee Walker, had slipped through the settler hierarchy in Australasia, from a clerical job in Melbourne to a dangerous position as supercargo on a New Hebrides trading schooner, living on the boat for months at a time before his violent death at native hands. This was no idealized empire life, or death. In that sense he was a failure – and he knew himself to be such – and he was then a bad colonist, slipping about on the unsteady ground where colonist and colonized met. There were those who failed through no fault of their own – poor land, poor prospects, an economic downturn – and those culpable in their own failure. But the beachcomber, the blackbirder, the remittance man: all these have their place in the histories of colonialism, even if they serve to embarrass the affable memoirists and raconteurs who populate the nostalgic modern literature of empire. It's an easy temptation to dismiss Connolly and Blackwood, Thomas and Bailey and the like as part of this colourful empire flotsam, men and women who in different ways fell for obvious temptations, for drink, adultery, miscegenation, peculation. Empire had its own ways of accepting and explaining their fall: they lacked character, spine, weren't manly, let themselves go. Medics packed their charges off to the East after passing them fit with wise words about drink in the tropics, knowing that much of their advice would be ignored. And trouble was only to be expected of the lower classes, routinely assumed to be intemperate sexually and in other ways. But Kipling's career began with his tales of the complications that arose in higher-ranking colonial lives in Simla summers, and Kenya's 'Happy Valley' of sybaritic remittance men overshadows much of the settler story. Shanghailander society was widely perceived as morally loose. Cosmopolitanism, concluded one Shanghailander historian, meant that foreign society stuck to the level of the lowest moral standards represented in the city by different national groups, but there were many 'with no standards at all'.[36] Intemperance certainly knew no class bounds. The bad colonist was woven into the empire tapestry. Organizations sifted people out, and people sifted themselves out. They drank, took to the cabarets, ran up debts, got entangled emotionally or physically. They weren't up to the job, could not hack it, could not make good. The bad colonist wasn't necessarily an evil colonist. Many of these people merely failed, and would have failed at home, but in Shanghai, living in or on the margins of a self-consciously 'fast' society, they were perhaps helped on their way. And the proximity of failure was often blithely assumed. Business taipan Jock Swire thought 'Shanghai for a young man fresh from home is the devil and none but the best English and hard bitten Scots can stick it'.[37] Yang Terrace, the Hanbury Institute, the United Services Association, the St George's Society, were all needed to help those who couldn't stick it. In 1936 the Salvation Army helped 205 men find work in Shanghai or leave the port, but mostly the latter.

The Yang Terrace Hostel therefore served as one still point in this turning world. The archives of the SMP Special Branch provide further snapshots of the Shanghai phase of many empire lives. Shanghai was after all just one port of call to those who were travelling empire's crooked paths. These were men and women sometimes living close to the law and off their wits, sometimes moving to Shanghai after failure elsewhere, sometimes too ashamed to head back to Britain. Cecil Jones was one such.[38] A former Indian Army officer, he resigned his commission in 1922 and bought a sheep farm in Australia. After this failed he took a civil service post in Nyasaland, but was jailed for 'criminal negligence in the keeping of his accounts'. After his release Jones went directly to Shanghai, arrived 'destitute', and was given a month's credit by the United Services Association in which to find a job. He called on Commissioner Martin to ask about openings (and on Special Branch to ask 'if there was any chance of his securing a job with the "local Chinese warlord"'), but with a criminal record could not be accepted. So he set himself up as a private detective and debt-collector. For this Jones needed some Shanghai nous, and he set up a partnership with former guardsman George Allen, dismissed from the SMP the previous year after five months' service (and some riotous nights at the Del Monte). Allen had tried his hand as a salesman in Singapore and then returned to Shanghai, losing a similar job there because of indebtedness. 'He is without doubt a thorough waster, and will in all probability end up in the British Court,' concluded the SMP before warning Jones off him. Jones then asked an old wartime colleague (of some 'social standing' and once on the committee of the United Services Association) to intercede and recommend him to the police ('He does not drink, and so far as I know has no vices' while 'his one object in life is to make good'). But, despite 'his considerable experiences as a prison superintendent', there was no position open. By 1932 Jones was sinking into debt, leading the Cathay Hotel to request via the SMP that he settle his accounts. He later gulled a new partner into contracting loans on his behalf. A 1937 report caustically commented on his plausible tongue.[39] As Tinkler wrote, so Jones talked, talking up his prospects, coming clean, striving hard. He appealed to the charity of old friends and local institutions ready to give a second shot at turning out right to a young man of good family who'd made a mistake. The files don't record the conclusion to this tale, but they do show how empire worked and how men worked empire, desperately.

Colonialism, therefore, was often about failure, and about moving on, trying something else, somewhere else, and about loneliness, longing, debt, disease, disaster and death. Men moved on from Shanghai and from the SMP, which served as a gateway to the empire world. They often left to 'make good', and they often succeeded. Some stayed on in China. Inspector George Matheson retired after twenty-five years' service in 1911, founded the Shanghai Mission to Rickshaws and lived on in the city until his death in 1937.[40] Constable Bookless stuck out his first contract in the SMP but later joined the Salt Gabelle, the Chinese salt tax inspectorate, serving for twenty-eight years before retirement in 1939. Other men took police posts in other concessions, down in Amoy, or up north in Tianjin. One man even joined the fundamentalist China Inland Mission.[41] George Matcham joined the SMP in 1919, stuck out one contract and then found work down in Hong Kong at the Race Club stables. The majority went further afield. Robert McLennan resigned at the end of his first term. He had 'no grouse' with the work, but intended 'eventually to join relatives in Australia'. He joined the New South Wales police, serving in Sydney until 1961. Sidney Reading left after four years' service and became a tram-driver in Brisbane. William Campbell resigned in 1929 to take up work through relations in Canada. When the rubber downturn cost him his job in Borneo M. R. L. Lingard joined the SMP in 1931, but moved back to another planting job in Borneo when the situation had improved in 1937. Fifteen years after resigning, William Burnell wrote from Bulawayo to request his superannuation. British empire was full of such men and women, moving through and on. The literature on settlement and settler culture in the dominions and in the African settler colonies mostly ignores the central fact of unsettlement, and of the unsettled, and this churning, turning world of the empire life.[42]

Migration statistics back up the anecdotal evidence of these Shanghai stories.[43] Between 1921 and 1941, 51,446 immigrants arrived in Rhodesia, but they were matched by 33,576 emigrants leaving the colony, representing two-thirds of the incoming total on average (in the first half of the 1930s, in the face of global depression, the proportion reached three-quarters). They moved back to, or on to, South Africa, or they moved elsewhere in Africa or beyond. Between 1923 and 1930 the equivalent 'turnover' in Kenya was on average 85 per cent. At sampled dates for New Zealand it was even higher: 1925: 71 per cent, 1928: 103 per cent, 1931: 83 per cent, 1934: 111 per cent.[44] Just over 780,000 Britons moved to British North America as migrants between 1919 and 1938, many of them assisted by government-funded schemes, but 310,000 British nationals left it to return to Britain. Between 1929 and 1938 the balance tipped in favour of returnees, who outnumbered those departing for Canada by 10,000. Over half a million Britons moved to Australia or New Zealand between 1919 and 1938; 200,000 moved back. Again, for 1929–38 there was a small net gain for Britain, of almost 13,000 returnees. The 1930s saw total emigration from Britain fall to less than a third of the levels of 1919–28, as the global economy changed, and as assisted-passages schemes were withdrawn, but returnee levels fell only to 83 per cent of the levels of the previous decade.[45] A steady flow of Britons came home. But from the evidence of these Shanghai lives it's clear that many of those moving back would have tried their luck elsewhere first. 'I am more of a citizen of the empire than of England,' wrote India-born former Shanghai policeman Basil Duke in 1942. After five years in the SMP – which followed stints as a farmer in New Zealand, a policeman in Samoa and a planter in India – he resigned to join the Sudan Political Service in 1938. 'It really is the duty of such to settle in the Empire if we want to keep it,' he wrote.[46] So if not Shanghai, then New Zealand; I failed here, perhaps I won't there. If not Shanghai, then perhaps the United States, if not the United States then perhaps Shanghai after all. Despite the tightening of entry requirements across the world in the 1930s, a man with a little capital, or some relatives, or the offer of a job, could still move on within an open empire world to try and better himself.

Then there were those who played it for all it was worth and certainly weren't much interested in making good (Kipling's 'Mandalay' again: 'Ship me somewheres east of Suez, where the best is like the worst,/ Where there aren't no Ten Commandments an' a man can raise a thirst'). The SMP Special Branch kept an eye on these, and also undertook reports for foreign consulates, from foreign police forces about arrivals from Shanghai and suspects with a Shanghai past, as well as following up tip-offs about suspicious characters. James Barton, an MI6 officer based at the British Consulate-General, put in a request for information about one Darrell Drake, recently arrived in Hong Kong in October 1937 and 'regarded with suspicion on account of his close association with Japanese and certain undesirable foreigners'. No wonder, was the response, given his twenty-five-year Shanghai record of 'heavy gambling, fornicating, drunken bouts of whiskey drinking . . . and associating with many local shady characters' while serving as a highly respectable (and heavily indebted) teacher in the SMC's Public School for Boys. From the CID in Bulawayo, Southern Rhodesia, came a request in 1933 for information on a suspected prohibited immigrant, 'Ernest William Weekes', who claimed to have been a doctor in Shanghai in 1921–5 and to have 'been associated with the Fire Brigade'. In fact, Weekes had been a wharf supervisor, overseer and municipal fireman, and had left Shanghai suddenly with many debts outstanding, never having represented himself as a doctor. He surfaced in Australia in 1927 when a newspaper chronicled his various frauds in the city of Melbourne. 'I wonder if you have anything on record concerning the following chaps,' enquired the President of the Australian and New Zealand Society of Shanghai in August 1941. Yes indeed, was the response. Nick Boyle: nineteen years in Shanghai after a spell in Manila, 'A waster and a habitual drunkard and practically unemployable. He has no fixed abode at present and is believed to be sleeping out, or in cheap Chinese lodging houses.' Harry Kerrey, professional piano player, aged 46, living in Shanghai for ten years playing in local bands and cabarets, but too much a drunk to find a place in any band, and presently playing in a brothel on the Great Western Road. Council Chairman Brigadier Macnaghten found his name being bandied about in 1931 by a recent arrival from Singapore via Hong Kong. D. A. Rushton, alias D. A. Berkeley-Rushton, self-styled 'Manufacturer's Representative', was hopping from lodging house to lodging house just ahead of the bills and raising credit in ways which led inexorably to a court appearance in 1931. Meanwhile, 'Rush' claimed in a private letter, there was dinner with Macnaghten to prepare for, so perhaps his friend and creditor Betty Botsford could return his impounded dinner clothes? They weren't all British. Commissioner Springfield wrote from Singapore about a suspicious fellow passenger, a US subject who may have been a 'dope' smuggler. A quick check of the antecedents of this Belgian-Chinese Eurasian revealed her to be in the sex rather than the drug trade. A file was created in response to a change of address announcement in the *Shanghai Evening Post and Mercury* classifieds from 'MISS PAULETTE'. Paulette Goubert turned out to have arrived in Shanghai eighteen months previously, after spending time in Hong Kong and Singapore. The apartment was rented by the mistress of G. Lalourcey, French, who ran the Fantasio Café on 'Blood Alley' as well as a number of flats used for professional assignations in the Settlement and French Concession.[47] Drake, Weekes, Goubert and the others moved laterally through the world of empires, skipping this town when things got too hot or complicated, looking for better opportunities in that port, fudging details here, glossing over some facts there, as they accounted for themselves to immigration, passport and security officials. Colonial agencies within and across empires were drawing closer together, especially in the watch for drug smuggling, cross-border prostitution networks, and political radicals. But there was less cohesion than might be thought, especially before the mid-1930s, even within British empire. These files show a floating world of enterprising individuals taking full advantage in particular of the uncertain status of Shanghai and treaty port China, and moving through the open port cities of Asia and beyond. Some came adrift, some were beached, others moved steadily on.

The Special Branch files show too Shanghai's secret life, offering the police's partial view of the world of political radicals, fellow travellers and spies, who moved in and out of the open city, taking advantage of the confusions of multiple administrations and extraterritoriality. If Shanghai was the colonial world's gateway to China, it was also the Comintern's, and served as a staging post on the road to the subject peoples of empire. Rudnik and Moiseenko, whom we met in

Chapter 7 as the Noulens, used Belgian, Swiss and Dutch aliases, and their office served as the business hub for Comintern activities in China and beyond. Richard Sorge lived, worked and spied in the city in 1930–32, on his way through to his spectacular espionage successes in Tokyo.[48] For the Cold War warriors Shanghai was the home of a conspiracy. For General Douglas MacArthur's intelligence chief Charles Willoughby the Shanghai tendrils reached deep into American life, and the SMP's Special Branch files were acquired and then mined for information about American radicals (and Comintern assets) such as Agnes Smedley.[49] For disgruntled ex-MI5 officer Peter Wright, whose paranoia saw betrayal everywhere, the years his former chief Sir Roger Hollis spent in Shanghai working for BAT was the period in which he must have become a Soviet agent.[50] This was a hunch too far, but many of the men and women Wright termed the 'great illegals' – the undercover agents of the Soviet Union – had their Shanghai days. The SMP watched Sorge, it had files on Smedley, and both were listed in a May 1933 report as 'Suspected Soviet agents'.[51] Most of those watched were merely politically leftist, but the seemingly innocently radical could well turn out to be important. Not a lead was left unfollowed. Shanghai's MI6 agents kept in close contact with Special Branch and their letters pepper the files: '(Very secret) My dear Givens, I shall be most grateful if you can find out for me the present where-abouts of one . . .'; 'Recent information which has come to my hands'; 'a telegram has just been received from India'; 'the following infor-mation may be of interest'.[52] Colonial India, Singapore, Hong Kong and beyond were all intimately linked to the Shanghai enterprise through the MI6 office in the British Consulate on the Bund.

Mythic Shanghai loves all these worlds. André Malraux gave shape to foreign communist involvement in Shanghai politics in his *La Condition humaine*, and inter-war travel writing in France was infused by visions of Shanghai as the city of spying.[53] Jules Furthman's script for Josef von Sternberg's 1932 film *Shanghai Express* revelled in the taste of the city of sin. 'It took more than one man', notes Marlene Dietrich's louche 'coaster', 'to change my name to Shanghai Lily.' ('A coaster's a woman who lives by her wits along the China coast,' explains one character). The script was loosely based on the sen-sational 1923 hold-up of the Peking–Pukow express – the Blue Train

– during which the passengers were kidnapped by bandits. 'Most of them were Shanghai Jews of various nationalities and well known here,' gloated Tinkler at the time, 'I was tickled to learn that these birds were in clink.'[54] In May 1937 the treaty port press buzzed with news of yet 'another new book about this so-called glamorous and "wicked" city'. *Shanghai: The Paradise of Adventurers* appeared under the pseudonym G. E. Miller. The author, Mauricio Fresco, was Mexican Honorary Consul, and claimed high-mindedly that his book was aimed at 'putting an end or at least curtailing, nefarious activities of exploitation systematically practised by foreign adventurers of all classes and types'.[55] Coming from the Mexican Honorary Consul this was particularly rich; as we have seen, the position had long been deeply implicated in the large-scale organized gambling in the city of the 1920s. Fresco left hurriedly when his identity was revealed (accusing the SMP in print, and without evidence, of granting 'full protection' to British opium smugglers was a representative indiscretion), but the book remains in print, in Chinese, and the catchy title joined that list of monikers associated with Shanghai's name.[56] Allman took over the consulship again.

Most of the men and women in this chapter were hardly adventurers, but they made what they could of the strange Shanghai set-up. The big-time crooks that also concerned Fresco, such as American Frank Raven, were certainly the exceptions, although big fish and small fry both swam in the same extraterritorial pond. Over thirty years in Shanghai before 1935 Raven built up a banking and real-estate empire supposedly worth $70 million, sat on the SMC and with his associates ran the American Chamber of Commerce after 1927. In fact, Raven had systematically and comprehensively 'looted' his various operations, and the failure of this fraudulent empire caused a local banking crisis that wiped out the savings of many Shanghailanders. He was jailed for five years.[57] Another of Fresco's targets was the Hungarian Trebitsch Lincoln, amongst other incarnations sometime missionary, Liberal MP for Darlington, self-confessed German spy, putschist, scourge of the British empire and, in his Shanghai years, a Buddhist Abbot, Chao Kung.[58] The British Legation kept its notes on such concessionaires and shysters in a 'Bad Hats' file. The darker politics of the later 1930s would see these political and economic undergrounds blur in Shanghai, as intelligence agencies competed in what remained for them an open city.[59]

Such characters were accorded centre stage in mythic Shanghai, but the Shanghai 'adventurers' were really mostly smaller actors in the larger drama of empire and migration, sometimes unlucky, but sometimes wastrels, losers and grifters. They moved within a world opened through empire, and not yet fully closed by passports, visas and work permits – the paperwork barbed wire of the modern border. They negotiated restrictions here or there, and no visa was needed for landing in Shanghai. The mysterious Edwin Weekes, for whatever reason (a peripatetic illegal abortionist, perhaps, he had medical training and claimed to have qualified) worked his way through China, south-east Asia, Australia, France, South America, South Africa and Portuguese East Africa before reaching Bulawayo, changing his name as he went. Where he went next, the file doesn't show. Some of these people were bad colonists, others merely bad. But all of them were citizens of empire. They moved within it and within the broader world of empire opportunity, and empire anonymity. And they tried to drag it with them, to Nanchang, for example, like Maurice Tinkler, dressed on a torrid July evening only in the aura of empire and his white skin. It followed them, to Nanchang for example, in the shape of consuls and gunboats, not to back them up this time, but to bring them into line. Often, empire couldn't quite reach. Lincoln infuriated the China diplomats, but they could not touch him. Jerry Morgan, a Calcutta-born British subject who'd spent his youth in Australia and New Zealand, arrived in Shanghai via the Royal Engineers and Hong Kong. A club-owner and gambler, a boxing promoter (until barred for corrupt practice, which meant that it must have been very corrupt indeed), he was involved in shady business speculation as a middleman with Chinese and Japanese interests and was suspected of receiving stolen goods. He repeatedly failed to register with the British authorities and was a 'continual source of annoyance' to them.[60] Morgan played on his British nationality, but evaded being hemmed in by it; he was a product of the empire world, and he worked it. Others, equally a product of that world, tried to 'make good', in the face sometimes of overwhelming economic and political odds. Tinkler wrote of himself as serving an empire cause, damning his timid superiors for meekly surrendering his 'good old China' birthright. But – classic Shanghailander – he'd argued with them, face to shouting face, when he felt like it. And they might snatch him from Nanchang, but in Shanghai he was safe if he was careful.

Empire dislocated. It shattered the societies it subjugated, but it also shattered and disoriented British society. The men and women of empire were dislocated by the imperatives and opportunities of their lives. Empire sundered ties to family, home and place. For some, this was a happy escape, and they made new selves at safe distances, but others were uprooted and unsettled. Hundreds of thousands returned, having given up, retired or served their stint, but many, most, did not or could not. Weary of change, afraid of return, of being crushed by the cost and pain of reintegration – and what work waited such men and women in the hard 1920s and 1930s? – of finding themselves back where they began, they hung on or moved on. Sometimes, finally, they killed themselves, as if saying with the act: 'Nothing here, no going back, no moving on.' Maurice Tinkler's own dislocation was total. He'd renounced place, family and nation. By 1934 he had also come close to abandoning self, his (cheeky) self-restraint and obedience replaced by violent insubordination, his self-respect in doubt. His dress and presentation were awry. He did not look the viewer in the eye. But there was always rhetorical hope. Two phrases recur as men explained themselves in letters begging charity or positions. They wished to 'better' themselves and to 'make good'. Imperial living, perhaps more so than metropolitan living, laid greatest stress on character and spirit. A man might fail through no fault of his own, and try again. A man might fail morally, in settler eyes or his own, might fiddle the books, take a bribe, drink himself onto the street, but there was still space for picking himself up within the hardy world of empire, to start afresh, clean the slate. The 'pioneering' spirit was what he needed. Some commentators in the mid-1920s thought that domestic social insurance schemes were undermining this spirit, but its central place in the ideology and rhetoric of empire is clear. This was Maurice Tinkler's world between 1931 and 1935. He kept a tenuous hold on respectability, paying his Masonic dues, working as manager and not simply a resident at Yang Terrace, staying (it seems) just within the bounds of settler society. He must have talked the right talk with McIlvenny and the Salvation Army, for all that he argued violently, rudely, with the diplomats. But it was a thin line indeed that separated the violence of Nanchang, that bearded self, the gunboat, the hostel, the argy-bargy, from the low, fraught living of Connolly, Jones, MacQuarrie and the Shanghai bad hats. And in 1935 Tinkler made good. At least, he found a pretty secure job, with a reputable British firm, and it gave him a room and a route out of indigent waters.

10

Empire's Civil Dead

As Maurice Tinkler returned to work and Shanghai played, a new guidebook appeared in 1934 offering a florid manifesto for the post-1932 city. *All about Shanghai* hyped up the mythic city with a breathless 'Shanghai symphony', offering 'a blatant cacophony of carnality from a score of dance halls; scarlet women laughing without mirth; virgins in search of life; suicides; marriages; births; carols of vested choirs; cathedral chimes; Communists plotting; Nationalism in the saddle; war in Manchuria!' 'It's a great old town,' it concluded 'and how we hate it and love it.' Darwent's old guide was for residents; *All about Shanghai* was for a new type, happy to spend, with a yen for living fast. War spiced up the city. A snapshot of Shanghai's neon night introduced the visitor's options for making 'whoopee!': 'dog races and cabarets, hai-alai and cabarets, formal tea and dinner dances and cabarets, the sophisticated and cosmopolitan French Club and cabarets.' And cabarets and cabarets: 'Hundreds of 'em! High hats and low necks; long tails and short knickers; inebriates and slumming puritans. Wine, women and song. Whoopee!'[1] Cabarets dominate the advertising: the Canidrome Ballroom, 'rendezvous of Shanghai's elite ... presenting Buck Clayton & his Harlem Gentlemen'; the Venus Café, 'located in a world-famous spot – CHAPEI – scene of the Sino-Japanese hostilities in 1932'; the Ambassador, '100 of the prettiest Dancing Hostesses in all Shanghai for your entertainment'; the Majestic Café, 'the largest Cabaret in Shanghai ... 100 charming dance hostesses'. Once, cabaret Shanghai had been routinely censured or ignored. The *North China Daily News* wearily reprinted exposés of Shanghai sin from the overseas press. Such salacious reportage had made hay with the facts of Shanghai prostitution and the Russian predicament. Here now was upfront celebration at home, and the conjuring up of a city of louche danger, where the taxi-dancer waited for your pleasure in the former battleground of 'CHAPEI'.

Sobriety was more the style of the May 1935 'Shanghai development number' of an expatriate local monthly, the *China Journal*. British editor Arthur de C. Sowerby didn't neglect the cabaret world, but merely claimed that Shanghai's foreigners were fairly evenly divided between those who did, and those who never would. Despite the depression in trade, the evidence of the long-term Shanghai boom was profuse, never more so than in the smart establishments opening up, the cinemas ('legion in number') which thronged the city, the hotels, the entertainment centres, the department stores. New mills were being established, the utility companies opened ultra-modern plants. 'Shanghai as a whole is bound to advance,' claimed the journal, and its 'glorious past' would 'inevitably' be 'eclipsed by a more glorious future' in which Sino-foreign collaboration (to which lip-service was always paid) would play a more prominent role.[2] Commercial Shanghai was now at its zenith, wealth and cosmopolitan sophistication combining in a rich urban culture. The Settlement might lack 'cultural amenities' such as museums and galleries, but at least it loved its orchestra. And foreign cultural life paled into insignificance in the face of the leading role Shanghai played in China's vibrant cultural life. The city was the home of Chinese cinema, publishing and theatre. Physically Shanghai reached upwards. Looming over the racecourse now was the Chinese-owned Park Hotel, self-proclaimed 'Tallest Building of the Far East'. The *China Journal* made much of the almost complete twenty-storey Broadway Mansions building that faced the British Consulate from across the Suzhou Creek. Opposite the Cercle Sportif, Sir Victor Sassoon's Cathay Land Company was completing the large Grosvenor House complex. The Bund skyline which became the city's iconic emblem for decades even after 1949 was all but complete, with only the seventeen-storey Bank of China building to come (construction began in 1936 and the building was completed in 1939). The buildings stared out over Pudong across the water, sullenly proclaiming their importance to the dull flats and mill compounds that faced them. They were mostly designed by Western architects and built by Chinese contractors; by the 1930s their designers were incorporating elements that were Chinese-inspired, but a stolid, stone pomposity dominated.³

Much of the new celebration was conjured up by North American writers, impatient with colonial affectation, and happy to provide, as one guidebook did, 'a sort of composite of what Shanghai looks like,

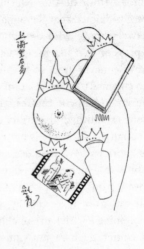

and feels like and smells like after, say, the third whiskey-soda'.[4] American society in the city was picking up confidence, moving out of the British shadow as America's Asia slowly grew more important to it. But Shanghai was mythologized by all of its residents. In his sardonic cartoons, published in book form in 1936, Xiao Jianqing caricatured the vices and brute contradictions of life in the hard-nosed city as lived in the canyon-like streets between the new high-rises and in the alleyway-house lanes. A Sikh policeman beats a beggar; the rickshaw pullers flock to the big-nosed foreigners, ignoring the hailing Chinese man; tarts accost a pedestrian in a 'Guizhou road night scene'; on 'culture street' (Foochow Road) a hawker offers pornographic post-cards to a young scholar. Female sexuality is unmastered. All relation-ships are based on power or cash. How was a 'virtuous lamb' to choose in a city where the flesh trade took so many forms: 'guide agencies', massage parlours, dancehalls, 'tableaux', and simple unpre-tentious prostitution? The dog-food delivery service comes thrice daily, watched by a hungry woman: 'Dogs are better than people.' The wet-nurse's child goes hungry. Always, there was the foreign threat: a buck-toothed Japanese goon squad; refugees from Manchuria beg underneath a poster advertising a dance hall; a foreign warship in the harbour, 'the spirit of peace' demonstrated by its heavy forward guns. Xiao's Shanghai is a city of greed, poverty, lust, licence and naked foreign violence. Skyscrapers rise above squatter shacks: heaven looks out over hell.[5] The city was all these things at once: as presented in *All about Shanghai*, as sketched by Xiao Jianqing, as proffered by Sowerby's *China Journal*.

The *China Journal* gave much space to the new civic centre complex north of the settlements at Kiangwan (Jiangwan). Here, a new town hall – in the 'Chinese Renaissance' style – opened in October 1933 at the centre of an impressive road system; administration buildings were inaugurated in December, with a municipal library and a museum opened by January 1937. Sports facilities and a hospital were also built.[6] With this ambitious plan the Greater Shanghai Municipality aimed now physically to outflank the settlements, re-zoning the entire city to draw its heart north to Kiangwan in preparation for rendition. But the Japanese invasion of Manchuria had put the Shanghai question on hold as the 1932 war brought new tensions. The war's resolution saw the 'demilitarization' of a zone extending twenty kilometres around the city, but this applied only to regular Chinese military units. The so-called 'Naval Landing Party', a 2,000-strong Japanese military force equipped with tanks and armoured cars, established itself in fortified barracks on the edge of Hongkew. This effectively meant the Japanese occupation of the area, with the force intermittently assuming police powers, 'arresting and detaining Chinese and foreigners, interfering with the Municipal Police at will, and holding manœuvres freely in the streets at any hour they wished'.[7] The official Japanese Residents' Association pushed the SMC for greater representation on the Council and in the police force. The 'onerous responsibility of administration' should be shared, and ought to represent (foreign) population size, while the reported 'discriminatory treatment' of the Japanese police should be ended. Some diplomatic rejigging of senior personnel was undertaken; it could not be avoided but was as token as possible.[8] In 1935 the Japanese attempted to change the make-up of the Council itself by putting up three candidates for election instead of the two usually proffered under the informal agreement which maintained a steady national quota (now 5 British, 5 Chinese, 2 US, 2 Japanese). The issue became more and more bitterly contested in the latter part of the decade. Incidents such as attacks on Japanese military personnel, notably the murder of a seaman in October 1935, were heavily politicized and used to support attacks on British hegemony. The Japanese claimed that little importance was given to the investigation, and relations even with senior Japanese personnel in the SMP began to fray.[9]

Things were changing more broadly in China for the British, whose position was evolving in the face of the triumph of Chinese nationalism. The old trading houses, which had concentrated on import-export trades, or on servicing that trade (insurance, shipping), were slowly being supplanted, by a new generation of multinational enterprises for whom China was just one item in an overseas portfolio, and for whom settler politics and polities really mattered not one jot. One such firm was Maurice Tinkler's new employer, the China Printing and Finishing Company, the Shanghai subsidiary of the Manchester-based Calico Printers' Association (CPA). Founded in 1899 and then representing some 85 per cent of the trade in Britain, the CPA had twenty-nine print works operating in England and Scotland by 1918. Between the wars, as Britain's cotton export market collapsed in the face of new competitors in India, China and Japan, the CPA steadily shut many of these works down and transferred production overseas, opening new plants in Egypt, India, Java and Australia. While Europe fought, Chinese entrepreneurs created a vibrant new industry largely based in and around Shanghai, and the China market was all but lost to British textiles by 1925. So Manchester came to the Huangpu instead and established a China foothold. In 1924 the CPA purchased a print works at Bailianjing and in 1932 it began construction of a brand new spinning and weaving mill, sited obliquely opposite the Bund across the Huangpu at Lujiazui, or 'Pudong Point'. The mill was needed because the printing plant had originally used Japanese-produced cotton and as a result was hit hard by anti-Japanese boycotts. To evade this problem and to 'exclude all taint of Japanese participation', the CPA opted to build its own cotton mill, through its Shanghai subsidiary, China Printing, importing machinery and personnel from Britain.[10] The CPA's archives are now in Manchester, and amongst the working papers of the firm were files and documents specifically dealing with Tinkler, or quite obviously written by him. In Shanghai, some papers of China Printing survive, providing useful details of this last phase of Tinkler's life.

The mill began production in the spring of 1935, and Tinkler began work that year as Labour Superintendent at the Pudong plant. Perhaps the Salvation Army employment bureau was approached for suggestions. Perhaps he'd already parted from them; perhaps not on such good terms. In any case, the mill would need a man with local knowledge, the Shanghai dialect, and the ability to supervise Chinese labour and the Russian security squad which guarded the mill. The ability to liaise with the police would be useful, and at least three ex-SMP men worked for the company, including Tinkler's fellow-1919 recruit Reginald Beer, who performed a similar role at the Bailianjing plant three and a half miles up the river opposite Nantao. Although it was physically close to the heart of the city, the Pudong Point site was outside the Settlement itself, for the Huangpu was the boundary. However, a number of foreign concerns had planted themselves on the cheaper Pudong shore and tried to squeeze under the Settlement's protective umbrella by virtue of their extraterritorial status. There was always a British naval vessel in port, while troops could be landed quickly to protect such British properties. The new manager reported in April 1932 that the site chosen 'afforded the greatest possible protection in case of trouble'.[11] It fronted the river, and was but a short hop away from the Bund. But even that ten-minute hop was a long journey in the Shanghailander imagination. British personnel at the plant, including Tinkler, routinely talked about crossing over to 'Shanghai', distancing themselves in this way from the city across the muddy water. Tinkler might have found a stable niche, but it was a doubly marginal one: it was outside the International Settlement, and it was also on the margins of the British staff at the plant. He was a local employee with no passage rights and no pension. His skills and desperation were equally matched, and so he was cheap. Neighbouring the mill were a British-owned dockyard, and a French-owned compound. Much of the 2,000-strong Chinese workforce lived in housing in the immediate vicinity of the compound. So, not much 'whoopee' there for a man about town.

Before 1939 there is not much in the records of the CPA in Manchester, or the remaining China Printing Company archives in Shanghai which throws direct light on Tinkler's peacetime activities at Lunchang (the company was often known simply by its Chinese brand-name). Like other unmarried employees, Tinkler had use of one of the rooms above the offices in a small, three-storey art-deco block that fronted the Huangpu by the main jetty, and which was separated from the main plant buildings by a stretch of unused ground. He messed with about eight other Britons who lived in the building, using a lounge and dining-room there, sharing the services of the 'flat coolies' and servants, the 'Number One Boy', and 'Number One Cook'. Tinkler's responsibilities included supervising the arrival and departure of the labour force, overseeing the security of the mill compound and regulating the workforce. New employees reported to the Labour Office which kept an eye on bona fides and drew up photographic identity cards. Liaison with the SMP was common. In September 1938 the force approached the company to ask for their help in arresting one of the women employees, wanted by the Chinese courts for misappropriation of funds. The force had no jurisdiction on the river, let alone in Pudong, but asked if the firm could have her brought over 'to Shanghai' on one of its launches. 'I shall . . . be glad if you will ask Tinkler to arrange this,' wrote the company's director to the mill manager.[12] Tinkler was probably also involved in running what China Printing's chairman labelled 'our detective service', which used Chinese informants to keep an eye on labour agitation and on the mood of the workforce.[13]

Labour unrest at the mill was a problem almost from the start. The company had aimed to import direct hiring practices, to avoid the entanglements with the Chinese underworld that resulted from the existing contract labour system in Shanghai and which would undermine direct control of the plant. This brought problems of its own, and there were strikes amongst different groups of the workforce in August and November 1935. Early March 1937 saw another strike and some sabotage of machinery, which led to a two-day lock-out and the closure of the whole mill. The managers had had no warning of the trouble, which ended with a conciliatory meeting of representatives and management.[14] Tinkler would have been deeply involved in the dispute, overseeing the 'detective service', the resolution of disputes on site and the clearing of labour from the mill when necessary. Tact was needed, and used. When the weavers' night shift arrived on 1 March and refused to work they were left alone 'as they were quite peaceful'. When the spinners began to get 'more unruly' on 3 March the foreign staff avoided confrontation 'under very provocative circumstances' and worked at negotiating with small groups of workers, playing them off against each other, before closing down and clearing the site.[15] The company liaised with the Chinese city government, especially as by early 1937 it was convinced that 'the forces in the labour camps are being marshalled for action' by, presumably, communist labour activists. In late March the Managing Director Clive Hargreaves was 'making friendly contact with Du Yuesheng', whom he described as 'probably much more powerful than any other individual outside the government'. 'He is – or was,' noted Hargreaves, 'a bandit with Headquarters in the French concession.'[16] Du was 'a Bandit, gangster and scoundrel', noted CPA chairman Lennox Lee after a visit to Shanghai in March 1938, but Hargreaves had done right to throw a party at the Park Hotel and invite him. China Printing as a result 'expect and hope to get extra consideration'. 'The police also employ him,' he added, laconically.[17] So Tinkler was effectively back doing police work, even detective work of a sort, but most of all providing that supervisory service that he had been recruited for, way back in 1919. It had little status, but it was likely to be more to his taste than the jobs he'd had since leaving the SMP.

Liaison with the SMP would have brought him into contact with the new men who were joining Gerrard's reformed force, and who were also joining Lodge Erin to which he still belonged. They differed significantly from the wartime servicemen who joined in 1919, and the navy men of the early 1920s. Gerrard's wholesale recruitment of Shaforce men had not exactly proved successful overall. 'The ex-soldier does not make a good policeman,' concluded Commissioner Martin in June 1929.[18] The Depression meant that the SMP could more easily select. The Council's London agents interviewed between 130 and 140 candidates in the early autumn of 1929, passing 94 of these through to a medical examination, and provisionally enlisting 61 men subject to character references from their local police forces. Frank Peasgood was one of those who passed and sailed out on 4 October with eleven others: 'one Scot one Welsh and ten English . . . None of our squad had left these shores before. Mostly leaving for better pay and prospects with a three year get out clause . . . I was running away from a coal mine.'[19] Peasgood enjoyed himself in Shanghai, as did Barney Wall, who had arrived in February 1932 just in time for the war. As he wrote home, the glow from burning Chapei filled his window. Wall found the force was agreeably full of his fellow Irishmen; the Chinese inspectors he trained with were 'jolly good sports' and pretty soon 'dead bodies no longer cause me surprise'. The cabarets failed to amuse him, but there was the police rugby team (which he captained), plenty of golf, Sunday Mass, and keeping up with the bad news from Ireland. A useful home-side contact recommended him for an early transfer to CID, and a 'marvellous job' in the Modus Operandi Section. He thought Shanghai 'artificial', lived a fairly quiet life (a Spanish girlfriend, in time), and had fun. But understanding peacetime Chinese politics, he concluded, was 'rather like trying to follow politics in Ireland'.[20] Former planter Jack d'Esterre Darby could not 'see one redeeming feature in Shanghai, and very few in the occupation of a Shanghai policeman, whose social status and salary is not very far removed from that of a rickshaw coolie'. And 'for pure "A" Grade concentrated filth,' he added, 'Shanghai stands in a class by itself.' Darby arrived in August 1933. Nanking Road and the Central District might present a 'truly magnificent spectacle', but he was dismayed by the noise ('continuous, even through the night'), and the ugliness of the cityscape. 'We are all formulating schemes of escape,' he claimed of his draft of 14 recruits, and the destination of choice was Brazil: 'as far as we can see most of the opportunities of today lie in that area.' Darby cleared out in October 1934 and headed to New Guinea, producing a 34-point list of grievances, amongst them: '6. Dust, muck, disease, noise. 14. Starved of sunlight and fresh air. 20. Bribery and corruption throughout the Force, *and not excluding the higher ranks*. 24. Social standing. 29. One is allowed a very small amount of private life.'[21] Basil Duke joined with the same draft, and spent much of his time fantasizing about running a plantation in Paraguay.[22] In the meantime pollution from the Shanghai Power Company's plant and the unsanitary conditions of the streets he patrolled got to him: 'rarely a day goes by when I am not sick in the street.'[23] Both were empire men, not prepared by their previous posts for the subservient position of the Shanghai policeman. Shanghai's urban extremes revolted (although Duke enjoyed the cabarets). For these two men, Shanghai was a necessary interlude while they waited for more amenable empire billets.

The March 1936 issue of the British-edited Shanghai monthly *Oriental Affairs* highlights the transitions and tensions the Settlement was facing in local Sino-foreign and Anglo-Japanese relations, and in relations between the Settlement and foreign governments. Work on the new Bank of China was beginning on the Bund while the Shanghai branch of the swanky department store Lane, Crawford and Co. was going out of business.[24] The annual Council elections were to be held on 23–4 March, and it was widely believed that the Japanese Residents' Association would again mobilize its members to try to break the Anglo-American hold on the Council. They did, but were defeated as the British Residents' Association and the Americans mobilized their voters in turn. Incompetent handling of the ballot boxes – several hundred Japanese ballots were overlooked – soured relations even further. In January and early February the US Court for China saw the trial for embezzlement of Frank Raven and a key lieutenant in the 'Raven Group' of companies. The integrity of the settler position was ill-served by the evidence which emerged about this large-scale fraud perpetrated by a man formerly seen as a leading citizen, who had as recently as early 1934 stepped down after a two-year stint on the Municipal Council. The integrity of the SMP was itself hit hard by the trial which began the day following the Raven judgement, of Sergeants E. W. Peters and W. A. Judd, in connection with the death of a Chinese beggar on 1 December 1935. (The accused in both trials had crossed paths in the foreign section of the massive Ward Road Gaol.) Peters was Charge Room Sergeant at Kashing Road station. Disregarding regulations, he had left this post at 3 a.m. in response to a report that the man, Mao Debiao, was lying in a road. Taking a police car, the two men had picked Mao up, taken him to the edge of a creek on the Settlement boundary and thrown him in. He was later pulled out and hospitalized but died of triple pneumonia. Both men lied to their superiors about the incident, appeared in court, charged with causing bodily harm, the day he died, and were subsequently charged with murder. They were acquitted, and then dismissed from the force. Although Special Branch tried to keep Chinese press comment under control, the damage was done. 'Even animals deserve our benevolence,' concluded the Chinese newspaper *Xinwenbao*, 'But a guiltless man was killed for no reason and no recourse took place.' On his return to Britain Peters collaborated with a journalist on a series of newspaper articles ('Ruined by Fight for his Honour' splashed the *News of the World*) and then a book, *Shanghai Policeman*, the greater part of which was concerned with a mendacious defence of what he described as his 'tactless mistake'. Judd stayed on for a few months working in Shanghai for Clarke's Inquiry and Protection Agency.[25] British juries were unwilling still to convict in such instances, although attitudes had changed. Assistant Commissioner Bourne displayed no hesitation in recommending bringing criminal charges even while Mao still lived, but a residual inclination towards avoiding bad publicity lingered: 'there is very strong evidence against them, and lack of action in court, when obviously called for, will lead to much undesirable comment for which there may be some justification.'[26]

This was all small beer, and war overshadowed settler embarrassments. On 16 February 1937 Mayor Wu Tiecheng unveiled a memorial to the unknown Chinese soldiers who died in the 1932 battle. But the war was far from over. A clash near Peking on 7 July 1937 led to Japanese and Chinese troops fighting throughout north China, and in August the conflict spread to Shanghai. Tensions developed locally after two Japanese spies were killed on 9 August. Chinese civilians began leaving Chapei in late July, and by 25 August there were an estimated 400,000 refugees in the Settlement. This was not 1932. This time the central government actively sought a fight, planning to shift the war to central China, confident that its superior numbers – and its German-trained forces – would prevail on the Shanghai battlefield, and that the proximity of the concessions would help it prevail at the diplomatic table. Small Japanese reinforcements backed by a formidable naval squadron were moved up. Up to 30,000 Chinese troops were in position by 12 August, and the local and national authorities rejected Japanese demands for their withdrawal. The SMC called out the SVC and police. 'Shanghai mobilizes to counter threat of war', headlined the *North China Daily News* on 13 August. Thousands of Japanese residents evacuated outlying areas, and all British and US nationals were urged to move south of the creek into the heart of the Settlement. Chinese refugees rushed south as fast as the clogged roads and barricades would allow. 'Today's entertainments', offered on the paper's masthead, included the usual fare: Hai-Alai at 8.00, greyhound racing at the Canidrome at 8.30, 'Entertainment' at D.D.'s Night Club and the Del Monte, 'Hollywood Cowboy' at the Metropol, and 'Alibi for Murder' at the Hongkew cinema.[27] Murder it was in Hongkew. The first shots were exchanged on 13 August and by the afternoon there were fierce artillery exchanges. But Chiang's Yangtsze strategy imploded as his soldiers were slaughtered in front of the Japanese defences in Chapei. In the north, Tianjin fell. By the end of the year, after a bitter and hard-fought campaign, Nanking had fallen to the Japanese army. The victorious troops were allowed free licence to desecrate the city and its inhabitants in the literal and metaphorical 'Rape of Nanking'.[28]

Chapei burned again, but Maurice Tinkler had a lovely war. Lunchang stood between large Chinese forces in Pudong and the

Japanese battle cruiser *Izumo*, which was moored close by. Tinkler could talk with the Chinese at the landward gate, and liaise with the Japanese at the jetty. So he was back in no man's land, doing what he liked doing best, and did well, filing thrice-daily reports on the conflict around the mill, and receiving visitors – including Consul A. H. Scott and the navy's China Station Commander in Chief – who came to inspect war damage and the situation at the site.[29] When the fighting was over, Shanghai chairman Clive Hargreaves sent the file of reports back to the CPA board. They were 'loquacious', but would give them a sense of the dangers of the Shanghai enterprise.[30] On 14 August – 'Black Saturday' – when over 1,000 people were killed after Chinese planes dropped bombs on a Nanking Road thick with refugees during a botched attempt to bomb the Japanese warships, the mill was also hit by shell fragments and shut down, paying off the workforce and clearing the site. The company requested, to no avail, a detachment of British troops, seeking precedent in the fact that a unit had been sent to the print works in 1927. Tinkler stayed on site voluntarily well into September, usually with two other Britons and a skeleton Chinese staff. He moaned about a misbehaving refrigerator and asked for fifty pounds of ice to be sent over daily (as well as flags and maps, and the newspapers) on the launches which kept up a skeleton service to the compound. He relayed pedantically precise intelligence about Japanese and Chinese military activity, counting and identifying the shell types and the vessels, including, remarkably, a hospital ship he recognized from the Keelung–Kobe run he'd done in 1921. On

5 September Tinkler showed his bulletins to a visiting British naval commander as, he boasted, 'they contained a few items not known to the Navy'. Meanwhile, 'the *North China Daily News* account of yesterday's fight contains many inaccuracies,' he complained on 11 September, and was 'wilfully misleading'. Things were so quiet, in fact, that one passenger on a passing Moller Line vessel was up on deck sporting a bathing suit. Tinkler noted the location of Chinese emplacements and barricades, checked the security of the compound, ejected refugees (but kept an eye on those hiding in the abandoned French compound next door, noting laconically at one point that they had 'killed and eaten the police dog – Alsatian – which disappeared last night') and fixed up bomb damage. The Lunchang compound was hit several times, but never seriously, and the flats themselves were also accidentally machine-gunned by a Japanese destroyer. Some of the damage was still visible in 1997. Damage to neighbouring plants was reported, and casualties, too, of sorts: 'so far only two chickens have been killed,' he noted of the shelling of the Shanghai Dockyards company complex.

Laconic report gave way to outrage. On 20 August Tinkler described what he labelled a 'Brutal attack on sampan' (a small boat). A Chinese man, woman and their three children had sailed downstream, trying to pass the *Izumo* about fifty yards from the flats. 'Everything could be seen and heard plainly' from the cruiser, he wrote, but the sentries on board fired at the boat until it found sanctuary and shelter near the mill jetty. By that time the mother had been shot through the heart, the father wounded in the head, and a 13-year-old girl shot in the back. Tinkler signalled the cruiser to stop firing, dressed the wounds and spirited the survivors into the safer hands of the Customs service River Police. He rebuffed a Japanese party which came to the plant looking for them, and later pointed out to the cruiser's Flag Lieutenant 'in the politest manner' that, far from being 'spies and snipers', the occupants of the craft could be plainly seen and heard for what they were. He asked Hargreaves to have the British naval authorities lodge a 'strong protest' with the Japanese. Tinkler was off-handedly sarcastic about Chinese preparations in Pudong, and had little time for the volunteer units composed, as he saw it, of local gangsters (they probably were: several Green Gang leaders mobilized their networks to fight the invaders). 'All are irresponsible and in a truculent mood usually,' he declared, concluding, characteristically, that 'the whole of both of these collections of criminals should be shot forthwith'. (The phrase confirmed for me his authorship of most of this document.) But like most Britons he had cause to see close at hand the ruthless tenor of the Japanese assault. In 1932 the Shanghailanders had cheered on the Japanese from the security of the rooftops. In 1937 most knew that the Japanese attack was an attack on their position too, and saw that the military's treatment of Chinese civilians was random and reprehensible. On his visit in 1938, Lennox Lee talked with Chinese operatives about their experiences, and reported to the board about the rape of Nanking. In Britain the company contributed discreetly to the anti-Japanese China Campaign Committee. The Japanese were 'in possession' after 1937, but they would not win in the long run, and so CPA must maintain its Chinese bona fides.[31]

By 6 September the Chinese units in Pudong were growing suspicious of the curiosity being displayed by the British on site at Lunchang. Tinkler had been fishing widely for information, including the location of divisional headquarters and the numbers of the units, and had been asking the mill's small Chinese police squad for details, perhaps not as discreetly as he thought. General Zhang Fagui (whose siege of Canton in 1930 had kept the vacationing Tinkler corralled in the British settlement there) wired the municipal authorities, accusing him of being a Japanese spy and asking for guidance. Hargreaves refuted the charge immediately, but offered to move him if the Chinese wished and in the meantime ordered him not to leave the compound. He also used the sampan incident to argue instead that in fact 'the Chinese people owe Mr Tinkler a debt of gratitude for his action'.[32] Tinkler was later withdrawn from the site 'for other important work'[33] (the date is unclear, as is the work), but was back by 12 November when, together with Hargreaves and others, he walked through Pudong to the print works, which had been cut off for some time, and was communicating with the company headquarters by carrier pigeon. This was only one day after the Japanese army had occupied the whole area. Here again are echoes of 1924 and 1927, as Tinkler led the party through the battle zone to the works. For over twenty years now, he had been coming back to battlefields. Walking through them, fighting through them, picking up souvenirs as he went, unscathed so far as the twentieth century fought. The formal battle for Shanghai was now over, however, and from 13 August until late October it had consumed the best of the Chinese officer corps. Japanese casualties reached 50,000, and the bitter stalemate was broken only by two Japanese naval landings, one north of Wusong on 23 August, and the second in Hangzhou Bay on 5 November. This set the scene for a pincer movement which would trap Chinese troops in the city unless they withdrew. They fled, leaving behind at least 300,000 dead and wounded, fresh offerings for the Mayor's war memorial. One and a half million refugees sought sanctuary in the Settlement and Concession. Against diplomatic protests, Japanese commander General Matsui Iwane forced a victory parade through the Settlement on 3 December, marching 6,000 troops from the western edge of the Settlement to the Garden Bridge by the British Consulate-General, stomping along Nanking Road as Japanese residents 'emerged from Hongkew by the thousand' to cheer them on.[34] Matsui was warning Chinese and foreign residents of the fact of victory, and staking a claim: the Japanese did the parading now.

In Hongkew, Frank Peasgood kept another journal of the fighting.[35] Frank was based at Dixwell Road station, a few hundred yards from where the firing began. 'Nothing to write home about,' he reported at the end of day one. 'We have been through it before,' joked the police – British, Japanese and Chinese alike – 'We were here in 1932.' By the end of 14 August the station had been evacuated ('the Municipal flag being left flying to indicate the ownership of the property'), and one man had had his toes blown off. From Hongkew station they ventured out in police vans to rescue trapped civilians and to pick up bodies. They sent out squads to prevent looting, and sometimes worked to maintain what was left of the neutrality of the Settlement, answering calls to assist the Japanese Naval Landing Party when it suspected snipers were working within it, for example, although nothing had been done to prevent Japanese landings of men or munitions on the Yangshupu wharves. When rumours circulated of Chinese advances the police took defensive positions to prevent the station being taken over. On 17 August the Japanese informed them that they were about to bombard Chinese positions, and the post was evacuated; 260

stranded policemen were evacuated on a barge from the Shanghai power station on 18 August. Maintaining municipal dignity in such circumstances was tricky. Police work in such circumstances was dangerous, but a spot of danger was always useful for the record and might help promotion.[36] As soon as the fighting allowed, the SMP set up replacement temporary stations and substations, aiming not to give either side occasion to believe that the Settlement authorities had abandoned sovereignty by default. But the Japanese military were in no mood to be wholly diplomatic, and where they 'resented the presence' of the SMP close to the front lines, no presence was maintained, and in October most of Hongkew was declared to be 'prohibited' to the International Settlement police. 'Talk about a ringside seat at a Boxing match,' commented Frank Peasgood.[37]

Returning from leave in November 1937, Barney Wall described the concessions to his mother as 'islands in a sea of desolation'.[38] The high hopes of the *China Journal*'s development number were in ruins, literally. The Kiangwan civic centre was the location of fierce fighting, and was gutted. Peasgood wrote of the 'wonderful view' of key parts of the fighting their outposts presented, but this time there had been fewer untouched bystanders. Nanking Road had been turned into a 'foul charnel house' on 14 July. Bodies – and body parts – had been dumped on the racecourse; walls, hoardings and fences in China's busiest shopping street had been plastered with human detritus.[39] By 21 August almost 3,000 British women and children had been evacuated to Hong Kong. The intensity of the fighting had meant much heavier casualties in the Settlement itself, and Japanese forces proved less restrained than in 1932 when it came to international opinion, and to the international presence in China. The British Ambassador was machine-gunned by a Japanese aircraft, and had to be replaced as a result of his injuries. The US gunboat *Panay* was bombed and the survivors strafed by planes and Japanese craft. Prominent settler figures killed in the Nanking Road bombings included Frank Rawlinson, the now defunct Moral Welfare League's tireless opponent of Shanghai immorality. The Japanese immediately sought Chinese collaborators to re-establish civil administration, sponsoring first a 'Great Way' (Dadao/Ta-Tao) government in Pudong in December 1937, and then in October 1938 a Shanghai Special Municipal Government. British diplomats refused to recognize the legitimacy of the new authorities, and most foreigners continued using the label 'Dadao' long after the cluster of criminals and traitors who composed it was supplanted in Japanese affections by the Special Municipality which arrogated to itself the forms, titles and rights of the former Guomindang administration.

With the fall of Shanghai began the queer *gudao* ('solitary island') period, when the foreign settlements stood alone in a Japanese-occupied region. In one sense this was hardly new, as they had for almost a century resisted the exercise of national or local authority within their borders. But this time the local authority was ultimately in the hands of a foreign invader, while the Chinese government used the settlements as one base in the political, covert and economic war against this enemy. A new battle began in the settlements almost immediately, with spontaneous attacks by Chinese on Japanese civilians, as well as Koreans and other unfortunates deemed to look Japanese, such as a local Filipino boxer, who was 'badly mauled'.[40] But this type of action took more organized shape after the withdrawal of Chinese regular forces, when plain-clothes units began to attack the Japanese. On 3 December a grenade was thrown at Matsui's victory parade. On 27 December another was thrown at Japanese military launches on the Soochow Creek. The perpetrator was caught by two Chinese SMP constables, and, before being handed over to the Japanese military authorities, 'admitted being a member of a Chinese Military Plain Clothes Group whose purpose it was to harass the Japanese forces from the rear'.[41] From June 1938 onwards a vicious terror war was fought in the settlements between collaborationist and anti-Japanese units. Assassination, violent intimidation and bomb attacks took a heavy toll of collaborators, resisters, and the politically quiescent, forcing them to make a choice. Even cabarets were bombed, wartime puritanism passing bloody censure on those still dancing. The mêlée was compounded by competition between and within puppet administrations and organs, turf wars that developed over the criminal activity which provided the funds, such as narcotics, and the contested sovereignty on the western border of the Settlement. This locale became the headquarters of puppet activity and was renamed the 'Badlands'.[42] Frederic Wakeman gave shape to this era in his book

The Shanghai Badlands, laying out clearly how the waves of terror left Chinese in the city 'psychologically devastated' and anxious for peace, any peace.[43] Canadian policeman Ken Bonner tried to give some shape to it himself, pasting into a scrapbook cuttings about this battle for Shanghai: 'Bombs Explode, Bullets Fly as Shanghai Marks First War Anniversary', 'Six bombs hurled on eve of anniversary', 'Another "Ta Tao" official slain', 'Army officer assassinated', 'Salt Tax chiefs Riddled'. In its round-up for 1938, *Oriental Affairs* listed the victims of only 'the more important of the terroristic crimes': Tang Shaoyi, the veteran statesman who the Japanese hoped would lead a puppet republic; Gu Qingyi, chairman of the rice-dealers guild and member of a Japanese-sponsored Shanghai Citizens' Association; Chen Deming, chief of the shipping control office of the Dadao regime; Superintendent Lu Liankui, chief of the SMP's Chinese detectives.

Far from being a lone island, the city was a key battlefield in the spreading undeclared war. These campaigns stoked up Japanese-SMC and Anglo-Japanese tensions, slowly internationalizing the conflict. Settler Britons strove to hold fast to an idea of a neutral Shanghai, which maximized benefit for all parties. The more pragmatic SMC tried to neutralize the threat of Japanese occupation by working to suppress anti-Japanese activity. On 1 January 1938 it had issued an emergency proclamation stating that any person committing an offence against armed forces in the Settlement would be liable to be handed over to the armed forces concerned, promising rewards for information about 'terrorists', and authorizing the SMP to search all premises for weapons. After the first wave of attacks in July it issued a further decree which made those illegally possessing arms or explosives liable to expulsion.[44] In this it acted as it always had, collaborating with local *de facto* authority, whether it was Sun Chuanfang or the Nationalist Special Municipality. But this time there was also broad pro-Chinese sympathy, and much suspicion of the ultimate aims of the Japanese. Shanghai tensions also grew out of growing strains in Anglo-Japanese relations developing due to the role of Hong Kong and later Burma as conduits for supplies to the Nationalists, and over Tianjin. There the British and French municipal authorities were accused of not aiding the suppression of local anti-Japanese activity, and the concessions were barricaded by Japanese forces from

December 1938 to February 1939, and then again on 14 June 1939 over the question of extradition of Chinese 'terrorists' to the Japanese authorities. Down south, the tiny International Settlement at Kulangsu (Gulangyu), off the port of Amoy (Xiamen) was blockaded after 11 May, and this was lifted only when two Japanese SMP officers were appointed to the British-run force.[45] There was no escaping such tensions in Shanghai. Full control of the Northern Districts was not returned to the SMC, and only a skeleton SMP presence was allowed. The Soochow Creek became the northern border of a rump Settlement; Japanese soldiers guarded the bridges. 'Space does not permit', sighed *Oriental Affairs* in its round-up of 1938, 'a record of the numerous incidents which occasioned protests by the British government ... assaults upon and the arrest of British subjects, including military men; occupation, and denial of access to British properties north of the Soochow Creek; interference, and in some cases, seizure of British vessels ... etc.'[46] The Japanese were clearly no longer playing the balanced game of empires. China was to be theirs alone.

The China Printing and Finishing Company faced more than its share of such problems. The immediate issue facing them was that Pudong, where both installations were located, was under Japanese military occupation, and had been cleared of its Chinese population. The mill began to re-engage its workforce on 25 November, and had the mill running again four days later. 'Labour problems are a constant source of anxiety,' reported Lennox Lee in March 1938. The housing in which the mill workers had previously lived had been destroyed. Although a French hospital adjacent to the site was run as a hostel for a while, this led to ongoing problems with the Japanese. Most of the workers had fled into the security of the concessions, and the mill had to make arrangements for transportation to and from the city. A company launch towed barges which could accommodate 70 people (but which often carried closer to 250) from pontoons moored near the Garden Bridge on the Soochow Creek. The danger was not helped by the activities of the members of the Shanghai Rowing Club 'who apparently consider that other craft on the creek should on all occasions move aside to allow them free passage'.[47] War might come and go, but rowing should continue unimpeded in China's busiest harbour. Although there was a relaxation of the Japanese embargo on

Chinese residence in Pudong, most Chinese employees preferred the settlements, and the company itself kept its landward gates closed so that even those living locally had to cross over to Shanghai first to get to work. In the only surviving China Printing document to which he signed his name, Maurice Tinkler issued a notice to the senior Chinese staff at the mill on 10 May 1939. Henceforward they would not be allowed to travel on the launch itself, when it took the day shift back to Shanghai in the early evening, as 'they cannot be trusted not to capsize the launch when they all rush to one side to jump ashore'.[48] Instead, they would have to travel on the barges or await a slightly later boat. The issue seems petty and unremarkable, but it was to explode ten days later.

In April 1997, in a room at the Lunchang plant, known since 1958 as the Shanghai No. 10 Cotton Mill, I met 80-year-old Peng Hongfei. 'Jimmy' Peng, as he was then known, began work as a clerk at the plant in 1934, and later became personal assistant to the mill's then manager, James Ballard. For the first time I had direct Chinese testimony about Maurice Tinkler. Peng recoiled with distaste at the memory. He remembered Tinkler as 'tai ben' and 'tai liumang' – thick and loutish. According to Peng, Tinkler didn't mix with the other Britons much in the course of his work as they were mostly office-bound, and he supervised the arrival and departure of the labour force. Tinkler didn't go out with his colleagues at the weekends, mostly staying in his flat. He drank heavily. When no other Britons were about he brought Russian prostitutes over the river to his room. They weren't girlfriends, Peng insisted, they were prostitutes. He was the lowest of the British there. He was the thickest, his personal behaviour was distasteful, and his 'cultural level' was very low. Peng had begun working for a company later taken over by China Printing at the age of 13. He wasn't one of the English-speaking university graduates moving into the foreign business world, but he got on well with the British management and most of his colleagues, who treated him well. He was bright and adept. Peng spoke with visceral loathing of a man we know to have been a colonial racist, whose behaviour he would have found crude and repugnant. He didn't offer any personal examples of problems with Tinkler – although he would have been one of those barred from the launch after 10 May – but he claimed that the man had nothing else to do in his job most of the time, except harass the workers. Peng then embarrassed the plant's Communist Party Secretary, who sat in on the meeting, by repeating a piece of doggerel larded with sexual innuendo that he claimed Tinkler sang at women mill workers. All of this rings true to an extent (and, as we shall see, there is some documentary evidence as well). Peng may have misinterpreted some aspects of Tinkler's life, and the conventions and taboos of the small community of Britons living on site. The man he portrays is not wholly the man we know from the 1920s, but then again we know that the man had changed, and Tinkler, like Britons elsewhere in the colonial world, was not likely to hide his life from servants at the flats or Chinese staff, even if he hid it from his colleagues. And gossip would have spread amongst the workforce for whom Tinkler was the leading and direct daily face of the British presence at the plant. They would have met him when they joined the mill. They saw him every day at the jetty. They knew who he was.

A contemporary sketch after his death offers a more positive view. Here Maurice was 'exceedingly popular', 'particularly in sporting circles, having been a good cricketer and having taken an interest in light athletics'.[49] I can't find any evidence for this at all. But if the report offers any useful detail it may lie in the record of those who sent wreaths to his funeral. Aside from his colleagues, there were tributes from three fellow-masons from Lodge Erin, a journalist, and two serving and two former SMP men. There were also flowers from 'Iris', girlfriend or friend, former or present, we don't and can't know. There isn't much here to show that he moved beyond the narrow circles of lodge, police or China Printing. He's not likely to have been the sullen hermit Peng recollected, but he had always been fairly self-contained. We do know that Tinkler's job was at least stable, even if like most of his peers he found Shanghai no longer a city of easy pickings. By 1939 he was earning the equivalent of just £10 a month, and the exchange rate was on the slide (Detective Sergeant Barney Wall, with seven years in the SMP, wasn't earning much more). Between July 1937 and May 1939 the sterling equivalent of his earnings was cut by well over a third. This took place as the Japanese waged a fierce campaign to destroy the Chinese dollar and strengthen the position of a new currency issued by the puppet Central Reserve

Bank. And the cost of living was rising for foreigners. In the two years after August 1937 a quart of Ewo Lager rose in price by 50 per cent, 50 Craven 'A' cigarettes became twice as expensive, as did even a cheap whisky. Tinkler's mess bills rose, but at least he was spared the soaring rise in rents.[50] So Tinkler's progress after twenty years of work in China was negligible. By May 1939 he had £44 in savings (half of it in sterling), and just under £4 in the bank. He owed his tailor the equivalent of £5, and his mess bills were eating up his salary. He had a full wardrobe, but he had no possessions of any value. Tinkler owned twenty books, five albums of photographs, two boxes of medals and certificates, two stamp albums, a silver cigarette case, a couple of pieces of lacquerware. His rooms might have been robbed after his death – there was no trace of his masonic regalia, his watch, his ring – but he may already have pawned or sold some of these things. If, as Peng claimed, he never went 'to Shanghai' it was partly because he could not afford to. He didn't leave China because he could not afford to. He was trapped at Pudong Point.

And Pudong Point remained a hotspot. Labour tension at Lunchang was exacerbated by the economic crisis that developed in the city after the battle, and by the vicious Japanese proxy campaign against the settlements. According to one Chinese history of the Shanghai textile workers' movement, the outbreak of the Sino-Japanese War saw the raising of the political consciousness of some of the Lunchang hands at what was termed the 'old factory' – the Bailianjing print works – by a local primary school teacher. Chen Ren was a communist; in night classes he gave for plant workers he allegedly introduced them to Marx's *Das Kapital*, and mobilized numbers of them for political activity. But the same source also admits that events in May and June 1939 were 'extremely complex', and *Das Kapital* – even in translation – seems a less potent cause of labour mobilization than economic turmoil and events in the mill itself.[51] The official Guomindang-led labour movement worked after 1937 to avoid upsetting the delicate situation in Shanghai, and strike action in 1938 was down sharply on pre-war levels. But while actual earnings for Shanghai workers rose by about 20 per cent between 1936 and 1939, the cost of living doubled and contemporary estimates show real wages falling to 60 per cent of their 1936 levels. Rent and fuel were the biggest problem as a result of an almost threefold increase in the population of the settlements south of the Soochow Creek. In 1935 there were on average fifteen people in every house in the Settlement, by 1938 there were thirty-one.[52] The potential for labour unrest was strong and strike action increased in 1939. Insecurity compounded the situation, especially as the Japanese manipulated rice shortages in an attempt to undermine order in the unoccupied areas, with some degree of success.[53] Wildcat action lay behind the situation which developed at Lunchang. It began at the print works where, in early May 1939, plant activists made a series of demands for increases in rice allowances and wages. When this was refused they struck on 10 May.

The wider stage was set. The 24 May edition of the *North China Herald* surveyed the previous week's edginess in the Settlement. The SMC and the British and US consulates had suppressed four foreign-registered Chinese newspapers for publishing expressions 'detrimental to the maintenance of peace and order'. Puppet Mayor Fu Xiaoan wanted formal responses from the settlements to his demands for 'anti-terrorism' measures and recognition of the legitimacy of his regime. Japanese street unions were demanding that Japanese become an official language of the SMP. A man was murdered in Pudong for refusing the offer of a post in a puppet organization. Another man was arrested in the Settlement by the SMP, at the request of the Japanese, for alleged guerrilla activities. On 17 May 'Rabidly anti-British' pamphlets were scattered from a convoy of trucks by 'very young Chinese children' under Japanese armed guard and accompanied by a brass band that 'blared out stirring march tunes'. Anti-British parades were held on 19 May in Wusong, Chapei and Kiangwan. That same day 10,000 troops and police took part in a mobilization exercise in the settlements. Roads were closed, perimeter positions manned. Ninety ten-man patrols searched pedestrians in the French Concession; Reserve Unit Red Marias cruised the Settlement streets.[54] The authorities were ready, was the self-evident message. Lunchang's labour unrest spread downstream to the Pudong mill on 20 May. At 9.55 p.m. the SMP's Special Branch received a message that there was trouble at the plant. The labour force had refused to leave for two hours after work finished at 5 p.m. A British Naval guard landed and the Japanese were asked to use the puppet police to sort things out. 'This appears to be a labour dispute', the message concluded, but by 25 May the neighbouring street was plastered with anti-British posters: 'Down with Great Britain, the public enemy of the Yellow race', 'Confiscate all rights and interests of Great Britain', 'Do not serve in British commercial concerns', 'Keep in mind the Shanghai Incident of May 30th', and more in a similar vein. Special Branch opened a file on the strike, its officers submitting daily situation reports.[55] The strike leaders were soon receiving 'strike pay' from the puppet city government, and agitation seemed as if it would spread to the British American Tobacco plant and Jardine's Pudong wharf, as well as to the Jardine mills in Yangshupu. The affair took place at a tense moment, six days after a blockade of the British concession in Tianjin by Japanese was resumed, and shortly after the marches and leafleting reported in the *North China Herald*. 'All the evidence points to a concerted anti-British drive through the fomentation of labour troubles in British mills,' concluded Consul-General Phillips, 'almost certainly directed by higher Japanese authorities.'[56]

Matters had come to a head on 20 May, a day of violence and dispute at the Lunchang plant. At 9.30 that morning Number 3 Electrician Gu Jin'gen (Koo Kyung Kung), a 26-year-old Shanghai native, was dismissed. Gu had a record of labour agitation and 'general misbehaviour', having been sacked two months previously only to be immediately re-engaged, in a bid to avoid wider troubles. On 19 May he was allegedly 'found instigating the workers to strike', and the company later claimed that he was already an agent of the puppet local authority. 'Apparently acting in accordance with a pre-arranged plan', ran an SMP Special Branch report, Gu signalled the eighty mechanics to stop and picket the plant's electric motors. Meetings were held in a bid to encourage the mill workers to strike. The mill's score of British staff discussed matters with a series of delegations from the workforce, but the dispute continued long after the mill was supposed to close at 5 p.m. At 6.30, watched by about half the workers, Gu and other 'agitators', armed with iron bars, attacked the British staff who had congregated outside the mill offices. The British fled inside but were followed there by the crowd which caused 'considerable damage': 'At this juncture,' the report continued, 'Mr R. M. Tinkler, a former member of the Shanghai Municipal Police, armed

WOO LING DZUNG
(譯音) 吳林順
崇明人:年廿五歲

WOO EU KWEI
(譯音) 吳有貴
浦東人:年廿四歲

YANG KWUNG KWUNG
(譯音) 楊昆昆
上海人:年廿歲

KOO KYUNG KUNG
(譯音) 顧金根
上海人:年廿六歲

ZI LOONG LOONG
(譯音) 徐龍龍
上海人:年廿六歲

TSOONG TUH KUNG
(譯音) 鐘德根
溧陽人:年廿歲

himself with a pistol kept on the premises for protective purposes and deliberately fired one shot above the heads of the attackers who then retired and formed into small groups about the compound.' Another man had managed to leave the scene and phone the British Consulate-General, fearful that more violence would occur. By the time armed British seamen from HMS *Decoy* landed about 8 p.m., most of the mill workers had already left, crossing the river back to Shanghai in the company boats. As the seamen arrived, the remaining strikers fled the compound over the walls into Pudong. One of the Britons had been struck by an iron bar and was hospitalized.[57] The Japanese authorities immediately protested to the British Consul-General about the landing of the British force, which was replaced by a detachment of Seaforth Highlanders on 23 May. British marines were landed at the print works that same day. A fierce war of words erupted between the Japanese and the British. After written assurances were given that the Japanese 'would hold themselves responsible for the protection of the mill', the Highlanders were withdrawn from the mill and the marines from the works on 25 May. They were replaced by Japanese marines, 300 of whom were initially on duty at Pudong Point. 'I think that our action has had a salutary effect on the Japanese and may even have nipped in the bud other similar anti-British moves of which there have been signs lately', reported the Consul-General.[58]

Two things became clear in the aftermath of 20 May. The dismissal of Gu Jin'gen was certainly one cause of the strike, but another was Maurice Tinkler. Not because of the single pistol shot – although forbidding the company's staff to carry arms quickly became one of the strikers' demands – but because of incidents related to the transport barges, and because of his behaviour generally. One group of workers attempted to head off the growing politicization of the dispute by calling on Eleanor Hinder, director of the SMC's Industrial Section which dealt with labour disputes, to seek mediation and present a list of demands. These were:

1. Dismissal of Mr Tinkler.

2. No more beating of workers.

3. Wages be adjusted in accordance with the increased cost of living.

4. No dismissals on account of the strike and no loss of wages.

5. Management not to suppress the workers without reason.

6. Management to assist in the problem of transportation of workers.

The three representatives gave equal weight to Gu's dismissal and to the physical treatment of the workforce as the causes of the strike. The flashpoint was provided by the boats. The workers struggled to get places on the boats so as to get across the river more quickly once their shift was done, and Tinkler and his Russian subordinates were allegedly in the habit of using force to keep the numbers in each boat at safe levels, often beating people back to keep them out of the barges. On 20 May a Russian security guard had beaten a woman mill hand but, the workers maintained, Tinkler's own 'practices are . . . of the same type'.[59] Peng Hongfei later claimed that Tinkler 'hit and abused people', and there were also complaints about the searching of women operatives as they left by the security staff.[60] In the anti-British diatribes in the handbills circulated amongst the staff the issue of assaults on staff surfaced again and again. The plant labourers had economic grievances, but they also had their dignity to maintain. The issue of embarkation had come to a head. They were also furious about what they saw as a high-handed dismissal of their grievances on 20 May, when they alleged that their representatives had been threatened with dismissal and the demands rejected out of hand. But the primary cause of the strike, as these men saw it, was Maurice Tinkler's casual colonial violence.

With no settlement in sight, the company paid off all the workers. Japanese and puppet agents saw their chance. Operatives gathered at the Pudong Southern District Administrative Office, where they had received a 'Relief Fee' from the Chief of the Pudong Section of the Japanese Military Special Service Department. The Shanghai City Government's Police Bureau pasted up 'huge quantities' of anti-British posters.[61] On 28 May, a 'Chinese Workers' Support Committee' was contrived by Japanese and Chinese puppet officials, and two anti-British processions were held.[62] Nine hundred mostly women workers met on 1 June opposite the Pudong Administrative Office. Led by thirty members of the 'Anti-Communist Youth Group' (an organization known for its anti-British activities) and a small brass band, and escorted by thirty constables and twenty detectives of the Shanghai City Government Police Bureau, the women paraded through the streets, past British American Tobacco's mill to Lunchang where they 'stopped for half an hour during which they sang anti-British songs'. 'We strike, we strike. It is sacred, it is sacred. Let us unite wholeheartedly, and expel the British,' they choroused.[63] The 'Support Committee' was replaced by a 'Chinese Republic Workers' league' which led the strike, organized the parades and issued handbills and posters which strayed far from Pudong Point as they lambasted British perfidy over the century since 1842. Negotiations upriver at the print works reached a settlement that allowed for a return to work on 2 June, but that morning armed puppet pickets blockaded nearby roads and the works entrance and prevented reopening. The local Japanese units refused to intervene. 'It would seem', noted Special Branch chief Thomas Robertson in a note to the Commissioner, 'that the aim of the Japanese Special Service is to work up a hate out of which anything may happen.'[64]

On 6 June anything did. At 8 a.m. the morning launch arrived from Garden Bridge carrying a couple of foreign staff and a number of non-striking Chinese. They noted nothing unusual, but a contingent of strikers armed with sticks had made their way along the Pudong shore in sampans, and were waiting in hiding.[65] As the launch discharged its passengers they appeared and began to intimidate the 'loyal' Chinese, and the noise of the fracas reached the British residents in the flats. The two Japanese marines on duty were joined by reinforcements who attempted to keep the men under control. 'This was done', reported one eyewitness, 'by escorting them into the compound and immediately this was done the strikers broke away and ran towards the power house.' Inside the flats, two Britons, Herbert Stott and John Sharples, ran upstairs to Tinkler's room, where the mill firearms were kept. As they loaded the Webley pistols Tinkler prepared his own Mauser automatic and left the room first. Once outside, and seeing that the marines had made no attempt to stop the strikers reaching the power plant, and – it was assumed – attempt to wreck it, he tried to head them off himself, revolver in hand. Two of the marines headed him off in turn, and a struggle ensued. 'As I watched,' reported another Briton, 'several blows were exchanged between Tinkler and the Japanese, and eventually, Tinkler deliberately pointed his gun to the ground, away from anybody, and fired one shot.' Breaking away from them, he moved back towards the flats, apparently shaken by the fight, his mouth bleeding. While more Japanese marines arrived and cordoned off the flats, Tinkler, the two other armed Britons, Sharples and Stott, together with a fourth, William Chadwick, were surrounded by a number of marines. The Japanese had rounded up all Chinese in the compound, including the 'loyal' staff – which may have been the aim of the action – and were preparing to march them all off to their headquarters. Tinkler and the others now remonstrated with the troops, attempting to get them to release the nonstrikers, whose safety in Japanese and collaborationist hands they had very good reason to doubt. But none of the Japanese spoke English. 'At this point Mr Tinkler pointed his gun' at a Japanese officer 'and told him to get off the Plant, as they were more harm than good.' Sharples continued:

The officer then got angry, and the Japanese marines turned their attention to the foreigners, who were, Stott, Tinkler, Chadwick and myself. [We] then asked Mr Tinkler not to show so much force, but he had by this time lost his temper, and would not listen to us.

By this time another group of Japanese marines led by an officer arrived, and were concentrated around the foreigners. All the time, Mr Tinkler was threatening people with his gun, and the rest of the foreigners pleading with him to be quiet and not show any force. He was so mad and out of control that he threatened to hit us if we did not leave him alone, as the Japanese were making no attempt to save the Plant.

About this time, Commander Noji arrived. I told Mr Tinkler this, and said that as he (the Commander) spoke English we may get some arrangement, whereupon Mr Tinkler went up to him, threatened him with his gun, and told [him] and his men to get off the plant, as they had been no use. Commander Noji then withdrew a little and his men surrounded us – all had fixed bayonets, and all put a bullet in the breach of their rifles.

This was a very serious moment as Mr Tinkler was continually waving his gun about and would not listen to either Mr Chadwick, Mr Stott or myself.

While Sharples parleyed to one side with Lieutenant-Commander Noji Munesuke, head of the Pudong Japanese naval landing party, Chadwick and Stott persuaded Tinkler that it would be a good idea to withdraw to the flats and finish breakfast. 'He was obviously obsessed with the idea that the safety of the mill depended on him,' reported Chadwick. But next, continued Sharples, 'we heard a commotion around Mr Tinkler again, and I went up to him to try and pacify him. He told me that he was going for breakfast, but the marines had encircled him and would not let him pass.' Sharples tried to get Noji to call off his men, but while his back was turned one of them knocked the pistol out of Tinkler's hand, and then the group closed on him beating him to the ground with their rifle butts and not sparing him their bayonets, hitting him in the head and body. Sharples and Chadwick dived into the mêlée to try and stop this. The marines eventually pulled Tinkler, now bleeding badly, to his feet and held him up as Noji approached and hit him three or four times across the face with his scabbard. 'Until Tinkler was disarmed,' reported Chadwick, 'the Japanese showed great forbearance, but after disarming him they revealed nothing but bestiality.' The marines then started to pull him to the mill's landward gate. When he fell they dragged him along the ground by his legs and arms for twenty yards, before he managed to get up and walk to a waiting car, which took him and Sharples and guard to a Japanese hospital in Pudong.

He had been badly beaten all over, and had been cut in the head, thigh, buttock, hip and under the ribs, and bayoneted 'with considerable force'. At a 'crowded and tense' press conference the following day the Japanese naval spokesman claimed that 'for several hours Tinkler resisted all attempts to treat his wounds', but this was clearly a lie, and the journalists knew it.[66] None of his wounds was deep and a Japanese surgeon had immediately begun to patch them up. Sharples stayed with Tinkler as the Japanese refused to release him. Tinkler asked for brandy and morphine but neither was forthcoming. Sharples was sent away in the afternoon and rushed to the China Printing offices in Shanghai to report that although Tinkler had been well treated in the hospital he needed to be moved to a hospital in the Settlement. The British Consulate – visible from the Lunchang jetty – had moved swiftly into action, and so had the Japanese, who lodged a verbal protest about the incident almost immediately. Consul-General Philips dispatched a telegram to London giving a brief summary, and the information that the Japanese intended to detain Tinkler to ensure that he was 'adequately punished'. Vice-Consul Joe Ford was sent over to Pudong with company representatives, and went to the local headquarters of the Naval Landing Party.[67] Long and meandering discussions with Noji and others took place, but access to the injured Briton was refused, although Ford was assured by the Japanese surgeon in person that Tinkler's condition was not serious. A photograph published that evening in the Japanese newspaper *Tairiku Shimpo* showed the party around a table examining the empty cartridge case and the bullet, which the marines had recovered. Noji also refused to release the 'loyal' Chinese mill workers. Under the heading 'The Outrage: Beyond Expression', *Tairiku Shimpo* also published photographs of Japanese marines inspecting the compound in front of the flats, of a relaxed Lieutenant Commander Noji drawing on a cigarette, and of Maurice Tinkler, clearly uncomfortable, lying on a couch in the Japanese hospital. As the photographer took this propaganda snap, Tinkler's guts were haemorrhaging.[68] Ford returned to the Bund empty-handed mid-evening, but at 10 o'clock that night the Japanese Consulate rang to say that his 'condition had become so grave that his relatives should be notified'. The company doctor was rushed over to Pudong on a Japanese naval launch. Dr Korec found him in a 'very critical condition' and it was clear that he was suffering from severe internal injuries which had not been dealt with by the Japanese surgeon. Korec brought his patient back over the river. A *North China Daily News* journalist saw the party arrive at the Customs Jetty on the Bund. Tinkler lay on a stretcher carried by four Japanese marines: 'He looked pale and tired. He turned his head looking around but he did not talk.' 'He is injured all right,' snarled one of the China Printing officials.[69] An ambulance rushed the party to the Shanghai General Hospital in Hongkew, accompanied by Japanese officials who waited while a further operation was carried out. For diplomacy's sake a Japanese surgeon joined the team. The job was done by 2 a.m., but three hours later Richard Maurice Tinkler lay dead. 'The same operation, carried out at an earlier hour would most probably have been successful,' noted Korec, but Tinkler was too

昭和十四年
六月六日發行
六號
第二號

この暴戻！言語に絶す

〈光人不法發砲經過の事件を語る〉

②

写眞説明

① 現地
② 浦上天主堂
③ 現地へ駈けつける佐々木兵隊長
④ 原爆一号の殺された少年
⑤ ……殺された少年
⑥ 現場

佐々木兵隊長談

厳重抗議

weak, and had already lost too much blood.[70] He never woke from the anaesthetic.

It need not have happened, of course. British diplomats admitted to the Japanese that Tinkler's behaviour had offered 'considerable provocation', and to the Americans that he had 'completely lost control of himself.'[71] The coroner was to censure the marines for their 'entirely unnecessary and unjustifiable' bayoneting of the disarmed man, the Japanese surgeon for failing to recognize the seriousness of the injuries, and the Japanese naval authorities for denying him earlier access to a foreign doctor.[72] And in Tinkler's defence both consuls and company representatives argued that he had been under very great stress since the start of the strike. He was not the only one. Mill manager Ashworth was in such a state that he had already been removed from duty. Another man present during the altercation on 6 June died the following day of a heart attack. Tinkler's state may have been exacerbated by the fact that he was a target of the earliest strike demands, although nothing in the company records comments on this. He may have feared that not preventing destruction at the plant on 6 June would have compounded the potential problem and threatened his job. Securing the mill might have secured his fragile hold on a Shanghai livelihood. While one Russian security guard was eventually moved from his duties at the mill, the company nowhere mentioned this key initial demand of the strikers. Hargreaves noted instead to the CPA board that in the deaths at the plant the company 'had lost two of its best linguists'.[73] It was not only the Japanese who rewrote the event. Company director D. J. Sinclair had the awkward job of composing a letter of sympathy to Edith. He opted, it seems, for invention, claiming to have been told by one colleague that 'Tinkler's was a heroic soul which had to experience a gallant and heroic end'.[74] But there was, of course, little heroism shown in the early morning fracas on 6 June, and more bloody-minded, blind-eyed recklessness than gallantry. His colleagues could barely conceal their dismay at his behaviour – 'so mad and out of control' – endangering them all, as much as they condemned the Japanese actions after he was disarmed. Maurice Tinkler had stood his ground on a grey, sultry Shanghai morning, out of control and beyond reason, clutching his pistol, threatening the marines and his colleagues alike. He'd pushed

Fred West around; he'd punched and kicked the Nanchang gendarmes. This was how he lived. This was how he died. He'd lived a forward life, of force instead of reason, of violent language and violent action. He bullied and blustered, but now did so with the wrong people, at the wrong time, in the wrong place. Shanghai 1939 was no longer a city in which the servant of British empire held sway by force. That city was gone, but it lingered in memory, sparking this furious, futile, fatal act. When the news first came in over the wires, officials at the Foreign Office reminded each other of the Nanchang affair.[75] 'If the Japs say he fired on them I think it quite likely he did,' noted Consul Blackburn, settling his score. 'It's a pity', he then sneered, 'that so many of our disputes with the Japs are over such very vile bodies.'

I I

Aftermath

Noji had the gall to attend the funeral. He stood ten feet behind Holy Trinity's Dean Trivett, sporting a large black armband, and bowed 'reverently' as the hearse passed. Twenty of Tinkler's colleagues from the United Services Association led the procession, medals glinting in the bright June sun as they marched by the hearse through the Hongqiao (Hungjao) cemetery, west of the Settlement. From among them came the pall-bearers, who carried the coffin, draped with the Union flag, to what Hargreaves later decided should be a 'company grave', the upkeep of which would be met by the CPA. There was a large turnout from a shocked and wounded British community. Many had had their own minor altercations with Japanese sentries at the Garden Bridge, or else-where. Another man, Bertram Lillie, had recently died in a car accident along with a Japanese soldier during one such incident; 'there, but . . .', they will have thought. Even the British Ambassador was guarded by an armed escort from the SMP. In Hongqiao, the wild belligerence of Tinkler's mad June morning fell away. 'At present Might is Right', ran the inscription attached to one set of flowers. Wreaths came from col-leagues at China Printing, from 'Number One Boy', from 'Number One Cook'. There were many, too, from the SMP: 'Old Comrades at Sinza', 'Former Colleagues at Bubbling Well', 'Comrades of Ward Road Gaol Staff', 'Officers of the SMP', 'The Bodega', a bar run by an ex-policeman. Whatever else might have been said – and it was as likely to have been said in Shanghai as it was in the Foreign Office – Maurice Tinkler was one of them still: a Briton in Shanghai, and a former member of the SMP. They too were in the firing line, every day. From the funeral parlour to the cemetery the hearse had been escorted by an SMP motorbike and car. His death was announced in Police Orders.[1]

Saturday, June 24, 1939   THE DAILY MIRROR   Page 3

JAPS' WORST INSULT YET

Tribute to Briton Murdered by Japs

SOON after Mr. Chamberlain had referred in the House of Commons yesterday to the 'insult' by Japanese troops to a New Zealand woman reported from...

...official statement that this insult was the...

...ese, who was... ...ation shell... ...on women.

...okeless... ...t that he... ...s a silver... ...his own... ...pounded:

...of such... ...tually.

MEMBERS of the United Services Association carried the coffin of Mr Richard Maurice Tinkler, 42-year-old Briton, who died from Japanese bayonet wounds in Too-Tung, when the funeral took place in Shanghai.

British solidarity was stiffened by the excesses of the Japanese propaganda machine. At press conferences and in official statements the Japanese lambasted the 'insult' to their navy that Tinkler had inflicted through his actions. This version denied that he had been deliberately attacked. After being disarmed he continued to struggle, it was said, and so 'came into contact with' a bayonet. He'd then belligerently refused treatment at the hospital for hours. The meetings with the press were tense. Nobody believed the Japanese; they could hardly have believed it themselves. Stott and Sharples gave their painfully precise accounts of events on 6 June to the inquest at the

British Police Court, but no Japanese representatives appeared (and so, they later claimed, the judgement was biased). The coroner found it a 'deplorable story'. The bayoneting was 'entirely unnecessary and unjustifiable', the Japanese naval surgeon had failed in his duties and the naval authorities had been reprehensible in not permitting foreign medical access.[2] Note and counter-note were then exchanged by British and Japanese diplomats, but even the formal protest lodged in Tokyo by the British ambassador elicited no response. The ritual dance of the diplomats, those carefully choreographed steps neatly preserved in the Foreign Office records, was no longer appropriate to the new era taking shape. Details were certainly fed to Parliament, as a series of questions were tabled by MPs who asked for updates and for details of notes and responses. The 'unsatisfactory' nature of the events leading to Tinkler's wounding did not help the diplomats, but even if they might have agreed with the Japanese assertion that 'Had he but been less unreasonable even to the slightest degree, it would not have cost him his life for his violence', they could not allow his behaviour to define their response.[3] But then came the outbreak of the European war and Maurice Tinkler's posthumous career as the subject of an Anglo-Japanese 'incident' was left hanging in limbo.

His was an empire death, all the same. Bad news now travelled fast. The lonely facts from Shanghai were wired back by Reuters within hours. Edith first heard them on the midnight radio news on Tuesday, 6 June. The British papers followed the next day: 'Stop-Press News: Lancashire Man Injured by Japanese: Died in Shanghai Today' (*Manchester Guardian*); 'Lancashire Man Dies, Wounded by Japanese' (*Daily Dispatch*). And it was from the report in the Scarborough *Evening News* that Rachel Tinkler heard of her stepson's wounding and death. This was the first time that any in the family had heard of him for almost ten years now. It was a local death: 'Scarborough Associations: Dead Man's Step-Mother Resides Here' (Scarborough *Evening News*), 'Killed by Japanese: Mr R. M. Tinkler Stabbed in Shanghai: Penrith Milliner's Only Brother' (*Cumberland and Westmoreland Herald*). A *Daily Express* staff reporter descended on Edith, ringing the Foreign Office on her behalf trying to extract more detail, and more copy.[4] Edith had married, in October 1936, Thomas

Whalen, who wrote a letter in her name on 7 June to the Colonial Office. After some delay it reached the diplomats:

I would be grateful if you would be good enough to supply me with any information concerning Mr R. M. Tinkler who has been killed in Shanghai. He is my brother. I and my Aunt who lives with me are the only near relatives he has. We have not heard from him since he was here about 10 years ago on holiday. We should like a Correct account of what really happened. Whether he was still in the Police Force or not and the address of his employers and if he is still unmarried and any further particulars concerning him.

'Lord Halifax has no information as to whether Mr Tinkler was unmarried or not', replied the Far Eastern Department, and the diplomats developed a sceptical attitude towards the letters Edith and her husband sent. As the couple obviously knew so little about his circumstances, it was blithely assumed that they could only be interested in what money might be coming their way.[5]

In July, fearing that silence indicated the case was being forgotten, Edith wrote to her MP: 'My brother's death does mean a great deal to me & I do feel that the Government should not be allowed to forget it or that the Japs should be allowed to ignore the British Government's protest & that they should be compelled to make Reparation.' Her husband wrote in a similar vein to the Foreign Office the same day.[6] But the mandarins were not concerned with the human wounds left by the case, which for them was but one aspect of an evolving crisis in Anglo-Japanese relations. The Whalens were not the point; indeed, Maurice Tinkler was not really the point. Although they reserved the right to press the Japanese for compensation, and despite the fact that the 'deplorable' case elicited much continuing comment from their colleagues in other ministries, they were inclined to admit defeat and move on. In May 1940 Ambassador Craigie in Japan submitted a final note to the Foreign Ministry there, hoping 'that the Japanese Government may effect some degree of reparation' in order to settle the case. But the document reached London in the aftermath of the French collapse in the face of the German invasion, so it was no surprise that the diplomats felt that 'The present is of course not the time to press the case'.[7] China Printing pressed them over the broader issue of the ongoing strike, until that was resolved in November 1939. And the firm also became the main channel through which Edith Tinkler saw her brother's affairs sorted out. This was easier to resolve. There was no will. There was barely any money (and she did admit that money had for a moment seemed an issue, as her husband's business had just collapsed), and there would have been none at all if the firm hadn't defrayed the funeral costs and added an additional three months' salary to the estate. China Printing sent over a list of Tinkler's effects, and barring an iron and his coat hangers, and the items which could not be found, she asked for them all to be shipped back to her. Edith could not bear to have anything sold off in Shanghai. The trunks of clothes, albums, books and hats passed Customs in December 1939, the remains of a life with the man taken out. China Printing also sent an enlarged snapshot of her brother, and then in time a photograph of his gravestone, 'In Memory of Richard Maurice Tinkler who died on the 7th June, 1939, Aged 41 years, Late of the China Printing and Finishing Co. Ltd., Shanghai'.[8]

Lily learnt of his death from cold newspaper print. She pinned the clipping – 'Stabbed Briton dies' – into her commonplace book, transcribing a corruption of Laurence Binyon's elegiac verses, more usually associated with the dead of the Great War, perhaps now belatedly marking a death in Flanders.

> He shall not grow old
> As I, that am left, grow old,
> Age shall not wither him
> Nor the years contemn,
> At the going down of the sun
> And in the morning
> I shall remember him.

'I *shall* remember him,' she wrote. 'I have done – always. After nearly 20 years this is the only news I had of him.'[9] Distraught, she wrote to Edith, asking for a memento, 'for to me he remained very dear'. She had kept all his letters (which answers his query of seventeen years earlier: 'I wonder if she destroyed that wonderful collection of art and literature'). 'I had and do pray for him,' she continued, 'I have done regularly all the long years since Ulverston days.' Lily sought to memorialize his death, composing an obituary for their old school magazine, the *Ulverstonian*, and she might also have been the correspondent who submitted a short 'Appreciation' to the *Manchester Guardian*. 'Maurice Tinkler was indeed a true and worthy son of the British Empire,' she wrote for the school. 'In this country,' began the 'Appreciation', 'deeds which adorn British prestige are quickly recognised by the public, but in countries far from home they often pass unnoticed.' In both cases his was portrayed as an empire death, and an honourable, courageous death: 'he was proud to be an Englishman and knew no fear.'[10] In August, in Auckland, New Zealand, a stranger, the young Enoch Powell, was moved with sober fury to pen another commemoration.

R. M. Tinkler
Bayoneted by the Japanese at Tientsin, 6th June, 1939

Murdered, deny who can,
Here lies an Englishman;
The steel that through him ran
Was tempered in Japan.

Who then the murderer?
England, that would not stir,
Not though he died for her;
England, the slumberer.

His cries she would not hear
Because insensate fear
Had stopped the mother's ear;
But now revenge is near,

For while his land forgets
And bends the knee to threats
His vengeful spirit whets
The German bayonets.[11]

Powell conflated the China crises, placing Tinkler's death in Tianjin; but he knew an 'Englishman' when he saw one. Like Edith, he saw weakness in the British response but also the inevitability of war, and like Lily Wilson he also claimed for Maurice a different death, that of the patriot servant: 'Not though he died for her', for 'England'. But England, and by extension empire, betrayed Tinkler's valour. Powell's anger at appeasement and his fears for the consequences of war found shape in the reports he read of Tinkler's cold dying in Shanghai.

As war came, Shanghai talked the empire talk for all it was worth. Its plants and shipyards, its intelligence service, its sons, were all pledged loudly to the service of wartime empire. Shanghailanders ran bazaars, totted up the funds raised and looked to fund a Spitfire squadron, and they watched their Axis neighbours. Men took shifts in anti-sabotage squads, guarding the shipping in the harbour. It had done all this in 1914, cheering the recruits who sailed off home, and printing the (censored) chatty letters they sent back. But this was a different war, because there was also another enemy in waiting much closer to home. Shanghai lived on the sharp edge of this war for another two years. The men of the SMP also cast themselves as actors in the empire story. When the *North China Daily News* editorialized on the anniversary of Kipling's birth in 1941, it quoted amongst other verses from what it described as the 'Singer of empire', lines taken to heart by the Shanghai British: 'stand to your work and be wise.'[12] They stood to their work in Shanghai as empire thinking demanded, and as the British empire state requested. But it was never smooth, and the daily hurts of a class-riven society still poisoned attitudes. 'People out here make one a bit sick,' wrote Barney Wall in 1938, 'They haven't much time for us until they get in a jam and then we are great lads.'[13] 'We were treated', remembered Frank Peasgood, 'like the British always treat the troops. Discarded when not in use.'[14] Resentment at their low standing in Shanghailander society was the traditional gripe. Tinkler had once wished for a crisis so that people would know that 'the police was here'. Shanghailanders got their crisis.

Interwoven into the Foreign Office files on Tinkler's death are details of one of a growing number of violent clashes between the SMP and the puppet regime, and a serious escalation of local tension. Wallace

Kinloch was a 22-year-old former Scots Guardsman, who had joined the SMP in August 1938 along with fifty-four other men, including a strong contingent from the Metropolitan Police, and a group of soldiers discharged in Shanghai. This time they needed the soldiers. Kinloch was leading an armoured car patrol along Jessfield Road when parleying with puppet police turned into a fierce gun-battle, leaving two puppets dead and two wounded after they fired on him. The incident unleashed a further wave of anti-British activism: a mock funeral for the young Scot presided over by a huge caricature of him, an anti-British rally and then distribution of illustrated booklets to all members of the puppet police relaying the story while urging them to 'Never forget the 19 August incident: Chief Perpetrator Kinloch.'[15] This is what policing in Shanghai had come to. Fire-fights involving armoured cars on the borders of the Settlement, and waves of bloody terrorism within it. The booklet was a call for bloody revenge. A Danish member of the SVC was murdered that month for his alleged role in a much milder mêlée, and by the end of 1941 four senior officers of the SMP (three Chinese, and one Japanese) had been assassinated. Special Branch chief R. W. Yorke narrowly survived an attempt on his life on 6 September 1940. Yorke was ready, and shot first, but he took the hint – and settled his wife's nerves – by applying to retire.[16] Kinloch was eased out of Shanghai and into the Hong Kong police. There were fears for his own safety, but also the potentially 'disastrous results' which might stem from any connected confrontation.[17] Shortly after the outbreak of the war in Europe it seemed that the Japanese were preparing to back the seizure of the area, and negotiations were begun with the puppet Special Municipality. In October 1939 the SMP was involved in an hour long fire-fight on Jessfield Road, involving machine guns and grenades, with members of the puppet 'Special Service Corps of the National Salvation Army', despite an agreement on a 'de facto system of dual police control' which been in operation for some weeks in the Western District.[18]

War in Europe brought new problems to Shanghai. Men sought to resign to join the armed forces, but those on leave at home were asked to return in a message relayed by the Foreign Office and circulated by Pooks: 'British diplomatic authorities here advise imperial interests best served for the present by employees here remaining in posts. Hope

民眾於
憤怒之
餘,將之
禍首金
洛克之
肖像,
付諸一
炬!

that those now on leave will return to duty at end of leave, especially Police.' In the later retelling this became a message from the Foreign Secretary himself, asking the men to return.[19] At least two notes were circulated to each Briton asking him to stay, and conveying the authorities' support for the request. J. R. Hunt co-ordinated service recruitment at the Consulate, and was later at pains to point out that he had 'for all practical purposes ... barred' SMP members from joining up. They needed written permission from the Commissioner, and they would not get that if they could be held to their contracts.[20] The press played its part, printing story after story about police retirements, long-service presentations and such like, working to boost morale and work the men and their families into Shanghailander society. In the pages of the *North China Daily News* the men of the SMP were recast – at long last – as local heroes. But, inevitably, men managed to resign. David Bannerman Ross, a key figure in Special Branch since June 1930, and one of Tinkler's companions on the boat out in 1919, was one. He had already sent his children home earlier because of 'unsettled conditions'. The local Japanese press used the occasion to portray an SMP riven by disagreement over the war, with junior officers keen to leave en masse to join up. By July in 1940, thirty-eight men had already tendered their resignations (up from an average of twenty-four a year since 1935). Only ten of them, Commissioner Bourne claimed, were intending to join the forces. There hadn't exactly been 'normal tranquillity' over the previous decade, noted the chief of CID, as 'it has been one thing after another with the Police Dept getting the spade work to do'. Another officer bluntly noted that the main reason for the resignations was 'pecuniary'. The men no longer believed that 'the Council would be able to pay superannuation should anything happen to Shanghai'. In short, their savings would vanish, and so they resigned to make sure that they got their money. On top of that, and despite cost-of-living bonuses, many only 'just manage to make ends meet'.[21] Publicly, the force denied that there was any problem; privately, morale amongst all branches was again and again hammered.

Yorke resigned at the behest of his wife. Amongst the many changes to the character of the force in the years after Tinkler left was its evolution into a body of married men. Since restrictions on marriage had been eased in 1934 the quota had been routinely exceeded. By 1939 it worried the SMC, as quarters and allowances were adding substantially to Council expenses. Bourne defended the influence of marriage (sport ought to keep the rest 'pretty safe and healthy-minded'). This was all very well, argued the Council, but pretty soon they would all be married and the cost by April 1940 was 'frightfully high'.[22] Families meant responsibility, for the SMC and for the men of the force. The wives themselves formed a close-knit group. Accommodation went with the station, and as men were posted families moved with them. Paddy Fearnley remembered eight flats and houses in eleven years as her father John Smith moved from station to station. Life for the police families held all the benefits of Shanghailander comfort: servants, spacious accommodation, long leaves. Albert Cornwell and family lived off Bubbling Well Road, served by a 32-year-old 'Cook-Boy', Hu Ninggang, and a 38-year-old amah, Lu Aibao. Families also meant that SMP culture evolved, and its position within local society, too. In Shanghailander snobbery the policeman still cut no ice, but his wife and children of necessity took the force out of the bachelor barracks and much more prominently and in greater numbers into the schools, sports clubs, and other social institutions of British society. They met, and remember, fierce snobbery there, but change was in the air. There was change, too, in the perception of the spoiling perils of a China childhood debated in the *North China Daily News* when Tinkler arrived in 1919. Those men who could afford to send their children to Britain for their education – such as D. B. Ross – did so, although the Shanghai police salary made this difficult, but the children of the police were more often growing to adulthood in Shanghai. Some even followed fathers into the force. However, domestication and the financial uncertainty resulting from the SMC's revenue crisis and its attempts to economize, and from inflation, produced an unstable situation. Family responsibility might lead men to work efficiently and to stick out danger in order to gain promotion, or reward. But, as Bill Widdowson put it to Commissioner Gerrard in 1936, 'a man with fear in his heart for the future of his dependants is not a man fully equipped to combat crime in Shanghai'.[23]

Combat was the crucial word. In 1935 there had been an average of one exchange of fire with armed criminals every twenty days; by 1940 it was once every three and a half days. In 1935 police fired 192 shots, and were shot at thirty-four times. In 1940 they fired 962 shots, and were on the receiving end of 209 bullets. One policeman was killed in armed encounters with criminals in 1935, four in 1940, while another three were deliberately targeted and murdered by political assassins. The SMP kept a steady shooting average, though: it took fifteen shots to kill a criminal in 1935, and thirteen in 1940.[24] Barney Wall and his colleagues killed three men in November 1937 in a raid on a room in the Oriental Hotel on Nanking Road. But he took two bullets in his hands during the encounter. After they burst into the room Wall realized that there was a man concealed behind the open door:

The robber ... had a 'Mauser' sub-machine in his hands. I jumped him just as he was going to spray my two detectives from behind (range about 4 feet). As only the gun was showing from behind the door of the room I could not tell exactly where he was standing and, therefore, it would have been necessary for me to have emptied my gun over the entire area of the door. Also that would have taken a couple of seconds, during which time he might have let loose a hail of bullets. I accordingly grabbed the gun with my left hand and pushed the muzzle upwards. He then jumped from behind the door and using both hands, tried to turn the gun on me. But he was not strong enough. I then pushed him backwards at a table in the middle of the room, thinking to break his back over it but the table broke instead! As he fell back still holding the gun I jerked him to his feet but he still held on. In the meantime the room was full of flying bullets as the two detectives were bumping off the other two robbers. When the first shot hit my right hand my gun went flying. The second broke my left thumb with which I was holding the Mauser. I managed to retain a grip on the barrel with my fingers and kneed him good and hard anywhere but above the belt. He then staggered away leaving his gun in my hand and one of the detectives gave him one on the button. So you see, none of them left the room except feet first.[25]

Wall was single, and he was very lucky. DSI John Crighton was off duty and just alighting from a bus with his wife when he saw three men acting suspiciously on 19 April 1939. He took her across the road to cover in an alley, by which time the men were robbing a pedestrian at gunpoint. Noticing him load his pistol they fired at him and for the next few minutes he was involved in a chase and exchange of fire hampered by fading light and the presence of bystanders. But he freed the victim, and wounded one man, who was later arrested, and whose pistol was shown to have been used in twenty-six recent shootings, including murder. Through all of this Julia Crighton waited in the alley, probably wondering if any of the shots she could hear had killed her husband.[26] He received the police Distinguished Conduct Medal, second class. But changes to salaries, allowances and benefits for dependants put 'too high a penalty on heroism', and on these Shanghai medals, when assailants were much readier to fire on the police.[27] Canadian Mike Slater, killed on New Year's Eve 1936, was the first foreign officer to have been killed since 1929. A thousand men made up an impressive funeral cortège. The funerals which punctuated the next five years of Shanghai street life got no less impressive, but in essence, by mid-1939 the SMP was bloodily engaged in the first British engagements of the Pacific war, and this was a job for soldiers, not policemen.

The SMP, however, held the line. The force was at the peak of its efficiency, almost as if this was the crisis it had been preparing for since the disaster of 1925. Under Gerrard, the Shanghai Municipal Police had been redesigned, restructured, and retrained. Old corruption had been weeded out. The force was technologically up to date, equipped with radio vans and fully mechanized, and its weapons training programmes and urban disorder tactics were world leaders. There was no repeat of May Thirtieth. Police casualties were lower, too, all told. In the years of political crisis and the great armed robbery wave between 1924 and 1930, forty-three men were killed. In 1937–41, during five years of warfare and violent terrorism, twenty-seven died. The streets got more dangerous as more bullets flew in an increasing number of fire-fights, but on average fewer men, in a larger force, were killed. And no anti-imperialist politics can deny their courage. Albert Cornwell was one of five men awarded medals in early 1940. On 8 December 1939 he was on motorbike patrol with SI Bretherton when they passed an armed Chinese man running in the opposite direction. They turned and chased him, and he fired several shots at them at very close range before he was shot in the head. CPC 2969 was sitting undressed in his home six days later when he heard a hue and cry being raised outside after an armed street robbery: 'The constable, still partially undressed, responded and chased one of the robbers for some 500 yards to Haiphong Road where the culprit fired at the Police Officer. The shot did not take effect and [the] CPC grappled with the man, disarming and arresting him.' [28] It took more than medals, and financial rewards, to make an undressed, unarmed man risk his life like this. The men of the Shanghai Municipal Police believed in what they were doing, and they did the job.

Tinkler died just two months short of the twentieth anniversary of his arrival in the city in the steamy August of 1919. There were still fourteen of that year's recruits serving in June 1939, five of whom sailed out with him and whose anniversary was noted in the local press in August 1939.[29] Robert Andrew lasted only another month: 'If I stay here much longer I shall suffer a breakdown in health, a nervous breakdown,' he noted in his resignation letter. So thirteen men remained to mark their twentieth anniversaries in the SMP, seven from the second batch, six from the first, while a further two held senior positions in the gaol. They'd stuck it out. The past caught up with some: his wartime gassing was behind the health problems which forced Ernest Ling into early retirement in 1940. Drink finally got the better of another colleague, invalided to Australia in April 1941. On 1 November 1940 nine of the men were available to be formally presented with their Long Service Medals by council chairman and Jardine Matheson's taipan, W. J. 'Tony' Keswick. Henry Robertson was now Deputy Commissioner in charge of the reserve units and Sikhs. Vic Sharman was Divisional Officer running 'A' division, the three stations in the heart of the Settlement. CI Oswald Perkins ran Hongkew, a difficult task in the heart of Japantown. John Watson ran Yangtszepoo Road station further east. David Ross oversaw detective operations in the Northern Districts and James Barry the Eastern. The men of 1919 now dominated the higher levels of the SMP, but not the highest tier, Robertson excepted, and the force never resolved the question of how high it would appoint men from the ranks. Gerrard had been brought in from India. Bourne had assumed command in 1938, and was a Shanghailander product of the cadet system. Smyth, who became acting chief in 1941, had come from the Indian army in 1932 to run the Sikh branch. Dan Cormie finished his memoir with a philippic aimed at the 'Old School Tie' mentality, as he termed it, which pervaded the commissioned ranks of the force: 'patting each other on the back, hail-fellow-well-met, good Club men who enjoyed

their whiskey and sodas, likewise their good pay and high rank in the Force with not the remotest idea of what they were there for.' Like appointed like. 'What we needed was a good Chief,' he concluded, 'what we got was too pathetic for words.'[30]

By late 1939 the SMC was effectively bankrupt; those worrying about their superannuation had good cause. The Council had spent the 1930s living off the proceeds of the sale of its power generation and supply branch to a private company. The Japanese occupation of the Northern and Eastern districts cut it off from important revenue sources. The collapse in exchange rates also drained its funds, as it had extensive sterling and US dollar commitments – not least in pensions to foreign employees, but also to existing employees. Only a loan, brokered by British diplomats from the Hongkong and Shanghai Bank in 1940 kept it in operation. But the process saw British diplomats and the 'hongs on the bund' finally seize the initiative from the settler coalition. The 'semi-autonomous' SMC could not survive in the new politics of the China war and the growing Pacific crisis. British forces in Shanghai were increasingly drawn into policing issues, as their defence sector included the troublesome western area 'badlands'. The question of the Japanese share of Settlement authority arose again. 'Calculated and feverish' diplomat-sponsored gerrymandering was the key to defeating Japanese attempts to take over the Council through the 1940 election which was, claimed one journalist, 'perhaps one of the wildest in the history of suffrage'.[31] The Japanese applied pressure to the Russian and Jewish refugees – assassinating community leaders who did not kowtow – and nominally split Japanese properties, parcelling out 'ownership' to unenfranchised Japanese subjects to increase their electorate from 1,300 in March 1939 to 4,000 in March 1940. The British did the same, only better, and maintained the existing national balance on the Council.[32] But this was an untenable victory, and they knew full well that they could not do it again. Uncertainty hit morale, which was also undermined by the necessity for new economies in 1940. The disbandment of the Sikh Mounted Branch was a blow to Shanghailander pretensions, but changes to recruitment proposed by Bourne in April 1940 would have eventually seen, in peacetime, the end of the SMP as constituted and its evolution into a body of mostly Russian or Japanese staff, locally recruited.[33] But this was wartime, and in the meantime the leadership was concerned with maintaining morale as 'one thing after another' continued to hit the force.

It hit Chinese personnel the hardest. On 26 September 1939 a young married Chinese constable, father of two, was found bleeding to death, shot in the back of the head. His pistol was undrawn, and he had plainly had no warning of the attack. Strewn about the scene were small slips containing a stark warning from a puppet 'New Life China Salvation and Traitors' Extermination Group': 'You people work for foreigners as slaves. You have failed to reform yourselves despite warnings. We national salvation martyrs work for the heavenly way by exterminating you.' Officers tried to keep the message secret.[34] The timing was no accident; from late August onwards a wave of petitions from Chinese personnel had been received by the Commissioner. Even the highest paid could not 'live decently', and the danger to efficiency and honesty was obvious, even if there was as yet no real unrest. The SMC offered all it could afford. By September 1940 Deputy Commissioner Yao Zengmou noted that 'The lower ranks of the Chinese Branch cannot live on their present wages'.[35] The attack on Reginald Yorke was possibly connected to his role in examining puppet suborning of the Chinese personnel. The day prior to the shooting sixty men had been suspended on suspicion of taking a 'retaining fee' offered by the puppets as part of a programme designed to undermine the SMP. British diplomats put the number of Frenchtown police so suborned at 460.[36] By late November the crisis had deepened. Graffiti on the latrine wall at Bubbling Well station attacked 'chicken-feed' salaries and called on men to strike. On the night of 29 November 1940 men at Central and Louza stations did so. Bourne lambasted Council policy: 'we have been trading on the loyalty of our Chinese Police in the interests of economy.' Significant additions were made to salaries and allowances, and he was able to issue a conciliatory address, abolish 'undignified' punishment drills, downgrade the seriousness of other disciplinary offences, and urge the men, in coded language, to guard against aiding the Japanese. When the address was read out at Central men clapped their hands and shouted 'Manyi!' (satisfied).[37] But by November 1941 prices had increased by another third, and 'smouldering unrest' developed into strike action at the end of November.[38]

Satisfying the Chinese rank and file as crises arose was one thing, coping with relentless Japanese pressure was another. The SMC resisted for as long as possible Japanese demands for greater Japanese executive control in the force. The SMP's Japanese Branch had been formed only in 1916 when 30 men were recruited from the Tokyo Metropolitan force and there were about 260 Japanese men in the force by 1938. The Council had cemented a Japanese presence at senior level in 1934 with the appointment of a Japanese Deputy Commissioner, Tajima Akira, and his replacement as Assistant Commissioner by Uyehara Shigeru. Uyehara was a Japanese consular officer, who had come initially as a Superintendent from a post in London, and was married to a British woman. However Anglophile he might have been, he described himself and other senior Japanese officers in a memoir written in wartime as being excluded from active decision making by what he saw as a 'British intelligence unit' – his term for the cadre of British officers who ran the force. The memoir might be coloured by the time of its writing, but Uyehara reported that British personnel paid him and his senior Japanese colleagues no respect, and even deliberately avoided saluting him, and he assailed Bourne as 'the worst kind of colonial type of Englishman'. His memoir shows him working closely with the Japanese civil and military authorities – as Bourne and SMC Commissioner General Godfrey Phillips were, of course, with the British – and engaging in argument after argument with a 'vain and stubborn' Bourne.[39] In 1938 the SMC bowed to Japanese demands and appointed a Japanese Special Deputy Commissioner of Police. The post was filled by a consular police official, Akagi Chikayuki, known from his previous Shanghai service by many British officers and widely liked. Akagi's role was still circumscribed, but the groundwork was laid for integrating Japanese into the mainstream of the force, just as soon as they had learnt its official language, English, and absorbed its culture and practice. The latter caveats were of course designed to slow the process down interminably, and the force resisted implementation of an agreement to create a new police division which would cover Japanese Hongkew and which would be controlled by Japanese officers. Akagi was shot dead in June 1941. Uyehara Shigeru reportedly saw the SMC as 'tolerating and encouraging anti-Japanese terrorism in the settlement in order to harass Japanese efforts to create the New Order in Asia'.[40] But in fact it was just trying to survive.

The badlands situation spiralled out of the SMP's control. Whatever measures the Council and defence forces might take were undermined by the physical difficulty of enforcing order when the SMC controlled only the roads (and that control was anyway contested, as Kinloch found out), and the Japanese-sponsored authority controlled the districts they bordered. In fact, puppet control was fractured and fractious, and there was more and more battling within the regime. From 76 Jessfield Road the puppet 'Special Service Corps' – usually known simply as '76' after its address – viciously intimidated the waverers and potential opponents of the regime, kidnapping, extorting, bombing and assassinating. And the business of war included running and 'protecting' brothels and casinos. Gambling provided a major source of revenue for the collaborators, locally, and in Nanjing. In April 1940 '76' controlled at least 500 armed men. It was 'an appallingly grave menace to peace and order in Shanghai', wrote Godfrey Phillips, who had himself survived an assassination attempt on the morning of 6 January, when three armed men opened fire on his car. Thereafter he travelled with bodyguards, bullet-proof attaché cases to use as shields, and a pistol.[41] But the activities of nationalist agents were also worrying: 'I wonder if you can yet once again try to get Chungking to give orders to do the killings outside the settlement,' he begged British Ambassador Clark-Kerr in June.[42] Superintendent Tan Shaoliang, one of the most important Chinese figures in Special Branch, had been one of the latest victims, gunned down as an alleged traitor in April. In February 1940 Commissioner Bourne opened negotiations with the puppet police chief, Lu Ying, inviting him for a man-to-man talk at the Police Club officer's room at Central station. A series of often sharply worded meetings was held during 1940 with Lu and his Japanese 'advisers' in which Bourne – no diplomat, it must be said – aimed to tie the creation of a joint SMP–City Government force for the Western District to the suppression of Special Service Corps activities.[43] Only in December was agreement reached, and after ratification, a Western Shanghai Area Special Police Force (WSASPF) came into being on 17 March 1941, six weeks after SMC Chairman Keswick toasted puppet Mayor Chen Gongbo at the signing ceremony. So it was all smiles and cooled champagne, even though the killing continued.

Ken Bonner was one of fifty-eight foreign officers promoted and transferred to the new force, in his case to its Foreign Affairs Department, responsible for all cases involving foreign nationals. Bonner's papers contain a sheaf of carbon copies of the cases he worked on in this office. Here is the morose fodder of the police day – larceny, traffic accidents, domestic disputes – although with Shanghai characteristics: the suspicion, above all, of servants. But the papers also indicate the continued decline in public security in the model settlement. A Mr Bailey was robbed at gunpoint by four men on the upper deck of a bus. Two men dragged the conductor off another bus and beat him up because they were asked not to spit on the floor. Eighteen armed Chinese boarded each bus which stopped outside West End Gardens, home to various puppet organizations, and broke every window on board, apparently in retaliation for the company's attempt to get them to pay their fares. A Mr Lopes (British) was quietly but very strongly urged to mend relations with his neighbours, the bodyguards of a puppet Vice-Minister, one of whom he had slapped in the face; the men shook hands. Nobody was safe: British diplomat Sir Alan Mossop and SMP Special Branch chief William Duncan were among the larceny and burglary complainants, and tucked in the file, evidently for amusement's sake, was a copy of the report recording a burglary at Bourne's home in Frenchtown.[44] In September 1941 Bonner tried to transfer back to the SMP. Having given the force a 'fair trial' he found his colleagues from the puppet city police 'insolent' and obstructive, and saw little hope for any improvement. The foreign staff had no authority and weren't getting results. The badlands got no better. Bonner was essentially nothing more than a recording clerk, compiling statistics for the crime reports.[45] But he remained until late February 1942, when all foreign officers were withdrawn.

If morale was low amongst rank and file, it was little better amongst the senior officers, who attempted to resign within two months of the force's establishment, citing corruption and the lack of any real role as the reason (the WSASPF detective squad was effectively an autonomous organization not integrated into the force). Bourne asked them to stay: the importance of the foreign presence was political, and

the agreement represented a strengthening of the SMC's hands.[46] But in reality the SMC had finally all but abandoned its long-claimed sovereignty in the western area, and it had little control north of the Soochow Creek.

By the end of January 1941 vote-splitting had produced 12,500 British votes, but events at a special ratepayers meeting on 23 January 1941 confirmed for many the dangers of holding an election that year. The SMP expected trouble at the meeting, as the Japanese community strongly objected to budget changes being proposed, but they hadn't exactly expected the Chairman of the Japanese Ratepayers Association – a 'tub thumping demagogue', according to Phillips – to shoot Keswick at the podium after the vote was lost. A riot erupted amongst the 2,000 ratepayers crammed into the stands at the Shanghai Race Club, high farce mingling inimitably with high drama. Japanese ratepayers threw 'wooden chairs, flashlight bulbs, pot plants and other missiles' at those on stage. 'Ladies and Gentlemen,' announced the Danish Consul, who was in the chair, 'the meeting is adjourned.' 'Dastardly outrage', shrilled the *North China Daily News*, but Keswick was only lightly wounded, and it was now clear that the time for gerrymandering was past.[47] British diplomats, councillors, administrative officers and business leaders held a series of meetings to discuss suspending the Land Regulations, and replacing the elected council with an appointed body. The Shanghai Provisional Council agreement put in place a new body, nominated by the Shanghai consuls. The scheme had many benefits, not least the dilution of the overly prominent Anglo-American bloc through the introduction of Dutch, Swiss and German representatives.[48] The new Council first met on 1 May, and to all intents and purposes conducted business as usual thereafter, although there was an easing of some areas of potential conflict, and the new body had much greater tax-raising powers. This was altogether most useful for the diplomats, who had more important things to worry about, a fact they frequently now made very plain indeed. 'I do not think', noted Ambassador Clark-Kerr to the Shanghai Consul-General in February 1941 after the Keswick shooting, 'that wider Imperial interests are affected by these events in Shanghai.'[49] For British planners, despite the long lists of Shanghai's contributions to the war effort that were sent home by the Consul-General, Shanghai was beyond the bounds of British empire, and it ought to develop a sense of proportion.

Shanghai was not, after all, a colony and, when war threatened, British empire turned away from imperial sentiment to strict colonial fact. The International Settlement was an enclave in a foreign sovereign state, vulnerable in the extreme to a hostile occupying power, hundreds of miles from any British possessions. 'The real marvel to me is that we are still in control,' noted Keswick in January 1941.[50] It was not just that the Japanese had not bothered to take it over, but that British defence had been scaled back to the absolute minimum. In August 1940 the garrison was pulled out. Imperial defence schemes in Asia pivoted on Singapore; not even on Hong Kong. In October 1940 the authorities urged British residents to leave Shanghai if they had 'no good reason for remaining'.[51] For diplomats in London, the wires from Shanghai hummed with 'highly imaginative information' about local contributions to the empire and to Chungking (Chongqing: Chiang Kai-shek's wartime capital), and 'special pleading by local commercial interests, who are less concerned with the allied and free Chinese war effort, or strangling Japan, than with keeping their own businesses running'.[52] Since Japan had signed the Tripartite (Axis) pact in September 1940 the British had been steadily developing a range of sanctions to hamper Japanese aid to Germany and Italy. By July 1941 a comprehensive economic blockade of Japan was in operation. Shanghai businesses were badly hit, and begged for concessions, claiming that any resulting lay-offs in Shanghai plants would cause a public order crisis. But as Britons in the city followed the heart-stoppingly dark news of 1941 they knew Japanese action was only a matter of time. The SMP still buffered Japanese activity in the Settlement to an extent, but this was stymied by the agreement to co-operate, by the need to suppress anti-Japanese activism and so the veneer of neutrality, and by the fact that the police force was probably riddled with spies and informers. 'They were spying on the British,' claimed American journalist Carroll Alcott, 'and spying on themselves.'[53] The 'Shanghai News' pages of the *North China Herald* catalogued shooting after shooting, killing after killing: 'Armed robber shot dead', 'Gunman shoots Japanese', 'Another gambling den raided', 'Chinese Police Constable Shoots Sub-Inspector'. Shooting Japanese simply because they were Japanese was senseless, the paper pointed out, 'and creates endless inconveniences to many sympathisers' with the Chinese cause.[54] Even the sporting life brought little relief. When the SMP played a league match at the Canidrome Stadium with Shanghai's premier Chinese team in March 1941, 20,000 spectators rioted after a sending off. 'Swine, dogs, foreign loafers', they shouted, pelting the police with sticks, stones, bricks (and orange peel), and defying the hastily summoned Reserve Unit in their attempt to burn down the stands.[55] For his part, Tony Keswick had decided that imperial interests, and his own safety, would be better served elsewhere.[56] He was given a thumping send-off. A guard of honour from the Russian Regiment (now part of the SMP) was lined up on the Bund, together with other police and SVC units. Escorted by SMP motorcycles, he was driven to the Customs jetty, and here – as the police band played 'Aloha Oe' – Tony Keswick inspected the guard and 'bid adieu to Shanghai'.[57] Lucky him.

Others left with less fanfare. Commissioner Bourne, his circulars to his men notwithstanding, took long leave in mid-August 1941, departing to Canada with his family for a vacation. It was obvious that he would not be returning to the fray. Henry Smyth, Deputy Commissioner, and perhaps already a British MI6 agent, assumed command of the SMP. Men continued to resign from the lower ranks as and when their contracts allowed, and left Shanghai as and when they could find a berth, which was increasingly difficult. The class of 1938, which had included so many ex-soldiers, had their opportunity as their three-year contracts came up for renewal, and a substantial number left to join up. 'Another SMP Officer joins British forces,' noted one routine snippet in the *North China Daily News*, while Sergeant Duffy, reported another, was leaving 'for the south'.[58] They had to make their way to Hong Kong, Singapore or Australia to join up, no easy task as the wartime shipping situation worsened (Duffy never made it). John Killingbeck and Alexander Gammie headed for South Africa, Gordon Reynolds went to join the Indian Army, as did Douglas Henchman. The *North China Daily News* printed news and photos of Shanghailander recruits in India and Malaya, and sober notes on Shanghailander deaths in action. But men in mid-career, or with families, were trapped by financial uncertainty, above all, and anyway, the worst might never happen. Most Shanghailanders reasoned that it was not in Japanese interests to seize the Settlement; it was too useful all round. Others, less optimistic, were just too late. Ted Quigley submitted his resignation in October 1941, with effect from April 1942. Together with an Irish pal, David Orme, he intended to go to India to join the army. Pearl Harbor intervened. On 10 December 1941 Quigley asked to rescind his resignation, and six days later Police Orders cancelled the resignations of seven men who had been unable to get out in time.[59]

Frank Peasgood was on night duty at Louza station on the night of 7–8 December when 'everything went dead'. And so with the attack on Pearl Harbor war again came to Shanghai, this time discreetly, and the Japanese announced – through leaflets dropped on the sleeping city – their imminent arrival. Special Branch filed the leaflets, being nothing if not methodical. Aside from a short, sharp engagement in the harbour with the two remaining allied gunboats, there were no military targets. Smyth asked for, and was given, details of the numbers and positions of the Japanese troops in the Settlement. The councillors were asked to carry on as normal. There was not very much that the

Japanese had to do. There was no immediate mass internment because, after all, somebody had to run the city, and the British did it best. 'If we lose control of the situation,' Phillips had stoically noted in 1940, 'we shall at least leave a going concern in good order.'[60] The last thing the Japanese wished to do was empty the administration and public utilities of personnel, or risk serious disorder by closing down foreign plants. Japanese military force was needed elsewhere. An announcement issued on 8 December publicized the Council's agreement to the Japanese request that it 'should carry on its normal functions for the welfare of the Settlement'. The latter clause lay at the heart of all subsequent explanations of the startling scenario whereby British and American personnel administered the Japanese-occupied city, many of them into spring 1943. 'It wasn't morally wrong,' declared Fred West, 'We were still doing police work, we weren't working for the Japanese.'[61] On 20 December the Japanese Gendarmerie, following established procedure, requested that the SMP assist them in the arrest of eight British, three American, one Russian and two Chinese nationals, all accused of anti-Japanese activities. Here Britons in the force drew a line, except for the Chinese, whom they continued to arrest. The Gendarmerie fully understood the objection, merely remarking that they thought Britons in the SMP would prefer to help out, to make sure that such operations were carried out properly.[62]

Allied nationals were asked by the new Japanese Chairman, the 'highly intelligent' and 'charming' Okazaki, to resign from the SMC at the end of January, but many remained on the sub-committees which conducted most business long into 1942. Acting Commissioner Smyth resigned on 21 February (but remained as 'adviser' – although little advice was asked for – until his repatriation via neutral Mozambique in the summer); Godfrey Phillips resigned a few days later. 'Evidently,' commented A. H. Scott at the Foreign Office, 'there are some patriotic Britons at Shanghai', but then again, he mused, the Japanese might just be forcing these men out. 'Only in Shanghai today,' Phillips told the SMC at his final Council meeting, singling out German councillor A. Glathe, 'could a new friendship have come into being between two people whose countries were at war.'[63] On 6 December the diplomats had ordered Britons not to 'assist the enemy voluntarily', but the instruction is unlikely to have got through. It was only in March 1942 that a consensus emerged in London that it was in fact better for Britons to maintain themselves economically during the crisis by doing their job. The message sent through eventually followed Foreign Secretary Anthony Eden's line that British subjects had to decide which option 'embarrass[ed] the enemy war effort most', staying in post or abandoning it.[64] Most stayed. But if continuing to run the administration was justifiable, resuming events at the Shanghai Race Club, repatriated journalist H. G. W. Woodhead confessed on his return to Britain in late 1942, was indiscreet. 'Much propaganda use', he acknowledged, 'was made of photographs of leading "enemy" nationals leading in winning ponies.'[65] 'Only in Shanghai', indeed. The world of collaboration during the occupation has been explored elsewhere, but there was little of what might be described as classic, active treason. On top of everything else – and by far the great majority of Britons remained wholly loyal – there really wasn't much call for it. The SMC had already so adapted itself to Japanese demands to ensure its own survival prior to Pearl Harbor, that there was not much else that needed to be done.

Due decorum and cosmopolitan rhetoric – and, naturally, sound finance – remained dear to the men who now took over the running of the International Settlement. When they abolished the Orchestra they allowed it a final farewell performance; when they abolished the Shanghai Volunteer Corps, they held a reception to mark the placing of the Corps' colours 'in a place of dignity and honour' in the Council chamber.[66] Discharged officials were given the correct paperwork, due pensions and their superannuation. After twenty-three years' service 1919 recruit George Craik asked permission (granted) to keep his cap badge, as a souvenir. Precedents set during the First World War regarding employees' military service were revisited in order to inform new decisions. When the International Settlement was placed under the control of the Special Municipality on 1 August 1943, Okazaki praised the 'deep sense of civic responsibility' shown by Settlement residents and pleaded for sound finance to continue, and for the new administration to consult business and civic interests. The Council bowed out with a cocktail reception and handed its files, administrative machinery and personnel over to the Special Municipality.[67] For the Japanese residents of the Settlement, the take-over was to be nothing short of a complete disaster. Retaining the independence of the International Settlement was just as important to them, and to other Axis nationals. Japanese business interests were no keener than anybody else about the prospect of operating under puppet Chinese administration, which they regarded as inefficient and corrupt, and whose sponsorship of serious crime had been plainly seen. They were wary, too, of Japanese military interference in Settlement life. The gendarmerie jails, of course, contained a full quota of Japanese suspects, along with Chinese and other nationals. And the military was greedy for loot.

War had made Shanghai dull, although the cabarets did not close, and the gambling continued merrily. But inflation soared, housing became a real problem, and corruption slowly became ingrained. On 12 August 1942 the neon lights of the electric city were turned off for the duration. In the new Shanghai dark the SMC decided in October 1942 to legalize brothels, one decision its predecessors would have been happy to see. That same month 'enemy nationals' – Britons, Americans and other Allied civilians – were barred from cinemas, nightclubs, theatres, the racecourse, the Hai Alai stadium and the Canidrome, so at least British prestige was spared more shots of Shanghailanders at play. The Bund got a makeover. Sir Robert Hart and other empire worthies were lifted from their pedestals as Shanghailander statues were removed. Street names were changed wholesale and a Chinese flag was soon to fly over the SMC building. From India came high-level complaints to London that, despite plentiful opportunities, few Shanghailanders were making their way to Chinese-held territory.[68] But Shanghailanders would argue that they had family to look after, or were serving British interests by remaining in place, so as to resume operations when victory came. Some quite clearly feared for the financial consequences, the loss of pension rights, positions and superannuation. They also (self-)serve, some thought in London, who only stand and wait. There had been a clandestine stay-behind unit organized by the British Special Operations Executive (SOE), amongst whose personnel – incredibly – was sacked former CID chief W. G. Clarke, as well as former SMP Specials commander, W. J. Gande. Clarke was arrested on 17 December, and the rest of the group was scooped up pretty swiftly afterwards, then tried and jailed.

Clarke declined the chance of repatriation. Japanese suspicion of the extent of underground work by other British nationals led to a large number of men being arrested and ill-treated, but there is not much evidence of any other activity, although MI6 planned in 1944 to recruit amongst remaining Chinese and Russian SMP officers from the secret base run by Henry Smyth in Anhui province.[69] In the months before internment began life in fact went on pretty much as normal.

Policing certainly did. But Bourne was pensioned off in his absence. Two Deputy and three Assistant Commissioners were retired in February 1942, as well as three Superintendents. E. C. Baker was left in charge of the SMP's Traffic Branch, but there was no traffic, so the joke was rather on him. Thirty men who were on long leave in December 1941 were dismissed in their absence. In August the new commissioner forwarded to secretary Teroaka Kohei a list of seventy-two 'members of the foreign Branch whose services are no longer necessary and others retention of whose services is considered undesirable'. Pensions and gratuities were issued to the men, but they were booted out of their quarters. The gendarmerie solved the accommodation problem. In November twenty-one more men were discharged after being arrested in a sweep of about 350 allied nationals and detained in a military-run camp at Haiphong Road which held, altogether, about sixty-five policemen. 'Reorganization' of the SMP entered its final stage in early 1943, when the remaining Britons, and those still serving in the jail, were discharged together with a number of Russians probably considered too Anglophile. Barney Wall was one of the last to go.[70] Internment followed swiftly, and it was boring. The treatment the great majority of those interned received was bearable, but wearyingly dull as three summers and two winters of captivity passed. A third winter's internment would have seen a higher death rate due to malnutrition, but the horrors of camps in south-east Asia were not visited on the Shanghailander. Ten of Tinkler's peers from 1919 were interned. 'We were hungry for long periods,' noted businessman Hugh Collar, who led the Britons in Haiphong Road, but they never starved, and Shanghai hunger was hardly restricted to those in camp.[71] Even there the Japanese allowed a radio and distributed a newspaper, the *Shanghai Times*.[72] General internment began on 31 January 1943, and by the end of the year about 7,500 British,

American and other allied civilians in the city – barring the elderly and the infirm – were moved into a converted school, empty godowns and other installations making up 'Ash Camp', 'Pootung', 'Lunghwa', addresses, for the duration, of the Shanghailander.

The SMP carried on without the British. At the annual inspection on 16 April 1943 the remaining Japanese, Russian and other foreign personnel – who now included some Jewish European refugees – paraded behind the Police drum and fife band as usual, although they now marched Japanese style.[73] A Japanese Gendarmerie Major was appointed to run the CID. Reckoned 'very efficient' at the work in a post-war US intelligence report, he nonetheless 'permitted graft on a large scale' to win over detective personnel and was effectively head of the force. Gendarmerie officer Saito, placed in charge of the Special Branch – now restructured as a Foreign Affairs Section – operated a profitable extortion racket with some of his Russian officers. The SMP retained responsibility for most areas of policing, except sabotage, espionage or activities involving the military, but in fact the Gendarmerie retained ultimate control, and Commissioner Watari Seikan was purely a figurehead. By far the great majority of Russian officers remaining in the force were the subject of anti-British propaganda which highlighted their unfair treatment under the old regime (and they were also forced to swap compulsory English lessons for compulsory Japanese ones). In a newspaper interview Boris Maklaevsky, who had joined in 1922, noted that 'his work, no matter how hard he tried, was not given the same recognition as a British officer'.[74] This was, as we have seen, absolutely true, but many of his Russian and British colleagues were furious that he'd said it.[75] But Boris Maklaevsky made hay while the rising sun sparkled, although most men kept their heads down, and kept as great a distance as was possible and as was still diplomatic from active collaboration.[76]

War splintered the SMP in other ways. Its men were divided between those who had left Shanghai, or who were repatriated, and those who took part in the allied war effort. Smyth, Vic Sharman, former Special Branch chief Thomas Robinson and a few more got berths on one of the two repatriation ships that made their way to neutral Mozambique. Some names crop up in histories of the secret war in Asia. Here is Smyth working for MI6 at one of the closest allied bases to Shanghai.

Here is Bourne in India, with two of his former charges, setting up 'Bristol', a counter-espionage unit for SOE. (Keswick and Godfrey Phillips had also assumed important roles within SOE.) First SOE, and then American clandestine warfare recruits trained in small arms firing, and unarmed combat techniques, under William Fairbairn, who had devised and instituted the programmes which had for two decades prepared the Shanghai police. Fairbairn called on other ex-policemen, such as Dermot 'Pat' O'Neil, to help him. Ex-boxer Jimmy Fallace got as far as Hong Kong, joining the Naval Volunteer Reserve there in February 1941. Captured when the city fell, he was one of 2,000 prisoners of war on the *Lisbon Maru*, torpedoed on its way to Japan. Their captors locked the men into the slowly sinking vessel. Fallace survived, and with two others made his way ashore, and then all the way to the Nationalist capital Chungking and back to war.[77] Wallace Kinloch found himself interned for the duration in Hong Kong. Having joined the Naval Volunteer Reserve in the colony in 1940, John Basil Smith found himself a prisoner of war there, too. In England, E. W. Everson, still drawing his pension from Pooks (he hadn't worked since leaving Shanghai), became a commander in his local home guard unit. Ernie Peters worked in a munitions factory. Former commissioner Kenneth McEuen, now blind, was living freely in Japan.

While groups were dismissed or interned, the force in Shanghai was also sundered by nationality. Rivalries and bitterness previously suppressed by police discipline – or police surveillance – were given free rein, and even encouraged. Indians in particular were actively targeted by the Japanese. The SMP delivered a full and proper funeral for Halvidar Dalip Singh, killed by an armed robber (himself an SMP detective) on 18 July 1943, to demonstrate where Indian interests lay, and how much better Indians were being treated.[78] Over a thousand Shanghai residents joined Subhas Chandra Bose's Indian National Army when a branch was established in the city, but their primary purpose, US intelligence concluded later, was as propaganda fodder.[79] Some ended up much closer to the battlefields. Ex-soldier Kartar Singh joined the SMP in December 1940, having worked as a watchman in the city for five years. In December 1942 he was sent with twenty-six other Indians to Penang, where he studied at a somewhat ramshackle clandestine warfare school, before moving on to Rangoon, where he joined the Indian National Army and surrendered to the advancing British in May 1945.[80] But for most of the 2,800 Indians in the city – including many of the police, who were dismissed in 1944–5 – the war was a period of hideous destitution and uncertainty, and it severed relations with local Britons, who saw them as collaborators, and who had always queried their 'loyalty'.

At the end of the war, the ex-policeman will tell you, they sat in their camps, plans all laid for taking the stations back over, and then they got an awful surprise at liberation. They knew about the abolition of the settlements by the puppet regime from the pages of the *Shanghai Times*, but seemed not to know that the British and the Americans had signed treaties with China to the same effect. 'We didn't realise Churchill had given Shanghai back to the Chinese,' remarked Frank Peasgood. 'We were all flabbergasted when we learned,' wrote Barney Wall in December 1945. The British diplomats had at long last solved their Shanghai problem. They'd signed it away, 'and our jobs with it', added Wall.[81] All that was left to do, as far as the diplomats were concerned, was negotiate the fine detail with the incoming Guomindang administration. The men of the SMP had other ideas, and they bombarded the authorities with letters and petitions. Somebody owed them a living; they had stuck to their posts at the orders of the government, which had then proceeded to abolish their livelihoods. 'For serving "Imperial interests",' claimed R. G. Hargraves, 'we had not only lost our homes, but our jobs had been given away as well.'[82] They were fit and ready to work, and some, like Dan Cormie and Bill Widdowson, found temporary work establishing an Auxiliary Military Police unit for the Americans. But if new Shanghai would not take them – and the new city police bureau employed only a small cadre of Russians – then, they said, the empire should.

Empire was hardly keen. Malaya said no, and Hong Kong only wanted men to cover rehabilitation leave taken by its own former internees. But the Foreign Office decided that it owed it to the men to get them employment. In their camps in Shanghai they drew up their *curricula vitae* and penned their awkwardly formal requests. Henry Robertson dashed off reference after reference for his former subordinates. With no other prospects in view, most men were keen to take any position, anywhere. 'I wish to state that I would prefer a job abroad dealing with natives,' announced William White. Albert Kyte stated a preference for work out East and his potential use in the 'supervision and control of native labour'. They offered themselves for plantation work, Customs services, police forces, anything. Former Deputy Commissioner Smyth, now working in the police department of the British administration in Germany, lobbied the Foreign Office to send them to him. The diplomats got working. And so the great majority of the men of the SMP were released from internment and were removed from the city for new beats in different climes. By mid-1946, twenty-four had joined the War Crimes Commission in Singapore, and eight the naval police there; fifty-three men went on one-year contracts to Hong Kong, although some stayed on; fifty were offered jobs in Germany, and fifty-nine with the British Military Administrations in former Italian colonies in North Africa.[83] Such barren exile was about as far away from the Bund, from Blood Alley, the Nanking Road, Shepherd's, Jimmy's Kitchen and the Shanghai life as it was possible to imagine.

There was, therefore, this final and most comprehensive offering of Shanghai policemen to the empire diaspora. Very few men took their expertise into organizations fighting the Cold War, but the Special Branch archive itself was the most substantial legacy of Shanghai's anti-communist policing.[84] On the whole, they had to find new places in a changed world. At least sixty of those who had been serving in the early 1940s made their way to Australia. There were a dozen men in Hong Kong in 1957; John Watson, who'd sailed out with Tinkler, ran a pub there until the early 1960s. Some younger men, such as the recruits of 1938, managed to get colonial police service postings, but most had been in mid-career and were too old. After working in relief organizations in China, Bill Widdowson took himself off to New Zealand, 'where the over 40s are still considered to be very useful', as he told the British Ministry of Pensions.[85] Barney Wall moved to the Philippines, working until 1972 before retiring to a Dublin he'd left in 1927; Dan Cormie ran a private security firm in Hollywood; Ted Quigley tried just about everything after police work in north Africa, including a trawling business in Australia. Canada's Mounted Police absorbed Commissioner Bourne; Ken Bonner worked in the pipe and steamfitting trade in Los Angeles and then Seattle. In June 1955 Jack

Albon formed a Shanghai Police Association in Sydney, which kept in touch with lobbying efforts in London, but mostly put its efforts into holding dances. 'Remember your own special mates, the blokes you drank with and sometimes fought and of course went to cabarets with,' he wrote in one circular. 'You must admit,' he continued, 'we were unique.' There was an annual SMC bash in London, but not many ex-police attended; 'the price of booze there is not conducive to really letting one's hair down,' noted Albon, and in any case the organizer 'never did much have time for the police', however unique. Old tensions were not forgotten. A 1957 survey of the Sydney men showed that some found police-related work, but others worked in clerical posts. Ted Baldock and Eddy Markland ran a fruit and vegetable business together in Bondi; Bill Munnings was a golf club steward, F. A. 'Tiny' Pitts – who had had a rough few weeks in Bridge House, the Japanese Gendarmerie headquarters – was production manager at a baking plant; Tom Darvill managed a hotel. Albon himself worked for the Egg Marketing Board.[86] A few stayed on in Shanghai until the communist take-over in 1949 and even beyond, working for the Consulate, or for relief agencies. (Former Inspector Collison was in a Shanghai gaol in April 1951, charged with smuggling gold.) Within a few years of the new regime's establishment they, and most remaining foreigners, had gone.[87] But on the whole, after the surrender of the concessions, to use a phrase of Wyn Curtis (whose husband Ben spent nineteen years in the force), all their skills, that training, that Shanghai nous, were now just 'about as useful as a cup of cold tea'.[88]

Barney Wall found a bill awaiting him on his return. Mr Ernest Bevin – the Foreign Secretary – required repayment of the repatriation passage, as well as monies advanced during internment. Bevin's ministry was tight when it came to money. Negotiations with the new authorities in Shanghai over winding up the SMC dragged on until 1950, when the Foreign Office gave up, allocated a lump sum of £1.5 million to the Council's former British employees and set aside £70,000 per annum for their pensions.[89] It wasn't much. Those with no savings outside China before the war were destitute. Fred West was 'left with nothing but my clothes and a Red Cross sponge bag'. On return to England he 'grafted'. The former Chief Inspector and head of Bubbling Well station, one of the Settlement's trickiest postings, initially worked as a petrol-pump attendant. Frank Peasgood, who hadn't been home for twelve years, opted to return to Britain, turning down the offer from an old mate of a post in the Hong Kong police on the way home. He found work eventually in the prison service. Chinese employees got nothing. In January 1947 'several hundred' ex-SMP constables, mostly now working for the Special Municipality, 'crowded into' the British Consulate demanding monies owed them. It was 'very unpleasant', wrote Consul-General Ogden. Two days later Shanghai's Mayor Wu himself had to spend an hour and half trying to persuade a second gathering to disperse. Two hundred ex-CPCs petitioned Ogden in August, as did the 616 members of the 'Ex-SMC Foreign Staff (Non-internees) Association', that is (mostly) the Russians. Mayor Wu found funds for the CPCs, but nobody felt they owed the Russians.[90] Slovak Edward Papp joined the SMP in 1921. He had been loyal to his British salt, he declared (although he worked on in the SMP until March 1945), and he fled from Shanghai to Paraguay in the face of the communist victory. Now 'bereft of his country, home, family and property', he petitioned the United Nations and the British Ambassador for assistance, as he and his wife were 'mostly eking out a mere existence, counting the days when the Almighty will relieve us from ourselves'.[91] The British had mostly made their way back to Britain, to small towns and villages they hadn't seen for years, migrating with the rest of the retirees in time to the Sussex coast, to Dorset. Others found new small worlds in Bondi, Sydney, Adelaide, Queensland. Some kept up with each other, swapping gossip and a 'yarn about old faces and places'.

They tried, before they left, to settle accounts. And when they remember wartime they remember their own first. The men of the SMP who had joined the War Crimes unit carried out a 'considerable part' of investigations throughout south-east Asia, but they did not forget Shanghai. By the end of 1947 this process was already being wound down, and the army sifted out the ex-SMP, who were mostly now too old for short service commissions.[92] One of those who remained was Albert Kyte, who got his chance to stay out East. Together with John Watson, and the dead man's father, Kyte was active in the bringing to trial of men accused of responsibility for the one fatal war crime committed against an SMP officer, Chief Inspector Bill Hutton. (Inspector Sam Sharrock, shot dead in the badlands in January 1942, was reckoned instead to have been the victim of an avenging criminal gang.) Hutton had joined the SMP in 1924. Married to a Russian, the Perthshire native was one of the men interned in Haiphong Road. He was arrested there, with a colleague, John Watson, on 3 August 1943 after being accused by one of the Sikh guards – all of them were SMP – of attempting to suborn him to take messages out of the camp. There are elements of truth somewhere in this story. The pair were taken to the Kempeitai Headquarters on Jessfield Road, and for ten days were interrogated, tortured and starved. After a series of savage beatings Hutton spent five days 'trussed . . . like one would a pig'. When Watson was allowed to see him the man 'was a pitiable object, still bound, filthy dirty, eyes staring and he was attempting to bark like a dog'. Two days after the men were returned to Haiphong Road Hutton was evacuated to a mental hospital, and died that night. At some point before his release he had used a nail to scratch the word 'Killed' on one side of his groin, and 'Murd[er]' on the other. On his feet he had scratched 'Look', 'At'. A fortnight after his release Watson saw the Sikh back in camp. 'Bastard, why you no die?' the Sikh asked him.[93] Hutton's former colleagues aided his elderly father's persistent campaign to get those responsible tried. 'On reading of my son's death his mother died of a Broken Heart and I am only living', he wrote, 'to see the Criminals or those who support them brought to Justice.' Two men were arrested, but then released in April 1948 as the target date for completing war crimes trials expired. After a public outcry in Hong Kong and Shanghai – 'England the slumberer' again seeming to fail Britons in the East – and after Hutton turned up unannounced at the Army Judge Advocate's Office in London with a sheaf of witness statements, the case was relaunched, and two men were convicted and jailed in Hong Kong in December 1948.[94]

Watson told his former colleague Harold Bretherton that the Shanghai British felt 'let down badly' by the lack of any prosecutions in China outside Hong Kong. The Americans had done a thorough job, and the Chinese had prosecuted numbers of Indians.[95] It looked a little like incompetence, but a lot more like a slur on the Shanghailanders, and on their loyalty, especially in view of the queer unresolved months that followed Pearl Harbor. In fact, the whole war crimes process was fatally compromised by the political need to restore relations with Japan in a Cold War world, and so 'lost sight of' the victims.[96] Shanghailanders articulated their own suffering in the pages of the relaunched *North China Daily News*, which carried angry letters from ex-inmates of Bridge House, from 'V.I.C. Tim', 'Forgotten', 'Disillusioned'. 'The price of empire', the Revd Darwent had written in his fusty old Shanghai guidebook, 'is that the bones of its soldiers and sailors lie on every foreign shore.'[97] The Shanghai dead and the unequivocal fact of internment became for Shanghailanders an unchallengeable mark of their inclusion in the British empire story. They paid the price; their bones lay on the Shanghai shore. In books and articles ever since they have remembered the dark days of internment, revisiting Hutton, Sharrock and Bridge House, while pushing the other story, of accommodation with the victor, to the edge of memory.

And Maurice Tinkler, too, was remembered. In January 1946 the Consulate sent papers about his death to the British Military staff office in Shanghai, for possible investigation as a war crime. The issue was referred to London. For the Foreign Office it raised some difficult questions and some disagreement. Tinkler had been killed over two years before war broke out in December 1941, so how could it be called a 'war' crime? G. V. Kitson, who as Consul in Shanghai had dealt with the case in 1939, argued that, as China had lobbied successfully in 1944 for the period covered by war crimes to be dated back to 7 July 1937, the killing of Tinkler was part of 'Japan's undeclared war in China'. Noji's full name was not known to them, nor any details of his unit, but it was agreed that a search for information should be made. The case was referred to the British War Crimes team in Shanghai.[98] The trail then runs cold, as did perhaps the search for information. Tinkler's name appears on none of the lists of British war crimes victims in the China theatre that I have found. In September 1948 the Secretary of the China Association in London, a business-lobbying group which represented British China interests, wrote to the army's Judge Advocate General about the Hutton trial. He then raised the issue of Maurice Tinkler's 'brutal' killing, and outlined the bare facts of the case. If Noji and others responsible were brought to trial, he argued, 'this Association and Tinkler's late employers ... would do everything possible to produce the necessary evidence'. But whatever the diplomats had argued in 1946 the army now saw differently. The War Crimes machinery had been mostly wound up towards the end of 1947, and a note scribbled on the letter stated baldly: 'This is not a war crime.' No state of war existed at the time of Tinkler's death, noted the reply, and only incidents occurring after the outbreak of the European war were covered.[99] So Maurice Tinkler died three months too early for any redress to have been made. There would be no settlement, and there would be no accounting. He was already history.

12

We Are the Dead

I too am a creature of the empire world. Grandfather Bickers served in the wartime Indian army, and then later as a school head in both colonial Malaya, and independent Malaysia. With the 1st Gurkhas he saw wartime duty on the North-west Frontier, in Iraq, and in Persia. At King George V School in Seremban he taught the sons and daughters of the new Malay and Chinese elites before and after Malaysian independence. My father served as a crewman in the Royal Air Force, working on the Britannia aircraft which served the supply routes of the diminishing empire in the 1960s, and then on helicopters in the Crown Colony of Hong Kong. In the family atlas he drew in the routes he flew 'down the line': Lyneham to El Adem, on around Nasser's corner to Aden. In his logbooks are recorded the trips out further, to Changi via Khormaksar, Muhharaq, Gan; Changi to Kuching during the 'confrontation' with Indonesia; the Nairobi–Lusaka shuttle after UDI in Rhodesia. He spent a year on his own in Sharjah, and a weekly postcard of an Arabian scene was part of the world I grew up with. His father-in-law spent the war years with the RAF in Khartoum. My own early memories gain colour and sensory impression only with our arrival at Hong Kong's Kai Tak international airport in 1971, at the start of a three-year stay at Flat 1, Block 1, Sunderland Road, Waterloo Road, Kowloon. From that day on I have known what empire means, even for the son of an airforce sergeant: the flat in the compound, Ah Hing the amah, the school which worked to make little Britons, cricket in the oddest of places. And on my mother's side are the immigrant Irish, another long tale of British colonialism. Empire is present in a broader family history, with paternal ancestors, like almost every Briton's ancestors, working over the seas in Burma,

India, South Africa, and Australia, some buried there too. There's George Sidney Bickers, a gas engineer in the Transvaal in 1899. George Bickers emigrating to Australia in 1853 on the *Rattler*. Ellen Dyer, dead in Rangoon in the early 1900s, her husband, an Archdeacon and a chaplain on the Bengal establishment since 1885. There were missionaries in Africa. Earlier still James Bickers and his brothers, linen-drapers in Southwark, sold cotton goods made from raw materials secured through empire. I make no special claims here. I'm not even sure of all the details; this is just normal family background. Mine was mostly a family of middling Yorkshire farmers who branched out as drapers and milliners based in Leeds and then in London. Empire was incidental, and nothing special. It did not run in this family, as it sometimes did – fathers in service overseas packing their sons back off to schools which prepared them for another round of imperial service.[1] Members of the Bickers family emigrated, sojourned, served within that world, and retired home or came back to better themselves, or else they settled, or died there. Empire was the stuff of stories, civic ritual, education, imagination, infusing all these lives, from Yorkshire to New South Wales.[2] It was seamlessly integrated into the ordinary wide world of the British experience.

It still is. Looking for Maurice Tinkler led me to Grange, Ulverston, Shanghai, Manchester, Edinburgh, to factories and archives, to parks and schools, and to bungalows and houses in Britain, where the forgotten servants of empire and its adjuncts still live. As you enter the Shanghailander's home you wonder who lives across the street, and where they were: Uganda, Trinidad, Hong Kong? Who has ever talked with them? Do the neighbours know? Inside the Shanghailander's home, surrounded by mementoes – if they were lucky, if these were not looted during internment – these men and women chat easily enough about their past – and the things they remember. Frank Peasgood could still bark out the Shanghainese commands which began the policing day, and remembered still the quiet details of another life and world. Fred West chuckled at the thought of police corruption. Jimmy Fallace just sighed as he remembered the city on the river; for 'it was', he said, 'a lovely place'. They have had time enough to mull over China memories, and also the seeming injustice of it all. Frank was still angry at being sold out, as he saw it, by the

British government after the end of the war. Only in November 2000 was any compensation (an ex-gratia payment of £10,000) grudgingly granted wartime prisoners of the Japanese, including civilian internees, 'in recognition of the unique circumstances of their captivity'.[3] This was little enough, and long enough in coming, to stoke anger further. To cap it all, they find themselves traduced, as they see it, in popular culture, most notably by J. G. Ballard's unromantic portrayal of the interned British in his 1984 novel *Empire of the Sun*, and then by the film of the book. They refused to read it as fiction, their anger aroused at such betrayal by one, seemingly, of their own. After all, Ballard's father was in Tinkler's story, too, as a China Printing director and plant manager, and the young Ballard, a Shanghai Cathedral Boys' School pupil, did his time with the rest of them in Lunghwa camp. And so when you have listened to this, nodded and taken your notes, you go home and look again at your own neighbours, and wonder what history is theirs.

And the dead live, too, in the memories of relatives, lovers and friends, in the boxes stowed away in attics and cupboards, scraps and letters, ephemera which once meant something, undated photographs, and in the romanticized legends which remake meaningless Shanghai death as epic (such is the power of the mythic city), such as 'murdered' Sam Sherlock, who died in fact of meningitis. As the book was researched I found myself communicating with dozens of relatives and descendants of the Shanghai policemen, scattered, as their fathers and grandfathers were scattered, through Australia, New Zealand, Canada, the United States and back in Britain. As family historians research their backgrounds they find themselves tracing such empire stories. For the descendants of the empire migrants this raises no eyebrows, but for the still-British it might. Some were surprised to find a Shanghai connection, were not sure what it meant, whom these men served, and usually assumed that there was some official and colonial connection, that this was empire service. The papers they possess form an invaluable proxy archive for the SMP, but it is the photographs which most bemuse. Great heavy volumes which often lack captions; the scenes portrayed surreal even with them. Here are the albums of Sub-Inspector Robert William Thomas, who joined the SMP in 1897, and left in 1910, working next as a policeman in British

Columbia before retirement in Leicester. This image shows Sergeant Gibson, posing in a rickshaw in front of a police station, framed by two smirking Europeans shouldering rifles; Sikhs stand in line behind. This one shows Thomas, who headed the Mounted Branch, leading an elaborate funeral along Nanking Road, brass band behind him, a coffin draped with the Union flag. Page after page of CID chief William Armstrong's albums contains portraits of Chinese rural folk, mostly women. Several shots portray a coyly smiling Chinese woman, hiding behind trees; a girlfriend, a companion? Then there is what must be his personal knife collection. Armstrong's other albums, filled with executions, beheadings, strangulation, death by slicing, were destroyed. But death and punishment fill the other collections of the Shanghai policemen, sanguine memorials.

Richard Maurice Tinkler has had three stone memorials, three gravestones, and his sister and Lily Wilson sought and left other forms of remembrance, in public and in private. His photograph hangs still on his old school wall. Edith partly blamed herself for his death, writing in 1970 that 'I was responsible in the first place for his ever going to China'.[4] In 1967 she tried to bring him back, writing to the Foreign Office asking to have his remains returned and buried at Grange, his 'native town'.[5] She even asked if she could go herself to fetch him. Perhaps the violence of the developing Cultural Revolution in China prompted her to write, but the same situation also made such requests impossible. The Consul was forbidden to visit the cemetery, and was later expelled. 'Perhaps you could draw some comfort', wrote a Far East Department official, 'from the thought that he is not alone but lies with many others of his countrymen who gave their lives in the Far East.' So the diplomats were polite, as ever, but could do nothing, as ever. There Tinkler stayed, but the trunks that had been returned from Shanghai were kept until Edith's age and changing circumstance meant finding somewhere else for them. In 1969 she wrote to Philip Noel-Baker, a winner of the Nobel Peace Prize who as a Labour MP had pestered the government about Tinkler's death in the autumn of 1939 and with whom she had then corresponded. (Odd that the telling of this life of violence can be framed by tangential encounters with two idealists, the other being Norman Angell in 1914, who campaigned for peace and disarmament.) 'I have never ceased to feel contempt', she wrote, 'at the ineptitude of what need not have happened.' Edith wanted advice on what to do with her brother's papers, 'in which he indicts diplomats and statesmen of that time'. 'He served his country *well* and conscientiously,' she added, 'he never appears to have had many thanks apart from a few medals and citations.' Noel-Baker passed on the letter to the Imperial War Museum, which set in motion the transfer of the documents, and the process by which I came to be handed them in October 1989. Edith was then still alive, but unwell, and it was only some years after her death in 1992 that I realized this, and located the Tinkler family. 'May I say', she had written to the museum in 1970, 'that for all these past years I have had a kind of obsession that "somebody ought to do something".'[6] She tried this herself, doing something, bringing him home, getting his death noticed, noted. He had, she complained privately, 'been crucified by the British government just like Christ', such was the insensate, impotent anger to which her brooding 'obsession' gave rise.[7] She had also asked the Royal British Legion to have his name added to the war memorial at Grange-over-Sands. They had agreed in early 1969 to try to get this done, but nothing came of it (the memorial belonged to the council anyway, and was not theirs for the altering). The memorial to the thirty-four Grange dead of the First World War, and seventeen of the Second does not include his name. Strictly speaking, Maurice did not fit. It was not a memorial that could accommodate such an out-of-kilter death.

But Maurice Tinkler was brought back to Grange, in a sense, as his name is recorded on the fresh tombstone which marks Alfred and Edith's grave, placed there after her death in 1992.[8] And there is also still, by chance, a stone in Shanghai. This now lies not in Hongqiao Cemetery, but in the 'Foreigners' Section' of the former International Cemetery, now better known as the Song Qingling Memorial Garden. Song had been married to Sun Yat-sen (and her sister to Chiang Kai-shek), and was a leading non-party figure in communist China. Shanghai's foreign cemeteries fared badly after 1949. British diplomats had long worked to protect the dead and their memorials, but there was little they could do in the new Shanghai. New Shanghai had no respect for cemeteries. The sites – Bubbling Well, Shantung Road, Pahsienjao – are now mostly parks or were built over. You can still see the remains of the odd tombstone in Jing'an Park (Bubbling Well), but this site was ordered to be cleared in late 1953, the local government liaising with British diplomats over the removal to a suburban cemetery of the remains of some 7,000 graves. There was tremendous pressure on land as the city developed – although remaining Shanghai Britons put the decision down to 'local cussedness' – and there was also symbolism in the drive. The British paid particular attention to the removal of some sixty service graves, and were disgusted to find, when the operation was over, that the Chinese had deliberately effaced from the stones all supplementary details identifying these men as soldiers, chiselling away the words, leaving deep horizontal scars on the stone. 'The object . . . was undoubtedly to turn back the clock, that is to eliminate from local historical remains . . . any evidence that foreign troops had fought or died in China,' thundered the Consul. Ex-policeman Harold Gill, now working for the Consulate, reported on this 'desecration', photographing sample tombstones. But it was not just service careers that were thus obliterated: one of the stones he photographed commemorated Robert John Morrow, an Armagh native who had joined the SMP via the RIC, and who had been gunned down on duty in 1907.[9] This was part of a broader drive. New Shanghai 'began to wash clean the filth and stains inflicted by the colonialists', it turned the racecourse into a park and a parade ground; the clubhouse became a cultural site, first an art museum, then the city library, and in the 1990s again the municipal art museum.[10] The Shanghai Club became a seamen's hostel. Proud records of the 'New Shanghai' were published to mark the tenth anniversary of the new dispensation, using photographs to contrast the corrupt, decadent past with the wholesome, egalitarian present and creating new myths for the mythic city. The 'former "Paradise of Adventurers"', noted one, 'has become a healthy, vigorous city.'[11] The dead were turned over too. The foreign-owned Hongqiao Cemetery was abandoned, and then turned into a factory site (only a small section now survives as a park). After 1976 surviving tombstones from various sites were re-created at the International Cemetery, which survived the turmoil of the previous decade largely because it housed the Song family tombs.[12] So here, in rows in a quiet, shady section of the garden, lie 576 small tokens for the Hongqiao dead.

In April 1997, after a tip-off from a friend, I cycled out there. It is a small plot, a little overgrown, but sweetly landscaped, in which are set rows of small concrete memorials. On these rest the names copied from the original stones, mostly just the names, or approximations of them (perhaps the only details which survived such desecration that had been noted in 1953). The hands which shaped the stencils and which applied them were not comfortable with roman letters, and some may already have been eroded or damaged. 'Harth Raeburn' (Martin? Gareth?), 'J. H. Howard', 'E. G. Schvetz', 'Li Young Son' lie side by side, mostly shorn of details, of dates, kin, and the token comforts and euphemisms of the tombstone: 'resting', 'in peace', 'sleeping'. Somebody has found an ancestor's grave here, and provided a smarter marble stone. And in the shadow of a hedge, underneath a small tree, lies one marked simply:

So after all this his name is still inscribed on Shanghai, and weathered in the east China air.

Edith proffered the idea of a commemorative plaque to the museum when she donated the papers, but the documents instead form the memorial. They have been used by a handful of historians over the years, although it is the virulent racism which usually finds its way into the texts. But, aside from Dan Cormie's incomplete, candid memoir, there is no other record quite like them of the police years in Shanghai. There are or were other accidental or incidental reminders, if you look for them as I have looked. On a wall at the Ulverston Victoria High School is the photograph of the puppy-cheeked army recruit; on a wall in an Edinburgh home an enormous photograph of the funeral cortège at Hongqiao; on a wall in Pudong, until the plant was razed in 1997, the words 'The China Printing and Finishing Co. Ltd.' were still clearly visible (I first saw them in 1991). The mill's water tower was still pitted with shrapnel damage from the summer and autumn of 1937. Tinkler would have recorded that hit in his reports to Hargreaves. The block of flats, his last residence, still stood. So this was where he would have walked, this was where he came that day, the strikers running this way, the altercation round about here (this patch now built over). This was the path they took him along to the waiting car, the Naval Landing Party headquarters, death. The machinery inside the sheds seemed of the period and now stood idle, the plant shut for good and awaiting the wreckers. It was there that Peng Hongfei talked with me for an hour or so about the man, and the events he well remembered taking place in the grounds outside our window. Other odd traces remain. Because of Powell's poem, Tinkler is indexed in biographies of that politician, his death forming a strange (unexplored) footnote in somebody else's life. The copy of Widdowson's *Police Guide and Regulations* that I received on an inter-library loan had been initially issued to the man who inherited Tinkler's number; the copy of G. E. Miller's *Paradise of Adventurers* had belonged to Hargreaves. And in attics in Nottingham and in Edinburgh were stored other documents, and drawings. Just as she had promised in 1939, Lily Wilson – 'pensive maiden' – never forgot. His letters have gone, but her commonplace book is annotated as late as September 1977 with brief comments about Maurice, and about betrayal. This was fifty-eight years after he had left, when she had meditated on 'life's sum total . . . Summer & you – and a remembered kiss!' She made a visit to Hong Kong in later life, perhaps – surely – a pilgrimage of sorts, for China itself was then closed to foreign tourism. Lily died a month after I first looked at Maurice Tinkler's letters.

Edith had her own reasons for her 'obsession' with doing something about her Maurice, perhaps mostly linked to the long loneliness of a life without mother, father, and her idealized brother, 'the greatest personality I have ever known'.[13] But she was also partly voicing in her own way the puzzled dismay of those finding the China enterprise, and the empire itself, unremembered, unfashionable, and unwanted. As decolonization became an accepted and unchallenged fact of the British experience by the end of the 1960s, empire became an embarrassment. Anti-imperialism moved into the cultural and political mainstream. The prolonged US intervention in Vietnam came to define in retrospect the whole saga of the Western enterprise in Asia. Radical scholarship galvanized itself to map out the contours of the imperialist assault and identify the roots and long history of anti-colonialism, the better to counter the one and celebrate the other. Radical became reflexive, the small change of political and cultural life. In Britain in particular, South Africa's apartheid and the politics of settler Rhodesia's Unilateral Declaration of Independence came to define the character of the colonial: reactionary, violent, racist – although it is not as if either place lacked British supporters, or immigrants. Anti-empire feeling holds sway in popular culture, casting Paul Scott's policeman Ronald Merrick as the sneering, violent face of imperial practice, or, more flippantly, laughing at it all, and reworking empire as a *Carry On*. Because of all this it became alien at last. Only in the aftermath of empire did it come to be perceived as a wholly different world, another country, cut off from and out of British society and politics, excised from home-side. The retreat from empire led to this great fracture, and to the growth of an idea that all that business was wholly of the past, done and dusty. And nobody was much interested for a long time in what the servants of empire had to say, or what they had to remember.

It was bad enough, on return, to cope with the loss of status and the creature comforts of empire life.[14] It was tiring, disorientating, to find yourself also recast, whatever you were then, memsahib, midwife, missee, civil servant, engineer, agronomist, nurse, medical officer, Shanghai policeman. It was tedious to not be understood, to be somehow always on the defensive about what you did, how you lived, and how different and normal it all was back then and over there. It was all made to seem like dirty work, and re-imagined as an enormous system of repression and control in which there is no room for nuance, or innocence. The (colonialist) boot stamps on the (colonized) face until independence dawns, and the administrators depart. So you get fed up with defending yourself against the ignorant present, against the ignorant interviewer. You close ranks. Meanwhile, families, however sympathetic, have heard all of the Shanghai stories before, and are not much interested in listening again and again. Often the historian's visit turns out to be the first time in years, a decade, that anyone has asked about that life. 'When I left,' recalled Frank Peasgood, 'I missed the rattle of mahjong pieces when on night patrol, the "He-ho" of the carriers of weights on both ends of a bamboo pole, the singing of foremen to their workers to get them working in unison. I had long recovered from all that,' he continued, 'until . . . you came along.'[15] And so it comes pouring out, irrepressibly, all the long afternoon fuelled by cup after cup of strong tea. And some of the refugees from empire also thought it would be easier to re-integrate if they downplayed the Shanghai stuff, or else they were content to close the chapter and get on. Age and the scattering of community made keeping in touch a little more awkward with every passing year.

Then there are the dead. On church walls and in school chapels you find recorded the empire dead as sons, daughters, parents, pupils. There is a memorial to the 'Civil Services of the Crown in India', unveiled in Westminster Abbey in 1958 ('They served India well'), there, too, were placed plaques for the Colonial Service (1966), and the Sudan Civil Service (1960). In Guildford Cathedral there is a memorial to the Palestine Police, but for much of the official dead, for the thousands of men and women who died on empire service, or as empire collateral, there is no lasting memorial. The military dead, yes, but not the civil dead of empire life and work. Much of the memorialization of British empire instead takes place in private, or in the work of the family historians, or the scholarship of former officials, writing up that history of the China consular service here, that administrative branch there.[16] There are, sometimes were, associations of this group and that group: the Palestine Police Old Comrades Association (thirteen branches in Britain, Australia and New Zealand), groups of ex-Indian Civil Service, or ex-Indian Political Service, or

Indian Police. Mostly, however, it is part of that remembered but mostly unobserved past, just a fact of family life, like my family life, and so a wholly normal part of the island's story – which means, whether immigrant to Britain or migrant from it, Britons share this past. British families were complicit in a world that was first internationalized through empire.

The literature on the First World War has broadened over the years to look at the impact of war on the societies concerned, on European culture, and then on the long aftermath, on a generation of survivors who worked out complex rituals to remember and understand the gaping wounds left in families and communities.[17] All proportion duly considered, there is nothing to help the remembering of the real life of the empire world. Empire's own memorials won't do; its street-hogging statues are too double-edged a testament to the difficult past. The Marine bayonets the Chinese soldier on the Mall; out of sight, the police officer tips the wink to his subordinates and the servant is tortured; Everson seizes his rifle and fires; Dyer sets up his squads to shoot in Amritsar; populations are relocated; communities are punished. The business of empire required dirty hands as well as fine ideals. The only dirt showing on the statues' hands comes from city pollution and pigeons. But empire was also a British graveyard, and graveyards need memorials. Those studying the political economy of health argued controversially that empire had a sharp impact on the health of subject populations.[18] But the 'relocation costs' borne by British men and women, while varying from colony to colony, were immense overall – 'staggering' was Philip Curtin's term for the nineteenth-century death toll amongst British and French troops. Such costs remained high even after safer environments for empire work were created through developments in medical understanding and treatment, and improvements in sanitation and public hygiene. Curtin acknowledged the 'terrible weight of individual human tragedy' involved hidden by his statistics.[19] Tragic, too, the separations, the family ties sundered, the washed-up wrecks of those who gave in to empire temptations. No surprise, then, that empire's servants feel unacknowledged, and that Shanghai's ex-internees re-imagined their police work as empire work, and as national service – which of course was not the point of the contracts they signed with the Shanghai

Municipal Council – for which they deserved, they felt, if not recognition, then at least in the first instance a replacement job.

In Edith's rereading, too, Maurice Tinkler first and foremost served his country, through service in the Shanghai Municipal Police, through his military liaison work in 1924, and in 1927, and through the fact of his death at Japanese hands. In death, Tinkler became for his family, former lover and colleagues, another man, living and dying ('Here lies an Englishman') as a true servant of his country, and his empire. But we have also seen how much he hated England, Britain, Britons, British diplomats and British statesmen. Through empire life he was able to see Britain as it really was (as it really was in his jaundiced view). Shanghai, for all its frustrations, allowed him to become someone else, at least initially, although circumstances and the tightening of international borders seem to have prevented his taking that last step away and aside into what he evidently saw as the American alternative. It was easier for those close to Richard Maurice Tinkler to remember him differently, easier to accept his dying as an act of imperial self-sacrifice, or, on the part of his colleagues, to see his murder as a war crime. It was far easier to misread the criticisms and rants in his letters as pungent ultra-patriotism; far easier to skip over the more unpleasant passages, the frightened student in the cell, the foul hatred of missionaries, the flippant childish wish to shoot, shoot, shoot and kill on the Shanghai street in June 1925; far easier to do that, than to cope with the messy bloody-mindedness of either his life or his death. The point of Tinkler's life, the point of empire life for most – not all, but most – was not settler idealism, not loyal service on behalf of an imperial project, not the wish to dominate or 'civilize'. Maurice Tinkler lived in a world in which empire was the fact of life, ingrained. And 'A white man can get a job out here'. He took that job; he did that job; he didn't come home.

But what a story. The letters and archived files speak it for the mute stones in Grange and Shanghai. Maurice Tinkler lived in this widened world of empire, walked that Shanghai beat, took the rickshaw, the houseboat, the Yangtsze steamer, the SS *Hiye Maru*. He circled the globe, stopping in at the empire ports: Port Said, Aden, Colombo, Penang, Singapore, Hong Kong; and then Kobe, San Francisco, Panama and onwards. Camera ready, Maurice snapped the gunboat on the Huangpu, the Annamite on Rue Consulat, the Buddha at Kamakura. He travelled, talked (harangued) and took it all in. He wrote some of it down, meditating on its past, on his place in a developing (but now in his time declining) empire story. This enigmatic empire variation was set to a Chinese landscape littered with tombstones like the ones he found in Amoy in 1930, dead British seamen and soldiers remembered by inscriptions 'full of romance'. Tinkler's last words home in January 1930 linger in the memory: 'Travel is a wonderful thing. I would like to go on forever.' You catch your breath as you realize that this is the final letter, and that this is how, unknowing, he signed off (from Edith, 'forever'). Of course, he never signed off from Shanghai. Maurice Tinkler was a man ensnared. It was a good life (if you didn't weaken, as many weakened), and even when it wasn't it seemed such a better life. Best then to hang on in, and wait for something to turn up. You could get by with a little bluster, if you lived a little harder for the moment there in Shanghai. China Printing turned up, and then so did all the rest of it, and all the things I don't know and can't now know. But for Tinkler I do know that there was no going back. Others like him, who joined with him or afterwards, moved on through, others returned. It was all a question of finding your billet somewhere, and sticking it out, about luck and judgement, and he didn't always have either. But shame was also a burden; that and something to do with pain and loss in 1922, something I don't know. Maurice Tinkler was brought back into the British story after his death – brought home – and recast as patriotic servant, otherwise it all seemed a colossal waste. But it would be difficult to recast the violence; violence in thought, in action, the coarsening of the Shanghai life, the punch, the kick, the colonial reflex. This story has highlighted the enormous harm, and the enormous self-harm of empire, and it is very hard finally to give in to sympathy. Tinkler's is a story of individual and state violence and of the exercise of power abroad over peoples and places weakened in the face of British might. He is no empire hero. (In the final analysis there is perhaps no room any more for empire heroes.) But this is also a story of ordinary British lives created in the interstices of the grand narrative of the rise and fall of British empire, of ordinary men and women living in the ordinary empire world.

In Shanghai itself, the site of this story, these stories, the language of anti-imperialism is now muted, with far less emphasis on stylized foreign villainy on display in histories and in museums than was the case before the 1990s. The last memorials erected by the settlers have gone, pulled down during the occupation, during the Guomindang reoccupation (when the roads were renamed), or after 1949. Politics retains an anti-imperialist reflex, but scholarship is more neutral, and fragments retain a place in Shanghai's popular memory, most notably the Sikh policeman. But hapless Inspector Everson remains caricatured, caught for ever at killing time. In one recent painting he rides a charger, his firing squad (its Chinese personnel conveniently excised) a line of sniping Sikhs. Chinese innocence falls bleeding to the road as the bullets fly.[20] There is a 'May Thirtieth Martyrs Memorial', a wall with bas-reliefs depicting class solidarity in the face of foreign bullets, which sits as close as city planning has allowed to the actual site of the shooting. But this token political gesture is ignored as the city does its shopping, although it stinks of urine, so it serves a very different practical purpose from that intended. There is, however, one spot which does dwell still on the ordinariness of that policing past. The exhibition rooms at Shanghai's Public Security Museum on Ruijin Road survey the decades before 1949, and you can get a sense here of how some of the old policing practices have survived in the normal procedure of the present force (which occupies the stations and barracks built for the SMP and the Frenchtown police). The SMP even has a memorial of sorts, seen mostly only by new recruits to the Public Security Bureau (for no one else bothers with such a museum). The exhibition starts with one of the re-created 'Shanghai old streets' that are popular in the city's other tourist sites. Here, three life-size figures of SMP policemen model their respective uniforms, a Sikh, a European and a Chinese standing side by side. Their backdrop is a blown-up photograph of the guarded entrance to Louza station after May Thirtieth. It brings a smile to the face, to see them on display like this, rendered harmless in wax. But it is a little awry, and after puzzling awhile you realize why. I can't vouch for those teeth, but that European is too short. He would not have made the grade at Pooks, on Fenchurch Street, London EC3: 'not less than 5ft. 10in in height' said the advertisement. The man would surely have been refused an interview. To get it right, to catch it as it really was, well, you really have to remember the size required of these men, and how they stood tall, back then, back there, in those miles and miles of crowded, stinking, noisy Shanghai streets.

Acknowledgements

First and foremost I am especially grateful to Pat Tinkler and her late husband John, and their family, who welcomed me into their home and allowed me to look at and reproduce Maurice Tinkler's letters, documents and photographs. Roderick Suddaby, Keeper of the Department of Documents at the Imperial War Museum, somewhat inadvertently set this project rolling in 1989, and I am grateful for his assistance, keen eye, and goodwill, as I have revisited the museum and the Tinkler papers over the years. Mrs Judith Baldry, formerly of the Manchester City Archives and Local Studies unit, rooted out important documents long after my visit and was tremendously helpful. Keith Renshaw dug out the commonplace book his aunt Elizabeth Benson (Lily Wilson) had kept from 1919 into the 1970s and was extremely helpful in providing me with information about the family. In Shanghai I owe a debt of thanks to Li Yihai, Zhao Nianguo and colleagues at the Shanghai Academy of Social Sciences, and to former director Shi Meiding, Ma Changlin, Ma Jinghua and colleagues at the Shanghai Municipal Archives who made available the service records of Maurice Tinkler and his colleagues. Marcia Ristaino's patience was remarkable, and I am heavily indebted to her for securing important materials used in chapter 8. My thanks also go to Alex Ward, curator of the Grand Lodge of A. F. & A. Masons of Ireland at Freemasons' Hall, Dublin, for locating and supplying important documents; to Judith Walker at the Salvation Army International Heritage Centre; to the archives staff at the Institute of Modern History, Academia Sinica, Taiwan; and to the puzzled archivists and librarians in the Caribbean who responded to my red-herringed inquiries.

Time out to complete the writing of this book was funded by the Leverhulme Trust Research Fellowship Scheme, and tolerated by my colleagues at the Department of Historical Studies, University of Bristol. Research expenses and time were also funded by the University of Bristol Faculty of Arts Research Fund, the Universities' China Committee, the British Academy/ESRC China Exchange Scheme, and Nuffield College, Oxford, to all of whom I am extremely grateful. For permission to quote from copyright materials or to reproduce them I am also grateful to Charles Causley, the Literary Executors of the late J. Enoch Powell, Daniel G. Cormie, and Coats PLC, as well as Charlotte Havilland at John Swire and Sons.

This project would hardly have found such riches were it not for the help, enthusiasm and good cheer of the numerous relatives and descendants of the men of the SMP, some 150 of whom have corresponded with me, sharing information, donating images and documents. In particular I am extremely happy to record large debts of gratitude to Paddy Fearnley and Cecil Uyehara, for providing vital papers and for allowing me to quote from them, and also to Helen Allan, Harry Bonner, Marina Booth (née Crank), Daniel Cormie, Charles Darby, Matt Dudley, Ivor Everson, Caroline Gray, Bonnie Hewer, Marigold Hogan, Audrey Horne, Jane Kavanagh, Patricia Maddocks, Nicholas Solntseff, Jackie Tanner, Richard Thomas and Bill White for their help or for allowing me to use their materials in this book. Mark Sellar, Jim Herlihy, Christine Thomas at the Metropolitan Police Archives, David Mahoney and Peter Robins generously shared information and materials. I am especially grateful to Peter, whose good cheer and good leads proved invaluable. I am most sorry that he did not live to see the book in print, but I do hope that he would have felt that this book does the job. Scott Armstrong was rather more tolerant than he should have been, but I am pleased to be able to use photographs from his great-uncle's albums in the book. The late Mabel and Frank Peasgood were stalwart supporters of this project, and I am grateful to them – and to the memory of Frank's bluff decency and instructions that I keep a due sense of proportion and spend more time with my family and less with the SMP. Fred and Michael West, Jimmy Fallace, and Peng Hongfei all found time to talk engagingly to me about their Shanghai pasts and I learnt a great deal from them all.

For their encouragement, advice or help in this and related projects I owe thanks to Bernard Alford, Marie-Claire Bergère, Chiara Betta, Tim Brook, Timothy Barrett, Christine Cornet, John Darwin, Penny Galloway, Jos Gamble, Hatano Takehiko, Christian Henriot, Peter Hibbard, Tess Johnston, Bill Kirby, Françoise Kreissler, Rodney Lowe, Brian Martin, Cathy Merridale, Kirsty Reid, Philip Richardson, Alain Roux, Rosemary Seton, Brendan Smith, Steve Smith, Andy Thompson, Gary Tiedemann, Hans van de Ven, Bernard Wasserstein, Jeff Wasserstrom, Ian Wei, Xiong Yuezhi, Zhang Shunhong, Zheng Zu'an, and especially Fred Wakeman, so open with his time and advice for a (then) young graduate student from England in 1991. Charles Mason, Frances Wood, Elizabeth Buettner and R. John Pritchard provided invaluable references and materials, and I owe them all many thanks, as I do Professor Robert Gohstand, Project Director of the Old China Hands Archive, California State University, Northridge, who helped provide illustrations and whose library and collections I wish all success. I am particularly indebted to the following friends who have also read the manuscript at various stages and provided challenging commentary thereon: Jocelyn Alexander, Heather Bell, Tim Cole, Margaret Jones, Rana Mitter and Nicky Saunter. None of them is responsible for this text, of course (which is a great relief for at least one of their number).

This project was awarded the first Institute of Historical Research Prize in 2000. This is an important and stimulating competition and I wish it a long life. My thanks go to all concerned, and especially to those who established it: Toby Mundy, then of Weidenfeld and Nicolson, now of Grove Atlantic, and Professor David Cannadine, Director of the Institute, and to the latter as well for his support then and later. The competition provided a focus and a stimulus to move on speedily with the project. I am lucky indeed to have found an encouraging, like-minded and enthusiastic agent in David Miller, and a fine editor in Simon Winder at Penguin. Their keen interest has been a tremendous boon, and a great incentive to put a stop to it all. At Penguin I'd also like very much to thank Louise Ball and Chloe Campbell, and Elizabeth Stratford.

Edward and Judy Williams supplied the room, for which I am immensely grateful. Personal encouragement and much, much more besides came from Joan and Bob Bickers, Amy and Chas Bickers, Lisa Clothier, Mike Bullen, Adam Brookes, Susan Lawrence, Heather Bell, Neil Shepherd, Simon Firth, Jennifer Summit, Carol Murphy and the late, lovingly lamented Ray Hills. Kate, Lily and Arthur made sure this book took much longer to write than would otherwise have been the case, for which I am grateful beyond words.

Ranks in the Shanghai Municipal Police, Foreign Branch

(highest to lowest)

Commissioner of Police (before 1919 Captain Superintendent)

Deputy Commissioner

Assistant Commissioner

Superintendent

Chief Inspector

Inspector

Sub-Inspector

Sergeant

Probationary Sergeant (before 1929 Constable)

Note on Currency

'Travellers will find two kinds of money used in Shanghai and the treaty ports – taels and cash, dollars and cents; the former Chinese, the latter introduced by foreigners . . . The tael (Tl.) is the commercial currency of the port . . . it is not a coin, but a weight of silver, in the form of a shoe. It is seldom seen: where one does see it, it is in paper.. . . The most universally used coin in the Settlements is the Mexican dollar ($), a handsome piece of silver; it weighs just about 1 oz. There are nominally 100 copper cents to the dollar. The actual number varies from 100 to 140. . . . All the leading banks issue notes for one, five, ten dollars and upwards. . . . The tael is roughly one third more than the dollar . . . Let the newcomer always remember to take account of exchange' (Revd C. E. Darwent, *Shanghai: A Handbook for Travellers and Residents*, 2nd edn. (Shanghai: Kelly and Walsh, 1920), pp. v–vi).

Salaries and rents were expressed in taels, but everyday expenditure was made in and priced in dollars. In 1935 the tael was replaced by the *Fabi*, a national, uniform currency, commonly referred to as the dollar. After 1935 all transactions were quoted in and paid in 'dollars'.

Romanization of Chinese Words and Names

I have aimed at being clear, rather than absolutely consistent, in romanizing Chinese names and place-names. Tinkler and his contemporaries refer in their letters and books, and in interviews, to Nanking Road, the Yangtsze, Foochow, etc., rather than Nanjing Road, the Yangzi and Fuzhou as they would be written in the modern official romanization system used in China (which is known as 'pinyin'). I have usually followed their contemporary usage in the text, indicating in parentheses and in the index the pinyin romanization, except when I refer to Chinese names, where I have used pinyin. On occasion, not having the original Chinese characters for a name, I have used the romanization that I found in the source concerned. I have also used pinyin where I think it the more recognizable variant today, for example Pudong and Huangpu.

Illustrations

Frontispiece: RMT in countryside near Taihu lake, November 1923, Tinkler family.

p. 14. Frank Peasgood on patrol, from E. W. Peters, *Shanghai Policeman* (London: Rich and Cowan, 1937).

p. 23. RMT, France, July 1917, Tinkler family.

p. 26. 'Carry on!', illustration by RMT, January 1919, in Lily Wilson's commonplace book, with kind permission of Keith Renshaw.

p. 29. Officer cadet Tinkler, 1918, Catterick camp, Tinkler family.

p. 48. Shanghai street scence, early 1920s, Mary Evans Picture Library.

pp. 66–7. 'Omnia Juncta in uno' ('All together in one' – the SMC's motto): Chinese, Sikh and European SMP personnel, *c.* 1930s, P. T. Goffe papers (Goffe is standing to the left), with kind permission of David Mahoney.

p. 74. Dealing with an armed assailant: from W. E. Fairbairn, *Scientific Self-defence* (London: D. Appleton and Co., 1931), copy courtesy of Peter Robins.

pp. 78–9. Execution of armed robbers, Shanghai, *c.* mid-1920s, two pages from R. J. White photo albums, with kind permission of Bill White, and courtesy of Professor Robert Gohstand, Project Director of the Old China Hands Archive, California State University, Northridge.

p. 85. Probationary Sergeant Sam Sherlock and colleague, *c.* 1929–30, courtesy of Jacqueline Tanner.

p. 93. 'Types of the SMP' by 'Sapajou' (Georgii Avksent'ievich Sapojnikoff, d. 1949), from an SMP Christmas card (mid-1920s), courtesy of Helen Allan.

pp. 98–9. A. L. Crompton and RMT (left); Central Police Station (centre); A. E. Balchin and RMT (right); Central Police Station, Shanghai, 16 October 1921, Tinkler family.

p. 113. SMP ambulance in action, *c.* mid-1920s, William Armstrong collection, with kind permission of Scott Armstrong.

p. 131. Detective Tinkler, undated but *c.* 1921–3, Tinkler family.

p. 136. Lodge Erin Crest, Tinkler papers, Imperial War Museum.

p. 139. Lily Wilson drawn by RMT, undated c. 1919–21, loose in Lily Wilson's commonplace book, reproduced with kind permission of Keith Renshaw.

p. 148. Shura at Tsingtao (Qingdao), c. 1927–8, Tinkler family.

p. 167. May Thirtieth incident victim Chen Baozong's bloodstained shirt, Academia Sinica, Institute of Modern History Archives, Chinese Foreign Ministry Republican Archives, 03-40, 24-(3), reproduced with kind permission and assistance of the Archives staff.

p. 171. Demonstrators in front of Wing On department store, Nanking Road, 1 June 1925, William Armstrong collection, with kind permission of Scott Armstrong.

p. 173. Entry in E. W. Everson's appointment diary, 1 January 1926, with kind permission of Ivor Everson.

pp. 178–9. Shanghai Defence Force barricade, Hulton-Deutsch/CORBIS.

p. 181. Barricade at entrance to the International Settlement shortly after being rushed by deserting Russian mercenary troops seeking refuge, 22 March 1927, William Armstrong collection, with kind permission of Scott Armstrong.

p. 203. Vancouver–Yokohama–Kobe–Shanghai, 6 January to 28 January 1931: postcard of the SS *Hikawa Maru*, pasted into RMT photograph album, Tinkler family.

p. 219. Advertisement from the *Shanghai Police Gazette*, November 1933.

p. 224. RMT, Nanchang, 11 May 1934, Tinkler family.

p. 238. Advertisement from the *Shanghai Police Gazette*, November 1933.

p. 251. The Shanghai War Memorial on the Bund, 1930s, AKG Berlin.

p. 254. The pleasures and violences of 1930s Shanghai: sardonic cartoons from Xiao Jianqing, *Manhua Shanghai* (Cartoon Shanghai) (Shanghai: Shanghai jingwei shuju, 1936).

pp. 264–5. A group of refugees on the Bund during the Sino–Japanese War, 14 August 1937, Hulton-Deutsch/CORBIS.

p. 266. Chapei burning, 22 November 1937, Hulton/Keystone.

p. 279. Suspected labour activists, CPA's Lunchang plant, May 1939, US National Archives, RG 263, Shanghai Municipal Police Special Branch files, D 6968.

pp. 286–7. 'The outrage': 1. The site of the shooting. 2. British and Japanese officials examine the evidence. 3. Tinkler's Mauser and other CPA pistols. 4. Lieutenant-Commander Noji Munesuke. 5. RMT in Japanese custody. 6. More evidence. *Tairiku Shimpo*, 6 June 1939, US National Archives, RG 263, Shanghai Municipal Police Special Branch files, D 6968.

p. 291. Cutting from the *Daily Mirror* and *Daily Express*, 24 June 1939, Tinkler family.

p. 298. Burning Jock Kinlock, from anti-British propaganda booklet: *Wu wang ba, yijiu Huxi canan* (Never forget the 19 August massacre) (Shanghai: no publisher, 1939), US National Archives, RG 263, Shanghai Municipal Police Special Branch files, D 9391.

pp. 304–5. SMP medal parade *c.* 1940, courtesy of Matt Dudley.

p. 311. Shanghai Municipal Council, 1940 (Tony Keswick in the Chairman's seat, American J. W. Carney to his right, Yu Xiaqing to his left), with kind permission of John Swire and Sons.

p. 334. RMT's tombstone, Song Qingling Memorial Garden, Shanghai (author's photograph).

Notes

Abbreviations

ACP	Assistant Commissioner of Police
CCP	Chinese Communist Party
CDI	Chief Detective Inspector
CI	Chief Inspector
CID	Criminal Investigation Department
CP	Commissioner of Police
CPA	Calico Printers' Association
CPC	Chinese Police Constable
DC	Deputy Commissioner
DSI	Detective Sub-Inspector
DI	Detective Inspector
IWM	Imperial War Museum
IO	Intelligence Office
NARA	National Archives and Records Administration
NCDN	*North China Daily News*
NCH	*North China Herald* (= the weekly edition of *NCDN*, hence most citations in the notes are to *NCH*)
NRA	National Revolutionary Army
OHBE	*The Oxford History of the British Empire*
OSS	Office of Strategic Services
PRO	Public Record Office
SDF	Shanghai Defence Force
SI	Sub-Inspector
SMC	Shanghai Municipal Council
SMP	Shanghai Municipal Police
SVC	Shanghai Volunteer Corps

I

The Empire World

1. *Partnership for Progress and Prosperity: Britain and the Overseas Territories*, Cm. 4264 (London: HMSO, 1999).

2. The two best general introductions are: P.J. Marshall (ed.), *The Cambridge Illustrated History of the British Empire* (Cambridge: Cambridge University Press, 1996), and A. N. Porter (ed.), *Atlas of British Overseas Expansion* (London: Routledge, 1991). There are two recent single-volume histories which contain much meat for disagreement: Lawrence James, *The Rise and Fall of the British Empire* (London: Little, Brown and Company, 1994), and Dennis Judd, *Empire: The British Imperial Experience from 1765 to the Present* (London: Basic Books, 1996); but still the most fun is the Jan Morris trilogy: *Pax Britannica: The Climax of an Empire* (London: Faber and Faber, 1968), *Heaven's Command: An Imperial Progress* (London: Faber and Faber, 1973) and *Farewell the Trumpets: An Imperial Retreat* (London: Faber and Faber, 1978); all repr. Harmondsworth: Penguin.

3. For a survey of the debate see John Darwin, 'Decolonization and the End of Empire', in Robin Winks (ed.), *The Oxford History of the British Empire* (hereafter *OHBE*) volume v: *Historiography* (Oxford: Oxford University Press, 1999), 541–57, and Darwin, *Britain and Decolonization: The Retreat from Empire in the Post-War World* (London: Macmillan, 1988). For regional and thematic surveys see the essays in Judith M. Brown and Wm. Roger Louis (eds.), *OHBE*, volume iv: *The Twentieth Century* (Oxford: Oxford University Press, 1999).

4. Felix Driver and David Gilbert, *Imperial Cities: Landscape, Display and Identity* (Manchester: Manchester University Press, 1999), in particular their introduction, 'Imperial Cities: Overlapping Territories, Intertwined Histories', pp. 1–17; Anthony D. King, *Global Cities: Post-Imperialism and the Internationalization of London* (London: Routledge, 1990), 73–81.

5. Two surveys: John M. MacKenzie, *Orientalism: History, Theory and the Arts* (Manchester: Manchester University Press, 1995); Jeffrey Auerbach, 'Art and Empire', in *OHBE*, volume v: *Historiography*, 571–83.

6. P. J. Marshall, 'Imperial Britain', *Journal of Imperial and Commonwealth History*, 23 (1995), 379–94; one attempt at correction is the set of essays in Stuart Ward (ed.), *British Culture and the End of Empire* (Manchester: Manchester University Press, 2001).

7. William C. Kirby, 'The Internationalization of China: Foreign Relations at Home and Abroad in the Republican Era', *China Quarterly*, 150 (1997), 433–58.

8. Morris, *Farewell the Trumpets*, Penguin edn., p. 11; a different perspective – but one no less suggestive of the ordinariness of empire in British life – is presented in David Cannadine, *Ornamentalism: How the British Saw Their Empire* (London: Allen Lane, 2001), appendix, 'An Imperial Childhood?', 181–99.

9. 'Admonitions of the Instructress to the Court Ladies' (Nüshi zhen), attributed to Gu Kaizhi (*c.* 345–406 CE); Charles Mason, 'The Admonitions Scroll in the 20th Century', paper presented at a colloquy on 'The Admonitions Scroll: Ideals of Etiquette, Art and Empire from Early China', London, 18–20 June 2001.

10. James L. Hevia, 'Loot's Fate: The Economy of Plunder and the Moral Life of Objects "From the Summer Palace of the Emperor of China"', *History and Anthropology*, 6:4 (1994), 319–45.

11. John King Fairbank, *Trade and Diplomacy on the China Coast: The Opening of the Treaty Ports, 1842–1854* (Cambridge, Mass.: Harvard University Press, 1953); Rhoads Murphey, *The Outsiders: The Western Experience in India and China* (Ann Arbor: University of Michigan Press, 1977); James Polachek, *The Inner Opium War* (Cambridge, Mass.: Harvard University Press, 1992).

12. Robert Bickers, *Britain in China: Community, Culture and Colonialism, 1900–49* (Manchester: Manchester University Press, 1999), 22–66; Marek Kohn, *Dope Girls: The Birth of the British Drug Underground* (London: Lawrence and Wishart, 1992).

13. Peter Richardson, *Chinese Mine Labour in the Transvaal* (London: Macmillan, 1982).

14. Michael Summerskill, *China on the Western Front: Britain's Chinese Work Force in the First World War* (London: Michael Summerskill, 1982).

15. Imperial War Museum, Tinkler papers, R. M. J. Martin 'to whom it may concern', 20 October 1930.

16. Antony Best, *Britain, Japan and Pearl Harbor: Avoiding War in East Asia, 1936–41* (London: Routledge, 1995); Nicholas R. Clifford, *Retreat from China: British Policy in the Far East 1937–41* (London: Longman, 1967). The one – but contemporary – exception is Robert W. Barnett, *Economic Shanghai: Hostage to Politics, 1937–1941* (New York: Institute of Pacific Relations, 1941), 66.

17. Marcia Reynders Ristaino, 'White Russian and Jewish Refugees in Shanghai, 1920–1944, as Recorded in the Shanghai Municipal Police Archives, National Archives, Washington, D.C.', *Republican China*, 16:1 (1990) 51–72; United States National Archives and Records Administration, Washington, DC (hereafter NARA), RG 226, E182, Shanghai OSS station records, Box 12, folder 77, 'The "Special Branch" of the Shanghai Muni-

cipal Police', 8 January 1947, 'Sale of Shanghai Police Files', 20 April 1949.

18. Ma Jinghua *et al.*, 'Jiu Shanghai zujie dang'an de xingcheng yu guanli' (The Composition and Management of the Archives of the Concessions of Old Shanghai), *Dang'an yu shixue* (Archives and History), 1996, part 2, pp. 78–80. In 2001 the archives produced a systematic guide to the structures and history of the two concessions, the first in any language: Shanghai zujie zhi bianji weiyuan hui (eds.), *Shanghai zujie zhi* (Annals of the Shanghai Concessions) (Shanghai: Shanghai shehui kexue chubanshe, 2001).

19. Best, *Britain, Japan and Pearl Harbor*, 71–86.

20. The honourable exception in the China case is Warren I. Cohen, *The Chinese Connection: Roger S. Greene, Thomas W. Lamont, George E. Sokolsky and American–East Asian Relations* (New York: Columbia University Press, 1978).

21. Joan Alexander, *Voices and Echoes: Tales from Colonial Women* (London: Quarto, 1983); Eric Lawlor, *Murder on the Verandah: Love and Betrayal in British Malaya* (London: HarperCollins, 1999); Margaret Shennan, *Out in the Midday Sun: The British in Malaya 1880–1960* (London: John Murray, 2000); James Fox, *White Mischief* (London: Jonathan Cape, 1982); Elspeth Huxley, *Out in the Midday Sun: My Kenya* (London: Chatto and Windus, 1985); Anton Gill, *Ruling Passions: Sex, Race and Empire* (London: BBC Books, 1995).

22. The literature is surveyed in the essays collected in Frederick Cooper and Ann Laura Stoler, *Tensions of Empire: Colonial Cultures in a Bourgeois World* (Berkeley: University of California Press, 1997), and in the editors' introduction, 'Between Metropole and Colony: Rethinking a Research Agenda', 1–56. But see Nicholas Thomas, *Colonialism's Culture: Anthropology, Travel and Government* (Oxford: Polity Press, 1994), and Nicholas Thomas and Richard Eves, *Bad Colonists: The South Seas Letters of Vernon Lee Walker and Louis Becke* (Durham, NC: Duke University Press, 1999).

23. The pioneer here is Anthony Kirk-Greene; see, most recently, his *Britain's Imperial Administrators, 1858–1966* (Basingstoke: Macmillan, 2000). Two surveys which take in the men on the job at home and abroad are: John Cell, 'Colonial Rule', *OHBE*, volume iv: *The Twentieth Century*, 232–54; Ronald Hyam, 'Bureaucracy and Trusteeship in the Colonial Empire', ibid., 255–79.

24. One exception: Kenneth R. Balhatchet, *Race, Sex and Class under the Raj: Imperial Attitudes and their Critics, 1793–1905* (London: Weidenfeld and Nicolson, 1980).

25. Exceptions can be found in the essays collected in: David Anderson and David Killingray (eds.), *Policing the Empire: Government, Authority and Control, 1830–1940* (Manchester: Manchester University Press, 1992), and

Policing and Decolonisation: Politics, Nationalism and the Police, 1917–65 (Manchester: Manchester University Press, 1993). The standard contemporary account is Charles Jeffries, *The Colonial Police* (London: Max Parrish, 1952).

26. Charles van Onselen, *The Seed is Mine: The Life of Kas Maine, a South African Sharecropper, 1894–1985* (Cape Town: David Philip, 1996); Henk van Woerden, *A Mouthful of Glass*, trans. Dan Jacobson (Johannesburg: Jonathan Ball Publishers, 2000).

27. Amongst others which have made full use of these records see: Nicholas R. Clifford, *Spoilt Children of Empire: Westerners in Shanghai and the Chinese Revolution of the 1920s* (Hanover, NH: Middlebury College Press, 1991); Brian G. Martin, *The Shanghai Green Gang: Politics and Organised Crime, 1919–1937* (Berkeley: University of California Press, 1996); S. A. Smith, *A Road is Made: Communism in Shanghai 1920–1927* (Richmond: Curzon Press, 2001); Patricia Stranahan, *Underground: The Shanghai Communist Party and the Politics of Survival, 1927–1937* (Lanham, Md.: Rowman & Littlefield, 1998); Frederic Wakeman Jr., *Policing Shanghai 1927–1937* (Berkeley: University of California Press, 1995) and *The Shanghai Badlands: Wartime Terrorism and Urban Crime 1937–1941* (Cambridge: Cambridge University Press, 1996).

28. Some exceptions: Chiara Betta, 'Silas Aaron Hardoon (1851–1931): Marginality and Adaptation in Shanghai' (unpublished Ph.D. thesis, University of London, 1997); Maisie J. Meyer, *From the Rivers of Babylon to the Whangpoo: A Century of Sephardi Jewish Life in Shanghai* (forthcoming Lanham, Md.: American University Press, 2003); Marcia Reynders Ristaino, *Port of Last Resort: The Diaspora Communities of Shanghai* (Stanford, Calif.: Stanford University Press, 2002); Frances Wood, *No Dogs and Not Many Chinese: Treaty Port Life in China, 1843–1943* (London: John Murray, 1998).

29. Maochun Yu, *OSS in China: Prelude to Cold War* (New Haven: Yale University Press, 1996).

30. The term 'China-centred' comes from Paul A. Cohen, *Discovering History in China: American Historical Writing on the Recent Chinese Past* (New York: Columbia University Press, 1984), which outlines the contours of the earlier debates.

31. E. W. Peters, *Shanghai Policeman* (London: Rich and Cowan, 1937); Maurice Springfield, *Hunting Opium and Other Scents* (Halesworth: Norfolk and Suffolk Publicity, 1966); Ted Quigley, *A Spirit of Adventure: The Memoirs of Ted Quigley* (Lewes: Book Guild Ltd., 1994). There are two unpublished memoirs in private hands: Daniel G. Cormie, 'The Memoirs of a Shanghai Policeman' (no date), and Uyehara Shigeru, 'Memoir: Life of a Japanese Diplomat, 1892–1968. An Unpublished Manuscript'.

32. Tahirih V. Lee, 'Introduction: Coping with Shanghai: Means to Survival and Success in the Early Twentieth Century – A Symposium', *Journal of Asian Studies*, 54 (1995), 7.

33. Peters, *Shanghai Policeman*, opposite p. 40.

34. William L. Cassidy, *Quick or Dead: The Rise and Development of Close-Quarter Combat Firing of the Self-Loading Pistol and Other One-Hand Guns* (Boulder, Colo.: Paladin Press, 1978); Allen Pittman, 'William E. Fairbairn: British Pioneer in Asian Martial Arts', *Journal of Asian Martial Arts*, 6:2 (1997), 44–55. Various SMP men are bit part players in Tintin's Shanghai adventure, *The Blue Lotus* – Richards and Brown snatching the young reporter on the orders of Dawson, the corrupt 'Chief of Police' – the Sikh toughs bested as they try to give Tintin a beating. Hergé's work was first published in book form in 1936, after serialization in *Le Petit Vingtième* as 'Tintin au Extrême-Orient' in 1934–5. It first appeared in English translation as *The Blue Lotus* in 1983.

35. A high-profile example, Xie Gengxin, was briefly in the SMP before joining the French concession police. He spent twenty-five years in a labour camp after 1951: Joseph Shieh, with Mari Holman, *Dans le jardin des aventures* (Paris: Éditions du Seuil, 1995).

36. A. J. A. Symons, *The Quest for Corvo: An Experiment in Biography* (London: Cassell, 1934); Hugh Trevor-Roper, *Hermit of Peking: The Hidden Life of Sir Edmund Backhouse* (Harmondsworth: Penguin, 1978).

2

Before Shanghai

1. This information is derived from personal communications from the late Mr J. E. Tinkler, and from marriage certificates and photographs in the possession of the Tinkler family; see also *The Times*, 16 April 1904, p. 9.

2. Tinkler family papers.

3. J. Bulmer (ed.), *History, Topography, and Directory of Furness & Cartmel* (Preston: T. Bulmer, 1911), 359; I am grateful to Mr B. Dower, headmaster of the Ulverston Victoria High School in 1995, and to his staff, for providing copies of the *Victorian*.

4. Unless otherwise noted, all references to and quotations from Tinkler's correspondence are from the letters now preserved in the Department of Documents, Imperial War Museum. To the 36 letters from Shanghai (to Edith and Fanny Tinkler, 1919–1930) and 3 wartime letters originally deposited by Edith Whalen, another 12 wartime letters, and a small pocket diary were

added in 1995. I have not given individual references to what is essentially a modest collection of documents.

5. Tinkler family papers. The document was unwitnessed, and therefore unacceptable in English law.

6. 'Instructions to Applicants', R. M. Tinkler, personal file, Shanghai Municipal Archives, Records of the Shanghai Municipal Police, U-102-3-89 (hereafter SMA, Tinkler file).

7. *Victorian*, 27 (Easter 1914), no page.

8. Public Record Office, Kew (hereafter PRO) WO 95/1349, 24 Bn Royal Fusiliers War Diary (hereafter War Diary), 22 April 1916. This file is the source for the account in this chapter of the Battalion's experiences.

9. Edmund Blunden, *Undertones of War* (Harmondsworth: Penguin, 1937), 88, 136.

10. Tinkler family papers, citation dated 16 December 1917.

11. Imperial War Museum (hereafter IWM), Department of Documents, 'Some Experiences of the German Push 1918, by 50214 Pte W. A. Hoyle, 24th RF, 2nd Division'.

12. Tinkler family papers, printed commendations; *Supplement to the London Gazette*, 15 November 1918, p. 13455; War Diary.

13. IWM, RMT to Edith, 13 October 1917; War Diary, 2 October 1917, and Operation Orders No. 11, 2 October 1917.

14. *Victorian*, 38 (Christmas 1917), 377.

15. Shanghai Municipal Council, *Report for the Year 1919 and Budget for the Year 1920* (hereafter, for example, SMC, *Annual Report 1919*), 262a; SMA U-102-5-160, 'List of Men who Served in the British or Allied Forces during the War', Hongkew Station, 15 May 1922.

16. Lily Benson, 'In Memoriam Richard Maurice Tinkler DCM', *Ulverstonian*, 6:2 (1939), 34; *Victorian*, 42 (Christmas 1919), 460; personal information.

17. Tinkler family papers, RMT to Mrs Tinkler, 1 February 1918; to Edith, 29 January 1917 or 1918.

18. Jay Winter, *The Great War and the British People* (London: Macmillan, 1985), 244–5.

19. Tinkler family papers, Elizabeth Benson to Edith Whalen, 2 November 1939.

20. *People*, 16 March 1919–25 May 1919, *passim*. The SMP notice first appeared on 23 March 1919 and ran until 11 May 1919.

21. *Barrow News*, 23 April 1904, p. 5.

22. Winter, *Great War and the British People*, 267.

23. Details here and below from SMA, Tinkler file.

24. Winter, *Great War and the British People*, 84, 92. Ulverston Victoria

Grammar School sent 219 old boys to the forces; 27 were killed: *Victorian*, 42 (Christmas 1919), 447, 451.

25. Unless otherwise noted, all information on these men, here and elsewhere in the book, comes from their personnel files, held in the Shanghai Municipal Archives. These files are presently closed to researchers, but I have listed those I have used on pp. 389–90.

26. Quaker MP John Bright, in a speech in October 1858. The context is provided by James L. Sturgis, *John Bright and the Empire* (London: Athlone Press, 1969), 90–93.

27. Christopher R. Browning, *Ordinary Men: Reserve Police Battalion 101 and the Final Solution in Poland* (New York: HarperCollins, 1992).

28. SMC, *Annual Report 1919*, 45a.

3

Shanghai 1919

1. Jazz band leader Whitey Smith's, Manila: Philippine Education Company, 1956.

2. Revd C. E. Darwent, *Shanghai: A Handbook for Travellers and Residents*, 2nd edn. (Shanghai: Kelly and Walsh, 1920), p. xiv.

3. Ibid. 72.

4. Ibid. 2. Elements of Wright's *Twentieth Century Impressions* (see n. 8 below) are distributed freely throughout Darwent's guide, whose first edition appeared in 1912, four years after the former volume. A comprehensive survey of the Bund's architecture is to be found in: Jon W. Huebner, 'Architecture on the Shanghai Bund', *Papers on Far Eastern History*, 39 (1989), 127–65.

5. Robert Bickers and Jeffrey N. Wasserstrom, 'Shanghai's "Chinese and Dogs Not Admitted" Sign: Legend, History and Contemporary Symbol', *China Quarterly*, 142 (1995), 444–66.

6. Darwent, *Shanghai*, 6.

7. Ibid. 8–9.

8. Arnold Wright (chief ed.), *Twentieth Century Impressions of Hong Kong, Shanghai and Other Treaty Ports of China* (London: Lloyds Greater Britain Publishing Company, 1908), 688.

9. Quoted in P. D. Coates, *The China Consuls: British Consular Officers, 1843–1943* (Hong Kong: Oxford University Press, 1988), 105–6.

10. SMC, *Annual Report 1918*, 95b.

11. SMC, *Annual Report 1919*, 61a.

12. Wright, *Twentieth Century Impressions of Hong Kong, Shanghai*, 646–55; Darwent, *Shanghai*, 11.

13. Darwent, *Shanghai*, 15.

14. Ibid. 12.

15. Wellington K. K. Chan, 'Premier Department Stores on Nanjing Road, 1917–1937', in Sherman Cochran (ed.), *Inventing Nanjing Road: Commercial Culture in Shanghai, 1900–1945* (Ithaca, NY: East Asia Program, Cornell University, 1999), 31; *North China Herald* (hereafter *NCH*), 7 September 1918, p. 586, 23 August 1919, p. 511.

16. Darwent, *Shanghai*, 28–9.

17. Quoted in F. L. Hawks Pott, *A Short History of Shanghai: Being an Account of the Growth and Development of the International Settlement* (Shanghai: Kelly and Walsh, 1928), 259.

18. Wright, *Twentieth Century Impressions of Hong Kong, Shanghai*, 502; anon., 'History of Cricket in Shanghai', *Social Shanghai*, 12:6 (1912), 325.

19. Darwent, *Shanghai*, 30.

20. Tinkler family papers.

21. W. H. Widdowson (comp.), *Police Guide and Regulations. 1938* (Shanghai: n.p., 1938), 308.

22. Marie-Claire Bergère, *The Golden Age of the Chinese Bourgeoisie 1911–1937* (Cambridge: Cambridge University Press, 1989), 64.

23. Wright, *Twentieth Century Impressions of Hong Kong, Shanghai*, 646–54.

24. O. M. Green, *The Foreigner in China* (London: Hutchinson and Co., 1942), 92–3; University of Toronto, Thomas Fisher Rare Books Library, J. O. P. Bland papers (hereafter Bland papers): 'Memoirs', ch. 6, p. 8.

25. Darwent, *Shanghai*, 84.

26. Based on the 1930 figures in *Report of the Hon. Mr Justice Feetham, C.M.G., to the Shanghai Municipal Council*, vol. ii (Shanghai: North China Daily News and Herald, 1931), 170. The general average is lowered by the Russian presence. About one in five British Settlement residents had a vote.

27. PRO: FO 228/3175, Sir Everard Fraser to Sir John Jordan, 13 December 1918.

28. J. V. Davidson-Houston, *Yellow Creek: The Story of Shanghai* (London: Putnam, 1962), dedication.

29. F. C. Jones, *Shanghai and Tientsin: With Special Reference to Foreign Affairs* (London: Oxford University Press, 1940), plan 1.

30. The phrase itself dates from 1869, when it was inserted into the Land Regulations: *Report of the Hon. Mr Justice Feetham*, vol. i, pp. 74–5.

31. PRO: FO 228/3175, Sir John Jordan to Sir James Jamieson, 16 August 1919.

32. *NCH*, 7 August 1862, pp. 122–3; PRO: FO 228/3175, Sir Everard Fraser to Sir John Jordan, 13 December 1918.

33. Bland papers, 'Memoirs', ch. 9, p. 7.

34. Wright, *Twentieth Century Impressions of Hong Kong, Shanghai*, preface. Other volumes in the series featured the dominions, and formal colonies such as Ceylon, as well as such areas of British informal influence as Egypt, Siam, Uruguay and Argentina.

35. W. A. Thomas, *Western Capitalism in China: A History of the Shanghai Stock Exchange* (Aldershot: Ashgate, 2001).

36. SMC, *Annual Report 1920*, 271a–275a.

37. SMA: U 1-3-1974, N. O. Liddell to Brooke-Smith, 16 March 1922.

38. Details from SMC, *Annual Report 1919*.

39. George Lanning and Samuel Couling, *The History of Shanghai*, vol. i (Shanghai: For the Shanghai Municipal Council by Kelly and Walsh, 1921).

40. SMA: U 1-3-1114, Commissioner of Revenue to Acting Secretary, 11 September 1923.

41. SMC, *Annual Report 1919*, 102a; B. R. Mitchell, *British Historical Statistics* (Cambridge: Cambridge University Press, 1988), 58.

42. Christian Henriot, *Prostitution and Sexuality in Shanghai: A Social History, 1849–1949* (Cambridge: Cambridge University Press, 2001), 84–5.

43. 'Vice Conditions in Shanghai: Report of the Special Vice Committee', *Municipal Gazette*, 19 March 1920, p. 84, *North China Daily News* (hereafter *NCDN*), 24 January 1921, in NARA: SMP D 3572.

44. Maurice Springfield, *Hunting Opium and Other Scents* (Halesworth: Norfolk and Suffolk Publishers, 1966), 31.

45. Darwent, *Shanghai*, 168; Oliver Ready, *Life and Sport in China* (London: Chapman and Hall, 1903), 46–72, quotation from p. 46. On the shooting life see also J. O. P. Bland, *Houseboat Days in China* (London: Edward Arnold, 1909) and C. Cradock, *Sporting Notes in the Far East* (London: Griffith Farran Okeden & Welsh, 1889).

46. Wright, *Twentieth Century Impressions of Hong Kong, Shanghai*, 363–4.

47. Robert Bickers, ' "The Greatest Cultural Asset East of Suez": The History and Politics of the Shanghai Municipal Orchestra and Public Band, 1881–1946', in Chi-hsiung Chang (chief ed.), *Ershi shiji de Zhongguo yu shijie* (China and the World in the Twentieth Century) (Taibei: Institute of History, Academia Sinica, 2001), 835–75.

48. First published in Shanghai in 1890 after appearing in serial form as essays in *NCDN* in the late 1880s, Smith's lively primer was reprinted many times well into the twentieth century; on Smith, see Charles W. Hayford, 'Chinese and American Characteristics: Arthur H. Smith and his China Book', in Suzanne Wilson Barnett and John King Fairbank (eds.), *Christianity in China: Early Protestant Missionary Writings* (Harvard Studies in American–East Asia Relations; Cambridge, Mass.: Harvard University Press, 1985), 153–74.

49. Eileen P. Scully, 'Prostitution as Privilege: The "American Girl" of Treaty Port Shanghai, 1860–1937', *International History Review*, 20:4 (1998), 855–83.

50. SMC, *Annual Report 1920*, 273–4a.

51. SMC, *Annual Report 1919*, 105a.

52. Darwent, *Shanghai*, 16.

53. Joseph T. Chen, *The May Fourth Movement in Shanghai: The Making of a Social Movement in Modern China* (Leiden: Brill, 1971).

54. SMC, *Annual Report 1919*, 89a–90a.

55. SMC, *Annual Report 1918*, 58a–89a; *Annual Report 1919*, 93a–95a.

56. Kuai Shixun (ed.), 'Shanghai gonggong zujie shigao' (Draft History of the Shanghai International Settlement), in *Shanghai gonggong zujie shigao* (Draft History of the Shanghai International Settlement) (Shanghai: Shanghai renmin chubanshe, 1979), 498–547; Bryna Goodman, 'Democratic Calisthenics: The Culture of Urban Associations in the New Republic', in Elizabeth Perry and Merle Goldman (eds.), *Changing Meanings of Citizenship in Contemporary China* (Cambridge, Mass.: Harvard University Press, 2002), 70–109.

57. Shanghai Shi danganguan (ed.), *Gongbuju dongshihui huiyi lu* (Minutes of the Shanghai Municipal Council) (Shanghai: Shanghai guji chubanshe, 2002) (hereafter Minutes of the SMC), vol. 20, 26 November 1919, p. 182, 29 December 1919, pp. 201–3.

4

The Shanghai Municipal Police

1. SMC, *Annual Report 1905*, 20.

2. SMA: U 102-5-406/2, R. C. Aiers to ACP Crime, 3 August 1928.

3. See the various accounts in David Anderson and David Killingray (eds.), *Policing the Empire: Government, Authority and Control, 1830–1940* (Manchester: Manchester University Press, 1993).

4. SMA: U 102-3-825, A. Hilton-Johnson, Acting Captain Superintendent, to Secretary, SMC, 3 August 1914.

5. Bland papers: Box 13, W. E. Leveson to J. O. P. Bland, 8 September 1906, 4 November 1907.

6. Sir John Pratt, quoted in Richard W. Rigby, *The May 30 Movement: Events and Themes* (Folkestone: Dawson, 1980), 34.

7. Bland papers, Box 13, W. E. Leveson to J. O. P Bland, 4 November 1907; W. E. Leveson to J. O. P. Bland, 30 August 1913.

8. SMC, *Annual Report 1901*, 424.

9. Revd C. E. Darwent, *Shanghai: A Handbook for Travellers and Residents*, 2nd edn. (Shanghai: Kelly and Walsh, 1920), 126–7. A less complacent view of gaol conditions is given in Frank Dikötter, *Crime, Punishment and the Prison in Modern China* (London: Hurst and Company, 2002), 314–20, 'Life inside Ward Road Gaol'.

10. SMC, *Annual Report 1917*, 39a; SMC, *Annual Report 1918*, 42a.

11. SMC, *Annual Reports 1912–18*.

12. SMA: U 1-3-3507, memorandum by W. G. Clarke, 18 May 1928.

13. SMA: U 1-3-2790, enclosure in Commissioner of Police to Sterling Fessenden, 30 October 1928; U 1-3-3507, CP to acting secretary, SMC, 14 August 1928.

14. Frank Peasgood interview, 2 February 1996.

15. *Report of the Police Enquiry Committee appointed under Resolution XI, passed at the Annual Meeting of Ratepayers, 20th March 1907* (Shanghai: Kelly and Walsh, 1907). See also *NCH*, 16 August 1907, pp. 398–401.

16. Clive Emsley, *The English Police: A Political and Social History*, 2nd edn. (London: Longman, 1996), 206; Richard Hawkins, 'The "Irish Model" and the Empire: A Case for Reassessment', in Anderson and Killingray (eds.), *Policing the Empire*, 19.

17. New Zealand in 1903, for example, Richard S. Hill, 'The Policing of Colonial New Zealand: From Informal to Formal Control, 1840–1907', in Anderson and Killingray (eds.), *Policing the Empire*, 66.

18. SMC, *Annual Report 1912*, 26a–27a.

19. SMA: U 1-3-1579, B. L. Atkinson to McEuen, 24 June 1916; SMA U 1-3-3896.

20. Interview with Frederick G. West, 13 September 1996.

21. SMC, *Annual Report 1908*, 271.

22. W. H. Widdowson (comp.), *Police Guide and Regulations. 1938* (Shanghai: n.p., 1938), 596–7.

23. W. E. Fairbairn, *Scientific Self-Defence* (New York: D. Appleton and Co., 1931), pp. vii–viii. This was first published as *Defendu (Scientific Self-Defence)* (Shanghai: North China Daily News and Herald, Ltd., 1926).

24. William L. Cassidy, 'Fairbairn in Shanghai: Profile of SWAT Pioneer', *Soldier of Fortune* (September 1979), 66–71; Brandon L. Sieg, 'How Western Perceptions Influenced the Martial Arts in Old Shanghai', *Journal of Asian Martial Arts*, 6:2 (1997), 33.

25. SMA: U 102-5-406/4, 'Test Dictation'.

26. Municipal Council, Shanghai, *Police Guide and Regulations* (Shanghai: Kelly and Walsh, 1926); Widdowson, *Police Guide and Regulations*.

27. SMA: U-102-5-215/6, 'Questions for Examination of Constables for Promotion to the Rank of Sergeant, 30 June 1925'.

28. Arnold Wright (chief ed.), *Twentieth Century Impressions of Hong Kong, Shanghai and Other Treaty Ports of China* (London: Lloyds Greater Britain Publishing Company, 1908), 404.

29. Eileen P. Scully, *Bargaining with the State from Afar: American Citizenship in Treaty Port China, 1844–1942* (New York: Columbia University Press, 2001); Anatol Kotenov, *Shanghai, its Mixed Court and Council* (Shanghai: North China Daily News and Herald, 1925); Tahirih V. Lee, 'Risky Business: Courts, Culture, and the Market Place', *University of Miami Law Review*, 47:5 (1993), 1335–414.

30. Darwent, *Shanghai*, 54, 11; Thomas papers.

31. SMC, *Annual Report 1919*, 49a, 71a.

32. One man claimed to have witnessed between 200 and 250 executions, explaining that he was 'irresistibly drawn to them time and time again' out of 'morbid curiosity', and photographed many: IWM 79/2/1T, E. J. Roper, 'The Revelations of a Hangman', 2.

33. Daniel G. Cormie, 'The Memoirs of a Shanghai Policeman', 10.

34. SMC, *Annual Report 1918*, 42a–43a, *Annual Report 1917*, 27a.

35. SMC, *Annual Report 1914*, 44a–45a.

36. *NCH*, 6 March 1926, p. 430.

37. Interview with Frederick G. West, 13 September 1996.

38. F. L. Hawks Pott, *Lessons in the Shanghai Dialect* (rev. edn., Shanghai: Commercial Press, 1924), 76.

39. Cormie, 'Memoirs of a Shanghai Policeman', 48.

40. Cormie, 'Memoirs of a Shanghai Policeman', 15.

41. *NCH*, 19 September 1908, pp. 744–5; K. M. Bourne, 'The Shanghai Municipal Police: Chinese Uniform Branch', *Police Journal*, 2:1 (1929), 26–36.

42. SMA: U 102-5-40, 'Shanghai Municipal Council. Police Force. Chinese Branch. Terms of Service', 1 December 1921; U 1-3-2790, enclosure in Commissioner of Police to Secretary, SMC, 30 October 1928.

43. Bourne, 'Chinese Uniform Branch', 27.

44. SMC, *Annual Report 1915*, 25a, SMC, *Annual Report 1917*, 26a.

45. SMC, *Annual Report 1897*, 30; Bourne, 'Chinese Uniform Branch', 30.

46. SMA: U 1-1-1098, Police Daily Report, 17 May 1913. 'Kompo' ('Subei' is the usual term in Mandarin) was Shanghainese slang for natives of the poverty-stricken part of Jiangsu province north of the Yangtsze. Subei people were looked down upon by Shanghainese: on the creation of this identity see Emily Honig, *Creating Chinese Ethnicity: Subei People in Shanghai, 1850–1980* (New Haven: Yale University Press, 1992).

47. SMA: U 1-3-2659, E. I. M. Barrett to Secretary, SMC, 8 April 1929.

48. *Shanghai gonggong zujie Gongbuju jingwuchu Huapu zhiwu shunzhi*

(English title given as: *Shanghai Municipal Police Rules and Regulations for the Chinese Branch*) (n.d., *c.* 1931).

49. Sherlock papers, Samuel Sherlock to Jim Sherlock, undated, *c.* 1929–30. Sherlock joined in 1929 and died of cerebro-spinal meningitis in March 1931.

50. SMA: files U 1-3-2277, U 102-3-814, U 102-3-1007.

51. SMA: U 1-1-1098, Police Daily Report, 10 June 1913; SMA: U 102-5-158, 'SMP dismissals file, 1908–41'.

52. SMA: U 1-3-3590.

53. SMA: U 1-3-1677.

54. Minutes of the SMC, vol. 20, 29 December 1919, p. 201.

55. SMA: U 1-3-2429, 'Disaffection among Sikhs (1923–30)'; NARA: RG 263, SMP D 8/8, T. P. Givens to R. C. Aiers, 21 June 1929.

56. David Omissi, *The Sepoy and the Raj: The Indian Army, 1860–1940* (Basingstoke: Macmillan, 1994), 26.

57. Cormie, 'Memoirs of a Shanghai Policeman', 11–12.

58. Interview with Frederick G. West, 13 September 1996.

59. David Arnold, *Police Power and Colonial Rule: Madras 1859–1947* (Delhi: Oxford University Press, 1986), 71–2.

60. Minutes of the SMC, vol. 20, 2 January 1918, p. 205.

61. SMC, *Annual Report 1918*, 21a–23a; SMA U 102-5-23, A. F. Grimble to K. J. McEuen, 6 April 1916.

62. *NCH*, 30 May 1900, p. 956.

63. SMA: U 102-5-160, 'Return Showing Men Having Joined the SMP from the British Army (Shanghai Defence Force)', 18 April 1929.

64. Some were only wartime volunteers or conscripts, and these figures are also skewed by the existence of records specifically listing military recruits. The SMP was obliged to repatriate those discharged from the Army or Navy in Shanghai even if they left its service before the first three years were up.

65. Ted Quigley, *A Spirit of Adventure: The Memoirs of Ted Quigley* (Lewes: Book Guild Ltd., 1994), 75.

66. SMA: U 1-3-1709, Staff Committee Minutes, 11 June 1928.

67. Widdowson, *Police Guide and Regulations*, 100.

68. SMC, *Annual Report 1910*, 55–65.

69. PRO: FO 1092/226, Magistrate's Notebook, 18 December 1919; *NCH*, 20 December 1919, pp. 775–8; Minutes of the SMC, vol. 20, 29 December 1919, p. 198.

70. SMA: U 102-5-37, Acting CP, Hilton-Johnson to Secretary SMC, 18 May 1920, 'Municipal Salaries Commission'.

71. SMA: U 1-3-321, 'Terminations and Dismissals File, 1920–21'.

72. 'Report of the Municipal Salaries Commission', *Municipal Gazette*, 9 April 1921, p. 113.

73. Mike Brogden, *On the Mersey Beat: Policing Liverpool between the Wars* (Oxford: Oxford University Press, 1991), 7, 14–18.

74. Ibid. 36–60; Widdowson, *Police Guide and Regulations*, 30.

75. Darby papers, Jack Darby to mother, 7 December 1933, letter to Dick, 30 April 1934.

76. Sherlock papers, Samuel Sherlock to Jim Sherlock, undated, *c.* 1929–30.

77. Cormie, 'Memoirs of a Shanghai Policeman', 12.

78. Municipal Council, Shanghai, *Police Guide and Regulations*, 68.

5

Shanghai Detective

1. Marek Kohn, *Dope Girls: The Birth of the British Drug Underground* (London: Lawrence and Wishart, 1992).

2. Maurice Springfield, *Hunting Opium and Other Scents* (Halesworth: Norfolk and Suffolk Publishers, 1966), 38.

3. Percy Finch, *Shanghai and Beyond* (New York: Charles Scribner's Sons, 1953), 4.

4. 'Mixed Court Report for November', *Celestial Empire*, 25 December 1920, p. 724.

5. *NCH*, 4 June 1927, p. 421.

6. SMA: U 1-3-1349, 'Police Force: Chinese Branch (1921–32)', R. C. Aiers to Commissioner of Police, 6 August 1930; U 102-5-40, 'Chinese Branch: Revised Terms of Service, Pay, etc., 1924–30', T. P. Givens to Commissioner of Police, 26 April 1926.

7. *Celestial Empire*, 13 November 1920, p. 382; SMC, *Annual Report 1920*, 51a–52a; Christian Henriot, *Prostitution and Sexuality in Shanghai: A Social History, 1849–1949* (Cambridge: Cambridge University Press, 2001) 157, and Gail Hershatter, *Dangerous Pleasures: Prostitution and Modernity in Twentieth-Century Shanghai* (Berkeley: University of California Press, 1997), 157–64.

8. NARA: SMP D 8/2, DSI Tinkler, 'Work of Station Detectives', 30 January 1929.

9. Revd C. E. Darwent, *Shanghai: A Handbook for Travellers and Residents*, 2nd edn. (Shanghai: Kelly and Walsh, 1920), 22.

10. NARA: SMP D 8/4, H. J. Schmidt, 'Russian C. I. D. Branch', 14 May 1929.

11. NARA: SMP D 8/3, 'Instruction Classes of Japanese Detectives', 19 June 1927.

12. *Celestial Empire*, 9 December 1922, p. 535.

13. John Pal, *Shanghai Saga* (London: Jarrolds, 1963), 104. The closeness of relations in Shanghai is also clear in such memoirs as American journalist Carroll Alcott's *My War with Japan* (New York: Henry Holt and Company, 1943), 98–127.

14. Ross McKibbin, *Classes and Cultures: England 1918–1951* (Oxford: Oxford University Press, 1998), 511–13.

15. James Huskey, 'Americans in Shanghai: Community Formation and Response to Revolution, 1919–1928' (Unpublished Ph.D. thesis, University of North Carolina, 1985); Eileen P. Scully, *Bargaining with the State from Afar: American Citizenship in Treaty Port China, 1844–1942* (New York: Columbia University Press, 2001).

16. Edgar Snow, 'The Americans in Shanghai', *American Mercury*, 20:80 (1930), 437–45.

17. McKibbin, *Classes and Cultures*, 524.

18. George Orwell, *The Road to Wigan Pier* (1937; London: Secker and Warburg, 1959), 143–4.

19. SMA: U 102-5-37/3, A. Hilton-Johnson to Municipal Salaries Commission, 1 June 1920.

20. McKibbin, *Classes and Cultures*, 54.

21. SMC, *Annual Report 1921*, 71a–87a.

22. Theses are rough figures, as many men who joined and left the force before the turn of any given year do not show up in the statistics to hand, which are based on service at 31 December in any year. Many such men have been identified, but not all.

23. Figures calculated from SMC, *Annual Reports 1900–39*; Philip D. Curtin, *Death by Migration: Europe's Encounter with the Tropical World in the Nineteenth Century* (Cambridge: Cambridge University Press, 1989), 6.

24. W. H. Widdowson (comp.), *Police Guide and Regulations. 1938* (Shanghai: n.p., 1938), 603–13, 'Diseases to Guard Against'.

25. *China Weekly Review*, 1 October 1927, p. 116.

26. Daniel G. Cormie, 'The Memoirs of a Shanghai Policeman', 50; Wall papers; see also comments from Basil Duke quoted in Harriet Sergeant, *Shanghai* (London: Jonathan Cape, 1991), 152–3.

27. SMA: U 1-3-1571, John Forkin file.

28. SMA: U 102-3-922; U 1-3-2134, 1471, 2111, 3590.

29. Cormie, 'Memoirs of a Shanghai Policeman', 53.

30. PRO FO 917/3622, probate file.

31. Interview with Frederick G. West, 13 September 1996.

32. Brian G. Martin, *The Shanghai Green Gang: Politics and Organised Crime, 1919–1937* (Berkeley: University of California Press, 1996).

33. SMA: U 1-3-2425, K. J. McEuen to Acting Secretary SMC, 2 May 1923.

34. SMA: U 1-4-2695, 'Narcotics and Drugs Control: Chinese Government Measures', CID report, 12 July 1937.

35. Answer: send him to the Police Hospital, with an escort and a note explaining the circumstances: Widdowson, *Police Guide and Regulations*, 83.

36. Cormie, 'Memoirs of a Shanghai Policeman', 40–41.

37. Harold Gill papers, 'Twenty five years etc.'

38. SMA: U 1-3-2425, K. J. McEuen to Acting Secretary SMC, 2 May 1923.

39. SMA: U 1-3-2425, E. I. M. Barrett to Secretary SMC, 29 November 1926.

40. SMA: U 1-3-2426 'Opium raids: Rewards for Informers, etc., 1923–30', Commissioner of Police to Acting Secretary, SMC, 24 July 1923.

41. Springfield, *Hunting Opium and Other Scents*, 42 (on the Special Squad see pp. 42–6, but note that Springfield was much more interested in discussing sport than his work; SMA: U 1-3-2425, E. I. M. Barrett to Secretary SMC, 29 November, 1926.

42. SMC, *Annual Report 1925*, 35; *Annual Report 1926*, 33.

43. SMA: U 1-3-2425, R. M. J. Martin to Secretary SMC, 12 November 1926, A. Hilton-Johnson, Memorandum, 28 October 1926.

44. Martin, *Shanghai Green Gang*, 60–74.

45. SMA: U 1-3-2660, Commissioner to Secretary SMC, 8 April 1929.

46. Martin, *Shanghai Green Gang*, 126–34.

47. SMA: U 1-3-2425, CDI Givens, 'Opium Traffic in Shanghai and its Effects upon Crime', IO report, 23 October 1926.

48. SMA: U 1-3-2660, E. I. M. Barrett to Secretary, SMC, 8 April 1929.

49. Ibid.; Norwood F. Allman, *Shanghai Lawyer* (New York: Whittlesey House, 1943), 93–6. The memoir is less than candid about this activity.

50. SMA: U 102-5-165, K. M. Bourne to Commissioner of Police, 9 July 1928 and enclosures.

51. SMA: U 1-3-2660, Commissioner of Police to Secretary SMC, 8 April 1929.

52. NARA: SMP D 9655, 5 January 1940.

53. SMA: U 1-3-2660, Commissioner of Police to Secretary SMC, 29 January 1930.

54. Cormie, 'Memoirs of a Shanghai Policeman', 42–3.

55. Henriot, *Prostitution and Sexuality in Shanghai*, 291–311.

56. *All about Shanghai and Environs: A Standard Guide Book* (Shanghai: University Press, 2nd edition, 1934), 43.

57. Finch, *Shanghai and Beyond*, 34–49, quotation p. 36.

58. *Celestial Empire*, 31 July 1920, p. 225.

59. SMA U 1-3-466, Frank Rawlinson to Chairman, SMC, 2 August 1922; K. J. McEuen to Secretary, SMC, 16 August 1922.

60. SMA U 1-3-467, Isaac Mason to Secretary, SMC, 23 March 1926; E. I. M. Barrett to Secretary, SMC, 26 March 1926.

61. *NCH*, 20 April 1929, p. 105.

62. W. E. Fairbairn and E. A. Sykes, *Shooting to Live with the One Hand Gun* (Edinburgh: Oliver & Boyd, 1942), 80.

63. Cormie, 'Memoirs of a Shanghai Policeman', 32–3; SMC, *Annual Report 1927*, 34.

64. *NCH*, 12 January 1929, p. 69.

65. NARA: SMP CS 178, 30 December 1930.

66. NARA: SMP D4009, 'Prevention of Opium Running', 2 August 1932.

67. NARA: SMP D 4008; SMA: U 1-3-1677, 1543

68. SMA: U 102-5-406/1, SMC, *Study of Chinese* (1922 edn.).

69. SMA: U 102-5-2, report by Sergeant Lewis (Specials), 15 March 1932.

70. SMA: 102-5-471/3, 'Watch Committee Extracts', R. M. J. Martin to DC Divisions, 11 March 1931.

71. SMA: U 1-3-1775 'Death and Wounding by Police Shooting Affray', Watch Committee Minute, 15 September 1924.

72. SMA: U 1-3-1775, Commissioner of Police to Secretary, SMC, 28 February 1929.

73. Fairbairn and Sykes, *Shooting to Live with the One Hand Gun*, 68, 5.

74. *NCH*, 28 April 1923, p. 214.

75. Details from testimony presented in PRO: FO 1092/356, Rex *v.* J. F. Gabbutt and A. E. Balchin, 19–25 April 1923.

76. SMA: U 102-5-471/1, Minutes of the Watch Committee, 27 April 1923.

77. *NCH*, 28 April 1923, p. 261

78. SMA: U 102-5-471/1, Minutes of the Watch Committee, 27 April 1923.

79. SMA: U 102-5-471/1, Minutes of the Watch Committee, 27 April 1923; 4 May 1923; 20 July 1923.

80. F. L. Hawks Pott, *Lessons in the Shanghai Dialect* (rev. edn., Shanghai: Commercial Press, 1924), 76.

81. Minutes of the SMC, vol. 22, 1 May 1923, pp. 74–5, 13 June 1923, p. 87, 11 July 1923, p. 93.

82. Minutes of the SMC, vol 21, 30 June 1920, p. 133; *NCH*, 23 August 1924, p. 306; 6 September 1924, p. 387; SMC, *Annual Report 1924*, 56.

83. Arthur Waldron, *From War to Nationalism: China's Turning Point 1924–1925* (Cambridge: Cambridge University Press, 1995).

84. SMA: U 102-3-320, R. M. Tinkler, 'Appeal against Punishment Inflicted on the Undersigned', 12 September 1931.

85. SMC, *Annual Report 1924*, 51, 53–5; *NCH*, 20 September 1924, p. 466.

86. SMA: U 102-5-471/2, Council minutes, 29 October 1924.

87. Cormie, 'Memoirs of a Shanghai Policeman', 63–4.

88. SMC, *Annual Report 1927*, 122.

6

'Learning to be a man'

1. *NCH*, 9 March 1927, p. 470.

2. Revd C. E. Darwent, *Shanghai: A Handbook for Travellers and Residents*, 2nd edn. (Shanghai: Kelly and Walsh, 1920), 167–8.

3. Maurice Springfield, *Hunting Opium and Other Scents* (Halesworth: Norfolk and Suffolk Publishers, 1966).

4. Ross McKibbin, *Classes and Cultures: England 1918–1951* (Oxford: Oxford University Press, 1988), 390–97; on dancing and dance halls, see Andrew Field, 'A Night in Shanghai: Nightlife and Modernity in Semicolonial China, 1919–1937' (Unpublished Ph.D. thesis, Columbia University, 2001).

5. PRO: FO 917/2656, 2879, 2316; SMA: U 102-5-156, 'Personnel Matters 1908–1928'.

6. Gill papers, 'Twenty Five Years etc.', undated.

7. Marcia Reynders Ristaino, *Port of Last Resort: The Dispora Communities of Shanghai* (Stanford, Calif.: Stanford University Press, 2002), 52, 69; Zou Yiren, *Jiu Shanghai renkou bianqian de yanjiu* (Research on Population Change in Old Shanghai) (Shanghai: Renmin Chubanshe, 1980), 145–6.

8. NARA: SMP IO 4880, 'Russian Refugees at Woosung'; Ristaino, *Port of Last Resort*, 37–41.

9. SMA: U 1-1-130, SMC Orchestra and Band Committee Minutes, 25 May 1928.

10. Ronald Hyam, 'Concubinage and the Colonial Service: The Crewe Circular (1909)', *Journal of Imperial and Commonwealth History*, 14:3 (1986), 170–86.

11. PRO: WO 32/2526, 'Shanghai: Operation of Brothels in the International Settlement 1927–1935'; NARA: SMP D8984(c), 14 April 1939.

12. F. H. H. King, *The History of the Hongkong and Shanghai Banking Corporation*, vol. iii: *The Hongkong Bank between the Wars and the Bank Interned, 1919–1945: Return from Grandeur* (Cambridge: Cambridge University Press, 1988), 286.

13. SMA: U 102-5-471/1, Extracts from the Watch Committee Minutes, 11 February 1927.

14. SMA: U 1-3-217; U 102-5-471/1, Extracts from the Watch Committee Minutes, 11 February 1927. In fact, Parker rose to become an Inspector in 1941, the same year in which he filed for divorce.

15. Daniel G. Cormie, 'The Memoirs of a Shanghai Policeman', 15. A description of the process of selecting such a 'companion', although in this case in Canton in 1921–2, is given in Victor Purcell, *Memoirs of a Malayan Official* (London: Cassell, 1969), 129–33. NARA: SMP D 8984c contains lists drawn up in 1938 and 1941 for the US military authorities of servicemen renting rooms in the city, and the names, ages, nationality and occupations of the women they maintained in them.

16. Cormie, 'Memoirs of a Shanghai Policeman', 28–9.

17. SMA: U 102-5-156, 'Personnel Matters 1908–1928'.

18. SMA: U 102-5-406, Commissioner of Police to T. I. Vaughan, 18 August 1930; U 1-4-2052, 'Marriage: Police Branch'.

19. SMA: U 102-5-156, 'Personnel Matters 1908–1928'.

20. Anne-Marie Brady, 'West Meets East: Rewi Alley and Changing Attitudes towards Homosexuality in China', *East Asian History*, 9 (1995), 97–120; SMA: U 102-5-158, 'SMP Dismissals File, 1908–41'.

21. SMA: U 102-3-873.

22. SMA: U 1-4-1475, 4168; 3584; U 102-5-156, 'Personnel Matters 1908–1928'.

23. Cormie, 'Memoirs of a Shanghai Policeman', 54.

24. SMA: U 102-3-26; Cormie, 'Memoirs of a Shanghai Policeman', 62–3.

25. Interview with Frederick G. West, 13 September 1996.

7

The End of the 'Good Old China'

1. PRO: FO 228/3998/1 29a, Sir Erich Teichman minute on Chinkiang No. 1, 1 March 1929.

2. Hoover Institution archives: J. E. Jacobs papers, Box 2, Mixed Court Assessor's file, 4405. Jacobs was the American assessor at the trial. This discussion of the crisis is drawn from: Richard W. Rigby, *The May 30 Movement: Events and Themes* (Folkestone: Dawson, 1980); Nicholas R. Clifford, *Spoilt Children of Empire: Westerners in Shanghai and the Chinese Revolution of the 1920s* (Hanover, NH: Middlebury College Press, 1991), 97–158; S. A. Smith, *A Road is Made: Communism in Shanghai 1920–1927* (Richmond: Curzon Press, 2001), 89–107; SMC, *Annual Report 1925*, 48–54, 60–78.

3. Academia Sinica, Institute of Modern History Archives, Chinese Foreign Ministry Republican Archives, 03-40, 24-(3).

4. SMC, *Annual Report 1918*, 43a; SMC, *Annual Report 1919*, 65a.

5. Telephone interview with Ivor Everson (son), 7 September 2001.

6. Derek Sayer, 'British Reaction to the Amritsar Massacre, 1919–1920', *Past and Present*, 131 (May 1991), 130–64.

7. SMA: U 1-3-1718, 'Strikes in Settlement (1922–32)', A. Hilton-Johnson to Secretary and Commissioner-General, SMC, 26 March 1922.

8. Putnam Weale, *Why China Sees Red* (New York: Dodd, Mead & Co., 1925), opposite pp. 99, 130, 131.

9. SMA: U 1-3-2896, 'Council's Publicity Work, June–August 1925'.

10. Smith, *A Road is Made*, 110.

11. SMA: U 1-3-2901, S. Fessenden to Senior Consul, 8 July 1925.

12. SMA: U 1-3-2901, K. J. McEuen to S. Fessenden, 19 December 1925.

13. *NCH*, 30 January 1926, p. 191.

14. SMA: U 1-3-592, Secretary, SMC, to E. W. Everson, 11 January 1926; Everson family papers: E. W. Everson appointment diary, 1 January 1926.

15. SMC, *Annual Report 1898*, 34.

16. NARA, SMP IO 6232.

17. Collected as Arthur Ransome, *The Chinese Puzzle* (London: George Allen & Unwin, 1927).

18. Quoted in Rigby, *May 30 Movement*, 95–6.

19. Discussed and reproduced in Paul A. Cohen, *History in Three Keys: The Boxers as Event, Experience, and Myth* (New York: Columbia University Press, 1997), 255.

20. SMA: U 1-3-227, 'Chinese Clubs and Associations: Applications for Free Licenses, etc.'.

21. C. Martin Wilbur, *The Nationalist Revolution in China 1923–28* (Cambridge: Cambridge University Press, 1983).

22. Mao Zedong, 'Report on an Investigation of the Peasant Movement in Hunan' (1927), *Selected Works of Mao Tse-tung*, vol. i (Peking: Foreign Languages Press, 1965), 47–8.

23. SMC, *Annual Report 1926*, 52.

24. *NCH*, 7 July 1928, p. 13.

25. National Maritime Museum, Papers of Sir Louis Keppel Hamilton, HTN 250(a), letter to mother 16 September 1927; British Library, Oriental and India Office Collections, Ms.eur.e.400/1, J. Bazalgette to parents, 11 October 1927.

26. PRO: FO 228/3883/12. S. Barton to Sir Miles Lampson, semi-official, 2 April 1928: moreover, claimed Barton, he supplied the 'brains of the force until 1925'.

27. NARA: SMP D 4820. This paragraph is based on Brian G. Martin, *The Shanghai Green Gang: Politics and Organised Crime, 1919–1937* (Berkeley: University of California Press, 1996), Clifford, *Spoilt Children of Empire*.

28. *China Year Book 1928*, 1006, quoting *NCDN*. Nothing has yet surfaced

from the SMC archives to definitively endorse the plausible picture of foreign complicity, specifically Sterling Fessenden's, which was offered by John B. Powell, *My Twenty-Five Years in China* (New York: Macmillan, 1945), 158–9.

29. NARA: SMP IO 7804.

30. Patricia Stranahan, *Underground: The Shanghai Communist Party and the Politics of Survival, 1927–1937* (Lanham, Md.: Rowman & Littlefield, 1998); Frederick S. Litten, 'The Noulens Affair', *China Quarterly*, 138 (1994), 492–512; Frederick Wakeman Jr., *Policing Shanghai 1927–1937* (Berkeley: University of California Press, 1995), 147–51; Robert Bickers, *Britain in China: Community, Culture and Colonialism, 1900–49* (Manchester: Manchester University Press, 1999), 131–7.

31. *The Security Service 1908–1945: The Official History* (Kew: Public Record Office, 1999), 103–5.

32. SMC, *Annual Report 1927*, 46, *Annual Report 1930*, 91; Parks M. Coble Jr., *The Shanghai Capitalists and the Nationalist Government, 1927–1937*, 2nd edition (Cambridge, Mass.: Harvard East Asian Monographs, 1986), 32–5, 45.

33. I. I. Kounin (comp.), *Eighty-five Years of the Shanghai Volunteer Corps* (Shanghai: Cosmopolitan Press, 1939), 126–36, 242–67; Marcia Reynders Ristaino, *Port of Last Resort: The Diaspora Communities of Shanghai* (Stanford, Calif.: Stanford University Press, 2002), 58–62; the only volume dedicated to the history of this unit is: E. M. Krasnousov, *Shankhaiskii russkii polk, 1927–1945* (The Shanghai Russian Regiment, 1927–45) (San Francisco: Izd-vo 'Globus', 1984).

34. SMA: U 102-5-2, file 4, 'Employment of White Russians' [1927].

35. Christian Henriot, *Shanghai 1927–1937: Municipal Power, Locality and Modernisation* (Stanford, Calif.: Stanford University Press, 1993); Wakeman, *Policing Shanghai*, 60–77.

36. SMA: U 1-3-3119, 'Chinese Courts in the Settlement, 1926–'.

37. SMA: U 1-3-2485, S. Fessenden, 'Application of the Stamp Tax Law in the International Settlement', 22 March 1930.

38. SMA: U 1-3-2790, E. I. M. Barrett to Secretary, SMC, 20 February 1928, 20 June 1928.

39. SMA: U 1-3-2790, S. Fessenden to E. I. M. Barrett, 4 October 1928.

40. SMA: U 1-3-2790, S. Fessenden to E. I. M. Barrett, 12 October 1928.

41. PRO: FO 371/13241, F6363/6363/10 1928; FO371/13930, F3502/250/10 1929; SMA: U 1-3-2790, Council minutes, 29 May 1929.

42. Barrett stayed in England, working as paid secretary of various golf clubs until he was knocked off a bicycle and died in 1950. Clarke returned to Shanghai and set up a private detective agency.

43. SMA: U 1-3-2425, E. I. M. Barrett to Secretary, SMC, 14 December 1927.

44. *NCDN*, 3 May 1928, p. 1; *NCH*, 21 January 1928, p. 140; 18 February 1928, p. 259.

45. Quotations from correspondence and testimony in SMA: U 1-4-2662-3, 'Gambling: Greyhound Racing Club vs Council'; Maurice Springfield, *Hunting Opium and other Scents* (Halesworth: Norfolk and Suffolk Publishers, 1966), 86–7; John Pal, *Shanghai Saga* (London: Jarrolds, 1963), 136–140. Pal played a role in running Luna Park, and the Canidrome.

46. Revd C. E. Darwent, *Shanghai: A Handbook for Travellers and Residents*, 2nd edn. (Shanghai: Kelly and Walsh, 1920), p. xv.,

47. This paragraph and the following are based on: *NCH*, 11 May 1929, p. 231; 29 June 1929, p. 520, 'Police Report for May'; *Shenbao*, 4 May 1929, p. 15; *China Weekly Review*, 22 May 1929, pp. 446–7; Minutes of the Shanghai Municipal Council, vol. 24, 21 May 1929, p. 393, 29 May 1929, pp. 397–8.

48. SMC, *Annual Report 1928*, 52.

49. Interview with Frederick G. West, 13 September 1996.

50. SMA: U 1-3-374, A. Chamberlain to W. Beatty, ACP Musketry, 11 August 1925.

51. NARA: SMP D 2113, *China Forum*, May 1932, p. 13.

52. SMA: U 102-5-471, Extracts from the Watch Committee Minutes, 15 January 1926, 23 April 1926; U 1-3-374, 'SMP Arms and Ammunition 1920–32'.

53. 'How Riots are Dealt with in the Settlement', *Oriental Affairs* (February 1936), 67–70.

54. SMA: U 102-5-215(3), 'Armed Robbery at Mr Kuroda's House', and file, February–June 1929.

55. *NCH*, 1 June 1929, p. 353; 29 June 1929, p. 157; Norwood F. Allman, *Shanghai Lawyer* (New York: Whittlesey House, 1943), 96–7; SMA: U 1-4-2662-3, 'Gambling: Greyhound Racing Club vs Council'.

56. *NCH*, 3 August 1929, p. 172.

57. 'New Police Eastern Depot', *NCH*, 19 January 1929, p. 108.

58. Daniel G. Cormie, 'The Memoirs of a Shanghai Policeman', 57.

59. The main source for the rest of the chapter is Tinkler's SMP personnel file.

60. SMA: U 1-3-320.

61. SMA: U 102-5-56, 'Memorandum for the Special Economy Committee by Commissioner of Police', June 1940.

62. SMA: U 1-3-320.

63. Letter to author, 8 June 1999.

64. SMA: U 1-3-320.

65. SMA: U 1-3-320.

66. Cormie, 'Memoirs of a Shanghai Policeman', 51–2.

67. George Orwell, *The Road to Wigan Pier*, (1937; London: Secker and Warburg, 1959), 145–50 (quotations from pp. 146–7).

8

What We Can't Know

1. In this case Atherton, California, *China Journal*, 22:5 (1935), A16–A17.

2. SMA: U 102-5-157 contains papers dealing with Tinkler's discharge and related financial matters.

3. NARA, RG 83, Ship passenger arrival records, M 1383, passenger and crew lists of vessels arriving at Seattle, Washington, 1898–1953, Roll 163, SS *Hiye Maru*, 12 November 1930.

4. Helen Foster Snow, *My China Years: A Memoir* (London: Harrap, 1984).

5. *NCH*, 14 June 1939, p. 455; NARA: SMP D 6968, cutting from *Shanghai Times*, 8 June 1939.

6. These were supplied by the Grand Secretary's Office, Freemasons Hall, Dublin.

7. SMA: U 102-5-157.

8. *NCH*, 12 January 1932, p. 51.

9. US Consulate, Shanghai, 'The Employment Situation and Living Conditions for Americans in Shanghai, China' [1934], typescript, Library of Congress.

10. Macdonald: SMA: U 102-5-31/1; King: U 1-3-1579; others: personnel files or private information.

11. *NCH*, 30 November 1932, p. 326.

12. NARA: SMP D 7622, 'Ex-policemen Resident in Shanghai, 17 November 1936'.

13. Details from SMA: U 1-3-1678.

14. *The North-China Desk Hong List* (Shanghai: North China Daily News and Herald, 1938).

15. Alain Corbin, *The Life of an Unknown: The Rediscovered World of a Clog Maker in Nineteenth-Century France*, trans. Arthur Goldhammer (New York: Columbia University Press, 2001), 212.

16. Ibid. 210.

17. Carl Crow, *Handbook for China*, 5th edn. (1933; facsimile edn., Hong Kong: Oxford University Press, 1984), 40.

18. Interview with Peng Hongfei, 9 April 1997.

19. Robert Bickers, *Britain in China: Community, Culture and Colonialism, 1900–49* (Manchester: Manchester University Press, 1999), 27–31; Ivan

Hannaford, *Race: The History of an Idea in the West* (Washington, DC: Woodrow Wilson Center Press, 1996), 325–68.

20. Rodney Gilbert, *What's Wrong with China* (London: John Murray, 1926), 199–200.

21. This paragraph and the next are based on Bickers, *Britain in China*, 148–51; SMC, *Annual Report 1932*, 15–36; Parks M. Coble Jr., *Facing Japan: Chinese Politics and Japanese Imperialism, 1931–1937* (Cambridge, Mass.: Harvard University Press, 1991); Douglas Jordan, *China's Trial By Fire: The Shanghai War of 1932* (Ann Arbor: University of Michigan Press, 2001); Christian Henriot, *Shanghai 1927–1937: Municipal Power, Locality and Modernisation* (Stanford, Calif.: Stanford University Press, 1993), 65–102.

22. Hallett Abend, *My Years in China, 1926–41* (London: John Lane The Bodley Head, 1944), 195.

23. *NCH*, 18 August 1931, pp. 219, 237–8; 25 August 1931, pp. 272–3.

9

Adrift in the Empire World

1. For a reassessment see Elizabeth Buettner, 'From Somebodies to Nobodies: Britons Returning Home from India', in Martin Daunton and Bernhard Rieger (eds.), *Meanings of Modernity: Britain from the Late-Victorian Era to World War II* (Oxford: Berg, 2001), 221–40.

2. Carl Crow, *Handbook for China*, 5th edn. (1933; facsimile edn., Hong Kong: Oxford University Press, 1984), 230–32; published as *Traveller's Handbook for China*, 3rd edn. (1921), 168–9.

3. Wall papers, letter to Joe, 27 February 1934.

4. Information on the firm comes from: *The Memoirs of Tan Kah Kee*, ed. and trans. with notes by A. H. C. Ward, Raymond W. Chu and Janet Salaff (Singapore: Singapore University Press, 1994), 331–4; C. F. Yong, *Tan Kah Kee: The Making of an Overseas Chinese Legend* (Singapore: Oxford University Press, 1987), 41–82.

5. IWM: Tinkler papers, RMT/2, Leslie M. Smith to R. M. Tinkler, 14 August 1934.

6. Crow, *Handbook for China* 230–31.

7. William Wei, *Counterrevolution in China: The Nationalists in Jiangxi during the Soviet Period* (Ann Arbor: University of Michigan Press, 1985), 76–81; *NCH*, 21 March 1934, p. 447.

8. *China Year Book 1935*, 91.

9. *NCH*, 28 March 1934, p. 487.

10. PRO: ADM 116/3067, 'Yangtsze General Letter No.6, 1 July 1934–31 August 1934'.

11. *Jiangxi minguo shibao*, 15 July 1934. I am grateful to Liao Qun, and to Xiao Zhiwen for locating references in this newspaper, held in the Jiangxi Provincial Academy of Social Sciences library.

12. Ibid. 25 July 1934; *Hankou ZhongXibao*, 29 July 1934, p. 2, *NCH*, 1 August 1934, p. 162.

13. PRO: FO 371/23458, F5525/528/10, J. F. Brenan minute, 10 June 1939.

14. *China Press*, 28 July 1934, p. 9.

15. PRO: FO 232/40, dossier 50L, 1934.

16. PRO: FO 371/23458, F5525/528/10, A. D. Blackburn to J. F. Brenan, 7 June 1939.

17. *China Press*, 28 July 1934, p. 9; *NCH*, 1 August 1934, p. 162; *China Weekly Review*, 4 August 1934, p. 399.

18. PRO: FO 371/23458, F5525/528/10, J. F. Brenan minute, 10 June 1939.

19. This and other details from: Salvation Army, International Heritage Centre, London, North China Territory Annual Reports, 1932, p. 10; 1933, p. 9; 1934, p. 23; 1935, pp. 14–16.

20. David F. McIlvenny, 'The Men's Hostel', *Crusader* (November 1934), 8.

21. Daniel G. Cormie, 'The Memoirs of a Shanghai Policeman', 50–51.

22. *NCH*, 20 February 1935, p. 292; NARA: SMP D5665, clippings: *Shanghai Sunday Times*, 21 February 1937; *Shanghai Evening Post and Mercury*, 20 September 1937.

23. NARA: SMP D 8741, 'Mr James Dunbar Blackwood: Applicant for Employment in the Shanghai Municipal Police'.

24. NARA: SMP D6612, 'Memorandum on H. J. Connolly', 28 March 1938.

25. SMA: U 1-3-3894.

26. Revd C. E. Darwent, *Shanghai: A Handbook for Travellers and Residents*, 2nd edn. (Shanghai: Kelly and Walsh, 1920), 62; PRO: FO 369/2018, K6379/210, H. Phillips, 'Inspection of Shanghai Consulate-General', 25 March 1928.

27. SMA: U 102-5-156, 'Personnel Matters 1908–1928'.

28. SMA: U 102-5-158, ' SMP Dismissals File, 1908–1941'; NARA: SMP D5867, 'Applicants for SMP (Specials)'; D 7622, 'Ex-policemen Resident in Shanghai, 17 November 1936'.

29. Bob Moore, *Don't Call Me a Crook: My True Autobiography*, ed. Pat Spry (London: Hurst and Blackett, 1935), 274–304, quotations from pp. 276, 278.

30. Marcia Reynders Ristaino, *Port of Last Resort: The Diaspora Communities of Shanghai* (Stanford, Calif.: Stanford University Press, 2002), 88.

31. SMA: U 1-4-623, 'Mental Hospital: Indigent Patients'.

32. SMA: U 1-3-813, 'Mental Hospital: Indigent Patients'.

33. Charles Causley, *Collected Poems* (London and Basingstoke: Macmillan, 1992), 29.

34. SMA: U 102-5-157, 'List of Men who Resigned in the Year', 1927–32, 16 January 1933.

35. *Bad Colonists: The South Seas Letters of Vernon Lee Walker and Louis Becke* (Durham, NC: Duke University Press, 1999).

36. J. V. Davidson-Houston, *Yellow Creek: The Story of Shanghai* (London: Putnam, 1962), 167.

37. School of Oriental and African Studies: Swire papers, 1079, China Sundries 1926–7, J. K. Swire to G. W. Swire, 11 May 1925.

38. NARA: SMP D 3002, 'C. Y. Jones'.

39. NARA: SMP D 8162, 'Norman Christopher Begley, Enlistment into British Regular Army'. Begley had encountered Jones.

40. *Oriental Affairs* (January 1938), 29.

41. India Office Library and Records, Bazalgette papers, letter to parents, 17 October 1928.

42. Exception: Dane Kennedy, *Islands of White: Settler Society and Culture in Kenya and Southern Rhodesia, 1890–1939* (Durham, NC: Duke University Press, 1987), 91; Michael Roe, ' "We can die just as easily out here": Australia and British Migration, 1916–1939', in Stephen Constantine (ed.), *Emigrants and Empire: British Settlement in the Dominions between the Wars* (Manchester: Manchester University Press, 1990), 114–17.

43. It gets little attention in Stephen Constantine, 'Migrants and Settlers', in Judith M. Brown and Wm. Roger Louis (eds.), *OHBE*, vol. iv, pp. 163–87.

44. Kenya, Rhodesia: calculations from tables in appendix to Kennedy, *Islands of White*, 195–205; G. T. Bloomfield, *New Zealand: A Handbook of Historical Statistics*, table II.16, 'External migration 1861–75'.

45. Figures calculated from tables in G. F. Plant, *Overseas Settlement: Migration from the United Kingdom to the Dominions* (London: Oxford University Press, 1951), 174–80.

46. Duke papers, letter to mother, 21 June 1942.

47. NARA: SMP D 8120, 'Darrell Drake'; D 4436, 'Ernest William Weekes'; N 1050, 'R. H. (Nick) Boyle and H. Harry Kerrey'; D 2610, 'Report on D. A. Rushton'; D 2118, 'Miss J. Miller alias Mrs Jossett Miller'; D 8245, 'Character Sketch of "Miss Paulette" '.

48. Frederick S. Litten, 'The Noulens Affair', *China Quarterly*, 138 (1994), 492–512; F. W. Deakin and G. R. Storry, *The Case of Richard Sorge* (London: Chatto and Windus, 1966).

49. Charles A. Willoughby, *Shanghai Conspiracy: The Sorge Spy Ring, Moscow, Shanghai, Tokyo, San Francisco, New York* (New York: E. P. Dutton and Company, 1952); Janice R. MacKinnon and Stephen R. MacKinnon,

Agnes Smedley: The Life and Times of an American Radical (Stanford, Calif.: Stanford University Press, 1988); Richard J. Aldrich, *The Hidden Hand: Britain, America and Cold War Secret Intelligence* (London: John Murray, 2001), 274–6.

50. Peter Wright, *Spy Catcher: The Candid Autobiography of a Senior Intelligence Officer* (Victoria, Australia: William Heinemann, 1987); Anthony Glees, *The Secrets of the Service: British Intelligence and Communist Subversion, 1939–51* (London: Jonathan Cape, 1987), 304–99.

51. NARA: SMP D 4718.

52. NARA: SMP D 3528, D3852, D 7085.

53. Michael B. Miller, *Shanghai on the Metro: Spies, Intrigue, and the French between the Wars* (Berkeley: University of California Press, 1994), 239–59.

54. John B. Powell was one of those held up: *My Twenty-Five Years in China* (New York: Macmillan, 1945), 92–124; excerpts in Barbara Baker (ed.), *Shanghai: Electric and Lurid City* (Hong Kong: Oxford University Press, 1998), 133, 135.

55. NARA: SMP D 3307, clipping from *China Press*, 2 June 1937.

56. G. E. Miller (pseud. Mauricio Fresco), *Shanghai: The Paradise of Adventurers* (New York: Orsay Publishing House, 1937), 155. There was no truth to this charge, but – and this was its root – the SMP certainly acted on tip-offs from 'feuding' or rival drug gangs: Frederic Wakeman Jr., *Policing Shanghai 1927–1937* (Berkeley: University of California Press, 1995), 37–8; SMA: U 1-3-2425, K. J. McEuen to Acting Secretary SMC, 2 May 1923.

57. Eileen P. Scully, *Bargaining with the State from Afar: American Citizenship in Treaty Port China, 1844–1942* (New York: Columbia University Press, 2001), 187–94.

58. Bernard Wasserstein, *The Secret Lives of Trebitsch Lincoln*, rev. edn. (Harmondsworth: Penguin, 1989).

59. Bernard Wasserstein, *Secret War in Shanghai: Treachery, Subversion and Collaboration in the Second World War* (London: Profile Books, 1998).

60. NARA: SMP D8268.

10

Empire's Civil Dead

1. *All about Shanghai and Environs: A Standard Guide Book* (Shanghai: University Press, 2nd edn., 1934), 43–4, 73.

2. Shanghai: Past, Present and Future', *China Journal*, 22:5 (May 1935), 217.

3. Jon W. Huebner, 'Architecture on the Shanghai Bund', *Papers on Far Eastern History*, 39 (1989), 127–65.

4. Maurine Karns and Pat Patterson, *Shanghai: High Lights, Low Lights and Tael Lights* (Shanghai: Tridon Press, 1936), p. iii.

5. Xiao Jianqing, *Manhua Shanghai* (Cartoon Shanghai) (Shanghai: Shanghai jingwei shuju, 1936).

6. Stuart Lillico, 'The Civic Centre at Kiangwan', *China Journal*, 22:5 (May 1935), 225–9; Christian Henriot, *Shanghai 1927–1937: Municipal Power, Locality and Modernisation* (Stanford, Calif.: Stanford University Press, 1993), 177–84.

7. William Crane Johnston, *The Shanghai Problem* (Stanford, Calif.: Stanford University Press, 1937), 288–90; 'The Japanese Naval Landing Party: A Visit to Headquarters', *Oriental Affairs*, 7:2 (May 1935), 77–9.

8. SMA: U 1-4-1862, Secretary-General, Japanese Residents' Association, to A. D. Bell, 25 May 1933.

9. Uyehara Shigeru, 'Memoir: Life of a Japanese Diplomat, 1892–1968. An Unpublished Manuscript', ch. 3, pp. 21–5.

10. *Fifty Years of Calico Printing: A Jubilee History of the Calico Printers' Association* (Manchester: Calico Printers' Association, 1949); Simon Pitt, 'The Political Economy of Strategic and Structural Change in the Calico Printers' Association 1899–1973' (London Business School, unpublished Ph.D. thesis, 1990); David M. Swann, 'British Cotton Mills in Pre-Second World War China', *Textile History*, 32:2 (2001), 195–200; Manchester Central Library and Archives, M75, Calico Printers' Association archives (hereafter CPA), Board Minutes No. 18, 30 April 1935; Board Minutes No. 14, 13 November 1931, 23 August 1932; Board Minutes No. 15, 20 December 1932.

11. CPA: Board Minutes No. 14, 19 April 1932.

12. SMA: Q 199-1-60, D. J. Sinclair to C. Ashworth, 9 September 1938.

13. CPA: 103.4, C. R. Hargreaves to L. B. Lee, 28 March 1937.

14. SMA: Q 199-1-145, 'Notice to Operatives', 29 November 1935; Q 199-1-151, 'Notice to Operatives', 31 August 1935; 'Notice to Spinners and Doffers', 4 March 1937; *NCDN*, 4 March 1937, p. 10, 5 March 1937, p. 10, 6 March 1937, p. 10.

15. CPA: 103.4, C. R. Hargreaves to L. B. Lee, 28 March 1937.

16. Ibid.

17. CPA: Board Minutes No. 23, 'Report on a visit to the C.P.F. & Co's Mills and Works, Shanghai', L. B. Lee, March 1938.

18. SMA: U 1-3-1710, R. M. J. Martin to Secretary, SMC, 27 June 1929; U 102-5-406/4, R. M. J. Martin to T. I. Vaughan, 18 August 1930.

19. Letter to the author, 8 June 1999.

20. Wall papers, quotations from letters to mother, 6 March 1934, 15 June 1936, and to Joe, 2 May 1935.

21. Darby papers: letter to Dick, 30 April 1934; undated sheets, *c.* September 1935.

22. Duke papers, letter to Pat, 13 November 1941.

23. Letters quoted in Harriet Sergeant, *Shanghai* (London: Jonathan Cape, 1991), 150, 152.

24. *Oriental Affairs*, 5:3 (March 1936), 136.

25. *NCH*, 12 February 1936, pp. 278–80, 19 February 1935, pp. 321–2; NARA: SMP D7137; SMA: U 1-4-2566, 'Police force: Maltreatment of Prisoners'; cuttings in SMA: U 102-3-774, E. W. Peters, personnel file; E. W. Peters, *Shanghai Policeman* (London: Rich and Cowan, 1937), quotation from p. 233.

26. SMA: U 1-4-2566/4, K. M. Bourne to Secretary, 3 December 1935.

27. *NCDN*, 13 August 1937, pp. 9–10.

28. See chapters 5 and 6 of Hans van de Ven, *War and Nationalism in China, 1925–45* (London: Routledge, 2003).

29. CPA: 1254, 'Summary of Events Concerning Mill from about the Time of the of [*sic*] Hostilities onwards,' and 'Complete Report and Observations Made During the Sino-Japanese Trouble starting 6 p.m., Wednesday, 18th August, 1937', enclosures in C. R. Hargreaves to L. B. Lee, 7 December 1937. Most of this unsigned report is clearly Tinkler's work.

30. CPA: 1254, C. R. Hargreaves to L. B. Lee, 7 December 1939.

31. CPA: Board Minutes No. 25, 26 September 1939.

32. CPA: 1254, Zhang Fagui to Mayor Yu Hongjun; C. R. Hargreaves to Mayor Yu Hongjun, both 6 September 1937.

33. IWM: C. R. Hargreaves to R. M. Tinkler, 10 January 1938.

34. *Oriental Affairs*, 9:1 (January 1938), 13.

35. Peasgood papers, 'A History of "C" Division, Shanghai Municipal Police, during the Sino-Japanese Hostilities August 1937 to February 1938', and appendix, 'An Extract from the Personal Diary of a Police Sergeant' [by Frank Peasgood].

36. Smith papers, Muriel Smith to Dorothy Turner, 26 September 1937.

37. Peasgood papers, 'An Extract from the Personal Diary of a Police Sergeant', 91.

38. Wall papers, letter to mother, 10 November 1937.

39. Hallett Abend, *My Years in China, 1926–41* (London: John Lane The Bodley Head, 1944), 254.

40. *NCDN*, 19 August 1939, pp. 3, 5.

41. Peasgood papers, 'A History of "C" Division, Shanghai Municipal Police, during the Sino-Japanese Hostilities August 1937 to February 1938', 56.

42. John Hunter Boyle, *China and Japan at War: The Politics of Collaboration* (Stanford, Calif.: Stanford University Press, 1972), 282–6; Gerald E. Bunker,

The Peace Conspiracy: Wang Ching-wei and the China War, 1937–1941 (Cambridge, Mass.: Harvard University Press, 1972), 262–4; Frederic Wakeman Jr, *The Shanghai Badlands: Wartime Terrorism and Urban Crime* (Cambridge: Cambridge University Press, 1996).

43. Wakeman, *Shanghai Badlands*, 135.

44. Ibid. 39.

45. Antony Best, *Britain, Japan and Pearl Harbor: Avoiding War in East Asia, 1936–41* (London: Routledge, 1995), 71–86; Nicholas R. Clifford, *Retreat from China: British Policy in the Far East 1937–41* (London: Longman, 1967), 111–26; SMA: W1-0-129, *Kulangsu Municipal Council Report 1939*, 5–6.

46. SMC, *Annual Report 1937*, 21; *Oriental Affairs*, 11:1 (January 1939), 48.

47. CPA: Board Minutes No. 23, 'Report on a Visit to the C.P.F. & Co's Mills and Works, Shanghai', L. B. Lee, March 1938; SMA: Q 199-1-60, D. J. Sinclair to Committee, Shanghai Rowing Club, 18 May 1939.

48. SMA: Q 199-1-145, 'Notice to All Clerks, No. 1s, and Students', 10 May 1939.

49. *NCDN*, 10 June 1939, pp. 7–8.

50. *Oriental Affairs*, 12:3 (September 1939), 119–20.

51. *Shanghai fangzhi gongren yundong shi* (History of the Shanghai Textile Workers' Movement) (Shanghai: Zhonggong dangshi chubanshe, 1991), 272–8.

52. Figures taken from SMC, *Annual Report 1940*, 26; Robert W. Barnett, *Economic Shanghai: Hostage to Politics, 1937–1941* (New York: Institute of Pacific Relations, 1941), 52–62.

53. Between 14 and 18 December that year, 75 rice shops were attacked and looted by crowds in the Western District of the International Settlement. See the Special Branch report, 'Rice', dated 21 December 1939, enclosed in SMA: U 102-5-32/7.

54. *NCH*, 24 May 1939, pp. 322–3.

55. NARA: SMP D 6968 'Labour Dispute in the China Printing and Finishing Works – Pootung', reports: 20 May, 25 May 1939.

56. PRO: FO 371/23498, F5066/528/10, Shanghai Tel. No. 82, 27 May 1939.

57. NARA: SMP D 6968, 'China Printing and Finishing Company – Strike Situation in Pootung Mill', 27 May 1939; *NCH*, 24 May 1939, p. 328.

58. NARA: SMP D 6968, cutting, *NCDN*, 30 May 1939; PRO: FO 371/23498, F5065/528/10, Shanghai Tel. No. 80, 25 May 1939.

59. NARA: SMP D 6968, Eleanor H. Hinder, Industrial Section SMC, 'China Printing and Finishing Company Strike', 26 May 1939.

60. Interview with Peng Hongfei, 9 April 1997, Shanghai.

61. NARA: SMP D 6968, 'Strike of Workers of China Printing and Finishing Works, Pootung – Present Situation', 25 May 1939.

62. NARA: SMP D 6968, 31 May 1939.

63. NARA: SMP D 6968, report, 2 June 1939.

64. NARA: SMP D 6968, memo dated 2 June 1939.

65. This paragraph is based on inquest testimonies collected in PRO: FO 371/57638, and the papers in file F528/10, 1939, in FO 371/23498–9. See also *NCH*, 21 June 1939, pp.516–17.

66. NARA: SMP D 6968, cutting from *China Press*, 8 June 1939.

67. The late Mr Ford, asked about the incident in 1990, no longer recollected it.

68. NARA: SMP D 6968, cutting from *Tairiku Shimpo*, 6 June 1939.

69. *NCH*, 14 June 1939, p. 454.

70. PRO: FO 371/57638, copy of 'Doctor's Certificate', Dr W. Korec, 7 June 1939.

71. PRO: FO 371/23499, Ambassador R. L. Craigie to Japanese Minister for Foreign Affairs, 17 June 1939; NARA: RG 84, Shanghai Post Files, 394.4123/1, Shanghai No. 480, 8 June 1939.

72. PRO: FO 371/23498, F6195/528/10, Shanghai No. 90.

73. CPA: Board Minutes No. 24, 13 June 1939.

74. IWM: D. J. Sinclair to Edith Whalen, 29 July 1939.

75. PRO: FO 371/23458, F5525/528/10, A. D. Blackburn to J. F. Brenan, 7 June 1939.

11

Aftermath

1. *NCDN*, 10 June 1939, pp. 5, 7.

2. *NCH*, 14 June 1939, p. 435; 21 June 1939, pp. 516–17; coroner's report in PRO: FO 371/57638.

3. PRO: FO 371/23498, F5988/528/10, R. G. Howe minute, 14 June 1939; FO 371/23499, F11086/528/10, Consul-General for Japan to HBM Consul-General, Shanghai, 4 September 1939.

4. Various cuttings in CPA: M75/No. 159, CPA newscuttings scrapbook.

5. PRO: FO 371/23498, F7651/528/10, A. H. Scott note, 25 July 1939.

6. Both letters in PRO: FO 371/23498, F7651/528/10.

7. PRO: FO 371/24663, F3469/31/10, Tokyo No. 253, 6 May 1940 and note by A. H. Scott, 4 July 1940.

8. This file is in CPA: 39.4, 1939–49 correspondence sequence, Green no. 1239.

9. Lily Benson papers, commonplace book.

10. E. J. Benson, 'In Memoriam; Richard Maurice Tinkler, D.C.M.', *Ulverstonian*, 6:2 (July 1939), 33–4; E. J. Benson to Edith Whalen, 13 June 1939, Tinkler family papers; cutting ('Mr R. M. Tinkler: An Appreciation'), in CPA: M75/No. 159, CPA newscuttings scrapbook.

11. Enoch Powell, *Dancer's End and The Wedding Gift* (London: Falcon Press, 1951), 27. The place and date of composition are from Powell's annotations to his own copy of this volume. I am grateful to Roderick Suddaby for bringing this poem to my attention.

12. *NCH*, 22 January 1941, p. 120.

13. Wall papers, letter to mother, 29 January 1938.

14. Letter to author, 8 June 1999.

15. PRO: FO 371/23498, Shanghai No. 298, 26 August 1939; NARA: SMP D 9391.

16. NARA: SMP N 359; SMA: U 102-3-813, R. W. Yorke, personnel file.

17. PRO: FO 371/23456, Clark-Kerr to Foreign Office, No. 974, 3 September 1939.

18. PRO: FO 371/23457, F12567/12568/84/10, Shanghai No. 360, Shanghai No. 568, 26 October 1939.

19. Foreign Office to John Pook & Co., 12 October 1939 (F10840/990/10, 1939): Robins collection, Widdowson papers has one copy; Ted Quigley, *A Spirit of Adventure: The Memoirs of Ted Quigley*, (Lewes: Book Guild, 1994) 146.

20. PRO: WO 208/378a, Lt.-Col. J. R. Hunt, 'Note on Position of British Personnel of Shanghai Municipal Police', February 1943.

21. SMA: U 102-3-1549, D. B. Ross, personnel file; correspondence in U 1-4-1880, 'Police Force: Resignations'.

22. SMA: U 1-4-2052, 'Marriage: Police Force' (1934–42).

23. Correspondence with Paddy Fearnley, 2001–2, and her memoir, 'Shanghai 1929–1941'; Cornwell papers, 'Pao Chia Census Form', 14 July 1942; SMA: U 1-4-185, 'Police Force: Foreign Branch, Terms of Service', W. H. Widdowson to Commissioner of Police, 17 December 1936.

24. Figures calculated from reports in SMC, *Annual Reports 1935–40*.

25. Wall papers, letter to Joe, 1 March 1938.

26. File in SMA: U 102-5-212.

27. SMA: U 1-4-185, 'Police Force: Foreign Branch, Terms of Service', W. H. Widdowson to Commissioner of Police, and L. W. Hide to Commissioner of Police, both 17 December 1936.

28. Cornwell papers, undated news cutting (*c.* March 1940).

29. *NCH*, 16 August 1939, p. 281.

30. Daniel G. Cormie, 'The Memoirs of a Shanghai Policeman', 63–4.

31. Carroll Alcott, *My War with Japan* (New York: Henry Holt and Company, 1943), 318.

32. PRO: FO 371/23455, F7474/84/10, Herbert Phillips to R. Howe, 3 July 1939; Robert W. Barnett, *Economic Shanghai: Hostage to Politics, 1937–1941* (New York: Institute of Pacific Relations, 1941), 29–30.

33. PRO: FO 371/27631, F588/130/10, Shanghai No. 717, 12 December 1940; SMA: U 102-5-56, 'Memorandum for the Special Economy Committee by Commissioner of Police', *c.* April 1940.

34. NARA: SMP D 9454.

35. SMA: U 102-5-32/8, 'Pay of Chinese Constables. Part 1', Yao Zengmou to Commissioner of Police, 27 September 1940.

36. PRO: FO 371/24663, F5287/31/10, Shanghai No. 599, 16 September 1940.

37. SMA: U 102-5-33/10–15, 'Pay of Chinese Constables. Part 2'.

38. SMA: U 102-5-33/1-3, 'Pay of Chinese Constables. Part 3'.

39. Uyehara Shigeru, 'Memoir: Life of a Japanese Diplomat, 1892–1968. An Unpublished Manuscript', ch. 3, p. 10.

40. Ibid. 35.

41. PRO: FO 371/24663, Shanghai No. 267, 1 May 1940 enclosing G. G. Phillips to Senior Consul, 29 April 1940; the shooting may have merely been a warning, rather than an assassination attempt: NARA: SMP D 9639(c). On such units see Brian G. Martin, 'Shield of Collaboration: The Wang Jingwei Regime's Security Service, 1939–45', *Intelligence and National Security*, 16:4 (2001), 89–148.

42. PRO: FO 676/435, G. G. Phillips to Sir Arthur Clark-Kerr, 29 June 1940.

43. SMA: U 1-4-1160, 'Western Shanghai Area Special Police Force', 'Minutes of Conference, 4 March 1940'.

44. Bonner papers, WSASPF Foreign Affairs Branch reports, 21 March 1941–2 February 1942.

45. Bonner papers, letter dated 26 September 1941.

46. File in SMA: U 102-5-157.

47. PRO: FO 371/27631, F2091/130/10, Godfrey Phillips, 'Memorandum', 30 December 1940; A. E. Cornwell papers, statement dated 23 January 1941; *Municipal Gazette*, 13 February 1941, p. 45; *NCH*, 29 January 1941, p. 159.

48. The full composition was: Americans: 3; British: 3; Japanese: 3; Chinese: 4; Dutch, German, Swiss: 1 apiece. On the SPC see: SMA: U 1-4-1112, 'Council Membership (1941–43)'.

49. PRO: FO 371/27631, F534/130/10, Embassy to Shanghai No. 63, 6 February 1941.

50. PRO: FO 371/27631, F2091/130/10, W. J. Keswick to B. D. F. Beith, 6 January 1941.

51. *NCH*, 19 February 1941, p. 285.

52. PRO: FO 371/27973, F11750/285/10, Brenan minute on Shanghai No. 998, 3 November 1941.

53. Alcott, *My War with Japan*, 256.

54. *NCH*, 15 January 1941, p. 93, 22 January 1941, p. 120, 13 August 1941, p. 280.

55. *NCH*, 19 March 1941, p. 445.

56. PRO: FO 371/27631, F1956/130/10, Shanghai No. 232, 14 March 1941.

57. Undated clipping in SMA: U 1-4-1111, 'Council: Membership (1933–1941)'.

58. *NCH*, 23 July 1941, p. 123, 30 July 1941, p. 178.

59. Quigley, *Spirit of Adventure*, 146–7; SMA: U 1-9-1163, E. J. Quigley personnel file.

60. Minutes of the SMC, vol. 28, 8 December 1941, p. 133; PRO: FO 371/27631, F2091/130/10, Godfrey Phillips, 'Memorandum', 30 December 1940.

61. Interview with Frederick G. West, 13 September 1996.

62. NARA: SMP D8299/364, 20 December 1941.

63. Minutes of the SMC, vol. 28, 21 February 1942, p. 35.

64. PRO: FO 371/27634, F13613/130/10, Foreign Office to Shanghai No. 1204, 6 December 1941; FO 371/31677, F1495/1494/10, notes on Berne No. 499, 12 February 1942.

65. PRO: WO 208/378a, H. G. W. Woodhead, Chatham House lecture, 21 November 1942, 'The Japanese Occupation of Shanghai: Some Personal Experiences'.

66. *Municipal Gazette*, 1942 *passim*; quotation from 30 October 1942, p. 158.

67. SMA: U 1-4-966, 'Rendition of Settlement', Okazaki's comments are from 'Chairman's speech', 1 August 1943, and 'Radio Speech'.

68. PRO: WO 208/378a, General Sir Archibald Wavell to Chief of Imperial General Staff, 14 May 1942.

69. PRO: HS 1/172, B.B.232 to B.B.100, 7 April 1944. On SOE, see Richard J. Aldrich, *Intelligence and the War Against Japan: Britain, America and the Politics of Secret Service* (Cambridge: Cambridge University Press, 2000).

70. SMA: U 1-4-1884, 'Police Force and Gaol: Reorganisation (1942–43)'.

71. Hugh Collar, *Captive in Shanghai* (Hong Kong: Oxford University Press, 1990), 84.

72. W. G. Braidwood, 'Report on the Activities of the British Residents' Association Relief association of Shanghai, Dec. 1941–June 1943', typescript; Collar, *Captive in Shanghai*.

73. *Shanghai Times*, 18 April 1943, p. 3.

74. *Shanghai Times*, 27 January 1943, p. 3, 30 January 1943, p. 3.

75. NARA: RG 226, E182, Box 12, folder 77, 'The Outline of the Activities of the Foreign Affairs Section, Police Headquarters, During the Period of the Japanese Occupation of Shanghai', autumn 1945.

76. NARA: RG 226, E182a, Box 9, Folder 70, OSS reports, 'Shanghai Municipal Police, Saito', 11 October 1945, 'Shanghai Municipal Police, 1937–1945', 15 October 1945.

77. PRO: FO 371/35945, F511/219/23, Chungking No. 614, 29 December 1942; interview with J. W. Fallace, 23 August 2000.

78. *Shanghai Times*, 22 July 1943, p. 3.

79. NARA: RG 226, E182a, Box 8, Folder 59, 'Summary Report on Indian Political Affairs in Japanese-occupied China', 1 March 1946.

80. NARA: RG 226, E182a, Box 14, Folder 86, J. P. McCarthy, chief X-2 to Lt. Col. E. N. Harding, 23 August 1945, and enclosures.

81. Interview with Frank Peasgood, 13 March 1996; Wall papers, letter to mother, 22 December 1945.

82. PRO: FO 371/53590, F5485/44/10, R. G. Hargraves to Foreign Office, 5 April 1946.

83. The process is described in files F63/10 (1945), PRO: FO 371/46191–46193 and F44/10 (1946) in FO 371/53588–53592.

84. For General MacArthur's extreme right-wing intelligence chief, Charles Willoughby, the files opened up an 'astonishing vista' on pre-war communism and the groundwork it laid for postwar 'success': Charles A. Willoughby, *Shanghai Conspiracy: The Sorge Spy Ring, Moscow, Shanghai, Tokyo, San Francisco, New York* (New York: E. P. Dutton, 1952), 13–15, 271–5.

85. Robins collection, Widdowson papers, Widdowson to Ministry of Pensions, 14 January 1957.

86. Smith papers, Shanghai Police Association newsletters 1955–7. My thanks to Paddy Fearnley who made these documents and others available to me.

87. PRO: FO 371/92335, FC1583/5, Foreign Office minute, 13 April 1951. Two works which deal with the endgame and its aftermath: Beverley Hooper, *China Stands Up: Ending the Western Presence, 1948–50* (Sydney: Allen & Unwin, 1986); Antonia Finnane, *Far From Where? Jewish Journeys from Shanghai to Australia* (Melbourne: Melbourne University Press, 1999).

88. Robins collection, Winifred Curtis letter, 22 June 1978.

89. Wall papers; records of the 'Liquidation Commission' through which the negotiations were channelled are in PRO: FO 671/565–560; on compensation see FO 371/83232, FC1015/20, answer to Parliamentary question, 3 April 1950.

90. PRO: FO 671/565, Consul General to Mayor K. W. Wu, 13 January 1947, Shanghai to Embassy No. 28, 15 January 1947; FO 671/567.

91. Letters in file PRO: FO 371/110365, 'SMC Claims 1954'.

92. PRO: WO 268/102–4, Quarterly Historical Report of the War Crimes GHQ SEALF, 1946–7; on this process as a whole, see R. John Pritchard, 'Changes in Perception: British Civil and Military Perspectives on War Crimes Trials and their Legal Context (1942–1956)', unpublished paper. I am most grateful to the author for allowing me to see this paper.

93. PRO: WO 325/58, J. M. Watson, 'Report on Brutal Ill-treatment whilst in an Internment Camp' (undated); H. E. Aiers to Major Stephan, 2 October 1945.

94. PRO: WO 325/129, William Hutton to Secretary of State for War, 30 June 1948.

95. PRO: WO 325/129, Major H. Bretherton to Colonel New, 27 April 1948. For a considered if incomplete survey, see Philip R. Piccigallo, *The Japanese on Trial: Allied War Crimes Operations in the East, 1945–1951* (Austin: University of Texas Press, 1979), 96–120.

96. Pritchard, 'Changes in Perception', 26.

97. Revd C. E. Darwent, *Shanghai: A Handbook for Travellers and Residents*, 2nd edn. (Shanghai: Kelly and Walsh, 1920), 76.

98. PRO: FO 371/57638, 'Death of Mr R. M. Tinkler'.

99. PRO: WO 325/560, China Association to Judge Advocate General, 20 September 1948; Judge Advocate General to China Association, 22 September 1948.

12

We Are the Dead

1. Elizabeth Buettner, 'Parent–child Separations and Colonial Careers: The Talbot Family Correspondence in the 1880s and 1890s', in Anthony Fletcher and Stephen Hussey (eds.), *Childhood in Question: Children, Parents and the State* (Manchester: Manchester University Press, 1999), 115–33.

2. See the essays in John M. MacKenzie (ed.), *Imperialism and Popular Culture* (Manchester: Manchester University Press, 1986).

3. War Pensions Agency, *Leaflet 12: Ex-gratia Payment for British Groups who were Held Prisoner by the Japanese during World War Two* (Blackpool: War Pensions Agency, 2000).

4. IWM archives, Edith Whalen to Director General, Imperial War Museum, 15 October 1970.

5. IWM: correspondence in folder RMT/2, April–June 1967.

6. IWM archives, Edith Whalen to Philip Noel-Baker, undated, 1969; Edith Whalen to Roderick Suddaby, 16 November 1970.

7. Reported in private communication to author, 6 March 2002.

8. I am extremely grateful to local historian Frank Brooks, who searched for more information about this issue, and who located the gravestone.

9. PRO: FO 369/4909, KG1103/7, 'Minute of Meeting', 9 October 1953; FO 369/5108, Shanghai to Peking, 21 September 1954. See also FO 671/577–8, 581 'Foreign Cemeteries in China', 1953–4.

10. Quotation from introduction to Zhongguo duiwai wenhua tiehui Shanghaishi fenhui (ed.), *Shanghai* (Shanghai: n.p., 1958).

11. Ibid.; see also Dong Weikun, *Shanghai jinxi* (Shanghai Past and Present) (Shanghai: Shanghai renmin meishu chubanshe, 1958).

12. 'Foreign Tombs, Lost and Found', *Shanghai Star*, 5 April 2001, p.18.

13. IWM archives, Edith Whalen to Philip Noel-Baker, undated, 1969.

14. Elizabeth Buettner, 'From Somebodies to Nobodies: Britons Returning Home from India', in Martin Daunton and Bernhard Rieger (eds.), *Meanings of Modernity: Britain from the Late-Victorian Era to World War II* (Oxford: Berg, 2001).

15. Letter to author, 17 April 1996.

16. Patrick Coates researched the story of his former service in *The China Consuls: British Consular Officers, 1843–1943* (Hong Kong: Oxford University Press, 1988); Antony Kirk-Greene's *On Crown Service: A History of HM Colonial and Overseas Civil Services, 1837–1997* (London: I. B. Tauris, 1999) was commissioned as a parting memorial by the Corona Club, the social club of the colonial services, to mark its disbandment 'at the end of the century that has seen the end of empire' (Preface by J. H. Smith, CBE, p. xxvi).

17. Jay Winter, *Sites of Memory, Sites of Mourning: The Great War in European Cultural History* (Cambridge: Cambridge University Press, 1995).

18. One telling case history is Maryinez Lyons, *The Colonial Disease: A Social History of Sleeping Sickness in Northern Zaire, 1900–1940* (Cambridge: Cambridge University Press, 1992).

19. Philip D. Curtin, *Death by Migration: Europe's Encounter with the Tropical World in the Nineteenth Century* (Cambridge: Cambridge University Press, 1989), 161.

20. *Xueji* (Blood Sacrifice) by Ma Hongdao, in Pan Junxiang (ed.), *Shanghai lishi youhua xinzuo* (New Shanghai History Oil Paintings) (Shanghai: n.p., 1998).

Unpublished and Archival Sources

Public Archives

Academia Sinica, Institute of Modern History Archives
    Chinese Foreign Ministry Archives.
Freemasons Hall, Dublin, Grand Lodge of A. F. & A. Masons of Ireland
    Documents and notices relating to Erin Lodge No. 463, Shanghai.
Hoover Institution Archives, Stanford, California
    J. E. Jacobs papers.
Imperial War Museum, London
    E. J. Roper, 'The revelations of a hangman', IWM 79/2/1T.
    Papers of Richard Maurice Tinkler.
    Correspondence file relating to deposit of Tinkler papers.
    'Some Experiences of the German Push 1918, by 50214 Pte W. A. Hoyle,
        24th RF, 2nd Division'.
India Office Library and Records, British Library
    Ms.eur.e.400, Jack Bazalgette collection, Letters 1926–8.
Japanese Foreign Ministry Archives, Tokyo
    A-1-1-0, 30-5-1-1, 'Shanghai intelligence reports'.
Manchester City Library and Archives
    M 75 Papers of the Calico Printers' Association.
National Archives and Records Administration, Washington, DC
    RG 83 Ship passenger arrival records, M 1383, Passenger and Crew lists of
        vessels arriving at Seattle, Washington, 1898–1953, Roll 163.
    RG 84, Shanghai Post files
    RG 226 E182, Shanghai OSS station records, 1944–9.
    RG 263 Shanghai Municipal Police Special Branch Files.
National Maritime Museum, Greenwich
    Sir Louis H. K. Hamilton papers.
Public Records Office, Kew
    ADM 116/3067 'Yangtsze General Letter No. 6, 1 July 1934–31 August
        1934'.

FO 228 Embassy and Consular Archives China, Correspondence Series 1.

FO 232 Foreign Office: Consulates and Legation, China: Indexes to Correspondence.

FO 369 Foreign Office, General Correspondence, Consular.

FO 371 Foreign Office General Correspondence, Political.

FO 671 Embassy and Consular Archives China, Shanghai Correspondence.

FO 676 Embassy and Consular Archives China, Correspondence Series 2.

FO 917 Embassy and Consular Archives China, Shanghai Supreme Court, Probate records.

FO 1092 Shanghai Courts, China: Judges' and Magistrates' Notebooks.

HS 1 Special Operations Executive: Far East: Registered Files.

WO 32 War Office, Registered Files (General Series).

WO 95/1349 24 Bn. Royal Fusiliers War Diary.

WO 106 Directorate of Military Operations and Intelligence.

WO 191 Peacetime Operations, Shanghai Defence Force War Diary.

WO 208 Directorate of Military Intelligence.

WO 268/102–104 Quarterly Historical Report of the War Crimes GHQ SEALF, 1946–7.

WO 325 War Office: General Headquarters, Allied Land Forces (South East Asia), War Crimes Group: Investigation Files.

Salvation Army, International Heritage Centre, London

The Crusader.

North China Territory Annual Reports, 1932–5.

School of Oriental and African Studies Library and Archives, London

John Swire and Sons papers.

Shanghai Municipal Archives

Q 199–1 China Printing and Finishing Company records.

U 1–1 Shanghai Municipal Council *Annual Reports*; Police Daily Reports; committee minute books.

    The minutes of the SMC are in this series, but have been published as: Shanghai Shi danganguan (ed.) *Gongbuji dongshihui huiji lu* (Minutes of the Shanghai Municipal Council) (Shanghai: Shanghai guji chubenshe, 2002), 28 vols. In the text this is referred to as Minutes of the SMC.

U 1–3 Shanghai Municipal Council, Secretariat files, 1919–30.

U 1–4 Shanghai Municipal Council, Secretariat files, 1930–43. (These two series include many files relating to individual personnel matters, including U 1-3-320, which deals with Tinkler's resignation.)

U 102 Shanghai Municipal Police records: U 102–3 Personnel files; U 1-2-5 Administration files (in 1997 the personnel files had been redesignated as the series U 1-9₃ (*sic*)).

    The personnel files of the following men were made available to me. In the text, Tinkler apart, and unless otherwise specified, all references to these men are drawn from their personnel files: Albert H. Aiers, Alfred H. Aiers, R. C. Aiers, J. Allen, D. D. Anderson, R. C. Andrew, W. Armstrong, T. H. Aukett, F. Austin, S. G. N. Bailey, W. S. Baimbridge, E. C. Baker, R. W. Barnes, L. Barr, E. I. M. Barrett, J. Barry, R. H. Beer, W. J. R. Billing, J. Binks, C. Bishop, H. R. Bladon, K. M. Bourne, F. C. Bridger, A. M. Cameron, J. J. A. Campbell, F. J. Carnell, A. H. Chamberlain, C. B. P. Chard, W. B. O'Reilly Coleman, J. Coll, A. Cooper, A. C. Craig, C. Craig, D. K. Craig, G. H. Craik, A. Crichton, J. Crowley, P. Curtin, H. Diprose, P. Dowding, J. T. Duffy, W. B. H. Duke, T. Dunne, E. W. Everson, R. Eynstone, W. E. Fairbairn, J. A. Farrell, J. Fenton, H. J. Foxworthy, A. Gammie, F. W. Gerrard, H. F. Gill, E. L. Gladwish, J. Goodfellow, R. C. Hall, J. J. Hedley, A. D. Hendry, C. B. Henry, A. P. Hibberd, A. Hindson, H. R. Hotchkiss, W. Hotchkiss, E. S. C. Jackson, H. C. Jackson, I. James, G. Johnston, E. Knifton, J. U. J. Langridge, N. Lboff, Ping-chun Liang, E. W. J. Ling, M. R. L. Lingard, F. McAulay, C. J. S. Macdonald, A. McGillivray, H. McGregor, J. E. McGregor, A. Mackie, G. McRobbie, A. Marshall, G. D. Matcham, A. G. Miller, B. H. Munson, R. H. Norton, R. Ockwell, D. M. O'Neil, W. R. Parker, A. Paterson, H. E. Peck, F. W. Perkins, O. B. Perkins, E. W. Peters, E. E. Pilbeam, F. A. Pitts, P. J. Poole, P. B. Potapoff, C. Powell, E. J. Quigley, C. Rafalovitch, G. H. Reynolds, D. Robb, J. S. Robinson, D. B. Ross, T. Rossington, W. J. Ryle, A. H. Samson, W. G. F. Sandell, W. A. Segiuf, L. R. Sims, W. Slater, H. M. Smyth, S. E. Spurgeon, H. K. Stangaard, D. A. Stevens, J. Sutherland, J. Thomas, C. E. Thurgood, A. Turner, A. G. Wadey, B. J. Wall, R. W. Ward, W. N. Webb, C. Weed, J. H. Weeks, G. R. Welch, C. Wellings, I. B. Williams, J. Wilson, H. G. Wrede, S. Wyles, R. W. Yorke, C. Young, J. A. Young.

    W1 series, English-language printed matter.

University of Toronto, Thomas Fisher Rare Books Library

    J. O. P. Bland papers.

Papers in private hands

Elizabeth J. Benson (Lily Wilson), commonplace book, documents and photographs.

Kenneth R. Bonner papers.

Daniel G. Cormie, 'The Memoirs of a Shanghai Policeman' (no date), and other papers.

Albert Edward Cornwell papers.

Jack d'Esterre Darby papers.

W. Basil Hare Duke papers.

E. W. Everson family papers.

Harold Gill papers.

Frank Peasgood, photographs and papers.

Peter Robins collection: W. H. Widdowson, Walter Benjamin Curtis, Daniel G. Cormie.

Samuel Sherlock papers.

John (Jock) Smith and Angus Turner.

H. M. Smyth papers.

Robert W. Thomas papers.

Tinkler family papers: Letters, documents, photographs and other items relating to R. M. Tinkler and family.

Uyehara Shigeru, 'Memoir: Life of a Japanese Diplomat, 1892–1968. An Unpublished Manuscript'.

Barney Wall papers.

Interviews

J. W. Fallace, 23 August 2000, Deal, Kent.

Peng Hongfei, 9 April 1997, Shanghai.

Frank Peasgood, 2 February, 13 March 1996, Peacehaven, East Sussex.

J. E. Tinkler, 16 September 1994, Edinburgh.

Frederick G. West, 13 September 1996, Tunbridge Wells, Kent.

Ivor Everson, 7 September 2001 (telephone).

Index

Note: Page references in *italics* indicate illustrations. Where appropriate subheadings are in chronological order rather than alphabetical order. In some instances, under a main heading, a paragraph of chronological subheadings is followed by a paragraph of alphabetical subheadings, e.g., under SMP. The entry for 'Tinkler, Richard Maurice' has chronological paragraphs of the main periods of his life followed by alphabetical paragraphs on other topics.